Scotland's Muslims

Scotland's Muslims

Society, Politics and Identity

Edited by Peter Hopkins

EDINBURGH
University Press

Edinburgh University Press is one of the leading university presses in the UK. We publish academic books and journals in our selected subject areas across the humanities and social sciences, combining cutting-edge scholarship with high editorial and production values to produce academic works of lasting importance. For more information visit our website: edinburghuniversitypress.com

Edinburgh University Press Ltd
The Tun – Holyrood Road
12 (2f) Jackson's Entry
Edinburgh EH8 8PJ

Typeset in 10.5/13pt Sabon by
Servis Filmsetting Ltd, Stockport, Cheshire

A CIP record for this book is available from the British Library

ISBN 978 1 4744 2723 4 (hardback)
ISBN 978 1 4744 2725 8 (webready PDF)
ISBN 978 1 4744 2726 5 (epub)

Contents

Figures and Tables

Acknowledgements

Many thanks to all of the chapter authors for their timely contributions, and for responding to requests for revisions so quickly and efficiently. I am very thankful to funding from the Arts and Humanities Research Council (AH/K000594/1) for research into the everyday geopolitics of ethnic and religious minority young people in Scotland. This project was one of the many factors that motivated me to edit this collection. Many thanks to my collaborators on this project – Katherine Botterill, Gurchathen Sanghera and Rowena Arshad. And my thanks also go to Robin Finlay and Gurchathen Sanghera for their collaboration on a related project about Muslim youth and political participation in Scotland.

Notes on the Contributors

Fayaz S. Alibhai is a PhD student at the Alwaleed Centre, University of Edinburgh, UK.

Hengameh Ashraf-Emami is a PhD student in the School of Social Sciences, University of Northumbria, UK.

Reza Bagheri is Assistant Professor, University of Tehran, Iran.

Stefano Bonino is Lecturer in the School of Social Policy, University of Birmingham, UK.

Katherine Botterill is Lecturer in Human Geography in the School of Life, Sport and Social Sciences, Edinburgh Napier University, UK.

Robin Finlay is Postdoctoral Research Associate in the School of Geography, Politics and Sociology, Newcastle University, UK.

Peter Hopkins is Professor of Social Geography in the School of Geography, Politics and Sociology, Newcastle University, UK.

Maria Kristiansen is Associate Professor in the Department of Public Health, University of Copenhagen, Denmark.

Nasar Meer is Professor of Race, Identity and Citizenship in the School of Social and Political Sciences at the University of Edinburgh, UK.

Michael B. Munnik is Lecturer in Social Science Theories and Methods in the School of History, Archaeology and Religion, Cardiff University, UK.

Sheila Riddell is Chair in Inclusion and Diversity, and Director of the Centre for Research in Education Inclusion and Diversity, Moray House School of Education, University of Edinburgh, UK.

Gurchathen Sanghera is Lecturer in the School of International Relations, University of St Andrews, UK.

Omar Shaikh is Project Co-ordinator of the Colourful Heritage Project, Glasgow, UK.

Aziz Sheikh is Chair of Primary Care Research and Development, Usher Institute of Population Health Sciences and Informatics, University of Edinburgh, UK.

Asifa Siraj is an independent researcher.

Rebecca Syswerda completed a PhD in Geography at the University of St Andrews, UK, in 2014.

Elisabet Weedon was Senior Research Fellow and Depute Director of the Centre for Research in Education Inclusion and Diversity, Moray House School of Education, University of Edinburgh, UK. She is now an Honorary Research Fellow.

1

INTRODUCTION
Scotland's Muslims: Early Settlement, Current Context and Research Themes

Peter Hopkins

INTRODUCTION

On 12 December 2002, I met with a young Scottish Muslim at the Edinburgh Central Mosque to interview him as part of a research project about the everyday lives of young Muslim men in Scotland. Part of the interview focused on ideas about Scotland, Scottishness and Scottish national identities, and during his discussion the young man – whom I call Kabir, in order to protect his confidentiality – said:

> I'm Scottish Muslim because I'm Scottish and I was born in Scotland. So it's my culture, it's my background, it's my home. Muslim is my goal. Being Muslim is my philosophy or my belief system. It doesn't contradict my nationality in any way, because they deal with different questions, you know. It's like being a red square – sorry, that's a bad example – take a blue square. Red square is an alcoholic drink, isn't it? … That's not on purpose, I just want to differentiate. A blue square: it's blue and it's a square. Its being a square doesn't interfere with it being blue. Its being blue doesn't interfere with it being a square. They're just nothing to do with each other, but they complement each other and they make a complete blue square. If it wasn't blue, it wouldn't be a blue square, if you see what I mean. So, being a Scottish Muslim, you know, both of them go together and they make me who I am. They're part of what I am. They're not even complete of what I am, because it doesn't describe my character or personality, but they don't contradict each other in any way.

After completing the research, I contacted Kabir to ask if he would be interested in meeting with me again to discuss the findings of the research, and he agreed. I recounted the quote above to him and he then compared being a Scottish Muslim to being a 'vegetarian poet'. He said: 'I mean, if someone is a vegetarian poet, at a dinner party he might say he was a vegetarian, and in a literary circle he might say he was a poet. He wouldn't introduce himself as the other thing at a dinner – "oh no, I'm a poet" – he wouldn't say that, but primarily that is what he is' (see Hopkins, 2008a).

When I interviewed Kabir in 2002, there was very little research about Muslims in Scotland, aside from a small number of studies that mapped the ethnic minority population of Scotland's main cities (e.g. Jones and Davenport, 1972; Kearsley and Strivastava, 1974; Mann, 1992) and sociological analyses of the place of race and racism in Scotland (Miles and Dunlop, 1987; Dunlop, 1993). Constrained by factors such as the lack of census data and an interest in matters of race and ethnicity (rather than religion), the focus of much of this earlier work was upon 'ethnic minorities' or 'Pakistanis', and rarely did analysis explore the significance of Muslim identity in the Scottish context. Over the last fifteen years or so, there has been a growing interest in research about the everyday experiences of Muslims in Scotland and it is this growth that is one of the motivations for bringing together the contributors to this collection.

Returning to Kabir, his understanding of the relationship between his Muslim and Scottish identities demonstrates the ease with which he sees these different identities coming together in different places and at different times. This points to a second motivation for this collection. It would be rare to find Muslims in England identifying as openly and positively with being 'English Muslims'. Also, the phrase 'British Muslims' – although used widely – tends to lead to stereotypes about segregation, social isolation, extremism and so on. Clearly, the Scottish context provides a particular environment in which many Muslims feel able to affiliate strongly with the Scottish nation while also openly practising their religion. This context deserves special attention, rather than being subsumed under the problematic category of 'British Muslims'; the main aim of this collection is to do this. Muslims in Scotland constitute only 1.45% of Scotland's total population. However, Muslims are the largest religious minority group and are larger than all of the other religious minorities combined (Elshayyal, 2016).

The chapters in this collection explore the everyday lives, experiences, practices and attitudes of Muslims in Scotland. In order to set the context for these chapters, in this introduction I explore the early settlement of Muslims in Scotland and discuss some of the initial research projects that charted the settlement of Asians and Pakistanis in Scotland's main cities. I then discuss the current situation for Muslims in Scotland through data from the 2011 Scottish Census. Following a short note about the significance of the Scottish context, in the final section I discuss the main themes and issues that have been explored in research about Muslims in Scotland. In doing so, I introduce the chapters of this collection and their contribution to these literatures. The themes covered include: gender, generation and sexuality; national, ethnic and religious identities; residential segregation, suburbanisation and integration; racism, Islamophobia and securitisation; health, economic and educational inequalities; political representation, engagement and participation; and, finally, media representation and stigmatisation. Research about Muslims in Scotland has emerged from a range of different academic disciplines including criminology, education, human geography, religious studies and sociology, to name a few. Such work also has its origins in different debates and perspectives – such as feminism, ethnic and racial studies or multiculturalism – and uses diverse forms of research such as ethnographic work, interviews, surveys and so on. This has shaped the focus and type of research being conducted. This disciplinary and methodological diversity is reflected in the chapters of this collection.

EARLY SETTLEMENT, GROWTH AND CURRENT CONTEXT

According to Bashir Mann (2014), there has been a Muslim presence in Scotland since 1504, as King James IV (1488–1513) employed 'black more' (Moor) musicians. In the seventeenth century, there was also evidence of 'black trumpeters', and these were connected to the Scottish Life Guards and Moorish musicians in the Scottish regiments of the eighteenth and nineteenth centuries. Migrants from North Africa, particularly Morocco, tended to be referred to as Moors or Mores, and so Mann (2014) surmises that these people were Muslims. However, they did not remain in Scotland, and instead returned home once their employment came to an end.

From around the mid-nineteenth century, Indian seamen could be found in Scotland as they were recruited as lascars to work in cities such as Glasgow, which was now the 'Second City of the Empire' (Ansari, 2014: 36). There were also sailors from Bengal in Dundee working in the jute industry, and early sources mention places such as Aberdeen, Dumbarton and Clydebank as locations where Muslim migrants could be found (Ansari, 2014). Gilliat-Ray (2010) includes Glasgow in a list of British cities – alongside Cardiff, Liverpool and Hull – as an important settlement for Muslims. The records of the Glasgow Sailors Home also provide evidence of Muslim lascars; its report of 1903 found that around

5,500 of the annual nightly boarders were lascars (Ansari, 2004). Mann (2014) confirms that some of the earliest Muslims to settle in Scotland did so in the 1920s and were from the Indian sub-continent. Ansari (2004) refers to the success story of Nathoo Mohammed, who arrived in 1919 as a lascar and started peddling before becoming a successful wholesaler. In 1924, his younger brothers joined him, along with other relatives and friends. Ansari (2004: 47–8) quotes Ata Mohammed Ashrif, a close relative of Nathoo Mohammed:

> there were about 40 to 50 Indians in Glasgow, all living in Anderton and Port Dundass [sic] districts. They were mostly illiterate peasant farmers from villages in the Nakodar and Jagaron areas of District Jullandhar. There were also two or three Pathans, from the North West Frontier Province, a similar number of lascars from Mirpur in Kashmir, and Bengal. Many of these people were ex-seamen who had jumped ship ... two or three ex-soldiers who were in this country during the war had come back here after getting demobbed in India. All were engaged in selling door-to-door out of bags.

Given the challenges of such insecure work, many of these migrants moved to other places in Scotland such as Dundee, Aberdeen and Edinburgh in order to look for work (Ansari, 2004). Although the Depression years of the 1930s were very challenging for many of these migrants, with some returning to India, others persevered and when the economy picked up again in the mid-1930s more opportunities became available in Glasgow. Around 400 Muslim migrants from within a ten-mile radius of Nathoo Mohammed's village in India were now resident in Scotland, mostly in the Gorbals area of Glasgow but also in other locations, including the Highlands and Islands. This was one of the reasons behind the presence of around 300 Muslims living on the Island of Lewis, mostly in Stornoway.

The growing Muslim community lacked a formal meeting place until late 1933, when the Jamiat ul Muslimin (Muslim Association) opened in Glasgow, the third organisation of its kind outside of London (the others being in Manchester and Newcastle). For larger celebrations, a hall on Gorbals Street was used and, in 1942, a formal lease was entered into, turning this hall into a temporary mosque (this was located opposite the site of the current Glasgow Central Mosque). By the late 1940s, Muslim migrants from rural Indian backgrounds had taken up casual trading opportunities and lived in various locations across the UK, including Scotland. It is estimated that there were around 500 Muslims in Glasgow by the early 1950s (Mann, 2014), some of whom opened clothing wholesale warehouses and grocery stores. Mann (2014) also notes that the number of Muslim pedlars at this time started to decline, as some were taking up alternative forms of employment in shops and restaurants. Most Muslims lived in the Gorbals in Glasgow, an area characterised by overcrowding and poverty.

Mann (2014) notes that it was at this point – from the late 1940s onwards – that the family and friends of those who had already migrated to Scotland chose to migrate, too. As a result, the Muslim population is estimated to have reached 1,000 by 1954 (Mann, 2014). In 1954, Glasgow's Indian community founded the Indian Film Society, which began showing films on Sundays in cinemas across the city. In the late 1950s, some Muslims from Lancashire and the Midlands migrated to Scotland as the recession resulted in the reduction of employment opportunities in mills and factories (Mann, 2014). It is estimated that there were 2,500 Muslims in Glasgow by 1960 (and 5,000 in Scotland) but, with many newcomers arriving in 1961 and 1962, Mann (2014) claims that Glasgow's Muslim community reached 5,000 by mid-1962. James Dickie, a sixteen-year-old Glaswegian boy, in 1960 apparently became one of the first young Scots to convert to Islam at the Glasgow Central Mosque (Mann, 2014).

Some of the earliest research about ethnic minorities in Scotland tended to rely on the electoral register as a mechanism for identifying 'Asian' names, as the census did not include questions about religious affiliation or ethnicity. One of the earliest studies of the Pakistani community in Scotland was Jones and Davenport's (1972) work about the Pakistani community of Dundee, which they estimated to be around 500 to 600 in the early 1970s, only 0.3% of the city's population. They interviewed thirty-four Pakistani men, all of whom came from West Pakistan. Before moving, most were employed in farming or retail in Pakistan, and the main motivations for leaving Pakistan were to earn more money and have a better living. Two-thirds moved in 1961 or during the first half of 1962, and the first place in Britain where nine of the thirty-four settled was Dundee. Others initially arrived in West Yorkshire, the East Midlands, south-east Lancashire or Glasgow, and then moved on to Dundee. There were two who originally arrived in Stornoway, and one each in Aberdeen, Kirkcaldy and Wick. These migrants moved to Dundee due to a lack of opportunity in their initial areas of settlement. Some twenty-eight of the thirty-four men were married to Pakistani women, nineteen of whom joined their partners, mostly after 1964. Most were working in the jute industry which employed twenty-seven of the thirty-four men, and only one was unemployed. The vast majority lived centrally in Dundee, in the Hilltown, Stobswell and Hawkhill-Blackness areas.

Shortly after this initial study in Dundee, Kearsley and Strivastava (1974) completed a questionnaire survey to explore patterns of residential mobility of the Asian community in Glasgow. They observed that the vast majority of immigrants in Glasgow at the time were Indian and Pakistani, with the Black African and Caribbean population that is found in many other British cities being largely absent. The ethnic minority population of Glasgow was estimated at 12,000, or 1.3% of the city's population. The authors relied on the identification of names from the electoral register. In 1951, most of the Asian population lived in the Gorbals, Garnethill, Maryhill and the city centre. It is estimated that by 1961 there were around 3,000 Asians in Glasgow. While there was still an Asian presence in those areas identified in 1951, the population had dispersed somewhat, particularly into the Pollokshields and Govanhill areas in the south side of the city and Woodside in the West End. By 1971, Pollokshields and Woodside were the main neighbourhoods of residence, with continuing dispersal into other areas, including those mentioned above as well as into the area along Paisley Road West in the south side. It is estimated that there were 8,000 Asians in Glasgow in 1966 and 12,000 in 1971, although by this time much of the Gorbals area was being demolished so there were fewer Asians living there. In a later study, Bowes et al. (1990) completed work for Glasgow City Council on the ethnic minority population of the city and found that there were 17,821 people with Indian or Pakistani heritage who comprised 89.3% of the city's total ethnic minority population. The average household size was 5.2. The main areas of residence of this population were the Pollokshields and Crosshill areas in the south side of the city and Woodlands in the West End. Bowes et al. (1990) noted that at this time the ethnic minority population was highly concentrated, but that some people were starting to move into neighbouring areas. They also observed that some Asian families were moving into new private housing outside of the traditional areas of settlement, with some also choosing to move to the suburban areas of Giffnock, Bearsden and Bishopbriggs.

It was only in 1987 that one of the first studies of Edinburgh's ethnic minority community was completed (SEMRU, 1987). At this point, the estimated population of the Pakistani community of the Lothians was 4,000, and the study noted that this was an estimate given the absence of questions about ethnicity in the 1991 census. Most lived in Edinburgh in areas such as Leith, in the south side of the city, and in council housing in Wester Hailes on the outskirts of Edinburgh. Most of this population worked in restaurants, grocery stores and draperies.

A census question about ethnic origin was added in 1991, and Bailey et al. (1995) were able to examine the situation of Pakistanis in Scotland in more depth and more accurately than in previous studies. They noted that shipping companies, as well as the university sector, were important sources of early Asian settlement in Scotland. Although most have their origins in pre-1947 India, their geographical origins and religious views connect them more closely with a Pakistani heritage. In 1991, the Pakistani community in Scotland numbered 21,192, one-third of the ethnic minority community in Scotland and the largest minority group. Most lived in Glasgow (10,495), Edinburgh (2,625) and Dundee (1,157), although there were clusters of over 500 Pakistanis in Eastwood (918), Motherwell (631) and Kirkcaldy (505). Pakistanis were noted to have large households and the population to be relatively youthful, the largest group being between sixteen and thirty-nine years old. The Pakistani community at this time was also largely found in urban areas, with some rural areas of Scotland registering no Pakistanis.

In the 2001 Scottish census, two questions were asked about religion: one about current religion and the other about religion and upbringing. It was only through the introduction of these questions in the census that a comprehensive demographic profile of the Muslim population in Scotland could be developed, as previous research relied upon data on ethnicity or, before this, on the surnames in the electoral register. In 2001, 42,557 people identified as Muslim when asked about their current religion. As Table 1.1 shows, over 40% of this population lived in Glasgow and just under 16% in Edinburgh.

According to the 2011 census – the most recent census at the time of writing – there are 76,737 Muslims in Scotland, representing 1.4% of the total population. This is an increase in 79% from the total of 42,557 in 2001. Mann (2014) notes that 6–7% did not respond to the census question about religion and this factor, combined with the number of new arrivals, leads him to suggest that there could be over 85,000 Muslims in Scotland. Mann (2014) notes that there are over sixty mosques in Scotland as well as twelve Muslim councillors and two Muslim Members of the Scottish Parliament. In August 2014, Nosheena Mobarik became a member of the House of Lords.

In terms of geographical distribution, the majority of the Muslim population live in Scotland's main cities, particularly Glasgow, where nearly 42% of the Muslim population live (see Table 1.1). Edinburgh, Aberdeen and Dundee have 16.2%, 5.59% and 5% of the Muslim population of Scotland respectively. Notably, North and South Lanarkshire, East Renfrewshire and Fife are each home to around 3–4% of the

Table 1.1 Muslim population in Scotland by council area in 2001 and 2011

Council area	2001		2011	
	Total Muslim population	% of total Muslim population	Total Muslim population	% of total Muslim population
Total	42557	100.00	76737	100.00
Aberdeen City	1753	4.12	4293	5.59
Aberdeenshire	266	0.63	691	0.90
Angus	194	0.46	395	0.51
Argyll & Bute	118	0.28	186	0.24
Clackmannanshire	171	0.40	334	0.44
Dumfries & Galloway	204	0.48	406	0.53
Dundee City	2879	6.77	3875	5.05
East Ayrshire	215	0.51	374	0.49
East Dunbartonshire	768	1.80	1044	1.36
East Lothian	204	0.48	508	0.66
East Renfrewshire	1918	4.51	3002	3.91
Edinburgh, City of	6759	15.88	12434	16.20
Eilean Siar	59	0.14	61	0.08
Falkirk	796	1.87	1415	1.84
Fife	1496	3.52	2591	3.38
Glasgow City	17792	41.81	32117	41.85
Highland	392	0.92	691	0.90
Inverclyde	148	0.35	197	0.26
Midlothian	286	0.67	508	0.66
Moray	171	0.40	236	0.31
North Ayrshire	164	0.39	210	0.27
North Lanarkshire	1916	4.50	3315	4.32
Orkney Islands	8	0.02	20	0.03
Perth & Kinross	304	0.71	741	0.97
Renfrewshire	627	1.47	1313	1.71
Scottish Borders	107	0.25	256	0.33
Shetland Islands	56	0.13	96	0.13
South Ayrshire	140	0.33	246	0.32
South Lanarkshire	1118	2.63	2514	3.28
Stirling	353	0.83	578	0.75
West Dunbartonshire	218	0.51	344	0.45
West Lothian	957	2.25	1746	2.28

Muslim population. A majority of Muslims in Scotland are of South Asian heritage (65%), although this percentage is decreasing over time as Muslims in other ethnic categories – such as Black African – are increasing (Elshayyal, 2016). There are Muslims in each of Scotland's eight Parliamentary regions, although 75% of the Muslim population live in Glasgow, Lothian and North East Scotland (which includes Dundee and Aberdeen) (Elshayyal, 2016). Some thirteen electoral wards have a Muslim population of 5% or more, with Pollokshields and Southside Central, both in Glasgow, having a Muslim population of 27.8% and 15.7% respectively.

Muslims represent just under 40% of Scotland's Asian population, 15% of the Black population and 80% of the Arab population (Elshayyal, 2016). It is notable (see Table 1.2) that nearly 8% of Scotland's Muslim population identify as White, 71.5% as Asian, less than 7% as African and almost 10% as Arab. This indicates an increasing diversity among the Muslim population of Scotland which may be due to the dispersal of asylum seekers and refugees to Scotland. One possible explanation for the sizeable population of White Scottish Muslims may be due to them converting to Islam. There are, however, other possible explanations: migrants arriving from Central and Eastern Europe who are of Muslim heritage but see themselves as White; people wishing to distance themselves from being associated with Asian or other ethnic groups (and therefore identifying as 'White'); or a strategy towards integration with the white Scottish community and minimising differences.

The Muslim population of Scotland is a youthful one; although only 1.45% of the total Scottish population, Muslims represent 2.4% of children of school age (Elshayyal, 2016). According to the 2011 census data, 55% of the Muslim population are aged under thirty, 35% under twenty and 20% under the age of ten. Less than 5% are aged 65 or over. As Table 1.3 makes clear, for all age bands under forty, the percentage of the Muslim population in each age group is more than the overall population in Scotland, and is nearly double in most of these age bands. As Elshayyal (2016: 30) observes:

> for some areas of Glasgow and Dundee, wards with the most concentrated Muslim populations (constituting over 5% of the total), the percentage of Muslims among children of school age is very high. For instance, in the Pollokshields ward, where Muslims make up 28% of the overall population, the proportion of 5–15-year-olds who are Muslim is 48%.

This not only indicates the youthfulness of the Muslim population, but also points to the likelihood of this population continuing to increase in size, emphasising the importance of the research in this collection.

THE SIGNIFICANCE OF THE SCOTTISH CONTEXT

A key motivation for bringing this collection of contributors together is the recognition that there are unique characteristics of the Scottish

Table 1.2 Ethnic group membership of Muslims in Scotland

	Total Muslim population	Percentage of total Muslim population
White		
Scottish	2,501	3.26
Other British	694	0.90
Irish	61	0.08
Gypsy/Traveller	25	0.03
Polish	130	0.17
Other White	2,572	3.35
Total	**5,983**	**7.80**
Asian, Asian Scottish or Asian British		
Pakistani, Pakistani Scottish or Pakistani British	44,858	58.46
Indian, Indian Scottish or Indian British	1,954	2.55
Bangladeshi, Bangladeshi Scottish or Bangladeshi British	3,053	3.98
Chinese, Chinese Scottish or Chinese British	341	0.44
Other Asian	4,664	6.08
Total	**54,870**	**71.50**
African		
African, African Scottish or African British	4,779	6.23
Other African	272	0.35
Total	**5,051**	**6.58**
Caribbean or Black		
Caribbean, Caribbean Scottish or Caribbean British	31	0.04
Black, Black Scottish or Black British	224	0.29
Other Caribbean or Black	74	0.10
Total	**329**	**0.43**
Other ethnic groups		
Arab, Arab Scottish or Arab British	7,505	9.78
Other ethnic groups	1,657	2.16
Total	**9,162**	**11.94**
Mixed or multiple ethnic groups	1,342	1.75
TOTAL	**76,737**	

context that result in the experiences of ethnic minority communities being different from other places in the UK. Although there is an extensive literature about Muslims in 'Britain' (e.g. Gilliat-Ray, 2010; Hopkins and Gale, 2009), the vast majority of this work has focused upon centres of ethnic and religious minority settlement in England such as London, Birmingham and the northern mill towns. There has been a tendency to generalise from such studies to make all-encompassing

Table 1.3 Age profile of Muslims in Scotland

Age	Total Muslim population	Percentage of Muslim population	Total population of Scotland	Percentage of total population
0 to 4	8,283	10.79	292,821	5.53
5 to 9	7,249	9.45	269,617	5.09
10 to 14	5,942	7.74	291,615	5.51
15	1,070	1.39	62,278	1.18
16 to 17	2,196	2.86	126,266	2.38
18 to 19	2,550	3.32	142,282	2.69
20 to 24	7,187	9.37	363,940	6.87
25 to 29	8,555	11.15	345,632	6.53
30 to 34	8,546	11.14	321,695	6.07
35 to 39	6,842	8.92	340,056	6.42
40 to 44	5,590	7.28	394,698	7.45
45 to 49	3,671	4.78	410,929	7.76
50 to 54	3,170	4.13	375,827	7.10
55 to 59	2,130	2.78	330,891	6.25
60 to 64	1,229	1.60	336,522	6.35
65 to 69	831	1.08	261,198	4.93
70 to 74	886	1.15	220,594	4.17
75 to 79	492	0.64	178,114	3.36
80 to 84	226	0.29	124,525	2.35
85 and over	92	0.12	105,903	2.00
Total	76,737	100.00	5,295,403	100.00

conclusions about 'British Muslims'. However, the distinctive characteristics of Scotland may mean that it is problematic to generalise from work in specific cities in England and apply this directly to 'Britain'. This is why this collection of essays is needed. This is not to suggest that there is no racism in Scotland: far from it. Instead, it is about recognising the distinctive characteristics of Scotland's history, politics and society that make it different from England.

Scotland experienced significant Irish migration in the nineteenth century and this, combined with deindustrialisation, meant that there was less demand for migrant labour from South Asia there than there was in other UK locations (Smith and Simpson, 2015). Moreover, Dunlop (1993: 89) notes that:

> The analysis of racialisation, and the role of racism in it, adopts almost exclusively a British perspective, assuming that what has happened in England since 1945 has also happened in Scotland. Rarely, if ever, is any specific attention given to events in Scotland. This neglect is in part the rest of certain 'common-sense' interpretations or 'good race relations' that have, until recently, predominated within Scottish political discourse.

Clearly, then, the history and nature of migration to Scotland have distinctive characteristics compared to England. This is why the diversity, distribution and structure of Scotland's Black and minority ethnic population are different from those of other places in the UK (Hopkins, 2008b). In addition, and as noted by Dunlop (1993; see also Miles and Dunlop, 1987), there have been problematic assumptions that see Scotland as being good at 'race relations'; unfortunately, such assumptions continue where there remains a culture whereby issues of racism are disengaged with or displaced and deflected onto England, and imagined as an 'English problem' (Hopkins, 2016). This has had the worrying consequence of 'unwarranted complacency among Scottish decision-takers' (Hopkins and Smith, 2008: 105) when it comes to matters of race equality.

The specifics of Scottish politics and governance, alongside the civic nationalism associated with Scottishness and Scottish national identities, are also important aspects of the Scottish context compared to England (Hopkins, 2008b). The dominant discourse in Scotland has tended not to espouse a version of Scottish nationalism that promotes White supremacy; instead, the focus has been about promoting a civic form of nationalism and standing in opposition to Englishness (Smith and Simpson, 2015). Hepburn and Rose (2014) point out the stark contrast between the racist anti-immigration rhetoric of the British National Party and the UK Independence Party, in contrast to the Scottish National Party, which, they observe, is one of the most pro-immigration political parties in the UK. These distinctive aspects of Scottish history, politics, governance and society are important considerations for research about the everyday lives, experiences and aspirations of Scottish Muslims, and further justify the need for this collection. I now explore key themes in research about Muslims in Scotland, while introducing the chapters that follow.

GENDER, GENERATION AND SEXUALITY

Issues of gender inequalities, the place of men and women in Islam, and differences between Muslim men and women in different aspects of public and private life have been the focus of research about Muslims in Scotland. In some of my earlier work, I explored the ways in which young Muslim men in Scotland construct their masculine identities (Hopkins, 2006). This work challenged the stereotypical view of young Muslim men as either patriarchal and aggressive, or effeminate and academic. From focus group and interview data with young Muslim men in Glasgow and Edinburgh, I argued that the young men's masculinities were shaped by different markers of social difference, such as disability, class and sexuality, and so were not shaped by Islam alone. I also made the point that the masculine identities of young Muslim men are shaped in relation to the masculinities of other men, such as White working-class Scottish men. Furthermore, I argued that young Muslim men adopt contradictory masculine subject positions in promoting a form of 'sexist equality' whereby they claim to support equality between men and women while also enforcing sexist stereotypes about the position of women in society (Hopkins, 2009).

Research about Muslim women in Scotland followed shortly after work about Muslim masculinities. Siraj (2011) explored ideas of modesty and the wearing of the hijab (head covering) among Muslim women in Scotland and found that there were differences and similarities between women who wore the hijab and those who did not. Wearers of the hijab tended to see it as a form of 'modesty, virtue and respect' (Siraj, 2011: 716), while those who did not wear it viewed it as an unnecessary item of clothing. The focus upon gender issues is reflected in a number of chapters in this collection. In Chapter 5, Rebecca Syswerda explores the everyday lives of migrant Muslim women who have recently moved to Scotland. She focuses particularly upon their interactions with a community organisation and the challenges they face in terms of social isolation (see also Folly, 2015).

Interconnected with debate about gender issues, some of my own work has explored young Muslim men's negotiations of intergenerational relations (Hopkins, 2006). Muslim youth is often represented as being in conflict with its parents' generation; parents are regarded as traditional and conservative, and the younger generation is seen to be modern and liberal. In contrast to this, I found that young Muslim men in Scotland were respectful of their parents' generation, valued how hard they had worked for the family and admired the commitment that they demonstrated to their religious faith. Hengameh Ashraf-Emami discusses related issues of gender and generation in Chapter 8 of this collection. She explores the relationships between mothers and daughters, as well as fathers and daughters, the role of women's agency, and how intergenerational tensions are managed and negotiated.

Although much work has focused specifically upon gender relations, issues of sexuality have featured far less frequently. A significant exception to this is work by Siraj (2006, 2011a, 2011b, 2012), who claims that there is a lack of work on Islam and sexuality as a result of the ways that the Qur'an, as a heteronormative source, determines ideas around sexual morality and so represses debate about such issues. Continuing this important work, in Chapter 6 Asifa Siraj discusses the challenges facing three gay Scottish Muslim men as they struggle to negotiate the conflicting relationship between their sexuality and their religion.

NATIONAL, ETHNIC AND RELIGIOUS IDENTITIES

An important contribution of some previous research about Muslims in Scotland has been the attention given to the construction and contestation of Scottish national identities, and how these interplay with ethnic and religious identities. Saeed et al.'s (1999) work about the national and ethnic identities of sixty-three Glaswegian Pakistani teenagers is very significant here. Some 97% of the participants stated that they were Muslim and tended to adopt a mixture of ethnic, national and religious identity categories. When questioned about their ethnicity, 59% of the young people selected dual forms of identification; for example, 22% said they were Scottish Pakistani and 19% Scottish Muslim. After these options were provided by the researcher, 63% stated that they were Scottish Pakistani, with 88% of young people choosing bicultural forms of identification.

Similarly, in my own work I found that young Muslim men in Scotland tended to identify as Scottish Muslims and utilised a range of markers of Scottish national identity in doing so (Hopkins, 2007b). This included claiming a sense of Scottishness through markers such as place of birth, length of residence and a commitment to place, as well as upbringing and accent. This earlier work is supported by recent analysis of the 2011 Scottish census, in which almost 71% of the Scottish Muslim population identified as being Scottish, British or a combination of these. Nearly 25% identified as Scottish only and just over 29% as British only, while nearly 10% identified as both Scottish and British (Elshayyal, 2016). In Chapter 9, Omar Shaikh and Stefano Bonino explore issues connected with national, ethnic and religious identities through the work of the Colourful Heritage Project, a charitable community heritage project that aims to preserve and celebrate the lives and times of the early South Asian and Muslim migrants to Scotland. Similar connections to, and affiliations with, Scotland and Scottishness were found following an analysis of the several oral testimonies found on the project website. Although both religion and national identities are important to Muslims in Scotland, much work, including Chapter 9, points to the ways in which Muslims identify with multiple forms of identification, including transnational connections associated with their countries or regions of origin or their families' heritage (e.g. Qureshi, 2006; Qureshi and Moores, 1999).

RESIDENTIAL SEGREGATION, SUBURBANISATION AND INTEGRATION

Debates about Muslims in Britain partly emerged from work about race, ethnicity and migration, including research focusing on the measuring and mapping of ethnic residential segregation and patterns of settlement. It is not surprising, then, that research about Muslims in Scotland has also explored similar issues (e.g. Hopkins and Smith, 2008; McGarrigle, 2010; McGarrigle and Kearns, 2009). Mir (2007) studied patterns of suburbanisation among the Glasgow-based Pakistani community and found that there was a complex range of factors that encouraged them to move to the suburbs. This included the professionalisation of the community, alongside a desire for middle-class identities, access to good schools and green space, and the prestige associated with a suburban postcode. Also, in terms of residential clustering, Muñoz (2010, 2011) investigated the clustering of the Indian-Hindu, Indian-Sikh and Indian-Muslim population in Scotland, and found that there was a tendency for them to form residential clusters based on their religious affiliation. More recently, Bonino (2015: 84) observed that 'the Muslim community in Edinburgh (about 12,500 people, i.e. 2.6% of the total population in 2011) is quite widespread and dispersed throughout the city and this seems to favour closer contact and better integration within wider society'. In Chapter 13, Reza Bagheri explores the issue of integration and proposes that Muslims in Scotland follow a form of halal (permitted) integration, whereby they are able to fit in with Scottish society as a whole while maintaining unique aspects of their religious identity.

Most of the chapters in this collection focus upon the experiences of Muslims in Scotland's main cities, as this is where the majority of the Scottish Muslim population reside. The increasing dispersal of the Muslim population into new areas of settlement on the suburbs of these main cities, as well as to more rural and remote places, is worthy of further attention (see De Lima, 2003). Chapter 7 includes reflections on the experiences of young Muslims in Fife and Dumfries, and some of the chapters in this collection involve research in which Muslims outside the traditional areas of settlement were consulted. In this context, there has been relatively little research about Muslims' housing situations in Scotland, their negotiations of housing tenure, or their household size and composition. It is interesting to note from the 2011 Scottish census that 52% of Muslims in Scotland are owner-occupiers, 18% live in social housing and 28% are in privately rented accommodation. Furthermore, the percentage of Muslim heads of household under the age of thirty-five is double that of the Scottish population as a whole, and 25% of Muslims live in single-person households compared to 35% of the total population (Elshayyal, 2016).

RACISM, ISLAMOPHOBIA AND SECURITISATION

Contrary to common-sense and stereotypical ideas that Scotland is tolerant and inclusive, an important strand of research about Muslims in Scotland, and ethnic minority communities in general, has been about their everyday experiences of racism and discrimination. In an early study, Bowes et al. (1990) found serious cases of harassment among South Asian tenants in Glasgow. Incidents referred to by those who participated in the research included verbal abuse by 58%, personal attacks by 30% and attacks in the home by 20%. This is supported by later work, including studies about the everyday racism experienced by the Pakistani community in East Pollokshields in Glasgow (Hopkins, 2004a). Hussain and Miller (2006) found that 49% of the majority community in Scotland were identified as having Islamophobic attitudes. Kidd and Jamieson (2011) found that Muslims in Scotland often experience racism or sexual harassment in their own areas of residence. More recently, research highlighted everyday experiences of Islamophobia for many ethnic minorities in Scotland, not only Muslims (Hopkins et al., 2015). Many of the chapters in this collection provide further evidence that racism, discrimination and Islamophobia unfortunately remain a part of the everyday lives for many Scottish Muslims.

Interconnected with research about racism and Islamophobia have also been a number of studies connected with matters of citizenship and identity, particularly since the events of 9/11 which resulted in the heightened stigmatisation of Muslim communities in Scotland. Bonino (2015) found that Scottish Muslims' sense of religiosity has been strengthened following 9/11, as the Muslim community has generated greater internal cohesion (see also Bonino 2015b). In a study of faith communities and local government in Glasgow, a key finding by Clegg and Rosie (2005: 2) was that 'the Muslim community is perceived, by all faith groups surveyed, to be the group most under pressure. The pressure has increased since the events of 11th September 2001'. Similarly, Frondigoun et al. (2007) found that Muslims in Scotland felt under additional scrutiny after 9/11 and the London 7/7 attacks.

Blackwood et al. (2013, 2015) have explored Scottish Muslims' experiences and negotiations of misrecognition in airports. They interviewed thirty-eight Scottish Muslims in Dundee, Edinburgh and Glasgow. Participants adopted different strategies in order to manage the anxiety that they associated with encounters in airport spaces. Some avoided all airports or specific airports, travelled less often or considered their travel plans in more detail than they had previously. Some also talked about avoiding the gaze of others or changing their walking style. An important strategy was to come across as less visibly Muslim. A number of the chapters in this collection also focus on the everyday encounters negotiated and experienced by Muslims in Scotland.

HEALTH, ECONOMIC AND EDUCATIONAL INEQUALITIES

Experiences of racism and discrimination are often interconnected with other inequalities. Netto et al. (2011) undertook a review of the relationship between poverty and ethnicity in Scotland and found that, on income-based measures, Pakistani, Bangladeshi and Black households had higher rates of poverty than other ethnic groups. Some of the key findings from this work point to high rates of unemployment among some minority ethnic groups, links between economic disadvantage, ethnicity and poor health, as well as concerns about racial harassment in some areas. More recently, Elshayyal (2016) observed that there is clear evidence that White and minority ethnic Scots face disproportionate levels of poverty and deprivation, particularly among those who identify as African. In terms of employment, 31% of the Muslim population is economically active on a full-time basis. A significant proportion – 18.5% – are students, 42% of whom live in Glasgow (compared to the Scottish average of 6.2%) (Elshayyal, 2016). Some 29% of Muslims are self-employed. Muslims' experience of the workplace in Scotland is a notable omission from this collection and an area worthy of further exploration (although see Deakins et al., 2009; Ishaq and Hussain, 2010).

Like others areas of research, debates about health and well-being have tended to focus on the variable of ethnicity, rather than religion, with a notable exception being the work of Kristiansen et al. (2014) on Muslims with life-limiting illness in Scotland. In Chapter 2, Maria Kristiansen and Aziz Sheikh provide a comprehensive health profile of Muslims in Scotland. Although they point to the diversity of the Muslim population in terms of health behaviours, experiences and outcomes, they also note some overall patterns, such as relatively low levels of alcohol consumption. That being said, they also observe that health outcomes are shaped by a complex range of intersecting factors, including religion, culture and socioeconomic background, as well as community and social issues.

In terms of education, most research in Scotland that is relevant to the focus of this collection is on issues of race equality or the experiences of ethnic minority pupils (e.g. Arshad et al., 2004) in general, rather than a specific focus upon Muslim students. One exception to this is the report by Weedon et al. (2013) about the educational experiences of Muslim families in England and Scotland. Building upon this work, in Chapter 3 Elisabet Weedon and Sheila Riddell explore the education outcomes of Muslim pupils in Scotland, as well as the ways in which their parents use different forms of capital. They found that Pakistani pupils' achievement in Scotland matches or is above that of White UK pupils. All parents also wanted their children to perform well at school, with a small proportion also emphasising the significance of social and emotional skills. Families clearly regarded education as a vehicle for social mobility.

POLITICAL REPRESENTATION, ENGAGEMENT AND PARTICIPATION

As far back as 1970, Bashir Mann was the first Pakistani councillor to be elected anywhere in Britain (from a ward in Glasgow). The only UK Parliamentary constituency in Scotland that has been held by an ethnic minority MP is Glasgow Govan, in which Mohammad Sarwar was elected in 1997 to become one of the first Muslim MPs in the UK (Meer and Peace, 2015). His son, Anas Sarwar, held the same seat in 2010 and is now a Member of the Scottish Parliament (MSP) for Glasgow. In 2015, there were two ethnic minority MSPs elected in Glasgow: Humza Yousaf for the Scottish National Party (SNP) and Hanzala Malik for Labour (Meer and Peace, 2015). The Scottish Parliamentary constituency with the largest Muslim population is Glasgow Southside, in which 18.9% of the population identify as Muslim. This is currently Nicola Sturgeon's constituency (Elshayyal, 2016). Following an analysis of data from the Scottish census, Elshayyal (2016: 54) noted:

> Muslims are civically engaged, with a strong sense of national identity, and a particular sense of pride in their Scottishness, although there is clearly some work to do in translating everyday civic and political engagement into active participation in the electoral system.

Research about the political participation of young Muslim men in Scotland has demonstrated that they have a range of carefully considered political opinions and are conscious of the significance of the decisions made by politicians when it comes to international affairs (Hopkins, 2007a). Research has demonstrated that Muslim women in Scotland may feel the need to engage more fully in community and voluntary organisations and support networks, in order to resist the negative ways that they are represented in the media (Ali and Hopkins, 2011). Indeed, some Muslim women were found to have reasserted themselves in the public sphere and to be redefining spaces of civic engagement in doing so. More recently, Botterill et al. (2016) found that ethnic minorities in Scotland started to feel more insecure as a result of the Scottish independence referendum, as this raised questions for them about whether or not they would be entitled to be a part of an independent Scotland.

Building upon these debates, Chapters 4 and 7 explore the political participation of Muslims in Scotland, with a specific focus upon young Muslims. In Chapter 4, Robin Finlay, Peter Hopkins and Gurchathen Sanghera explore the ways in which young Muslims engage with formal political parties and issues, including debates about Scottish nationalism, the SNP and the Scottish independence referendum. However, in this chapter, young people's engagements with social movements – activism as well as charity work and volunteering – are also explored, demonstrating the different forms that young people's engagement with politics can take. Interrelated to this, Katherine Botterill, Gurchathen Sanghera and Peter Hopkins (in Chapter 7) also explore young Scottish Muslims' engagement with political issues. However, the focus here also includes young people's engagement with ideas about multicultural nationalism and representations of Muslims in the media (see also Chapter 11). Important work on ethnic minorities and politics in Scotland has also focused upon how political elites locate minorities with projects of nation building in the context of multinationalism and multiculturalism, which is the focus of Chapter 10 by Nasar Meer (see also Meer, 2015). Here, the focus is upon multiculturalism in Scotland and the ways in which MSPs locate ethnic minorities in their engagement with the 'national question'. This connects with Netto's (2008) earlier work about the involvement of ethnic minorities in the arts in Scotland. The ways in which Scottish nationalism is constructed as multicultural (or not) by organisations and funding bodies play an important role in the extent to which ethnic minorities are able to participate fully in and engage with such activities.

MEDIA, REPRESENTATION AND STIGMATISATION

A significant issue for Muslims in Scotland is the problematic way in which they are represented in the media, and how their religion is often misunderstood and stereotyped in troubling ways (e.g. Frondigoun et al., 2007; Kidd and Jamieson, 2011). A number of research projects – including some that are discussed in this collection – express serious concerns about the general lack of understanding about what it means to be a Muslim (e.g. Hopkins, 2004b). In Chapter 11, Michael Munnik takes up these issues of the media and representation, pointing out that journalists in Scotland tend not to take much interest in religion and, when they do, the focus tends to be on Christian sectarianism rather than on Islam or Muslims. He interviewed journalists who identify as Muslim or have contributed to coverage of Muslims in Scotland, and also observed newsrooms and related meetings. Muslims who work in journalism are keen to present a diversity of stories about the Muslim community and, in doing so, are eager to ensure that the Muslim community is not represented as homogeneous and lacking in diversity.

That being said, the media is only one of many outlets that play a powerful role in representing Muslims in Scotland, and future research could usefully extend this to other contexts including schools, colleges, universities and other institutions that have a role in representing Islam to the public. In Chapter 12, Fayaz Alibhai explores how Islam is represented in the spaces of the Edinburgh International Book Festival, building upon the research that he conducted there between 2011 and 2013. He explores the public spaces of the festival and the nature of the encounters that take place there. Such spaces play a potentially powerful role in terms of how they represent Muslims in Scotland and educate people about what it means to be Muslim. Given that previous research has called for education to help to improve how Muslims are regarded by others, such contexts could provide a useful platform for challenging stereotypical representations of Scotland's Muslim community.

MOVING FORWARD ...

This introductory review of research about Muslims in Scotland – and indeed many of the chapters in this collection – could be said to present generally positive narratives about the community. The dispersal of Muslims into new areas of settlement, their engagement with and involvement in politics, and their strong sense of attachment to Scotland together present an optimistic account about the everyday lives of Muslims in Scotland. Elshayyal (2016: 54) concludes her review of the Scottish census by noting that 'on balance, the data tells us a more positive story that has been told in England and Wales, and this should be acknowledged as encouraging' (Elshayyal, 2016: 54). These factors may be the reason why Scotland is sometimes seen as an example of good practice when it comes to debates about multiculturalism, integration and the promotion of good relations between immigrant and minority groups.

That said, research shows that Muslims in Scotland are forced to negotiate specific exclusions. Everyday experiences of racism and discrimination, health and other social inequalities, and negative media representations are just a few of the challenges that many Muslims in Scotland have to negotiate regularly. To compare the Scottish situation only favourably to that in England could lead to complacency about the situation in Scotland. However, regardless of whether or not the Scottish context is encouraging compared to that of other places, it is crucial that everyday racism, marginalisation and prejudice are challenged and resisted whenever possible. Only when these multiple inequalities are overcome will Muslims in Scotland be part of a fair and just society.

REFERENCES

Ali, R. and Hopkins, P. (2012). 'Everyday making and civic engagement amongst Muslim women in Scotland'. In W. Ahmad and Z. Sardar (eds), *Muslims in Britain: Making Social and Political Space*. London: Routledge.

Ansari, H. (2004). *'The Infidel Within': Muslims in Britain Since 1800*. London: Hurst.

Arshad, R., Almeida Diniz, F., Kelly, E., O'Hara, P., Sharp, S. and Syed, R. (2004). 'Minority ethnic pupils' experiences of school in Scotland'. Scottish Executive: Edinburgh.

Bailey, N., Bowes, A. and Sim, D. (1995). 'Pakistanis in Scotland: Census data and research issues'. *Scottish Geographical Magazine*,11(1), 36–45.

Blackwood, L., Hopkins, N. and Reicher, S. (2013). '"I know who I am, but who do they think I am?" Muslim perspectives on encounters with airport authorities'. *Ethnic and Racial Studies*, 36(6), 1090–108.

Blackwood, L., Hopkins, N. and Reicher, S. (2015). '"Flying while Muslim": Citizenship and misrecognition in the airport'. *Journal of Social and Political Psychology*, 3(2), 148–70.

Bonino, S. (2015a). 'Scottish Muslims through a decade of change: Wounded by the stigma, healed by Islam, rescued by Scotland'. *Scottish Affairs*, 24, 78–105.

Bonino, S. (2015b). 'Visible Muslimness in Scotland: Between discrimination and integration'. *Patterns of Prejudice*, 49(4), 367–91.

Botterill, K., Hopkins, P., Sanghera, G. and Arshad, R. (2016). 'Securing disunion: Young people's nationalism, identities and (in)securities in the campaign for an independent Scotland'. *Political Geography*, 55, 124–34.

Bowes, A. M., McCluskey, J. and Sim, D. F. (1990). 'The changing nature of Glasgow's Ethnic Minority'. *Scottish Geographical Magazine*, 106(2), 99–107.

Clegg, C. and Rosie, M. (2005). *Faith Communities and Local Government in Glasgow*. Edinburgh: Scottish Executive.

Deakins, D., Smallbone, D., Ishaq, M., Whittam, G. and Wyper, J. (2009). 'Minority ethnic enterprise in Scotland'. *Journal of Ethnic and Migration Studies*, 35(2), 309–30.

De Lima, P. (2003). 'Beyond place: Ethnicity/race in the debate on social exclusion/inclusion in Scotland'. *Policy Futures in Education*, 1(4), 653–67.

Dunlop, A. (1993). 'An united front? Anti-racist political mobilisations in Scotland'. *Scottish Affairs*, 3, 89–101.

Elshayyal, K. (2016). *Scottish Muslims in Numbers: Understanding Scotland's Muslim Population Through the 2011 Census*. Edinburgh: Alwaleed Centre for the Study of Islam in the Contemporary World, University of Edinburgh.

Folly, R. (2015). 'The subjective experiences of Muslim women in family-related migration to Scotland'. PhD thesis, University of St Andrews.

Frondigoun, L., Croall, H., Hughes, B., Russell, L., Russell, R. and Scott, G. (2007). *Researching Minority Ethnic Young People in Edinburgh and the Greater Glasgow Area*. Glasgow: Glasgow Caledonian University, Report for the Strathclyde and Lothian and Borders Police Forces.

Gilliat-Ray, S. (2010). *Muslims in Britain: An Introduction*. Cambridge: Cambridge University Press.

Hepburn, E. and Rosie, M. (2014). 'Immigration, nationalism and politics in Scotland'. In E. Hepburn and R. Zapata-Barrero (eds), *The Politics of Immigration in Multilevel States: Governance and Politics Parties*. Basingstoke: Palgrave.

Homes, A., McLean, C. and Murray, L. (2010). *Muslim Integration in Scotland*. Edinburgh: Ipsos Mori Scotland.

Hopkins, P. (2004a). 'Everyday racism in Scotland: A case study of East Pollokshields'. *Scottish Affairs*, 49 (Autumn), 88–103.

Hopkins, P. (2004b). 'Young Muslim men in Scotland: Inclusions and exclusions'. *Children's Geographies*, 2(2), 257–72.

Hopkins, P. (2006). 'Youthful Muslim masculinities: Gender and generational relations'. *Transactions of the Institute of British Geographers*, 31(3), 337–52.

Hopkins, P. (2007a). 'Global events, national politics, local lives: Young Muslim men in Scotland'. *Environment and Planning A*, 38(3), 1119–33.

Hopkins, P. (2007b). '"Blue squares", "proper" Muslims and transnational networks: Narratives of national and religious identities amongst young Muslim men living in Scotland'. *Ethnicities*, 7(1), 61–81.

Hopkins, P. (2008a). 'Young, male, Scottish and Muslim: A portrait of Kabir'. In C. Jeffrey and J. Dyson (eds), *Telling Young Lives: Portraits of Global Youth*, pp. 69–80. Philadelphia, PA: Temple University Press.

Hopkins. P. (2008b). 'Race, nation and politics: The difference that Scotland makes'. In C. Dwyer and C. Bressey (eds), *New Geographies of Race and Racism*, pp. 113–24. Aldershot: Ashgate.

Hopkins, P. (2009). 'Responding to the "crisis of masculinity": The perspectives of young Muslim men from Glasgow and Edinburgh, Scotland'. *Gender, Place and Culture*, 16(3), 299–312.

Hopkins, P. (2016). 'Deflections, displacements, disengagements'. In N. Meer (ed.), *Scotland and Race Equality: Directions in Policy and Identity*, pp. 30–1. London: Runnymede Trust.

Hopkins, P., Botterill, K., Sanghera, G. and Arshad, R. (2015). *Faith, Ethnicity, Place: Young People's Everyday Geopolitics in Scotland*. Newcastle-upon-Tyne: Newcastle University.

Hopkins, P. and Gale, R. (2009). *Muslims in Britain: Race, Place and Identities*. Edinburgh: Edinburgh University Press.

Hopkins, P. and Smith, S. J. (2008). 'Scaling segregation; racialising fear'. In R. Pain and S. J. Smith (eds), *Fear: Critical Geopolitics and Everyday Life*, pp. 103–16. Aldershot: Ashgate.

Hussain, A. and Miller, W. L. (2006). *Multicultural Nationalism: Islamophobia, Anglophobia and Devolution*. Oxford: Oxford University Press.

Ishaq, M. and Hussain, A. (2010). 'Ethnic minority sole traders' experiences of racial discrimination'. *Scottish Affairs*, 70, 29–38.

Jones, H. and Davenport, M. (1972). 'The Pakistani community in Dundee: A study of its growth and demographic structure', *Scottish Geographical Magazine*, 88(2), 75–85.

Kearsley, G. and Strivastava, S. R. (1974). 'The spatial evolution of Glasgow's Asian community'. *Scottish Geographical Magazine*, 90(2), 110–24.

Kidd, S. and Jamieson, L. (2011). *Experiences of Muslims Living in Scotland*. Edinburgh: Scottish Government.

Kristiansen, M., Irshad, T., Worth, A., Bhopal, R., Lawton, J. and Sheikh, A. (2014). 'The practice of hope: A longitudinal, multi-perspective qualitative study among South Asian Sikhs and Muslims with life-limiting illness in Scotland'. *Ethnicity and Health*, 19(1), 1–19.

Maan, B. (1992). *The New Scots: The Story of Asians in Scotland*. Edinburgh: John Donald.

Mann, B. (2014). *Muslims in Scotland*. Glendaruel: Argyll Publishing.

McGarrigle, J. L. (2010). *Understanding Processes of Ethnic Concentration and Dispersal: South Asian Residential Preferences in Glasgow*. Amsterdam: Amsterdam University Press.

McGarrigle, J. and Kearns, A. (2009). 'Living apart? Place, identity and South Asian residential choice'. *Housing Studies*, 24(4), 451–75.

Meer, N. (2015). 'Looking up in Scotland: Multinationalism, multiculturalism and political elites'. *Ethnic and Racial Studies*, 38(9), 1477–96.

Miles, R. and Dunlop, A. (1987). 'Racism in Britain: The Scottish dimension'. In P. Jackson (ed.), *Race and Racism: Essays in Social Geography*, pp. 98–116. London: Routledge.

Mir, S. (2007). 'The other within the same: some aspects of the Scottish-Pakistani identity in suburban Glasgow'. In C. Aitchison, P. Hopkins and Mei-Po Kwan (eds), *Geographies of Muslim Identities: Diaspora, Gender and Belonging*, pp. 57–78. Aldershot: Ashgate.

Muñoz, S. (2010). 'Geographies of faith: The differing residential patterns of the Indian-Hindu, Indian-Sikh and Indian-Muslim populations of Dundee and Glasgow'. *Population, Space and Place*, 16, 269–85.

Muñoz, S. (2011). 'Ethno-faith-burbs: religious affiliation and residential patterns of the Indian ethnic populations of Dundee and Glasgow'. *Journal of Intercultural Studies*, 32(2), 115–31.

Netto, G. (2008). 'Multiculturalism in the devolved context: Minority ethnic negotiation of identity through engagement in the arts in Scotland'. *Sociology*, 42(1), 47–64.

Netto, G., Sosenko, F. and Bramley, G. (2011). *A Review of Poverty and Ethnicity in Scotland*. York: Joseph Rowntree Foundation.

Peace, T. and Meer, N. (2015). 'The 2015 election: BME groups in Scotland'. In O. Khan and K. Sveinsson (eds), *Race and Elections*, pp. 26–9. Runnymede Perspectives. London: Runnymede Trust.

Qureshi, K. (2006). 'Trans-boundary spaces: Scottish Pakistanis and trans-local/national identities'. *International Journal of Cultural Studies*, 9(2), 207–26.

Qureshi, K. and Moores, S. (1999). 'Identity remix: Tradition and translation in the lives of young Pakistani Scots'. *European Journal of Cultural Studies*, 2(3), 311–30.

Saeed, A., Blain, N. and Forbes, D. (1999). 'New ethnic and national questions in Scotland: Post-British identities among Glasgow Pakistani teenagers'. *Ethnic and Racial Studies*, 22(5), 821–44.

Siraj, A. (2006). 'On being homosexual and Muslim: Conflicts and challenges'. In L. Ouzgane (ed.), *Islamic Masculinities*, pp. 202–16. London: Zed Books.

Siraj, A. (2011a). 'Meanings of modesty and the *hijab* amongst Muslim women in Glasgow, Scotland'. *Gender, Place and Culture*, 18(6), 716–31.

Siraj, A. (2011b). 'Isolated, invisible, and in the closet: The life story of a Scottish Muslim lesbian'. *Journal of Lesbian Studies*, 15(1), 99–121.

Siraj, A. (2012). '"Smoothing down ruffled feathers": The construction of Muslim women's feminine identities'. *Journal of Gender Studies*, 21(2), 185–99.

Weedon, E., Riddell, S., McCluskey, G. and Konstantoni, K. (2013). *Muslim Families' Educational Experiences in England and Scotland*. Edinburgh: Centre for Research in Education Inclusion and Diversity: University of Edinburgh.

2

HEALTH
The Health Profile of Muslims in Scotland

Maria Kristiansen and Aziz Sheikh

INTRODUCTION

Human happiness and well-being are, to a large extent, dependent upon the health of the individual. Similarly, healthy populations are an important prerequisite for societal progress and prosperity (Marmot et al., 2010; World Health Organization, 2015). In order to maximise individual and societal well-being, it is important that the health of all members and sections – that is, irrespective of age, sex/gender, disability, ethnicity, faith or any other protected characteristic – is maximised. A growing body of evidence, however, points to substantial, persistent differences in health outcomes between different ethnic and religious groups. There is, then, an imperative to develop societal and healthcare strategies that are responsive to the aspirations and needs of the diverse populations that now characterise the UK and many other industrialised countries (see, for example, Bhopal, 2013 or Ingleby et al., 2012, for an overview). Insight into the health of Muslims in Scotland is integral to such efforts. In this chapter, we discuss the health profile of Muslims living in Scotland, outline some of the factors shaping health among this diverse group and consider ways of addressing the healthcare needs of Muslims within the context of Scottish healthcare services.

HISTORY AND DATA AVAILABILITY

To understand the current health situation of Muslims in Scotland, it is important briefly to appraise the history of Muslim settlement into Scotland. As outlined in Chapter 1, the migration of Muslims into various parts of the UK started in the early nineteenth century. The first wave of migrants were people from the colonies of the British Empire, including Yemen, India and Malaya (Malaysia) (Ansari, 2004). Since then, migration of Muslims into Scotland has been driven by a need for labour, in particular in the trade and manual sectors, but also by interest in pursuing education, in particular among students from affluent families in South Asia (Ansari, 2004; Maan, 1992). Today, Pakistanis represent the largest ethnic groups among Muslims in Scotland, followed by Indians, Bangladeshis and Arabs. The Scottish Muslim community represents people from a number of different countries and with differing migration histories, ethnic identities and socioeconomic circumstances (Scottish Government, 2011). This diversity has increased further as asylum seekers and refugee communities from across the war-torn Middle East and parts of Africa have settled in Scotland in recent years (Scottish Refugee Council, 2013).

Our ability to outline clearly and understand the health profile of Muslims in Scotland is restricted by the limited data available on health status, health behaviours and use of healthcare services by religious groups. The 2001 Scottish census, which included questions on religious identity, upbringing and health outcomes, provided the first nationwide quantitative data source for studying the profile of Muslims in Scotland (Office of the Chief Statistician, 2005). This was followed by the 2011 census (National Records of Scotland, 2013), which also included questions on religious identity and health outcomes. These census-based analyses provide important, yet limited insights. For more detailed analyses, there is still often a need to infer from analyses based on ethnic groups; this is because religious identity is not routinely recorded in health systems. While such analyses can be very important, they have some inherent limitations in making direct inference to religious groups. For example, as most ethnicity-based analyses in the UK and Western Europe have been carried out among people of South Asian origin, data on more recent migrant groups from Muslim-majority countries is often not available. In the following discussion of health profiles among Muslims living in Scotland, we will, as far as possible, draw directly on data from studies investigating the relationship between religion and health. We will, however, also need to draw on data from studies investigating the relationship between ethnicity and health; when making such inferences, this will be explicitly stated in the text. Scottish data will be drawn upon whenever possible, but we will also include wider UK data in instances where we believe this is likely to offer insights that are transferable to a Scottish context.

HEALTH, DISEASE AND FAITH

To set the stage for this endeavour, it is important to note that health refers not only to the absence of disease or physical impairments, such as disability or pain. Rather, health, as defined by the World Health Organization (WHO), covers the physical, mental and social well-being of people, thus incorporating complex and ever-changing aspects related to how we feel and engage with others around us (World Health Organization, 1948). Expanded a bit further, health also has to do with the capacity to cope with the changing realities of human life, and some might add that spiritual dimensions are also for many people part of a healthy life (Huber et al., 2011; Larson, 1996; Grant et al., 2010).

How we as individuals understand health is shaped by a range of factors, including our individual life story and experiences with (ill) health, norms within families, cultural aspects and religious beliefs (Ahmed, 2008; Kleinman, 1988; Padela et al., 2012). Religion can be defined as 'a particular system of faith and worship expressive of an underlying spirituality and interpretive of what the named religion understands of "God" or ultimate reality' (Speck, 2011: 110). For the believer, this system of faith – or worldview – guides understandings and behaviours, and it provides a means of understanding and making sense of experiences in life, including illness. When understanding the relationship between Islam and health, it is important to be mindful of the fact that many Muslims have an understanding of Islam that is strongly shaped by local cultural beliefs and practices, which at times contrast sharply with the values of Islam. Within the comprehensive tradition of Islam, based on the Qur'an, the sayings of the Prophet and centuries of scholarship, a number of core values can be identified. These are, for example, the importance of an existentialist quest for truth, striving for learning and scholarship, being humble and law abiding, standing up for justice and serving – all – fellow inhabitants of our shared planet. While some Muslims identify strongly with this grand narrative and seek to fulfil the obligations it entails, others are less deeply engaged with the core tenets of their faith.

Within the Islamic tradition, the Arabic concept of *al-afiyah* is commonly used to describe the multidimensional concept of health. In translation, this concept encompasses safety from disease, grief and troubles, thus emphasising the dimensions covered by the WHO's concept of health and adding spiritual well-being. Among Muslims, religion may be reflected or translated into a wide range of practices, including the five daily prayers, dietary practices such as fasting during the month of

Ramadan, and an avoidance of substances and practices that are considered to be forbidden (for example, drug abuse or extra-marital sex). In addition, Islam encourages Muslims to be physically active, to avoid excessive eating, to reflect regularly upon and seek to restore mental and spiritual well-being, and to be constructive members of society. These practices have the potential to decrease the risk of adverse health outcomes through promoting healthy lifestyle choices and fostering mental health. In its approach to public health, Islam builds upon the principle that public interests often take precedence over private ones, thus emphasising the need also to take measures to promote societal well-being (Rathor et al., 2011).

How people understand and explain illness may also be shaped by religious beliefs (Ahmed, 2008; Padela et al., 2012). From an Islamic perspective, illness and ultimately death are perceived to be in accord with the will of Allah, and these major life events are thus predetermined as part of the journey of this life (Kristiansen and Sheikh, 2012; Winter, 2008). Illness and the suffering that this may entail are perceived to be a potential source of reward in the hereafter, and Muslims are – from a religious point of view – encouraged to find meaning and comfort in the belief and trust in the mercy of Allah (Khan, 1996). The belief that illness and its outcome for the person are ultimately determined by a divine power does not in any way exclude the role of the individual person in seeking to maintain good health and/or seek treatment. Religious guidance and rulings seek to protect health and well-being, for example through avoidance of smoking, alcohol, drugs, poor diet and unsafe sex, as outlined above (Padela and Curlin, 2013). Also, a number of different approaches to promote well-being are encouraged within Islam. This includes the intake of honey, recommended for its healing properties, spiritual practices such as prayers and reciting verses from the Qur'an, fasting and engaging more intensely in doing good, such as voluntary almsgiving and helping others (Ahmed, 2008). In terms of restoration of health and coping with disease, Islam strongly encourages Muslims to seek treatment through mainstream healthcare services and to follow the treatment plans outlined by medical doctors (Ahmed, 2008; Padela and Curlin, 2013). Agency is central to Islam, as each person is individually responsible for his or her actions in this life and will be held accountable for them after death. Health is regarded as a divine trust and avoidance of behaviours compromising the health and well-being of self and others, and taking timely steps to maintain good health is thus very important within the Islamic ethos.

Moving beyond health behaviours and responsible self-management of the individual, Islam also influences the role of family and friends in supporting the sick. Visiting the sick is a particularly meritorious practice in Islam, and the involvement of large numbers of close and more distant relatives and friends, particularly for critically ill patients, is often noted by healthcare professionals as a source of valuable social support, although large numbers of visitors may at times be at odds with the needs of other hospitalised patients and the routines at the hospital ward (Kristiansen and Sheikh, 2012). Social support provided by members of the religious community may consist of reciting key verses of the Qur'an, praying, offering condolences, preparing food and taking care of children, thus giving valuable support to the patient and his or her family. However, for Muslims living in Scotland, the availability of such supportive networks should not be assumed. Through the process of resettling into Scotland, family networks may have been dispersed, sometimes across several countries, and some, in particular recent migrants and those from smaller ethnic groups, may find themselves in a situation with few contacts to the wider Muslim community (Kristiansen et al., 2010).

The role of religious beliefs in explaining and managing illness has been the subject of a large number of studies in Muslim countries as well as in Western countries (Inhorn and Serour, 2011; Padela and Curlin, 2013; Kristiansen et al., 2014; Mir and Sheikh, 2010; Mygind et al., 2013). In a Scottish context, and through interviews with South Asian Muslim patients with life-limiting illnesses, their relatives and key healthcare professionals, the ways in which religious beliefs shaped the end-of-life experience among patients were identified (Kristiansen et al., 2014; Worth et al., 2009). The study showed that for those who were conscious of their religious identity and found this important for their outlook on life, religious beliefs helped them make sense of their progressive illness. Their faith served as a source of hope that enabled them to live with the many personal and social consequences of severe illness. This is partly due to a belief in God as a source of healing and partly because the belief in an afterlife helped them uphold a vision of what the afterlife would be like for them. In terms of self-management, the study found that conventional medicine was combined with religious practices such as prayers. Prayer served as a way of communicating with Allah and through this to ask for cure, relief of symptoms or more time with relatives, which emerged as a strong need, particularly in those who had young children. In terms of access to social support from religious communities, South Asian patients reported limited access to supportive networks, at times due to the stigma attached to severe illness, and the lack of room for voicing grief and frustration related to the experience of living with a progressive and untreatable illness (Kristiansen et al., 2014). At the same time, a sub-study among Muslim participants who were parents of young children reported unmet needs for support from mainstream health and social care services in Scotland (Gaveras et al., 2014). These studies thus underscore the need not to assume that Muslims are embedded within resourceful religious communities.

As noted above, for those Muslims who engage actively with their religious beliefs and practices, Islam often has a considerable influence on the ways in which they perceive and manage health and disease (Ahmed, 2008; Padela et al., 2012; Padela and Curlin, 2013). However, among the diverse group of Muslims in Scotland, the value placed upon religious identity and the importance of Islamic teachings for everyday life obviously may be more limited and fluid.

FAITH IN CONTEXT: DIVERSITY AND CONTEXTUAL FACTORS SHAPING HEALTH

As described, Islam as a religious outlook can shape how Muslims perceive health and illness, how people behave in relation to the multiple factors that shape health, such as substance abuse, physical activity or diet, and the ways that people cope with illness and seek healthcare. However, it is important to be aware of the great diversity within the Muslim community in Scotland and the multitude of contextual factors that influence their health status: Islam is one such factor. To understand the discrepancy between the principles, values and behaviours encouraged by Islam as a faith-based framework and the health profiles of Muslims in Scotland, we must therefore understand the intersecting and overlapping factors at play at the personal level and in communities, as well as structural factors that operate at a more distant level.

Muslims have in common a worldwide religion based on common core beliefs, as outlined in the Qur'an. However, the meaning carried by religious identity and the ways that faith shapes health and disease naturally differ between people and even within the life course of any individual person. These are informed by the personal beliefs and interpretations of the tenets of faith by each person, but are also shaped by context-related factors such as ethnic and/or religious identity, and the behaviour and values of people in one's social circles (for example family and friends), in addition to individual experiences such as the diagnosis of a fatal disease and the associated need to try to make sense of illness and death. As mentioned earlier, a range of cultural values and practices are evident among Muslims and may influence health and well-being. This includes, for example, consanguineous marriages that are relatively common within the Pakistani group and have been linked to adverse birth outcomes, and intake of *khat* – a narcotic substance commonly used among men of Somali origin (Khatib et al., 2013). Also, wider societal phenomena, such as marginalisation and discrimination, may influence the importance and understanding of religious identity and the ways in which religious minority groups engage with society, including healthcare institutions. This is because religious identity is simultaneously an internal, fluid process of making sense of the world and one's place in the cosmos, while on the other hand it is a socially constructed category shaped by interactions with wider society and with consequences for people's actions and possibilities. As such, (visible) religious identity such as wearing the hijab or having a name that is perceived to be signalling the Muslim faith may carry implications for the individual person in everyday life and in encounters within healthcare services (Johnson et al., 2004). For example, studies in the US describe how, after the 9/11 terrorist attack and with the increased US military presence in the Middle East in its aftermath, the Muslim population became subject to negative stereotyping and discrimination. Through this process, the population moved from being invisible citizens who were being assimilated into wider society to visible subjects of media and political discourse (Howell and Shryock, 2003; Jamal, 2008). Such societal processes have, in some cases, led to an increase in intolerance and discrimination towards Muslims in the West, perpetuated by processes of segregation, for example in residential areas and schools. In a study into experiences of discrimination and religious intolerance among Muslims in Scotland, drawing on a literature review, focus groups and a survey, the authors concluded that Muslim communities reported increased experiences of religious discrimination following the terrorist attacks in New York and London, and that this experience was compounded by perceived racial discrimination (Scottish Government, 2011). The same study found that, although religion was important to their identity, Muslims in Scotland were more likely to identify as Scottish than Muslims in England were to identify as English (Scottish Government, 2011). However, experiences of being 'othered' or singled out by their religious faith in some instances led to segregation, for example in terms of friendship and residential areas, based on ethnicity and religion (Scottish Government, 2011). Complex historical and sociopolitical processes may thus lead to negative stereotyping and religious profiling, and create boundaries between mainstream society and Muslims, with implications for health. For example, a lack of trust in healthcare professionals may impede timely access to healthcare or exposure to stressful events such as discrimination or hate crimes that may negatively influence mental health (Ahmed et al., 2011; Howell and Shryock, 2003; Inhorn and Serour, 2011; Sheridan, 2006). Both Scottish and other European studies point to similar developments in terms of increased experience of discrimination that is fuelled by the current debate on the presence of Muslims in Western Europe. As such, it is influenced by larger global developments such as terrorist attacks, Middle Eastern conflicts and recent changes in refugee/migration patterns into parts of the European Union (Hopkins and Smith, 2008; Hussain and Miller, 2006; Qureshi and Moores, 1999). Nevertheless, for many Muslims who have migrated to or were born in Western countries, the experiences and realities of everyday life are largely positive, despite the processes of potential stigma and discrimination that some perceive, as outlined above. Being part of democratic societies with protection of human rights and comprehensive access to a range of important welfare services, including education opportunities, social benefits and health-care services, is of utmost importance and often leads to increased levels of education, not least for descendants of migrants, greater economic prosperity and possibly increased life expectancy (Kristiansen et al., 2007; Kristiansen et al., 2015; Page et al., 2007).

In addition to the varying importance of Islam for Muslims, the Muslim community in Scotland is also very diverse in terms of a range of factors that influence health behaviours, health status and encounters with healthcare services. Of particular importance are the ethnicity and socioeconomic background of the individual person. Ethnicity is a multifaceted construct used to describe groups of people who identify with or are perceived to belong to a certain group due, for example, to shared language, geographical origin or cultural traditions (Bhopal, 2004). Among Muslims in Scotland, a range of different ethnic groups can be identified, with the main groups being Pakistanis, Bangladeshis and Indians, more recent migrants from Middle Eastern and African countries, but also converts of Scottish origin (Scottish Government, 2011). This ethnic diversity is important to take into consideration when describing and explaining health behaviours and health status among Muslims in Scotland. The link between ethnicity and health is complex and multifactorial (Winkleby and Cubbin, 2004). Health behaviours and health status vary substantially across different ethnic groups, often due to a complex interplay between cultural factors, such as dietary practices or physical activity patterns, contextual factors such as socioeconomic background and residential area characteristics (for example deprivation, inadequate access to services), and individual factors such as language competencies. These shape the ability to understand and use information and available services that promote and maintain good health (health literacy) (Bhopal, 2013; Kristiansen et al., 2007; Marmot et al., 2010; Winkleby and Cubbin, 2004). Poor levels of health literacy may lead to less optimal health behaviours, poorer health status and limited opportunities to obtain high-quality healthcare (Kickbusch, 2001; Nutbeam, 2008; Pleasant, 2014). For example, an inability to read and act upon written information on how to lower risks for diabetes or how to access a range of medical services may negatively affect health. Language barriers are, of course, often most pronounced among newly arrived migrants, but may also be present among refugees suffering from post-traumatic stress disorder (PTSD) following traumatic events during time of war and among people who lack education (Teodorescu et al., 2012). The availability of interpretation facilities with different sectors of Scottish healthcare services is important for these groups, as these help to ensure their equal access to high-quality services.

A further factor that contributes to the diversity in health among Muslims in Scotland is related to socioeconomic background and psychosocial resources among this community, including social capital. Socioeconomic background refers to the level of education, income and employment among people, and it is closely related to health behaviours and health status (Marmot and Wilkinson, 2001; Whitehead and Dahlgren, 1991). In general, the lower the socioeconomic background, the higher the risk of poor health (Marmot et al., 2012). This so-called social gradient in health often explains the differences in health status across ethnic/religious groups (Karlsen et al., 2012). Muslims in Scotland are disadvantaged on a number of socioeconomic parameters. According to census data, Muslims achieve lower levels of educational than other religious groups, have the lowest employment rate and, in particular, Muslim women are more likely than women of other religious backgrounds to be unemployed (National Records of Scotland, 2013; Scottish Government, 2011). Rates of self-employment are particularly high among Muslim men, and more than a third are employed in the wholesale and retail trade. In addition, Muslim households have the lowest overall wealth of religious groups in the UK, and Muslims are more likely to live in the most deprived areas of Scotland (National Records of Scotland, 2011). This finding may at least in part be explained by the bidirectional relationship between health and income, since higher levels of long-term illness among older Muslims and lower educational level among younger groups contribute to the tendency to live in deprived areas (National Records of Scotland, 2011). Although there is therefore evidence of socioeconomic disadvantage among Muslims in Scotland, some studies argue that the Muslim community, in particular those of South Asian origin, fare comparatively better in Scotland than is the case in the UK as a whole (Hopkins and Smith, 2008; Hussain and Miller, 2006; Maan, 1992; Masud, 2005). This is partly due to differences in the diversity and distribution of ethnic minority populations, and the relatively middle-class status of Muslims in Scotland compared to those living in England. However, it is also related to the particularities of Scottish identity, history and politics that have made Muslims in Scotland more likely to identify as Scottish, since their religious identity is primarily seen as cultural, not territorial (Hussain and Miller, 2006; Masud, 2005). Scottishness and Muslim identity are complex constructs that are partly related to self-perceived identity and feelings of belonging, and partly related to how others perceive one's identity and its (in)compatibility with larger notions of national identity. This dual relationship is illustrated by a qualitative study in a multi-ethnic Scottish neighbourhood, which highlighted how being seen by others as Scottish was not dependent upon personal religious beliefs and identity, but rather could be hindered by exhibiting certain behaviours and cultural codes, for example through wearing hijab, which appear to be contrasting with Scottishness (Virdee et al., 2006). Furthermore, in a recent study of self-conscious Muslim identities in Scotland, Bonino (2015) concludes that although the global stigmatisation of Muslims in the post 9/11 period had local ramifications in Scotland, it generally appears as a place of religious tolerance that is positive towards its Muslim population. Through qualitative fieldwork in Edinburgh among an ethnic diverse group of Muslims, Bonino found that younger Muslims display a strong affiliation to Scotland that further strengthens the notion of inclusive Scottishness that accommodates visible Muslim identities.

The relationship between socioeconomic background, religious identity and health among Muslims in Scotland is complex and changes with time. Muslim students rank high among those studying full-time in Scotland, which may point to future increased educational attainment levels and employment rates among this group, thus indicating upwards social mobility with time (National Records of Scotland, 2013; Scottish Government, 2011). However, at a European level, Muslims – and in particular the younger age groups – have been shown to have limited opportunities for social advancement, partly due to social exclusion but also shaped by the financial crisis, which may be a contributing factor to the feelings of hopelessness and alienation among certain groups of Muslims (European Monitoring Centre on Racism and Xenophobia, 2006).

In terms of psychosocial resources among Muslims in Scotland, individual and social factors related to personal resilience and coping strategies, social networks and experiences across the lifespan of the person may influence health status, health behaviours and encounters with healthcare services. Muslims, according to the 2001 census, are less likely to be divorced and more likely to live in larger households than other religious groups in Scotland (Scottish Government, 2011). Extended families often comprise a valuable source of practical support in everyday life and for those who are ill, but social roles and obligations may be a strain on the individual person, in particular on Muslim women (Gaveras et al., 2014; Dhami and Sheikh, 2000). Responsibilities for the well-being of extended families may hinder the ability to maintain one's own health, for example through regular physical activity, and to seek healthcare if symptoms arise, for example in terms of participation in screening programmes (Kessing et al., 2013). Financial obligations, for example sending remittances to family members in the country of origin, may be an additional responsibility for the breadwinners of the family, in particular for newly settled migrants with refugee status, thus reducing their financial capability to prioritise, for example, their membership of a gym (Kessing et al., 2013). Psychosocial vulnerability, for example resulting from exposure to trauma among refugees or competing priorities within extended family networks, reduces engagement in health promotion activities and negatively affects the ability to cope with disease, thus shaping health status and healthcare utilisation (Michealis et al., 2013). In addition, both Scottish and international studies of Muslims illustrate how recent migrants, in particular, and those with potentially stigmatising or life-limiting illnesses may be socially isolated and correspondingly be in need of formal social support, for example from health and social care professionals and patient associations (Gaveras et al., 2014; Kristiansen et al., 2014; Worth et al., 2009). Thus, although Muslims are generally embedded within larger families and wider social networks, the availability of social support should not be taken for granted.

Finally, factors operating at the community level may contribute to the health of Muslims in Scotland. Whereas close-knit communities in neighbourhoods with large numbers of Muslim families may facilitate social support and access to local resources such as mosques, restaurants serving halal foods and other services catering for the particular needs of Muslims, thus building social capital and facilitating access to culturally appropriate services, such neighbourhoods may also have negative health effects. Research conducted in England finds that Muslims are disproportionately more likely to live in so-called deprived areas, characterised by inadequate housing (for example overcrowded, lacking central heating), low incomes and high proportions of unemployed inhabitants, poor infrastructure and inadequate investment and action by local and national governmental actors (Choudhury et al., 2005; Jayaweera and Choudhury, 2008). In particular for children and adolescents, growing up in such neighbourhoods may pose a risk to their health due, for example, to a lack of safe areas to play and exercise, inadequate role models facilitating educational attainment and socialisation processes leading to normalisation of unhealthy behaviours such as smoking and drug abuse (Simons-Morton and Farhat, 2010).

DISEASE BURDEN AND HEALTH BEHAVIOURS

As discussed above, health is shaped by a wide range of individual factors and by factors operating in the immediate and wider social contexts. Furthermore, there is great diversity in health status across different ethnic groups, relating to genetics, health behaviours and exposure to health risks across the life course of the individual (Bhopal, 2013; Kristiansen et al., 2007; Norredam, 2015; Spallek et al., 2011). Some refugee groups and asylum seekers may, for example, have been exposed to high rates of infectious diseases, malnutrition and traumatic experiences in their country of origin and/or during migration, influencing their life-long risk of illness. Studies have found inadequate rates of vaccination coverage upon arrival, poor mental health and a high burden of infectious diseases to be more common among refugees, many of whom have fled wars and unrest in the Middle East. In the process, they have been exposed to periods of insecurity and a lack of appropriate preventive care and medical treatment (Norredam, 2015; World Health Organization, 2015). Furthermore, poor mental health has been found to be a concern among a range of ethnic minority groups, including residents of Muslim origin in the UK and across Europe (Inhorn and Serour, 2011; Laird et al., 2007; Norredam, 2015). Psychological distress is related to a range of individual and contextual factors, including, for example, experiences of assault, overcrowding, low standards of living, and absence of family and confidants that may be more common among

Muslims of lower socioeconomic background or refugees (Bogic et al., 2015; Karlsen et al., 2012; Kristiansen 2011).

As discussed above, Islam encourages certain behaviours that impact on health, whereas others are prohibited. Studies into health behaviours among Muslims in Scotland illustrate how health behaviours, although shaped by religious identity, are also influenced by intersecting factors such as gender, age, ethnicity, socioeconomic background and societal dynamics. A qualitative study among South Asians aged sixteen to twenty-six in Glasgow illustrated, for example, how Muslims' abstinence from alcohol was strongly linked to their Islamic identity; this sense of identity was seen as being jeopardised by drinking alcohol (Bradby, 2007). Although most Muslims abstain from drinking alcohol, the study showed that many of the Muslim men who were drinking would hide their intake of alcohol in order to protect their claim to be Muslim. Although the interviewees acknowledged the religious obligation to guard one's health and avoid wasting money, they perceived cigarette smoking to be less problematic than drinking alcohol. Gender differences, conflict between young people and the older generations, and social control featured strongly in the findings among the South Asians interviewed in Glasgow, as the risk of gossip and damage to reputation were strongly felt among young Muslim women. While substance abuse was seen to tarnish the reputation of both young men and women, the reputation of young men could in some cases be restored by the parents' status within the community, whereas damage to women's reputations was much more difficult to repair (Bradby, 2007). Religious and gender differences have also been found in other studies of risk behaviours relating to alcohol intake. For example, a questionnaire study among pupils aged fourteen and fifteen and with follow-up four years later found that religiously specific patterns of abstaining from alcohol were particularly high among Muslims and that women of South Asian origin observed this pattern of behaviour more than men (Bradby and Williams, 2006). Also, studies on key health behaviours among Muslims in Scotland associated with cardiovascular diseases, diabetes and different types of cancers have found that, in particular, South Asians are less likely to drink alcohol and smoke, whereas lack of physical activity, low consumption of fruit and vegetables, and a diet high in fat are relatively common among these groups, compared to the general White Scottish population (Scottish Government, 2012).

Self-rated health is a measurement found to be strongly related to future health problems and mortality (Heistaro et al., 2001; Kaplan et al., 2007). According to the Scottish Health Survey, Muslims are among the most likely to rate their health as poor (Scottish Government, 2012). In the Muslim group, 70% of respondents rated their health as 'very good' or 'good', which is lower than the Scottish average (76%) and considerably below the findings in other religious groups, such as Hindus (92%).

The burden of different types of diseases varies substantially between ethnic groups, as outlined above. A major quantitative study exploring ethnic differences in the development of cardiovascular disease among patients with type 2 diabetes in Scotland found people of Pakistani origin to be at higher risk of developing this health problem than White Scottish people (Malik et al., 2015). As is the case in the general population, and in particular among elderly people, multimorbidity, or the coexistence of more than one health problem, is common among Muslim groups in Western contexts (Barnett et al., 2012; Norredam et al., 2015). The Scottish Health and Ethnicity Linkage Study (SHELS) has provided strong and generalisable results, based on data from 4.65 (out of 4.9) million people included in the 2001 census of Scotland, that have been linked to registries representing nine years of National Health Service Scotland hospitalisation and death records. In terms of the cancer burden, this study found Pakistanis to be less likely to develop a range of cancers, including cancer of the lung, breast, prostate and colorectal system (Bhopal et al., 2012). Also, looking into upper gastrointestinal diseases among different ethnic groups in Scotland, the study found comparatively higher rates of oesophagitis among Bangladeshi women, higher risks for gallstone disease and pancreatitis among Pakistani women, and higher rates of Crohn's disease among Pakistani men than the White Scottish group (Bhopal et al., 2014a; Cezard et al., 2016). There is limited evidence regarding the burden of respiratory diseases among Muslims in Scotland. However, Pakistani men and women were found to have a higher risk of respiratory disease than the majority population in the comprehensive SHELS study (Bhopal et al., 2015). Ethnic variations in the burden of lower respiratory tract infections were found in the same cohort, with Pakistani men having a higher risk of being hospitalised for this adverse health event, but with higher chances of survival than the White Scottish population (Simpson et al., 2015). A study into ethnic variations in asthma hospital admission, readmissions and death in Scotland found Pakistanis to be at increased risk of hospitalisation for asthma, which may reflect variations in the quality of primary care provision or differences in cultural factors shaping self-management and health-seeking behaviours among Pakistanis with asthma, compared to the White Scottish population (Sheikh et al., 2016).

Finally, some infectious diseases are relatively more common among South Asians. One example is the hepatitis C virus, which is related to liver disease and has been found to be common among South Asians, partly due to transmission through medical treatment obtained in South Asia (O'Leary et al., 2013). The Scottish Health Survey found Muslims to be most likely to have good dental health, as measured by the number of natural teeth among respondents (Scottish Government, 2012).

Although the health profiles of Muslims in Scotland differ somewhat from the White Scottish population, changes do occur with time and across generations. This is exemplified by the study on alcohol and smoking behaviours among adolescents in Glasgow and in studies of changing dietary patterns and sedentary lifestyles among Muslim groups settling in Europe (Bradby and Williams, 2006; Smith et al., 2012; Spallek et al., 2011). Studies of the so-called healthy migrant effect also indicate that the lower risk of developing cancers among many ethnic minority groups in Europe, for example, is lost with time, due to changes in health behaviours such as smoking and sedentary lifestyles, but also due to exposure to different contextual risk factors (Norredam et al., 2014; Spallek et al., 2011).

The majority of studies into health among Muslims in Scotland have focused on the South Asian group, thus less is known regarding the health status of smaller, less-established ethnic groups. Nevertheless, diversity in health profiles across religious groups is relevant to policy makers and practitioners, as different risk profiles may have implications for prevention, screening and clinical care. An example of this is current discussions on the relevance and cost-effectiveness of population-based mammography screening programmes that often have low participation rates among Muslim groups, and in a Scottish context particularly among women of South Asian origin (Bansal et al., 2012; Kristiansen et al., 2012). Although disease rates vary considerably within the group of Muslim women of different ethnic backgrounds, these groups have been found to have low risk of developing breast cancers. However, they have a higher risk of developing diabetes, certain infectious diseases (such as tuberculosis and hepatitis among some refugee groups) and poor mental health that could be addressed in screening programmes tailored to the particular disease profile among groups of Muslims (Bansal et al., 2012; Norredam, 2015). However, with disease rates often converging towards the risk in the White Scottish majority population, it is important to ensure that health services, including screening programmes, are accommodating the diversity in disease risk across the entire population.

Finally, mortality in Scotland has been found to be lower among people of South Asian origin than in the majority population, although precise estimates of mortality differences are difficult to achieve due to the small number of deaths among South Asians (Millard et al., 2015). The observed lower mortality among both South Asian males and females is partly explained by the relatively younger age profile of this group (Scottish Government, 2011). However, with time, adaptations to health and social care services to meet the needs of an aging group of Muslims will be needed, as has happened in England and some parts of mainland Europe.

SEEKING HEALTHCARE IN SCOTLAND

Concern has been raised regarding the access to and quality of healthcare services for Muslims and other ethnic/religious minorities in Europe based on studies indicating differences across groups (Bhopal, 2013; Ingleby et al., 2012; Karlsen et al., 2012). Access concerns dimensions related to entitlement – that is, whether these groups have formal rights to services, for example through comprehensive health insurance schemes – but also relates to the ability of the individual to seek appropriate healthcare when in need. Inequities in health and healthcare refer to the presence of systematic, and potentially avoidable, differences in health status or access to and outcomes of healthcare among population groups defined according to socioeconomic background, geographical area or ethnicity, for example (Starfield, 2011). Inequity in health and healthcare continues to be the focus of a large body of research, numerous national and international policies and a wide range of interventions targeting individual, contextual and system-related factors shaping health and healthcare utilisation.

In Scotland, healthcare is mainly provided by NHS Scotland, thus enabling all permanent residents to access care that is free at the point of need; this is funded by general taxation. Prescribed medication is also available free of charge. Private healthcare and a range of alternative and complementary treatments can be purchased through private providers. As such, there is little reason to believe that Muslims are disadvantaged from seeking healthcare per se, although language barriers, health illiteracy, lack of social networks facilitating access to timely care and insecurities related to interfaith encounters on the part of both patients and providers do constitute barriers that may affect access to care for Muslims (Kristiansen et al., 2014; Gaveras et al., 2014; Smedley et al., 2003). In terms of quality of healthcare services, studies have found that outcome data such as mortality and readmissions following hospitalisation for respiratory disease was similar to, or at times lower than, those found among the White Scottish population, indicating that inequity in hospital healthcare provision is unlikely to be a major concern in Scotland (Bhopal et al., 2015). Similar findings have been reported for acute myocardial infarction when Pakistanis were found to have the highest burden of disease, but with a similar, or even better, chance of survival than the general population and with no difference in cardiac intervention at hospitals (Bansal et al., 2013). There is, however, likely to be greater variability in the quality of primary care provision.

A number of studies have explored experiences with illness and access to healthcare services among Muslim groups in Scotland. In a combined survey and focus group study with Muslims, Sikhs and Hindus in Scotland's major cities, there was a high level of satisfaction with NHS services, although Muslims were more likely to report problems of religious or ethnic discrimination in the NHS (Love et al., 2011). A qualitative study among South Asian Sikh and Muslim patients living with life-limiting illness, their families and healthcare professionals involved in their care highlighted key barriers to the provision of responsive, culturally appropriate care (Worth et al., 2009). These included resource-constrained services, instances of institutional discrimination, and limited awareness and understanding among the South Asian group of the role of hospices. Professionals perceived challenges in providing care for Muslims to relate to insecurity, for example as to how to raise the issue of death and the availability of support within extended families and the religious community, pointing to the need for increased awareness and support in case management within healthcare institutions (Gaveras et al., 2014; Kristiansen et al., 2014; Worth et al., 2009).

MUSLIM HEALTH IN SCOTLAND: REACHING THE GOAL OF EQUALITY

In 2002, the Scottish Executive (now Government), through the Health Department, launched the Scottish Health Act 'Fair for All', with the aim of ensuring that services provided by NHS Scotland were responsive to the needs of individual and communities – including ethnic minorities (Scottish Executive, 2002). This policy and the initiatives that it has sparked underpin the Scottish Government's ongoing commitment to meet the diverse health needs of the Scottish population, irrespective of differences related to, for example, age, gender, socioeconomic background, sexual orientation or religious and ethnic identity. By promoting an advanced and comprehensive response to ethnic and religious diversity, and by making public organisations accountable for achieving equal care for all, Scotland is at the forefront of European policy making in response to inequality in health (Lorant and Bhopal, 2010). Through a process of taking stock of the current situation and identifying good practices relating to service provision for faith and ethnic minorities within NHS Scotland, a number of systemic, mutually reinforcing recommendations were made. Performance indicators were developed as part of the initiative to make NHS Boards accountable for documenting progress. Recommendations include a need for a strategic and coherent approach, so that efforts to meet the needs of disadvantaged and increasingly diverse groups become part of organisations' mainstream activities; awareness raising at all institutional levels within NHS Scotland; more focus on needs assessments, facilitating better understanding and dissemination of good practices; facilitation of partnerships and cross-agency collaborations; engaging in dialogue with communities and building their capacity; and recruiting more ethnic minority staff (Scottish Executive, 2002). This comprehensive strategy lays an impressive foundation for future policy and practice development in Scotland and, combined with strong research groups working within the field of ethnicity and health across Scotland, the coming years will likely witness interesting progress towards reaching the goals of the policy. The strategy has later been reinforced by the UK Government's Equality Act from 2010 (UK Government, 2010).

In terms of identifying ways to move forward, the body of research into health behaviours, health status and quality of healthcare among diverse ethnic and religious groups in Europe has increased substantially in recent decades, with strong participation from the University of Edinburgh's Edinburgh Migration, Ethnicity and Health Research Group (EMEHRG). Studies have explored how to promote smoking cessation and prevent diabetes among South Asian groups in Scotland (Begh et al., 2011a; Begh et al., 2011b; Bhopal et al., 2014b; Douglas et al., 2013; Morrison et al., 2014; Wallia et al., 2014). However, we are still lacking robust insight into how to address inequalities in health and living circumstances successfully across increasingly diverse religious and ethnic groups. As health and disease are shaped by a range of exposures and behaviours across the life course of the individual person, there is a need for early interventions, focusing on promoting and supporting healthy behaviours and cultural resources in minority groups and preventing risk behaviours that lead to a higher disease burden among Muslims in Scotland. This needs to include identifying how to increase physical activity levels and an intake of a healthy diet among Muslims, and also how to maintain the lower prevalence of smoking generally found among Muslim women in the younger generations. Health promotion interventions could also build upon cultural resources among religious communities, including both the social networks, revolving around mosques and other meeting places, for example, but also exploring the potential importance of drawing on Islamic values and principles in, for example, interventions against smoking, gender-based violence or stigmatisation of people suffering from mental illness (Ghouri et al., 2006). Although few robust intervention studies have been carried out among Muslims in Scotland to date, general lessons can be teased out, based on the large bulk of knowledge related to principles for public health interventions. In particular, there is a need to combine individual-oriented health interventions that focus on increasing the awareness and skills of the person with more comprehensive community-based, structural interventions aiming to ensure that social networks processes, private and public service providers and the built environment of communities facilitate healthy living. A multisectorial approach is often needed when combining interventions at the structural and the individual level, thus necessitating involvement of a range of sectors including primary healthcare, urban planning, educational institutions, and non-governmental and private partners such as faith-based associations or private companies in a particular community. The importance of holistic approaches to health promotion was underscored in an interview study among men and women of Bangladeshi, Indian and Pakistani origin living in urban settings in Scotland, seeking to elucidate key factors motivating and facilitating physical activity, thus pointing to ways of designing successful interventions and services for these groups (Jepson et al., 2012). The importance of social contextual factors and motivators for health behaviour appeared central, as engaging in physical activity, for example through football and the gym for men, and walking and swimming for women, was motivated by the opportunity for social activity and enjoyment that this entailed. Role models were perceived to be important, as these would be able to inspire and motivate people to engage in physical activity. Thus, group-based physical activity interventions, facilitated through religious, community, friendship or family networks, could be relevant for this target group (Jepson et al., 2012).

Community involvement is vital to successfully addressing the multitude of individual and contextual factors framing the everyday life of Muslims in an inclusive way. As Muslim communities are unevenly distributed across Scotland, focusing on areas with large numbers of

Muslims would be advisable, in addition to ensuring that the expected increasing numbers of migrants and refugees from war-torn areas in the Middle East and Africa are included in interventions. In general, timely and comprehensive user and community involvement is important, both in research and service delivery. This is because involvement through needs assessments and consultations, for example, may support the identification of key areas to address and the appropriate ways of doing so (Davidson et al., 2013; Johnson, 2012; Liu et al., 2012). Communities may be defined according to geographical anchorage, for example by working with mosques and more informal faith-based centres that for many devout Muslims are important settings, gathering large groups of people. A range of religious and more 'mundane' activities are organised in these settings, including communal prayers (the five daily prayers, the Friday prayer, prayers at the end of festivities including the holy month of Ramadan and funeral prayers for the deceased), and Arabic and Islamic classes for children, but mosques may also serve as entry points in reaching the Muslim community for different health-related activities. An example of this took place in the Edinburgh Central Mosque in 2003 (Ghouri, 2005). A health fair was developed in close collaboration between local health authorities and representatives from the mosque, thus building upon recommendations set out in 'Fair for All', and in particular the need for closer involvement of groups and organisations within ethnic minority communities in the provision of services for these groups. Based on the health profile of the Muslim community, the fair focused on diabetes, high blood pressure, healthy eating and oral hygiene, in addition to disseminating information on cancer and local community services. The involved researchers concluded that the intervention was well received, with strong participation across the community, highlighting the potential for community-based services anchored within mosques and other religious community settings. However, given the cultural, linguistic and socioeconomic diversity among Muslims in Scotland, involvement of the target group for an intervention is not straightforward. Awareness of interest groups and power dynamics within more or less well-established and identifiable groups of Muslims and the associated risk of excluding some while including others is therefore important.

Guidelines for the adaptation of health promotion interventions for ethnic minority populations point to a number of recommendations, again underscoring the importance of extending the focus beyond individual-centred interventions to also include community- and ecological-level dimensions (Davidson et al., 2013). Although the evidence base for how to deliver effective interventions among Muslims is lacking, the literature suggests ways to adapt interventions throughout the various intervention phases, including conducting formative work with the target population, the importance of involving religious and spiritual leaders, recruitment from formal and informal networks, a focus on family-level approaches of high intensity, and addressing the physical and financial barriers affecting participation in the intervention. In addition, guidelines highlight the potential of utilising the mother tongue of the target group, encouraging social support and ensuring the use of validated measurement tools in evaluating the effect of interventions (Davidson et al., 2013; Liu et al., 2012; Nierkens et al., 2013; Wallia et al., 2014).

Ensuring timely diagnosis and access to high-quality, coordinated patient-centred care is central to addressing ethnic inequality in health. Although there is little evidence for any lack of access to such services in Scotland, a continued focus on ensuring awareness of relevant health and social care services and help in overcoming language barriers is important, in particular for women and newly arrived migrants and refugees (World Health Organization, 2015). This also entails a focus on provider and organisational dimensions, as it is important to ensure that individual healthcare professionals and the organisations in which healthcare encounters take place are able to provide culturally sensitive care. This involves continued focus on raising awareness of the importance of attending to cultural, religious and ethnic diversity in healthcare encounters and skill in doing so, for example as outlined in the literature on cultural competency training for healthcare staff (Fleckman et al., 2015; Kleinman and Benson, 2006). It also relates to the need for provision of religiously appropriate food for different groups, translation of material for patients and relatives, and an openness towards and awareness of the role that religious beliefs may play for the individual patient (Kristiansen et al., 2014; Scottish Executive, 2002). Besides provision of patient-centred, holistic care within healthcare facilities, psychosocial support for patients and carers must be ensured in the local community context and during periods of hospitalisation (Gaveras et al., 2014; Kristiansen, 2011; Mir and Sheikh, 2010).

While Scotland is surely at the forefront of ensuring policy development to address the needs of religious minorities, there is still a need to ensure that data on health behaviour, health profiles and outcomes of healthcare services are systematically and reliably collected and broken down according to religious, ethnic and socioeconomic group, in addition to key characteristics such as age and gender. This will enable continued research into identifying unmet needs, as well as successful developments, but it is also important for accountability and transferability of the Scottish experience to other countries.

CONCLUSION

We have discussed in this chapter how Muslims in Scotland constitute a very diverse group in terms of health behaviours, experiences and outcomes. While some overall patterns may be observed, some of which are directly influenced by Islamic values guiding behaviour, for example relating to the low intake of alcohol, many other aspects of behaviour and ultimately health outcomes are shaped by a complex interplay between religion, culture and socioeconomic background, and more contextual community and societal factors. The Scottish Government is strongly committed to reducing inequalities in health and healthcare outcomes across different religious, ethnic and socioeconomic groups in Scotland, and the framework provided by the 'Fair for All' report – in combination with the UK Equalities Act, 2010 – constitutes an excellent and unique opportunity to improve the quality of care provision for Muslims, as well as other faith groups, and indeed the wider community of which they are part (Scottish Executive, 2002; UK Government, 2010).

REFERENCES

Ahmed, A. A. (2008). 'Health and disease: an Islamic framework'. In A. Sheikh and A. R. Gatrad (eds), Caring for Muslim Patients, 2nd edn, pp. 35–43. Oxford: Radcliffe.

Ahmed, S. R., Kia-Keating, M. and Tsai, K. H. (2011). 'A structural model of racial discrimination, acculturative stress, and cultural resources among Arab American adolescents'. American Journal of Community Psychology, 48(3–4), 181–92.

Ansari, H. (2004). The Infidel Within: The History of Muslims in Britain since 1800. London: Hurst.

Bansal, N., Bhopal, R. S., Steiner, M. F. C. and Brewster, D. H. (2012). 'Major ethnic group differences in breast cancer screening uptake in Scotland are not extinguished by adjustment for indices of geographical residence, area, deprivation, long-term illness and education'. British Journal of Cancer, 106(8), 1361–6.

Bansal, N., Fischbacher, C. M., Bhopal, R. S., Brown, H. and Steiner, M. F. C. (2013). 'Myocardial infarction incidence and survival by ethnic group: Scottish Health and Ethnicity Linkage retrospective cohort study'. BMJ Open, 3(9), e003415.

Barnett, K., Mercer, S. W., Norbury, M., Watt, G., Wyke, S. and Guthrie, B. (2012). 'Epidemiology of multimorbidity and implications for health-care, research, and medical education: a cross-sectional study'. *The Lancet*, 380(9836), 37–43.

Begh, R. A. P., Aveyard, P., Upton, R. S., Bhopal, M., White, A., Amos, R., Prescott, J., Bedi, R., Barton, P. M., Fletcher, P., Gill, P., Zaidi, Q. and Sheikh, A. (2011a). 'Promoting smoking cessation in Pakistani and Bangladeshi men in the UK: Pilot cluster randomised controlled trial of trained community outreach workers'. *Trials*, 12(197).

Begh, R. A. P., Aveyard, P., Upton, R. S., Bhopal, M., White, A., Amos, R., Prescott, J., Bedi, R., Barton, P. M., Fletcher, P., Gill, P., Zaidi, Q. and Sheikh, A. (2011b). 'Experiences of outreach workers in promoting smoking cessation to Bangladeshi and Pakistani men: Longitudinal qualitative evaluation'. *BMC Public Health*, 11(452).

Bhopal, R. (2004). 'Glossary of terms relating to ethnicity and race: For reflection and debate'. *Journal of Epidemiology and Community Health*, 58(6), 441–5.

Bhopal, R. S. (2013). 'Inequalities, inequities, and disparities in health and health care by migration status, race, and ethnicity'. In *Migration, Ethnicity, Race, and Health in Multicultural Societies*, 2nd edn, pp. 163–95. Oxford: Oxford University Press.

Bhopal, R., Bansal, N., Steiner, M. and Brewster, D. H. (2012). 'Does the "Scottish effect" apply to all ethnic groups? All-cancer, lung, colorectal, breast and prostate cancer in the Scottish Health and Ethnicity Linkage cohort study'. *BMJ Open*, 2(5), e001957.

Bhopal, R. S., Cezard, G., Bansal, N., Ward, H. J. T. and Bhala, N. (2014a). 'Ethnic variations in five lower gastrointestinal diseases: Scottish health and ethnicity linkage study'. *BMJ Open*, 4(10), e006120.

Bhopal, R. S., Douglas, A., Wallia, S., Forbes, J. F., Lean, M. R., Gill, J. M., McKnight, J. A., Sattar, N., Sheikh, A., Wild, S. H., Tuomilehto, J., Sharma, A., Bhopal, R., Smith, J. B., Butcher, I. and Murray, G. D. (2014b). 'Effect of a lifestyle intervention on weight change in south Asian individuals in the UK at high risk of type 2 diabetes: A family-cluster randomised controlled trial'. *Lancet Diabetes and Endocrinology*, 2(3), 218–27.

Bhopal, R., Steiner, M. F. C., Cezard, G., Bansal, N., Fischbacher, C., Simpson, C. R., Douglas, A. and Sheikh, A. (2015). 'Risk of respiratory hospitalization and death, readmission and subsequent mortality: Scottish health and ethnicity linkage study'. *European Journal of Public Health*, 25(5), 769–74.

Bogic, M., Njoku, A. and Priebe, S. (2015). 'Long-term mental health of war-refugees: A systematic literature review'. *BMC International Health and Human Rights*, 15(29).

Bonino, S. (2015). 'Scottish Muslims through a decade of change: Wounded by the stigma, healed by Islam, rescued by Scotland'. *Scottish Affairs*, 24(1), 78–105.

Bradby, H. and Williams, R. (2006). '"Is religion or culture the key feature in changes in substance use after leaving school?" Young Punjabis and a comparison group in Glasgow'. *Ethnicity and Health*, 11(3), 307–24.

Bradby, H. (2007). '"Watch out for the Aunties!" Young British Asians' accounts of identity and substance use'. *Sociology of Health and Illness*, 29(5), 656–72.

Cezard, G. I., Bhopal, R. S., Ward, H. J. T., Bansal, N. and Bhala, N. (2016). 'Ethnic variations in upper gastrointestinal hospitalizations and deaths: The Scottish Health and Ethnicity linkage study'. *European Journal of Public Health*, 26(2), 254–60.

Choudhury, T., Malik, M., Halstead, J. M., Bunglawala, Z. and Spalek, B. (2005). *Muslims in the UK: Policies for Engaged Citizens*. EU Monitoring and Advocacy Program: Open Society Institute, available at www.openso cietyfoundations.org/sites/default/files/muslims-uk-policies-2005-20120119. pdf

Davidson, E. M., Liu, J. J., Bhopal, R., White, M., Johnson, D., Netto, G., Wabnitz, C. and Sheikh, A. (2013). 'Behavior change interventions to improve the health of racial and ethnic minority populations: A tool kit of adaptation approaches'. *Milbank Quarterly*, 91(4), 811–51.

Dhami, S. and Sheikh, A. (2000). 'The Muslim family: Predicament and promise'. *Western Journal of Medicine*, 173(5), 352–6.

Douglas, A., Bhopal, R. S., Bhopal, R., Forbes, J. F., Gill, J. M. R., McKnight, J., Murray, G., Sattar, N., Sharma, A., Wallia, S., Wild, S. and Sheikh, A. (2013). 'Design and baseline characteristics of the PODOSA (Prevention of Diabetes and Obesity in South Asians) trial: A cluster, randomised lifestyle intervention in Indian and Pakistani adults with impaired glycaemia at high risk of developing type 2 diabetes'. *BMJ Open*, 3(2).

European Monitoring Centre on Racism and Xenophobia (2006). *Muslims in the European Union: Discrimination and Islamophobia*, available at http:// fra.europa.eu/sites/default/files/fra_uploads/156-Manifestations_EN.pdf

Fleckman, J. M., Corso, M. D., Ramirez, S., Begalieva, M. and Johnson, C. C. (2015). 'Intercultural competency in public health: A call for action to incorporate training into public health education'. *Frontiers in Public Health*, 3(210).

Gaveras, E. M., Kristiansen, M., Worth, A., Irshad, T. and. Sheikh, A. (2014). 'Social support for South Asian Muslim parents with life-limiting illness living in Scotland: A multi-perspective qualitative study'. *BMJ Open*, 4(2), e004252.

Ghouri, N. (2005). 'Health fair in a mosque: putting policy into practice', *Public Health*, 119(3), 197–201.

Ghouri, N., Atcha, A. and Sheikh, A. (2006). 'Influence of Islam on smoking among Muslims'. *BMJ*, 332(7536), 291–4.

Grant, L., Murray, S. A. and Sheikh, A. (2010). 'Spiritual dimensions of dying in pluralist societies'. *BMJ*, 341, c4859.

Heistaro, S., Jousilahti, P., Lahelma, E., Vartiainen, E. and Puska, P. (2001). 'Self-rated health and mortality: A long-term prospective study in eastern Finland'. *Journal of Epidemiology and Community Health*, 55(4), 227–32.

Hopkins, P. E. and. Smith, S. J. (2008). 'Scaling segregation: Racialising fear'. In R. Pain and S. J. Smith (eds), *Fear: Critical Geopolitics and Everyday Life*, pp. 103–16. Aldershot: Ashgate.

Howell, S. and Shryock, A. (2003). 'Cracking down on diaspora: Arab Detroit and America's "war on terror"'. *Anthropological Quarterly*, 76(3), 443–62.

Huber, M., Knottnerus, J. A., Green, L., van der Horst, H., Jadad, A. R., Kromhout, D., Leonard, B., Lorig, K., Loureiro, M. I., van der Meer, J. W. M., Schnabel, P., Smith, R., van Weel, C. and Smid, H. (2011). 'How should we define health?'. *BMJ*, 343, d4163.

Hussain, A. M. and Miller, W. L. (2006). *Multicultural Nationalism: Islamophobia, Anglophobia and Devolution*. Oxford: Oxford University Press.

Ingleby, D., Krasnik, A., Lorant, V. and Razum, O. (eds) (2012). *Health Inequalities and Risk Factors among Migrants and Ethnic Minorities*, COST Series on Health and Diversity, vol. 1. Antwerp and Apeldoorn: Garant.

Inhorn, M. C. and Serour, G. I. (2011). 'Islam, medicine, and Arab-Muslim refugee health in America after 9/11'. *The Lancet*, 378(9794), 935–43.

Jamal, A. A. (2008). *Race and Arab Americans Before and After 9/11: From Invisible Citizens to Visible Subjects*, Syracuse, NY: Syracuse University Press.

Jayaweera, H. and Choudhury, T. (2008). *Immigration, Faith and Cohesion: Evidence from Local Areas with Significant Muslim Populations*. Joseph Rowntree Foundation, available at www.compas.ox.ac.uk/media/PR-2008-Muslims_Cohesion_Final.pdf

Jepson, R., Harris, F. M., Bowes, A., Robertson, R., Avan, G. and Sheikh, A. (2012). 'Physical activity in South Asians: An in-depth qualitative study to explore motivations and facilitators'. *PLoS One*, 7(10), e45333.

Johnson, J. L., Bottorff, J. L., Browne, A. J., Grewal, S., Hilton, B. A. and Clarke, H. (2004). 'Othering and being othered in the context of health care services'. *Health Communication*, 16(2), 255–71.

Johnson, M. (2012). 'User and community involvement in health and social care research with migrants and ethnic minorities'. In D. Ingleby, A. Krasnik, V. Lorant and O. Razum (eds), *Health Inequalities and Risk Factors among Migrants and Ethnic Minorities*. COST Series on Health and Diversity, vol. 1, Antwerp and Apeldoorn: Garant.

Larson, J. S. (1996). 'The World Health Organization's definition of health: Social versus spiritual health'. *Social Indicators Research*, 38(2), 181–92.

Kaplan, M. S., Berthelot, J., Feeny, D., McFarland, B. H., Khan, S. and Orpana, H. (2007). 'The predictive validity of health-related quality of life measures: Mortality in a longitudinal population-based study'. *Quality of Life Research*, 16(9), 1539–46.

Karlsen, S., Becares, L. and Roth, M. (2012). 'Understanding the influence of ethnicity on health'. In G. Craig, K. Atkin, S. Chattoo and R. Flynn (eds), *Understanding 'Race' and Ethnicity. Theory, History, Policy, Practice*, pp. 115–32. Bristol: Policy Press.

Kessing, L. L., Norredam, M., Kvernrod, A., Mygind, A. and Kristiansen, M. (2013). 'Contextualising migrants' health behaviour – A qualitative study of transnational ties and their implications for participation in mammography screening'. *BMC Public Health*, 13(431).

Khan, M. M. (1996). *Summarized Sahih Al-Bukhari* (Arabic-English). Hadith # 2092. Al-Madina Al-Munawwara, Riyadh: Dar-Us-Salam Publications.

Khatib, M., Jarrar, Z., Bizrah, M. and Checinski, K. (2013). 'Khat: Social habit or cultural burden? A survey and review'. *Journal of Ethnicity in Substance Abuse*, 12(2), 140–53.

Kickbusch, I. S. (2001). 'Health literacy: addressing the health and education divide'. *Health Promotion International*, 16(3), 289–97.

Kleinman, A. (1988). 'The personal and social meanings of illness'. In *The Illness Narratives: Suffering, Healing, and the Human Condition*, pp. 31–55. New York: Basic Books.

Kleinman, A. and Benson, P. (2006). 'Anthropology in the clinic: The problem of cultural competency and how to fix it'. *PLoS Medicine*, 3(10), e294.

Kristiansen, M. (2011). 'Migration and social support in relation to cancer screening and cancer care – A comparative multiple-methods study'. PhD thesis, University of Copenhagen.

Kristiansen, M., Irshad, T., Worth, A., Bhopal, R., Lawton, J. and Sheikh, A. (2014). 'The practice of hope: A longitudinal, multi-perspective qualitative study among South Asian Sikhs and Muslims with life-limiting illness in Scotland'. *Ethnicity and Health*, 19(1), 1–19.

Kristiansen, M., Kessing, L. L., Norredam, M. and Krasnik, A. (2015). 'Migrants' perceptions of aging in Denmark and attitudes towards remigration: Findings from a qualitative study'. *BMC Health Services Research*, 15(225).

Kristiansen, M., Mygind, A. and Krasnik, A. (2007). 'Health effects of migration'. *Danish Medical Bulletin*, 54(1), 46–7.

Kristiansen, M. and Sheikh, A. (2012). 'Understanding faith considerations when caring for bereaved Muslims'. *Journal of Royal Society of Medicine*, 105(12), 513–17.

Kristiansen M., Thorsted, B. L., Krasnik, A. and Von Euler-Chelpin, M. (2012). 'Participation in mammography screening among migrants and non-migrants in Denmark'. *Acta Oncologica*, 51(1), 28–36.

Kristiansen, M., Tjornhoj-Thomsen, T. and Krasnik, A. (2010). 'The benefit of meeting a stranger – Experiences with emotional support provided by health care professionals among Danish-born and migrant cancer patients'. *European Journal of Oncology Nursing*, 14(3), 244–52.

Laird, L. D., Amer, M. M., Barnett, E. D. and Barnes, L. L. (2007). 'Muslim patients and health disparities in the UK and the US'. *Archives of Disease in Childhood*, 92(10), 922–6.

Liu, J. J., Davidson, E., Bhopal, R. S., White, M., Johnson, M. R. D., Netto, G., Deverill, M. and Sheikh, A. (2012). 'Adapting health promotion interventions to meet the needs of ethnic minority groups: Mixed-methods evidence synthesis'. *Health Technology Assessment*, 16(44), 1–469.

Lorant, V. and Bhopal, R. (2010). 'Comparing policies to tackle ethnic inequalities in health: Belgium 1 Scotland 4'. *European Journal of Public Health*, 21(2), 235–40.

Love, J. G., Levecque, K., Van Rossen, R. and Ronda, E. (2011). 'Muslims', Hindus' and Sikhs' access to NHS services in Scotland'. *Journal of Epidemiology and Community Health*, 65(suppl. 1), A127.

Maan, B. (1992). *The New Scots: The Story of Asians in Scotland*. Edinburgh: John Donald.

Malik, M. O., Govan, L., Petrie, J. R., Ghouri, N., Leese, G., Fischbacher, C., Colhoun, H., Philip, S., Wild, S., McCrimmon, R., Sattar, N. and Lindsay, R. S. (2015). 'Ethnicity and risk of cardiovascular disease (CVD), 4.8 year follow-up of patients with type 2 diabetes living in Scotland'. *Diabetologia*, 58(4), 716–25.

Marmot, M., Allen, J., Goldblatt, P., Boyce, T., McNeish, D., Grady, M. and Geddes, I. (2010). *Fair Society, Healthy Lives ('The Marmot Review')*, available at www.instituteofhealthequity.org/Content/FileManager/pdf/fairsociety healthylives.pdf

Marmot, M., Allen, J., Bell, R., Bloomer, E. and Goldblatt, P. (2012). 'WHO European review of social determinants of health and the health divide'. *The Lancet*, 380(9846), 1011–29.

Marmot, M. and Wilkinson, R. G. (2001). 'Psychosocial and material pathways in the relation between income and health: A response to Lynch et al'. *BMJ*, 322(7296), 1233–6.

Masud, M. (2005). *Muslim Women Talk: Experiences of Muslim Women in Scotland Since the London Bombings: The Findings from Scottish Consultations Held in September 2005 as Part of the 'Muslim Women Talk Campaign'*, Glasgow: Amina – the Muslim Women's Resource Centre.

Michealis, C., Kristiansen, M. and Norredam, M. (2015). 'Quality of life and coping strategies among immigrant women living with pain in Denmark: A qualitative study'. *BMJ Open*, 5(7), e008075.

Millard, A. D., Raab, G., Lewsey, J., Eaglesham, P., Craig, P., Ralston, R. and McCartney, G. (2015). 'Mortality differences and inequalities within and between "protected characteristics" groups, in a Scottish cohort 1991–2009'. *International Journal for Equity in Health*, 14(142).

Mir, G. and Sheikh, A. (2010). '"Fasting and prayer don't concern the doctors … they don't even know what it is": Communication, decision-making and perceived social relations of Pakistani Muslim patients with long-term illnesses'. *Ethnicity and Health*, 15(4), 327–42.

Morrison, Z., Douglas, A., Bhopal, R. and Sheikh, A. (2014). 'Understanding experiences of participating in a weight loss lifestyle intervention trial: A qualitative evaluation of South Asians at high risk of diabetes'. *BMJ Open*, 4(6), e004736.

Mygind, A., Kristiansen, M., Wittrup, I. and Norgaard, L. S. (2013). 'Patient perspectives on type 2 diabetes and medicine use during Ramadan among Pakistanis in Denmark'. *International Journal of Clinical Pharmacy*, 35(2), 281–8.

National Records of Scotland, Statistical Bulletin (2013). *2011 Census: Key Results on Population, Ethnicity, Identity, Language, Religion, Health, Housing and Accommodation in Scotland – Release 2A*, available at www.scotlandscensus.gov.uk/documents/censusresults/release2a/StatsBulletin2A.pdf

Nierkens, V., Hartman, M. A., Nicolaou, M., Vissenberg, C., Beune, E. J. A. J., Hosper, K., van Valkengoed, I. G. and Stronks, K. (2013). 'Effectiveness of cultural adaptations of interventions aimed at smoking cessation, diet, and/or physical activity in ethnic minorities: A systematic review'. *PLoS One*, 8(10), e73373.

Norredam, M. (2015). 'Migration and health: Exploring the role of migrant status through register-based studies'. *Danish Medical Journal*, 62(4), B5068.

Norredam, M., Agyemang, C., Hansen, O. K. H., Petersen, J. H., Byberg, S., Krasnik, A. and Kunst, A. E. (2014). 'Duration of residence and disease occurrence among refugees and family reunited immigrants: Test of the "healthy migrant effect" hypothesis'. *Tropical Medicine and International Health*, 19(8), 958–67.

Norredam, M., Hansen, O. H., Petersen, J. H., Kunst, A. E., Kristiansen, M., Krasnik, A. and Agyemang, C. (2015). 'Remigration of migrants with severe disease: Myth or reality? A register-based cohort study'. *European Journal of Public Health*, 25(1), 84–9.

Nutbeam, D. (2008). 'The evolving concept of health literacy'. *Social Science and Medicine*, 67(12), 2072–8.

Office of the Chief Statistician (2005). *Analysis of Religion in the 2001 Census: Summary Report. A Scottish Executive National Statistics Publication*, available at www.gov.scot/Resource/Doc/36496/0029047.pdf

O'Leary, M. C., Sawar, M., Hutchinson, S. J., Weir, A., Schofield, J., McLeod, A., Cameron, S., McTaggart, C., Banday, S., Foster, R. R., Ahmed, S., Fox, R., Mills, P. R., Goldberg, D. J. and Anderson, E. (2013). 'The prevalence of hepatitis C virus among people of South Asian origin in Glasgow – results from a community based survey and laboratory surveillance'. *Travel Medicine and Infectious Disease*, 11(5), 301–9.

Padela, A. I. and Curlin, F. A. (2013). 'Religion and disparities: Considering the influences of Islam on the health of American Muslims'. *Journal of Religion and Health*, 52(4), 1333–45.

Padela, A. I., Killawi, A., Forman, J., DeMonner, S. and Heisler, M. (2012). 'American Muslim perceptions of healing: Key agents in healing, and their roles'. *Qualitative Health Research*, 22(6), 846–58.

Page, A., Begg, S., Taylor, R. and Lopez, A. D. (2007). 'Global comparative assessments of life expectancy: The impact of migration with reference to Australia'. *Bulletin of the World Health Organization*, 85(6), 474–81.

Pleasant, A. (2014). 'Advancing health literacy measurement: A pathway to better health and health system performance'. *Journal of Health Communication*, 19(12), 1481–96.

Qureshi, K. and Moores, S. (1999). 'Identity remix. Tradition and translation in the lives of young Pakistani Scots'. *European Journal of Cultural Studies*, 2(3), 311–30.

Rathor, M. Y., Rani, M. F. A., Shah, A. S. B. M., Leman, W. I. B., Akter, S. F. U. and Omar, A. M. B. (2011). 'The principle of autonomy as related to personal decision making concerning health and research from an "Islamic wiewpoint"'. *Journal of the Islamic Medical Association of North America*, 43(1), 27–34.

Scottish Executive (2002). *'Fair for All': Improving the Health of Ethnic Minority Groups and the Wider Community in Scotland*, available at www.sehd.scot.nhs.uk/publications/ffar/ffar1.pdf

Scottish Refugee Council (2013). *Improving the Lives of Refugees in Scotland after the Referendum: An Appraisal of the Options*, available at www.scottishrefugeecouncil.org.uk/assets/0000/5495/4087_SRC_Referendum_Report_V3.pdf

Sheikh, A., Steiner, M. F. C., Cezard, G., Bansal, N., Fischbacher, C., Simpson, C. R., Douglas, A. and Bhopal, R. (2016). 'Ethnic variations in asthma hospital admission, readmission and death: A retrospective, national cohort study of 4.62 million people in Scotland'. *BMC Medicine*, 14(3).

Sheridan, L. P. (2006). 'Islamophobia pre- and post- September 11th, 2001'. *Journal of Interpersonal Violence*, 21(3), 317–36.

Simons-Morton, B. and Farhat, T. (2010). 'Recent findings on peer group influences on adolescent substance use'. *Journal of Primary Prevention*, 31(4), 191–208.

Simpson, C. R., Steiner, M. F. C., Cezard, G., Bansal, N., Fischbacher, C., Douglas, A., Bhopal, R. and Sheikh, A. (2015). 'Ethnic variations in morbidity and mortality from lower respiratory tract infections: A retrospective cohort study'. *Journal of the Royal Society of Medicine*, 108(10), 406–17.

Smedley, B. D., Stith, A. Y. and Nelson, A. R. (2003). *Unequal Treatment. Confronting Racial and Ethnic Disparities in Healthcare*. Washington, DC: National Academies Press.

Smith, N. R., Kelly, Y. J. and Nazroo, Y. R. (2012). 'The effects of acculturation on obesity rates in ethnic minorities in England: evidence from the Health Survey for England'. *European Journal of Public Health*, 22(4), 508–13.

Spallek, J., Zeeb, H. and Razum, O. (2011). 'What do we have to know from migrants' past exposures to understand their health status? A life course approach'. *Emerging Themes in Epidemiology*, 8(6).

Speck, P. (2011). 'Spiritual/religious issues in care of the dying'. In J. Ellershaw, S. Wilkinson and C. Saunders (eds), *Care of the Dying: A Pathway to Excellence*, pp. 107–27. Oxford: Oxford University Press.

Starfield, B. (2011). 'The hidden inequity in health care'. *International Journal for Equity in Health*, 10(15).

Teodorescu, D. S., Heir, T., Hauff, E., Wentzel-Larsen, T. and Lien, L. (2012). 'Mental health problems and post-migration stress among multi-traumatized refugees attending outpatient clinics upon resettlement to Norway'. *Scandinavian Journal of Psychology*, 53(4), 316–32.

Scottish Government (2011). *Experiences of Muslims Living in Scotland*, Edinburgh: Scottish Government Social Research, available at www.gov.scot/Publications/2011/03/08091838/0

Scottish Government (2012). *Scottish Health Survey Topic Report: Equality groups. A National Statistics Publication for Scotland*, available at www.gov.scot/Resource/0040/00406749.pdf

UK Government (2010). *Equality Act 2010, c.15*, available at www.legislation.gov.uk/ukpga/2010/15/pdfs/ukpga_20100015_en.pdf

Virdee, S., Kyriakides, C. and Modood, T. (2006). 'Codes of cultural belonging: Racialised national identities in a multi-ethnic Scottish neighbourhood'. *Sociological Research Online*, 11(4).

Wallia, S. R., Bhopal, R. S., Douglas, A., Sharma, A., Hutchison, A., Murray, G., Gill, J., Sattar, N., Lawton, J., Tuomilehto, J., McKnight, J., Forbes, J., Lean, M. and Sheikh, A. (2014). 'Culturally adapting the prevention of diabetes and obesity in South Asians (PODOSA) trial'. *Health Promotion International*, 29(4), 768–79.

Whitehead, M. and Dahlgren, G. (1991). 'What can be done about inequalities in health?' *The Lancet*, 338(8774), 1059–63.

Winkleby, M. A. and Cubbin, C. (2004). 'Racial/ethnic disparities in health behaviors: a challenge to current assumptions'. In N. B. Anderson, R. A. Bulatao and B. Cohen (eds), *Critical Perspectives on Racial and Ethnic Differences in Health in Late Life*, pp. 450–91. Washington, DC: National Academies Press.

Winter, T. (2008). 'The Muslim grand narrative'. In A. Sheikh and A. R. Gatrad (eds), *Caring for Muslim Patients*, 2nd edn, pp. 25–34. Oxford: Radcliffe.

World Health Organization (1948). 'Preamble to the Constitution of the World Health Organization, International Health Conference, New York, 19–22 June 1946; signed on 22 July 1946', available at www.who.int/about/definition/en/print.html

World Health Organization (2005). *Health and the Millennium Development Goals*, available at www.who.int/hdp/publications/mdg_en.pdf?ua=1

World Health Organization, Regional Office for Europe (2015). *Stepping up Action on Refugee and Migrant Health. Towards a WHO European*

Framework for Collaborative Action, Outcome document of the high-level meeting on Refugee and Migrant Health, 23–4 November, available at www. euro.who.int/__data/assets/pdf_file/0008/298196/Stepping-up-action-on-ref ugee-migrant-health.pdf?ua=1

Worth, A., Irshad, R., Bhopal, R., Brown, D., Lawton, J., Grant, E., Murray, S., Kendall, M., Adam, J., Gardee, R. and Sheikh, A. (2009). 'Vulnerability and access to care for South Asian Sikh and Muslim patients with life limiting illness in Scotland: Prospective longitudinal qualitative study'. *BMJ*, 338(n/a), b183.

3

EDUCATION
Educational Outcomes of Muslim Pupils in Scotland and Parents' Mobilisation of Different Forms of Capital

Elisabet Weedon and Sheila Riddell

INTRODUCTION

This chapter examines the educational outcomes of pupils from Muslim families in Scotland and the forms of capital mobilised by their parents to achieve social mobility through education. Over recent decades, the experiences of Muslims in Scotland and the rest of the UK have been very mixed. On the one hand, Muslims have sometimes been seen as a security threat and a challenge to social cohesion (Commission on Integration and Cohesion, 2007). On the other hand, the UK Government has taken the lead across Europe in passing equality legislation relating to protected characteristics, including race and religion/belief. Systems have also been put in place for gathering and analysing administrative data to investigate the implementation of equality policies. Despite these efforts, across the UK there is still some variation in the type and quality of administrative data that is available, with Scotland having less data on ethnicity and religion than England due to low numbers in specific groups and the lack of individual pupil data. Across Scotland, there has been very little research on the social experiences and outcomes of Muslims, although Peter Hopkins has investigated the social identity of young Muslim men in Scotland (Hopkins, 2004), and Hussain and Miller (2006) have explored social attitudes on Anglophobia and Islamophobia. This paper, drawing on research funded by the Al Waleed Centre at the University of Edinburgh, attempts to address some of the gaps in the literature by exploring the educational outcomes of Muslim pupils in Scotland and the attitudes to education within Muslim families. The need for education, and especially for educational qualifications, has become increasingly important in recent years for all members of society, irrespective of their background. This is in part due to the growth of the knowledge economy and a changing labour market, but also because it is seen by governments as a means to promote social cohesion. The Scottish National Performance Framework recognises its importance, as the framework includes aims to increase the number of Scottish graduates as well as the number of school leavers in positive destinations.

The questions considered in this chapter are the following: What are the educational outcomes of Muslim pupils in Scotland? How do Muslim parents in Scotland mobilise various forms of capital to influence their children's educational outcomes? What is the relationship between economic and ethno-religious capital in influencing the educational outcomes and experiences of Muslim pupils in Scotland?

PREVIOUS RESEARCH ON THE EDUCATIONAL OUTCOMES OF MUSLIM PUPILS IN THE UK

Across the UK, there has been little analysis of the educational outcomes and experiences of Muslim pupils, as most of the available administrative data relates to ethnicity rather than religious background. Burgess et al. (2009), in an analysis commissioned to inform the work of the National Equality Panel, noted that it is difficult to disentangle the separate effects of ethnicity and religion. They reported that, in England, Muslim boys of Pakistani and Bangladeshi origin who are not in receipt of free school meals caught up with average test results between seven and sixteen years. Free school meals is a statutory benefit available to school-aged children from families that receive other qualifying benefits and that have been through the relevant registration process. Muslim girls from all ethnic backgrounds who were not in receipt of free school meals reached or exceeded average test results by the age of sixteen. Muslim pupils of Bangladeshi and Pakistani origin receiving free school meals also improved their position throughout secondary school, although the achievement of boys from these groups was still below average at age sixteen. The achievement of Bangladeshi girls receiving free school meals was above average by age sixteen, while that of Pakistani girls in receipt of free school meals was just below average. Burgess et al. suggest that analysis of pupils' achievement needs to take into account ethnicity, religion and social class.

The literature examining educational aspirations and achievement among a number of ethnic minority groups is larger, and it is worth noting that for certain ethnic minority groups ethnic origin can be used as a proxy for religion. This is particularly the case for those of Pakistani and Bangladeshi origin, as a large proportion of these groups identifies as Muslim (Weedon et al., 2013). Research in the UK has shown that young people from Chinese and Indian backgrounds achieve well above average at school, and a high number from these two groups go on to higher education. Earlier research on Pakistani pupils' attainment levels has shown that while they are below average at school, a higher proportion of pupils from this ethnic group go on to higher education than White pupils (Shah et al., 2010); however, more recent data indicates a change. While these differences in achievement between ethnic minority groups were in evidence, Hills et al. (2010) found that educational and economic differences between minority ethnic groups have been diminishing over time within the UK. In contrast, they noted that differences within groups relating to social class have been increasing. This is consonant with the general trend across Europe, where economic inequality has been widening since the 1980s, particularly in countries with neoliberal regimes such as the UK (OECD, 2007). Social class differences are mediated by both gender and ethnicity, with socially disadvantaged boys from minority ethnic groups having particularly poor educational outcomes. The UK, in particular England, presents a particular case where neo-liberal market policies provide a greater choice of different types of schools than in continental Europe. However, there are indications that the situation in Europe is changing (Butler and van Zanten, 2007).Whilst this chapter focuses on Scotland, the issues raised are likely to be relevant in other developed countries. Education is conceived as a positional good; that is, as something that confers benefits on the person who possesses educational qualifications. It has therefore become particularly important in either gaining or underpinning middle-class status.

EDUCATIONAL OUTCOMES AND FORMS OF CAPITAL

The development of social capital dates back over a century and broadly refers to the social networks and social relations that are developed both within the family and in the wider community. Plagens attributed the first mention of the term to Marx and noted its development by Dewey in relation to education (Plagens, 2011). According to Balatti and Falk (2002), there are a number of different, and at times conflicting, conceptualisations of social capital which, they argue, are in part due to the context within which it is used and the analysis performed. Within education Bourdieu, Coleman and Putnam have also refined and made extensive use of the concept. In addition to social capital, Bourdieu noted the importance of cultural, linguistic and symbolic capital. He used the concept to explore inequalities, for example in relation to education. According to him, the norms and values of middle-class families, which are embedded in the family and friendship relations, lead to enhanced opportunities for children from these families, while the networks and norms of working-class families lead to less beneficial educational opportunities. Social capital, according to him, was not always a positive asset; this is in contrast with Coleman, who viewed it as beneficial. According to Field (2005), although Bourdieu used the concept of social capital in relation to education, he stressed that economic capital was of greater importance.

A number of researchers (see Shah et al., 2010) have been particularly interested in why some young Pakistani men from working-class backgrounds are more likely than the White working class to continue to further and higher education. They explored educational achievements and outcomes focusing specifically on British Pakistani pupils. To account for the above-average participation in further and higher education, they used the concept of 'ethnic capital', drawing on Zhou's concept of 'ethnic social capital'. This refers to 'familial or ethnic shared norms and values as contributing to educational achievement among immigrant groups' (Shah et al., 2010: 1110). In their study of a group of sixty-four Pakistanis aged sixteen to twenty-six in Slough, they found that, while social class influenced the educational outcomes of middle-class Pakistanis, ethnic capital accounted for the higher than anticipated achievements of some working-class Pakistani boys. They also noted that it was necessary to include gender in the analysis: 'gender identities, constructed in relation to family expectations and peer influences, were a key factor in influencing their orientation towards education and career' (Shah et al., 2010: 1119).

These researchers commented on shifting cultural values, with Pakistani families increasingly having high educational and labour market aspirations for their daughters as well as their sons. In contrast, they noted different effects on some young working-class men of Pakistani origin, where a peer culture emphasising non-conformity and negative attitudes towards school affected some detrimentally. However, this did not apply to all young working-class Pakistani men. Shah et al. (2010) argued that the role and nature of ethnic capital mitigated the impact of class and peer group cultures, and this explains why a greater proportion of working-class Pakistani boys attend higher education. They also noted the impact of religion on working-class men's participation in higher education. Those who identified their religion as highly important and practised regularly were likely to have higher levels of education than those who did not. Furthermore, English data using free school meal entitlement (FSM) indicated a smaller impact of social class on some ethnic groups (e.g. Bangladeshi pupils), but a higher impact on Pakistani pupils (Archer and Francis, 2006). These researchers also stressed the need to recognise the interrelationship between social class, ethnicity and gender, and that an analysis that looks only at the average performance of specific ethnic groups masks the differences within these categories. Using Bourdieu's concepts of economic, social, cultural and symbolic capital, they suggested that within each ethnic group some parents are able to draw on privileged forms of capital to access the 'best' education for their children. Strand (2007), in his analysis of achievement of minority ethnic groups, noted that 'it is important not to over-generalise from group mean scores to all members of any ethnic group' (Strand, 2007: 103). Our analysis examines these differences within our sample but, before presenting our findings, we shall briefly outline our methodology. Overall, empirical research suggests that it is not feasible to examine parents' aspirations purely through the lens of ethnicity or religion. Rather, it is necessary to consider the impact of social class and gender too.

RESEARCH METHODS

The data reported on here comes from a larger project examining the educational experiences and outcomes for Muslim pupils in England and Scotland. It took place over a period of three years from January 2010 to December 2012. The main focus of the research was on family case studies but, in order to contextualise our findings, we drew on a range of secondary administrative data sources. The main ones were those relating to academic achievement and census data on religion and ethnicity.

Thirty-eight family case studies were conducted in total: thirteen in England and twenty-five in Scotland (Table 3.1). The case studies were based on recorded semi-structured interviews and observations made at the time of the interview. The sample was opportunistic and used a range of methods to contact Muslim families in a number of geographical areas in England and Scotland. These were deliberately chosen to reflect labour market diversity and patterns of settlement. In England, the family case studies were drawn from Central London, a city in the east of England and an area of industrial decline in the north-west. In

Table 3.1 Number of interviews and backgrounds of participants

National[1] background	No. of interviews with parent(s)	No. of interviews with children/young people	First-generation immigrant[2]	Second-generation immigrant[2]	Refugee/Protected status[2]	'Temporary' residents[2]	No. of parents with degree equivalent qualification[3]
Pakistan	21	33	11	10			14
Bangladesh	5	7	2	3			3
India	4	1	2	2			3
Malaysia	3	3				3	3
Iran	1	1				1	1
UK	2	4	N/A	N/A	N/A	N/A	2
Turkey	1	1				1	1
Iraq	6	8			6		5
Somalia	1				1		1
Afghanistan	1				1		1
Scotland	**30**	**41**	**15**	**15**	**8**	**5**	**21**
England	**15**	**16**					**13**
Total	**45**	**57**	**15**	**15**	**8**	**5**	**34**

1. In a small number of cases, the parent(s) had grown up in a different country; for those of Indian and Pakistani origin this was usually Kenya.

2. Refers to parent interviewed; in many families one partner was a second-generation immigrant and the other was first-generation. Immigration status was not known for three interviewees.

3. Refers to parents and includes degrees gained in other countries; a small number of parents had postgraduate degrees.

Scotland, interviewees lived in cities in the east and west of the country. Some participants were contacted through mosques, schools and universities, and others via other interviewees. National backgrounds were diverse, with interviewees reporting ten different countries of origin. All of the adults who participated self-identified as Muslim. A total of ninety-eight interviews were conducted between June 2010 and May 2012.

The adults whom we interviewed were generally well educated. About three-quarters had a degree-level qualification or equivalent. This does not reflect the level of qualifications among adults of Pakistani and Bangladeshi origin in the UK (Hills et al., 2010), although there has been a recent increase in degree-level qualifications among Bangladeshis and Pakistanis in the working-age population (Hills et al., 2013). There is evidence from the census for England that the younger age group (aged sixteen to twenty-four) of Pakistani and Bangladeshi origin are better qualified than their elders (Lymperopoulou and Parameshwaran, 2014). It is worth noting that many of the Pakistani participants mentioned that their parents were not educated to degree level and some described their parents as working class. This might suggest a certain degree of educational and social mobility among those of Pakistani and Bangladeshi origin living in the UK. They all described themselves as Muslims, but they differed in the extent of their everyday practices, and these practices were often related to culture as well as religion.

Thirty of the interviews with parents were with mothers only; five were with fathers only; two interviews were with both parents separately and three interviews were with both parents together. In nine of the case studies, the interviews with the children/young people, the parents were not present; in five out of these nine case studies the interviews were conducted with each individual separately, and in the remainder the children/young people were interviewed together. In one case, an older child was interviewed on her own and her younger siblings together. Parental consent was sought for the interviews with the children, and all participants, apart from the youngest children, were asked to sign a consent form. Participants were ensured of anonymity and the names used in the case studies are pseudonyms.

THE SCOTTISH EDUCATION SYSTEM

Scotland has a comprehensive schooling system with compulsory education between the ages of five and sixteen; a post-compulsory system with upper secondary up to the age of eighteen in schools, and further and higher education in colleges and universities. There are a number of private schools, particularly in the larger cities, but these cater for only about 4% of the total school population. The proportion of pupils attending private schools is higher in the Edinburgh area, where around 20% of the school population is privately educated (though a number of the pupils come from surrounding local authorities).

EDUCATIONAL ACHIEVEMENT: ADMINISTRATIVE DATA

There is limited statistical data available that examines school achievements according to religion. As mentioned above, we therefore use ethnicity as a 'proxy' for religion for pupils of Pakistani and Bangladeshi origin, as most self-identify as Muslims (Strand, 2007).

Although our focus is on Scotland, much of the existing literature is English. It is therefore worth noting some demographic differences between the two countries. At the time of our research, the overall White school population in Scotland was 93%, and Asian pupils (mainly of Pakistani origin) accounted for 3.2% of the population (Scottish Government, 2012). By 2015, the proportion of White pupils was marginally lower (91.6%) and the Asian population slightly higher, at 3.7%. In England, the overall White population is below 80% and Asian pupils constitute 10.3% of the population (Department for Education, 2013). As a result of these variations in population, a wider range of ethnic categories is used in England.

The Scottish Government publishes figures for achievement at the end of compulsory education that were based previously on Standard Grades and now on National 4 and 5 exams (approximately equivalent to Key Stage 4 in England). Figure 3.1 shows the average tariff scores achieved by Secondary 4 (S4) pupils by ethnicity for the period 2008–9 to 2010–11, which coincides with the time of our research. Chinese pupils, followed by Bangladeshi and Indian pupils, achieved the highest scores. Pakistani pupils achieved above-average tariff scores and performed better than White UK pupils, because of the high achievements of Pakistani girls. The scores of Pakistani boys are the same as those of White UK boys. Those in the 'Not Known', 'All Other Categories' and 'Black Caribbean' categories have the lowest tariff scores. It is likely that the 'All Other Categories' group includes recent arrivals such as asylum seekers and refugees who may not be proficient in English. The most recent data shows an improvement in the tariff score of Pakistani boys, indicating that they now perform above the level of White pupils

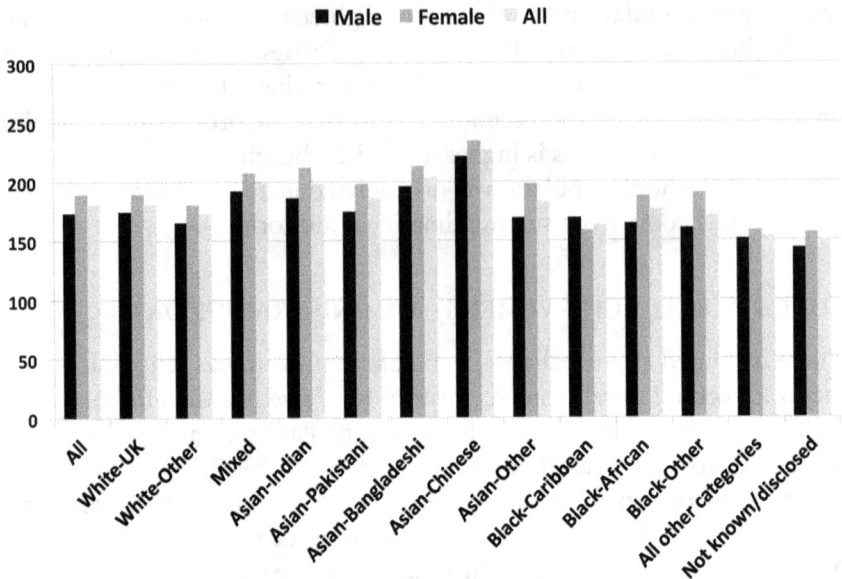

Figure 3.1 Three-year average tariff[a] score for Secondary 4 pupils by ethnic background, Scotland, 2008–9 to 2010–11

Source: Scottish Government, 2012

[a]'The Unified Points Score Scale is an extended version of the Universities and Colleges Admissions Service (UCAS) Scottish Tariff points system ... The tariff score of a pupil is calculated by simply adding together all the tariff points accumulated from all the different course levels and awards he/she attains' (Scottish Government, 2012)

(Scottish Government, 2014). This is in contrast to England, where pupils of Pakistani background perform below average (Department for Education, 2015).

Figure 3.2 provides information about Highers and Advanced Highers (roughly equivalent to AS and A levels). These are the qualifications required for entry to higher education. This again shows that Chinese pupils outperform all other groups. The proportion of Pakistani pupils gaining five Highers was slightly higher than for White pupils; a smaller proportion gained one or two Advanced Highers, but about the same achieved three or more Advanced Highers. Overall, Scottish Pakistani pupils perform above average, whereas in England their performance is slightly below average. The latest attainment statistics for Scotland show that this is still the case (Scottish Government, 2014). It is not possible to comment on the achievements at this level of Bangladeshi pupils, as the numbers are very small.

Figure 3.3 shows that in Scotland, Asian students, particularly those

1–2 @ SCQF level 6   3–4 @ SCQF level 6   5+ @ SCQF level 6
1–2 @ SCQF level 7   3+ @ SCQF level 7

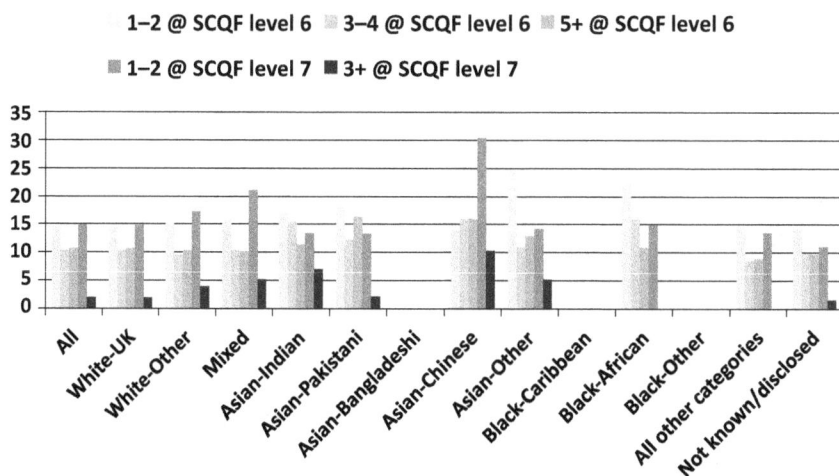

Figure 3.2 Highest qualifications attained by Scottish school leavers by ethnic background, level 6 and level 7 only[a], percentages[b]

Source: Scottish Government, 2012

[a]Level 6 is Higher qualifications; level 7 is Advanced Higher. Level 6 qualifications or above are required for university entrance; the most prestigious universities require a minimum of 5 Highers
[b]Based on total population within ethnic group
Note that: All other categories consists of: Black-Other, Asian-Bangladeshi, Black-Caribbean, Occupational traveller, Gypsy traveller, Other traveller and Other; numbers below 5 are not included due to confidentiality issues

of Chinese origin, are more likely to go to university than their White counterparts. This does not imply that White pupils in general are failing to access higher education in Scotland, but simply that the large variance in levels of achievement among the indigenous population reflects very large social class differences (OECD, 2007). It also suggests that the Chinese population in Scotland (and the UK) is not representative of the whole Chinese population, as the UK Chinese population has a high proportion of adults with degree-level qualifications (Hills et al., 2010).

Scottish data, measuring average tariff scores for S4 pupils according to levels of deprivation, shows significantly lower scores for those living in the 20% most deprived areas in comparison to the rest of the population. The average tariff score is 145 for pupils in the 20% most deprived areas, compared to 198 for those in other areas (Figure 3.4). Within the group of pupils of Pakistani origin, the difference is less, 178 compared to 207, but greater than it was in the three-year period 2007–10 (162 compared to 186) (Scottish Government, 2013). Data showing tariff

■ Higher education   ■ Further education

■ Training   ■ Employment

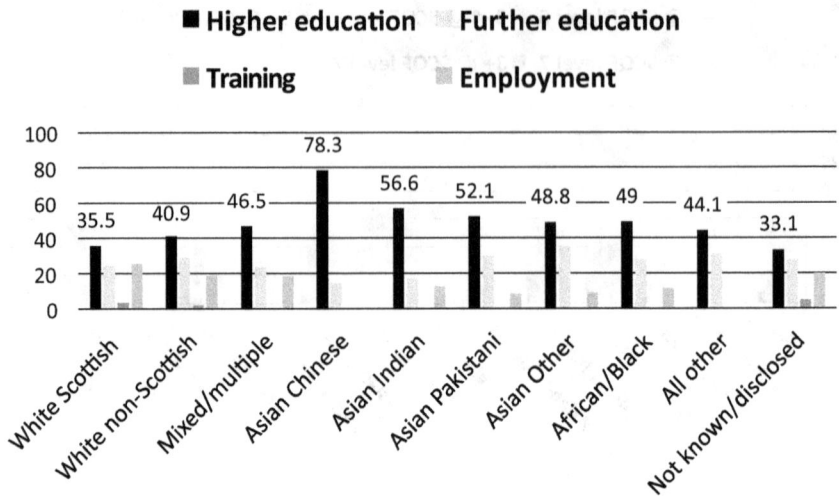

Figure 3.3 Initial destinations of Scottish school leavers, 2012–13

Source: Scottish Government, 2014

Note: this does not include the full range of categories as the focus is on the main destinations

■ SIMD 20 tariff score   ■ Other 80% tariff score

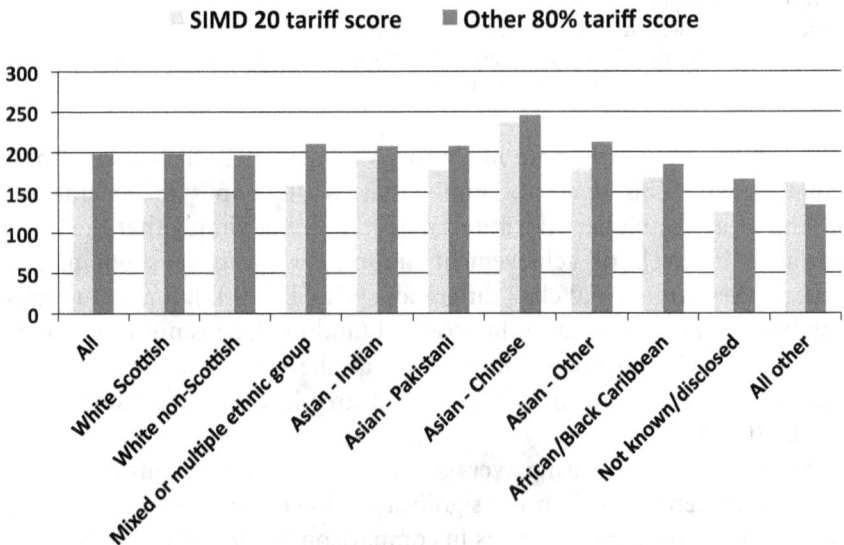

Figure 3.4 Average tariff score for S4 pupils, by ethnicity and SIMD,[a] 2011–12

Source: Scottish Government, 2013

[a]Scottish Index of Multiple Deprivation (SIMD) is the official measure of area based multiple deprivation used by the Scottish Government (http://www.scotland.gov.uk/Topics/Statistics/SIMD

score differences by the full range of deciles indicates a step progression with increasing tariff scores (Maxwell, 2013).

Overall, then, young Asian people, including a large proportion of pupils of Pakistani origin, have levels of attainment comparable to or above White UK/Scottish students and Bangladeshi pupils achieve above average. On average, pupils from ethnic minority backgrounds are more likely to go to university than White pupils. They are slightly more likely to attend less prestigious universities than the more elite institutions (Croxford and Raffe, 2014). A recent analysis of Scottish domiciled students attending Scottish universities showed a higher proportion of non-White ethnic minorities attending university than White students, and that students of Pakistani and Bangladeshi origin were considerably less likely to have at least one parent with university or equivalent level of education than White students. While the students with a Pakistani background were slightly less likely than White students to attend elite universities, this was not the case for the very small number of students with a Bangladeshi background. Although students of Pakistani origin account for only 1.9% of the Scottish domiciled student population, they account for 3% of the students studying medicine or dentistry.

It is clear that focusing on only ethnicity may well mask intra-group differences. There is evidence of a gap between pupils of Pakistani origin living in the 20% most deprived areas and those in other areas. However, the within-group differences for White UK/Scottish pupils are greater. Data for minority ethnic groups has to be treated with caution, as the number of pupils of Pakistani origin in Scotland is low. Analysis of achievement of White UK pupils consistently shows a very wide spread of attainment, reflecting the strong influence of social class. Research on widening access to higher education demonstrates the influence of school attainment on access to higher education (Riddell, 2016), and low attainment impacts on access to higher education irrespective of ethnic background. In Scotland, this was highlighted in an OECD report on the achievement of Scottish pupils (OECD, 2007).

PARENTS' AND YOUNG PEOPLE'S EDUCATIONAL ASPIRATIONS

This section draws on data from the Scottish participants in our study. As documented above, high aspirations among minority ethnic groups are common, and the same can be said for the Muslim parents and many of the young people in our sample. The quotes below from two of the

parents from two different Scottish cities highlight the value of education. One was a recent arrival and the other had been born and brought
up in the UK. These were typical of many of the parents:

> I would like to promote the idea [that] ... we invest in education and this
> is ... our intellectual property, intangible property and that is what I want
> to do with my children ... That is very important because ... we don't have
> money here, we don't have families here, this [knowledge] is our property.
> (Hanifa, mother, Iraqi refugee)

> Yes, yes, I expect all my kids to go to – Inshallah, we say – they will go
> to university and they will finish. That's what I'm, as a mum, I think a lot
> of parents would expect that ... Anything can happen but, so that's in my
> dreams. (Razia, mother, Bangladeshi origin)

In many cases, these aspirations were focused on academic achievement,
but a number of parents felt that the social and emotional aspects of
education were as important:

> I think I'd want them to feel confident first of all, happy in who they are,
> because I really believe if you don't know who you are then you just spend
> your whole life trying to figure out who you are. I want them to be passion-
> ate about something, it could be anything, it could be something academic,
> could be something outside school that they love, something like that, I want
> them to feel mentally and socially secure and what that means is having emo-
> tional confidence. That's really number one for me, so they're not going to
> get emotional confidence if you go OK, you've got your five grades whatever,
> A grades, you're perfect, that's not how to measure it. (Adifaah, mother,
> Pakistani origin)

Although parents had high aspirations, it was clear that the choice of
future education and career was generally left to the young people themselves, who often had similar high aspirations:

> I'm doing computer science and maths at an [ancient university] ... [as a
> career] I was thinking of software development, more into the computing
> side, I want to study maths but I don't actually want a job in that, but
> because I'm doing a joint degree in maths, I would also be able to go into
> finance if I had to, just like widen all the opportunities, get a lot more oppor-
> tunities for jobs ... Don't know what my parents want me to do. (Umar,
> Nuzhat's son (see Case study 1, below), aged seventeen)

Many parents recognised the increasing importance of academic creden-
tials in a labour market that they perceived as changing and increasingly
competitive, and this recognition was also evident among the older

children. At the same time, a small number of parents were concerned about the difficulties that their children may face because of their religion when going into higher education. This meant that some of the young people studied at universities close to home, so that they could continue living at home, or arrangements were made to ensure that they were not in the traditional type of student accommodation. Although some parents had concerns about their children moving away elsewhere to study, there were others who felt it would be good for their children to move away from home and gain new experiences:

> I said, 'if you really want to do it, go to Aberdeen or wherever ... live there ... if you get your grades and want to do something that is there, go there, live there'. She [daughter] said no. (Adeena, mother, Pakistani origin)

This brief overview demonstrates the importance placed on further and higher education, and also that there were differences among the parents in terms of emphasis on high academic achievement and whether it was acceptable for young people to live away from home while studying. It highlights the diversity within the Muslim population and the dangers of assuming that there is one 'Muslim' view or way of being. There were further differences relating to the ability of parents to realise their ambitions and the strategies that they used. These are explored below in three case studies. These case studies have been selected as they represent parents who were all brought up outside the UK (apart from one father); they had different levels of education; they differed in the way that they had used and gained knowledge of the education system; they had at least one child who had completed his or her school education; and the outcomes for the children also differed.

Case study 1

The family were of Pakistani origin. The father came from Kenya but had spent most of his life in the UK. Nuzhat, the mother, was born and brought up in Pakistan and came to the UK when she got married. They had three children, aged seventeen, sixteen and twelve. They lived on the outskirts of Sea City (a pseudonym), Scotland, in their own house in a small, modern development and they had extended family contacts in the city and elsewhere in the UK. Nuzhat was educated to degree level and was employed. Her first job was in administration, but she then obtained a job in education; her husband was working in finance, but was retraining to become a careers officer. Education was important and, according to Nuzhat, academic achievement had become more important to the UK Pakistani community in general, because the traditional labour market opportunities were no longer available:

> The other generation were mostly in the business in the shops, so they didn't get much [education] ... There are not many corner shops round now – there are supermarkets. Now all those men who had shops, they really want their children to do well in studies academically. It's improving in this generation. Because this is the third generation, like, I think our children will be the fourth generation here. (Nuzhat, mother)

Nuzhat had no specific occupational aspirations for her children, but it was clear that the importance placed on education had impacted on at least the two older children's ambitions. The children's primary and secondary schools had been selected because of their academic reputation. The parents had made a placing request to a secondary school outside their catchment area to ensure that the children did not attend the local school, which had a very poor academic reputation, and there had also been incidents of racism in the area. The secondary school attended by the children had above-average academic achievement and a higher than average percentage of pupils moving into higher education. Attending a school further from home was not without its difficulties, as it entailed either two bus rides or one of the parents taking the children to school.

Umar, the eldest son, was about to start studying at a prestigious university in a different city. Nuzhat expressed some anxieties about the difficulties that her children might face, particularly on the social side, when living away from home. However, there was no attempt to prevent the children from leaving home to study elsewhere. The concerns highlighted by Nuzhat about living away from home were also evident in other case studies, and one family had dealt with them by having one parent moving to live with the children while they completed their higher education, as shown below in case study 2.

Case study 2

The family were refugees from Afghanistan and arrived in the UK around ten years ago as asylum seekers. Both parents were well educated (Marid, the father, had a PhD from a UK university) and they had three children, aged twenty-three, twenty and seventeen. Their eldest, a daughter, was currently studying medicine, and their son was studying engineering. They were at the same pre-'92 university and the younger daughter was in sixth year at school. Scottish higher education institutions are often categorised as 'ancient', 'pre-'92' or 'old' and 'post-'92'. The ancient are the most prestigious and the post-'92 the least prestigious. Education was highly valued by the family; however, it was not considered acceptable for their children to live in traditional student accommodation. For that reason, Marid was living in their home in River City (a pseudonym) and working as a private tutor at the time of the interview. His wife was in rented accommodation in another Scottish city to be with her children as they completed their studies. Marid explained that this was because in their culture it was not acceptable for the children to live on their own.

This case study illustrates some of the tensions that arise for both parents and young people when they come to the end of their compulsory education. It also highlights the sacrifices that many of the parents are willing to make in order to ensure that their children have the best education possible and the importance that many parents attach to gaining good qualifications in order to ensure access to good-quality jobs and the parental support offered to the children. Not all parents were in the position to offer such support, and this was mainly due to a lack of social capital and economic resources, which related in part to the parents' own educational background. This is further explored in the case study below.

Case study 3

The family were of Pakistani origin. Ramsha, the mother, came to the UK when she was married. Her husband had lived most of his life in the UK, although part of his education took place in Pakistan. They lived in an area consisting predominantly of social housing in Sea City in an area that was ranked as one of the less affluent areas (SIMD quintile 2, SIMD 2012) of the city. It was an area where the schools had to deal with problems associated with social deprivation. Their accommodation was an upstairs flat with limited space. Although Ramsha's husband had some relatives in the UK, they lived far away, so they lacked extended family support. However, Ramsha had contact with others from the Pakistani community, including Nuzhat. She had enrolled on a college course to gain a qualification, but had left as the English was too challenging. There were four children in the family, two sons, aged eighteen and ten, and two daughters, aged twelve and eight. The two youngest children attended the local primary school, while Roshini, the twelve-year-old girl, was at the local secondary school that had below-average academic achievement and a lower than average percentage of leavers going on to higher education.

The elder son, who had attended the same secondary school as his younger sister, had experienced difficulties at secondary school. His mother attributed these difficulties to bullying. He had not wanted to attend school, had fallen behind with his education and left with low qualifications. Ramsha had struggled to make and maintain meaningful contact with the school, which contrasted with the experience she had had with the children's primary school:

> I lost this kind of contact with the high school at the end of, towards the end of the years. And I was always wanting to go and find out what it is my child doing and what he is not and what's the progress report. Even if you got a ten minutes or fifteen minutes to speak to the teacher, find out what your child is doing, what level they are doing, are they needing any help or not. And if you find out your child is needing help then you could specifically speak to that teacher to find out if there's any extra help they can do it ... I prefer if they send a letter [but this did not happen] ... Or maybe does, but just not in my knowledge. But in the start years, for a couple of years in the high school I went on to the parents' meetings. Then I lost [contact] completely. (Ramsha, mother of Pakistani origin)

Her son had wanted to study architecture and had started a college course after leaving school. He subsequently dropped out and was, at the time of the interview, working in a factory:

> I still wish he were back to the study. At the moment he's saying he will go back, but I'm not 100% sure about it. (Ramsha, mother)

Ramsha was not a disinterested parent. She was ambitious for her children, as was her husband. However, her English was not fluent and she struggled to engage with secondary teachers and, later on, with college staff. She seemed to lack sufficient knowledge and was not familiar with the culture of a secondary school, which led to less satisfactory outcomes for her elder son. The family also had limited economic resources and Ramsha was not working at the time of the interview due to health problems.

In all these cases, the parents' aspirations for their children were high. In the first two case studies, the parents' aspirations were being realised, but not in the third. The first two case studies indicate that the families possessed sufficient social and economic capital to ensure that their children would progress into higher education. It is unlikely that either of the families was wealthy. However, the educational background of the parents had allowed them to ensure that the children obtained the most from the compulsory school system. In the case of Nuzhat, it involved a placing request to an academically high-achieving secondary school; in

Marid's case it entailed helping the children with schoolwork to ensure that they achieved, in spite of attending a low-achieving primary school when they first arrived in the country. Ramsha, on the other hand, did not seem to be able to provide support with schoolwork, as her English was poor and her knowledge of the subjects was not good. It would seem, then, that Nuzhat and Marid had the necessary social capital and were sufficiently able to understand the norms and values of schools and higher education to ensure that their children could realise their ambitions. Ethnic capital possibly played a role in Nuzhat's case through her extended family, but it was not of relevance to Marid. Ramsha had some access to the knowledge of her ethnic community, but this was not sufficient to mitigate the effects of fewer social and economic resources.

DISCUSSION

This chapter set out to explore three questions. The first was: What are the educational achievements (based on administrative data) of Pakistani and Bangladeshi pupils in Scotland? As mentioned above, in the case of administrative data we used ethnicity as a proxy for religion in relation to pupils of Pakistani and Bangladeshi origin. The data for Scotland shows that Pakistani pupils' achievement matches or is above that of White UK pupils, and Bangladeshi pupils perform above average. This is in contrast with England, where Pakistani pupils achieve below average at Key Stage 4. Bangladeshi pupils, on the other hand, perform above average. The achievement of both these groups has improved in the period 2007–8 to 2011–12 and has continued to stay on or above average up to 2014.

The second question focused on the role of social and ethnic capital in the achievement of Muslim families' educational aspirations. It was clear that the parents considered portable educational qualifications to be essential. In Hanifa's words: 'we invest in education and this is ... our intellectual property, intangible property'. All wanted their children to achieve to their best ability, but a small number stressed that, while qualifications were important, it was just as important that their offspring developed socially and emotionally, as this was also necessary for success in the labour market. Many of the parents, such as Nuzhat, were aware of changes in the labour market, a decrease in low-skilled jobs and fewer opportunities for traditional work in small corner shops. The contraction of the manufacturing industry and the growth in supermarkets have contributed to these changes. This was similar to findings of Shah et al.'s (2010) study, in which they reported on young British Pakistanis' awareness of a changing labour market. This study also noted that parents considered education as a means to social mobility and that the greatest impact of 'ethnic capital' was likely to be seen among some working-class Pakistani boys, particularly those who were more religious. Our data suggests that ethnic capital does not always work to mitigate the effects of those from a lower socioeconomic background. Although religion and culture was important to Ramsha and her family and their main socialising was with people from her own culture, their access to the ethnic community and the high aspirations for her children shared with that community were not sufficient for the family to attain their aspirations. It was clear that socioeconomic circumstances such as lack of financial resources and a low level of parental educational qualifications made it more difficult for the family to realise their ambitions. In that sense, Bourdieu's view that a lack of economic and social capital can stand in the way of educational outcomes provides a better explanation of the outcomes for Ramsha's elder son.

It was clear that some families regarded education as a vehicle for social mobility. This was the case for Nuzhat and her family. Her husband's family, of Pakistani origin, had originally come from Kenya and had been shopkeepers, but her husband was in finance and was studying. Their older children were doing well at school as a result of the parents developing strategies to access a good school and supporting their children. The social capital available to the family through the networks of family and friends, as well as an understanding of the norms and values of the education system in the UK, had worked well for them. Although not wealthy, they were comfortably off and were able to access schools further from home. Marid's family did not have social capital in the form of a network of family in the UK. However, they did understand the norms and values of the UK education system. This came initially from Marid having studied for a higher degree at a prestigious UK university. As they moved to the UK, they were able to draw on this and Marid developed his knowledge further as a private tutor and contributor to school resources in his own subject area. It is likely that they would have been considered middle class in their home country and were now trying to ensure that they maintained this status in their new home country. In contrast, Ramsha and her family did not seem to understand the education system, particularly at secondary level, in order to be able to ensure the outcomes that they desired for their children. They had limited access to an extended family and, although Ramsha had links to the Pakistani community in the city, this did not seem to provide her with sufficient support to help her to understand the norms and values of the education system. In that sense, the family did not have sufficient social and cultural capital and they lacked economic resources. Although they potentially had access to ethnic capital, it was not sufficient to mitigate the effects of the lack of economic and social capital. It would seem, then, that parents with access to social and cultural capital, and to sufficient economic resources, were in a more advantageous position to ensure the educational outcomes to which they aspired for their children. Families living in more socially disadvantaged circumstances struggled more, in spite of their high aspirations and attempts to ensure a good outcome for their children. The third question to be considered was whether socio-economic factors affect educational outcomes of ethnic minority pupils and if there was evidence for an increasing gap within ethnic minority groups. It is impossible to provide a conclusive answer to this, as our qualitative data is limited and the administrative data does not provide sufficient detail. A tentative response to this question would be that there is some evidence to support a widening gap. This is based on the slight increase in the gap in achievement between those in the 20% most deprived areas (SIMD20) to those in other areas for Asian-Pakistani pupils in Scotland, although the most recent statistics show that the gap has not increased. There is also some support for this position from our data. However, this is not representative, and further research drawing on both quantitative and qualitative data would be required. This view is also supported by Burgess et al. (2009), who noted that sociodemographic differences were more likely to account for educational attainment than ethnicity or religion.

In conclusion, as other research has shown, ethnic minority and Muslim families have high aspirations for their children's education. It is also evident that social and cultural capital play an important role in parents' ability to support their children in achieving their ambitions. The data also demonstrates that reports on underachievement by Pakistani pupils cannot necessarily be ascribed to their ethnic background and that achievement within this group may well be more strongly affected by social class differences within this ethnic group.

REFERENCES

Archer, L. and Francis, B. (2006). *Understanding Minority Ethnic Achievement: Race, Class, Gender and 'Success'*. London: Routledge.

Balatti, J. and Falk, I. (2002). 'Socioeconomic benefits of adult learning to community: A social capital perspective'. *Adult Education Quarterly*, 52(4), 281–98.

Burgess, S., Greaves, E. and Wilson, D. (2009). *An Investigation of Educational Outcomes by Ethnicity and Religion: A Report for the National Equality Panel.* Bristol: CMPO, University of Bristol.

Butler, T. and van Zanten, A. (2007). 'School choice: A European perspective'. *Journal of Educational Policy,* 22(1), 1–5.

Commission on Integration and Cohesion (2007). *Our Shared Future.* London: Commission on Integration and Cohesion.

Croxford, L. and Raffe, D. (2014). 'Social class, ethnicity and access to higher in the four countries of the UK: 1996–2010'. *International Journal of Lifelong Education,* 33(1), 77–95.

Department for Education (2013). *GCSE and Equivalent Attainment by Pupil Characteristics in England, 2011–12, SFR 04/2013.* London: Department for Education.

Department for Education (2015). *GCSE and Equivalent Attainment by Pupil Characteristics in England, 2013–14, SFR06/2015.* London: Department for Education.

Field, J. (2005). *Social Capital and Lifelong Learning.* Bristol: Policy Press.

Hills, J., Brewer, M., Jenkins, S., Lister, R., Lupton, R., Machin, S., Mills, C., Modood, T., Rees, T. and Riddell, S. (2010). *An Anatomy of Economic Inequality in the UK.* London: London School of Economics.

Hills, J., Cuncliffe, J., Gambaro, L. and Obolenskaya, P. (2013). *Winners and Losers in the Crisis: The Changing Anatomy of Economic Inequality in the UK 2007–2010, Research Report 2.* London: CASE, London School of Economics.

Lymperopoulou, K. and Parameshwaran, M. (2014). *The Dynamics of Diversity: Evidence from the 2011 Census Briefing.* Centre on Dynamics of Ethnicity (CoDE), available at www.ethnicity.ac.uk

Maxwell, B. (2013). 'Improving equity in educational outcomes through curriculum for excellence'. Presentation at seminar, Educational attainment and inequality in Scotland, available at www.docs.hss.ed.ac.uk/education/creid/Projects/34ivh_ESRCF_Seminar_PPT_Maxwell.pdf

OECD (2007). *Quality and Equity of Schooling Scotland.* Paris: OECD.

Plagens, G. (2011). 'Social capital and education: Implications for student and school performance'. *Education and Culture,* 27(1), 40–64.

Riddell, S. (2016). 'Introduction to special edition on widening access to higher education in Scotland'. *Scottish Educational Review,* 48(1), 3–12.

Scottish Government (2013). *Pupils in Scotland 2012,* supplementary data published February 2013, available at www.scotland.gov.uk/Topics/Statistics/Browse/School-Education/dspupcensus/pupcensus2012

Scottish Government (2014). *Summary Statistics for Attainment, Leaver Destinations and Healthy Living (4): Attainment and destinations,* available at www.gov.scot/Publications/2014/06/9242

Shah, B., Dwyer, C. and Modood, T. (2010). 'Explaining educational achievement and career aspirations among young British Pakistanis: Mobilizing "ethnic capital"?' *Sociology,* 44(6), 1109–27.

Strand, S. (2007). *Minority Ethnic Pupils in the Longitudinal Study of Young People in England* (LSYPE). Warwick: University of Warwick.

Weedon, E., Riddell, S., McCluskey, G. and Konstantoni, K. (2013). *Muslim Families' Educational Experiences in England and Scotland: Final Report.* Edinburgh: CREID, University of Edinburgh.

4

POLITICAL PARTICIPATION
Young Muslims' Political Interests and Political Participation in Scotland

Robin Finlay, Peter Hopkins and Gurchathen Sanghera

INTRODUCTION

At the time of writing, politics within Scotland and the UK is experiencing a period of uncertainty, with issues such as Brexit, Scottish nationalism, the 'refugee crisis' and continued economic insecurity creating a complicated and unprecedented political climate. Scotland, for many, is considered to be expressing a distinctive politics to the rest of the UK (Mooney, 2013; McAngus, 2015), with the Scottish National Party (SNP) having strong representation in both the Scottish and UK Parliaments. With regard to the electorate, there is a sense that young people in Scotland have recently become more politicised (Baxter et al., 2015; Hopkins, 2015), with sixteen- and seventeen-year-olds having been given the right to vote in the Scottish parliamentary elections and the 2014 independence referendum. This contests the frequent narrative that young people are politically apathetic (Kimberlee, 2002), and adds to a growing body of work that seeks to examine and unearth the varied and complex ways in which young people engage with political issues (Brookes and Hodkinson, 2008; O'Toole and Gale, 2013; Pilkington and Pollock, 2015).

As highlighted in the Introduction, the Muslim population in Scotland is growing and 67% are aged thirty-four or under (National Records of Scotland, 2011). Young Muslims in Scotland, then, are an important demographic with regards to political participation. However, apart from the work of Hopkins (2007), there is a dearth of understanding of how young Muslims in Scotland are concerned with political issues (although see Chapter 7). The vast majority of research about Muslim experiences, political participation and racism still focuses on England (Hopkins, 2007). This is especially surprising when you consider that

Scotland provides a distinctive political and cultural landscape, and that examining political participation sheds light on pertinent processes with regards to young Muslims, such as integration, belonging and self-determination (Anwar, 2015).

This chapter examines the political participation and views of a variety of young Muslims, aged fifteen to twenty-seven, living in Scotland. We examine how different geographical scales impact on the political perceptions, identities and participation of young Muslims. The chapter is firmly grounded in the context of Scotland and examines how its political, social and cultural landscape can engender distinctive perceptions and engagements with political matters. However, we also analyse how the local/national intersects with the global, and examine the influence of international political events on political views and political participation.

Drawing on the work of O'Toole and Gale (2013), we adopt a broad interpretation of political participation, helping to show the emergence of more informal and everyday activism, along with more traditional engagement in mainstream politics. Overall, we demonstrate that there is a range of political participation and political interests, with young Muslims engaging with politics in a variety of ways, incorporating local, national and global issues. The forms of political participation that we analyse include engagement with mainstream Scottish politics, social movements and activism, and volunteering and charity work. Crucially, the chapter does not provide an exhaustive analysis of all the political participation that we have identified in the research, and certain nuances such as gender and ethnicity are not fully unpacked. Instead, it offers an insight into a selection of core political concerns and political participation conveyed by young Muslims.

The chapter is organised into three main parts. First, we provide some definitions of the key themes of analysis and recent research on young people, political participation and Muslim identities. Second, we provide an outline of the study that this chapter is based on. Third, we move to the empirical analysis and examine three key forms of political participation that are practised and articulated by the young Muslims who participated in the research.

POLITICAL PARTICIPATION, YOUNG PEOPLE AND MUSLIM IDENTITIES

Traditionally, political participation has been understood as participation in institutional and electoral politics (Brookes and Hodkinson,

2008; O'Toole and Gale, 2013). The patterns and extent of participation can vary, encompassing voting in elections, active campaigning and canvassing for political parties. The scale of electoral participation in the UK generally has two levels – national and local. However, with devolution of specific powers to Scotland, there are also now separate elections and parliamentarians elected to the Scottish Parliament. These different levels incorporate the electing of Members of Parliament (MPs), Members of the Scottish Parliament (MSPs) and councillors of local authorities.

Recently, however, there has been a broader shift in how political participation is conceptualised. O'Toole and Gale (2013), along with a number of other scholars (Bang, 2005; Brookes and Hodkinson, 2008; Pilkington and Pollock, 2015), have highlighted new and emerging forms of political participation that deviate from engaging only with traditional institutional politics. In a sense, it is a reconceptualisation of what is considered political. There are now what O'Toole and Gale (2013) call 'new grammars of political action', which incorporate social activism, protest marching, boycotting, blogging, e-activism, volunteering, community work and mentoring, to name a few. This is a move away from conceiving political engagement solely through conventional electoral practices, to understanding a number of non-conventional and non-institutional practices as highly political.

Symptomatic of the increase in new forms of political participation is generational change, with young people frequently considered to perceive and engage with politics in ways distinct from their parents' and grandparents' generation (Brookes and Hodkinson, 2008; O'Toole and Gale, 2013). Much has been written about young people and political apathy (Kimberlee, 2002; Pilkington and Pollock, 2015), with a number of scholars highlighting a disconnection between mainstream political parties and young people (Kimberlee, 2002). It is suggested that there is a lack of a fit with the agendas of the institutional political parties and the kinds of concerns and demands of young people, resulting in low levels of youth engagement in voting and formal political organisations (Kimberlee, 2002; Henn and Foard, 2014). However, a second interpretation is that political apathy does not necessarily equate with disengagement, as young people actually engage in politics differently and participate in less professionalised and formal ways (Brookes and Hodkinson, 2008; O'Toole and Gale, 2013). Young people, then, are considered key actors in the mobilisation and proliferation of 'new grammars of political action' (O'Toole and Gale, 2013), engaging with politics through mediums such as e-activism, blogging and social activism.

As Henn and Foard (2014: 362) point out, young people are better understood as 'engaged sceptics', rather than apathetic and disengaged. Key to these emerging forms of political participation are new technologies, with internet tools and social media playing a transformative role in how young people consume and engage with politics (Brookes and Hodkinson, 2008; Pilkington and Pollock, 2015: 5). Social media platforms such as Facebook and Twitter 'allow[s] young people to seek information, cross-check news articles, communicate with organisations and their members, get messages across to political teams and send petitions or contact politicians and municipal officials' (Pilkington and Pollock, 2015). New technologies can therefore facilitate young people to engage in politics from the relative comfort of their computer screens, but it can also be the catalyst for more embodied political participation, such as attending political rallies and campaigning. Although there is no doubt that technology allows for new forms of youth political participation, some scholars have questioned the 'quality' of the politics, arguing that it is a 'downgrading' of political participation and that online political publics can shut down political debate through 'selective exposure' and isolationism (Pilkington and Pollock, 2015). These debates open out broader questions about what is 'political', and demonstrate a hierarchy of political engagement for certain scholars. Another important interpretation of young people's political engagement are the notions such as 'anti-politics' (Pilkington and Pollock, 2015) and 'radically unpolitical' (Farthing, 2010). In brief, these ideas highlight how, through disengagement and a dislike of institutionalised politics, young people are 'acting very political by depriving politics of attention, labour, consent and power' (Beck and Beck-Gernsheim, quoted in Pilkington and Pollock, 2015: 7). Therefore, some scholars conceive a complete rejection of mainstream politics and non-political participation as a radical act, because it is a rejection of the hegemonic structures that control and organise society.

The political participation of young people, then, is interpreted in a variety of ways in academic literature, varying from the politically apathetic to agents of new forms of political participation. However, young people are not a cohesive and homogeneous group, with many other layers of identity being negotiated, influencing opportunities and perceptions about politics. Although the beliefs and affiliations of young Muslims in the UK have been put under great scrutiny by the government and the media (Mustafa, 2015), research that explicitly examines how Muslim youths engage with politics is only beginning to gain traction (Hopkins, 2007; O'Toole and Gale, 2013; Mustafa, 2015). Young

Muslim identities, in many respects, have been politicised, with frequent narratives of radicalisation and lack of integration circulating in political and media discourses (Poole, 2011). Therefore, external discourses have partly constructed young Muslim identities as a political issue and in some ways inherently political. A key question, then, is: How do youth identities that are so highly politicised by political and media discourses engage with and think about politics? Moreover, it is important to ask and explore how these processes of external politicisation and political participation are played out within the different contextual settings of the UK, such as Scotland.

As stated in the Introduction, the majority of research that has explored political engagement among young Muslims in the UK has been carried out in England, with the political concerns of young Muslims in Scotland receiving only a small amount of attention (Hopkins, 2007). With the rise in Scottish nationalism, the 2014 independence referendum and the very real possibility of a further referendum in the near future, Scotland has a distinctive sociocultural and political landscape, offering young Muslims a divergent social context for political participation and social engagement. There is a pressing need, then, to build on the work of Hopkins (2007) to examine how Muslim young people currently perceive and engage with politics in Scotland.

THE STUDY

The data discussed in this chapter is derived from a project about the political participation of young Muslims in Scotland. A qualitative methodology was applied, incorporating semi-structured interviews and focus groups. Overall, thirty-seven young people participated in the research, with twenty-six individual interviews carried out and three focus groups that included a total of eleven people. All of the young people were between the ages of fifteen and twenty-seven and identified as Muslim. The sample includes eighteen women and nineteen men. Glasgow dominated the residential location of the participants, with thirty-two living in the Glasgow/Paisley areas, three living in Edinburgh and two living in Dundee. This Glasgow-centric sample, we would argue, reflects the fact that around 42% of Muslims in Scotland are registered as living in Glasgow (National Records of Scotland, 2013), far more than any other area of Scotland. With regard to the country of birth of the participants, Scotland was the primary location, with twenty-three being born in Scotland, while fourteen listed countries outside of the UK, including Pakistan (7), Iraq (1), Azerbaijan (1), Somalia (1),

Eritrea (1), Indonesia (1), Spain (1) and Malaysia (1). Partly indicative of the high number of Pakistani-born participants and the high number of Muslims in Scotland with Pakistan heritage (around 58%), 65% of participants identified as having Pakistani heritage to some extent. The findings certainly speak more to the Pakistani Muslim experience than other ethnicities, and do not necessarily provide a representative sample of the different Muslim ethnicities that live in Scotland. Nonetheless, the sample provides an important insight into a wide variety of Muslim populations, including Scottish-born second-generation Muslims and those who have arrived from numerous different countries as migrants, refugees and asylum seekers. Finally, the quotes from participants used throughout this chapter are in an everyday, vernacular style. In order to maintain anonymity, all of the participant names used are pseudonyms.

ENGAGEMENT WITH MAINSTREAM SCOTTISH POLITICS: SCOTTISH NATIONALISM, THE INDEPENDENCE REFERENDUM AND THE SCOTTISH NATIONAL PARTY

Over the past thirty years, Scotland's political landscape has been in a state of transformation, forging what many consider a politically and socially distinct identity to other parts of the UK (Mooney, 2013). These distinctions are in part a symptom of a number of political and societal changes that have occurred over the past thirty years, such as the increased devolution of power to Scotland in the early 1990s, the formation of the Scottish Parliament in 1999, the 2014 Scottish independence referendum and the surge in support for the Scottish National Party (SNP). The years 2014 and 2015 are considered to have been highly 'tumultuous', with 'remarkable and profound developments in Scotland's political history' (Rosie, 2015: 383). During these years, the rise of Scottish nationalism was firmly crystallised and the build-up to the independence referendum in 2014 resulted in Scottish society becoming highly politicised. As Hopkins (2015: 92) points out:

> It was clear from the coverage from the Scottish independence referendum that many people – including young people – were deeply involved in, and engaged by, the whole process. Many were active in local campaigning, regularly campaigning in debates about the referendum; something about the Scottish independence referendum clearly captured the imagination of the Scottish people.

As Hopkins highlights, this was also a politically transformative period for young people, with sixteen- and seventeen-year-olds being granted the right to vote for the first time. As a result, many commentators have argued that the referendum sparked a political interest in young people, with an estimated 75% of eligible sixteen- and seventeen-year-olds voting in the referendum (Baxter et al., 2015).

From the perspective of the young Muslim people in the research, both the referendum and Scottish nationalism were significant topics when discussing their political participation and interests. The referendum, for a number of participants, was a process and period that engendered an interest and opportunity to engage with mainstream electoral politics. This was particularly the case for the Scottish-born Muslims who participated in our research. For example, the following extract is from a conversation with Fahad, a seventeen-year-old Muslim man, born and brought up in the south side of Glasgow, who spoke about how he became interested in politics:

> I think ... probably third year I picked up Modern Studies and the first thing we covered was British and Scottish politics. And I thought, this is interesting, because obviously we were sort of in the lead-up to the referendum, and of course everybody got, well the majority of people got very involved in that ... I did more research, watched 'Prime Minister's Question Time' and I thought 'I quite like this' ... I think it is to do with the way the referendum was played out. You know, you are choosing your future, and I think also, the SNP government was very clever in allowing sixteen-year-olds to vote in the referendum, and now at all Scottish elections. Because it is almost, I am no supporter of the SNP, but ... it is a confidence boost for a lot of young people.

The underlining of the importance of the referendum in this extract – which was conveyed in a number of other narratives that we collected – demonstrates that for many young Muslims, the referendum was highly conducive to initiating an interest in mainstream Scottish politics. It was not only the young White majority population that was being politicised by the referendum; young Muslims were also captivated by this politically unprecedented period. Fahad attributes his interest in politics not only to the referendum, but also to the fact that he chose Modern Studies as one of his school subjects, which involved studying material focused on politics during this period. It would appear, then, that this was a stage when politics became highly pertinent in Fahad's life, and the fact that sixteen- and seventeen-year-olds were given the right to vote in the referendum meant that he was able to participate actively in mainstream politics. As he states, the right to vote acted as 'a confidence boost for a lot of young people', and this was not limited to the majority population, but also functioned as a 'confidence boost' for young Muslims, encouraging them to engage and participate in mainstream Scottish politics too. A precursor to the referendum and the 'tumultuous' years of 2014 and 2015 was the rise of the SNP and the growing support for Scottish nationalism, which is another pertinent aspect to the political engagement and interests of a number of young Muslims in the research. For instance, Sara, a Scottish-born Muslim woman aged twenty-seven who lives in Edinburgh, is a member of the SNP. In the following extract, she talks about some of the reasons why the SNP appeals to her:

> With their economic policies and that, I'm not too keen. But with their social justice element and what they are doing in terms of that, I mean their whole kind of creating a healthier, fairer and more equal Scotland, the fact that they are recognising social isolation, mental health, they are trying to put human rights at the centre of everything. Whereas in Westminster at the moment they want to scrap that, which is frightening. I think they have a more open-minded approach and a more inclusive approach and that is what appeals to me and I think it appeals to a lot of young people, regardless if they are Muslim or not in Scotland.

As one would generally expect from a member of the SNP, Sara is also a supporter of Scottish nationalism and Scottish independence, and in the following extract she discusses why Scottish nationalism appeals to her:

> Well, I actually believe nationalism has generally been exclusive of people, but I think Scottish nationalism, we have kind of redefined nationalism, and that is why I feel kind of proud of the movement, if you will. I find it has been really inclusive, it's not about the colour of your skin, and it's not about where you come from, it's about what you want for Scotland. Overall, the kind of essence of Scottish nationalism has been inclusive. It is all about making Scotland a better place. So making sure politicians are accountable, making sure that our legislation is person-centric, have a human rights-based approach, and there is a social justice element to it. You know, I think that is what you kind of want from a movement and that is why I feel included in this movement. Other nationalist movements would probably exclude me for my background or the colour of my skin and things like that, but I feel we haven't really had much of that here and I feel really proud of that.

Sara believes, then, that the SNP's policies and the core ideology of Scottish nationalism are inclusive and are based on a strong notion of social justice, which she considers appealing to young Muslims and young people in general. This sense of Scottish nationalism as inclusive was conveyed by a number of participants, demonstrating that it is often perceived as a progressive, civic and liberal form of nationalism, rather than a conservative and ethnically defined one. It is a nationalist political ideology and movement that resonates with young Muslims, rather than overtly excluding and marginalising them, correlating with the understanding that the SNP and the independence movement have gained a growing support from ethnic minorities. In the following extract, we hear from Bahija, who is a politician in local Scottish politics, born and brought up in Scotland and living in Glasgow. In outlining the shift in support to the SNP, she said:

> And I think also just because at a UK level I think some Muslim like my mother, for example, who was always a Labour voter, hasn't voted Labour since the War on Iraq, she hasn't forgiven for that. So ... I think that has probably upset a lot of Muslims who traditionally voted Labour. Things like the War on Iraq, issues about immigration ... the whole kind of ... anti-terrorism kind of legislation, which is legislated at a UK level. I think that has sort of alienated some supporters. And whereas the SNP has been very good at courting them and sending out the right signals, 'oh we don't support that kind of rhetoric on immigration or terrorism legislation'. So they have become quite welcoming. So the government works, I think, with the Muslim community over a number of years to bring them over, so I think that probably kind of explains the kind of popularity of the SNP among the Muslim community in areas like Glasgow, where Muslim people traditionally voted Labour before.

In this extract, Bahija states that the SNP is perceived to offer a form of politics that is distinct from the UK-centric parties such as Labour and the Conservative Party. As a result, the SNP has ostensibly been able to disassociate itself from, and disagree with, contentious issues such as the Iraq war, increasing anti-immigration rhetoric and types of anti-terrorism legislation, which has helped to gain support from sections of the Muslim population, including young Muslims. This is highlighted in the previous quote from Sara, who asserts that the SNP appeals to her as it puts 'human rights at the centre of everything', unlike the politicians and policies in 'Westminster'. The SNP's supposedly distinctive brand of politics, which can disassociate the party from the legacies (war, austerity, immigration policy, economic crisis, and so on) of mainstream UK parties, is creating a political movement that young Muslims can identify with and actively support. Since the 'war on terror', it would appear that Westminster and its core political parties have become toxic and unattractive in the eyes of many young Scottish Muslims, while the SNP, on the surface, appears to offer an alternative ideology and legacy that is not visibly associated with the policies of Labour and the Conservatives. The SNP policies, then, have engendered the political engagement of some young Muslims, which, in turn, appears to assist with a sense of belonging and identification with Scotland. This demonstrates that political solidarity between young Muslims and mainstream political parties can help foster a sense of greater social inclusion and integration. These solidarities are frequently based on notions of social justice and human rights and, it is important to note, they are salient on both the local and the global scale. For example, the SNP's policies on local issues to do with poverty and free education in Scotland and their views on global issues, such as a more tolerant approach to refugees than the central UK Government, were frequently mentioned together in the conversations with those who supported the SNP. Therefore, these young Muslims have a wide range of political concerns, both local and global, and the SNP has managed to tap into these different concerns.

An additional salient factor that young Muslims stated as a reason for finding the SNP and politics in general appealing was that they that felt it included politicians with whom they could identify. For example, in the following extract, Fahad, a seventeen-year-old young Muslim man who was born and brought up in Glasgow, talks about the factors that have contributed to his interest in mainstream Scottish politics:

> I think all the political parties are quite good at appealing to a wide range of people. Umm, but especially for myself, because our MSP is a Muslim as well, Humza Yousaf ... that kind of encourages young Muslims to look up to somebody. You can be that person if you want to.

For Fahad, Humza Yousaf, the SNP politician who, at the time of writing, was the Scottish Government Minister for Transport and the Islands and MSP for the Glasgow Pollok constituency, is especially significant for his interest in and engagement with Scottish politics. Humza Yousaf, like Fahad, is a practising Muslim, from a similar area of Glasgow, and they share a Pakistani heritage. During our conversations with Bahija – a politician in local-level politics – she highlighted the impact of Muslim politicians on mobilising young Muslim political participation:

> You have got Humza Yousaf in the SNP, who is liked across the board. Liked, you know, by indigenous BMEs, he has got a broad appeal as well as Anas [Anas Sarwar]. So you have got two different parties. And then you have Tasmina [Tasmina Ahmed-Sheikh], who is an MP, who again is from a mixed background. So you know, I think it does make a difference.

It is therefore frequently perceived that Muslims in prominent political positions in Scotland are functioning as positive role models, providing young Muslims with the confidence to participate in and talk about politics. Certainly, those we spoke with who had a specific interest in mainstream Scottish politics considered Muslim politicians as an influential factor in their political engagement. However, we would argue that, although there is a presence of Muslims in Scottish politics (local and national), and they can engender young Muslims to participate politically, it is still very small in comparison to non-Muslim representation, and there is clearly still a need for more Muslims to be included in prominent political positions. Moreover, as in the Muslim population in general, the majority of Muslims in official political roles have been in Glasgow, so it is likely that their influence is more significant to young Muslims in the Glasgow area, and those living in other parts of Scotland may not be as greatly affected or aware of them as role models. Nonetheless, political role models for young ethnic minorities can engender a sense of self-confidence, which can result in greater political interest and participation.

We have explored how the institutional political geographies of Scotland shape young Muslims' engagement with and interest in politics. We have demonstrated that mainstream political processes and policies, which are specific to the Scottish context rather than the UK, are of interest to young Muslims and engender forms of political participation. The independence referendum, Scottish nationalism, the SNP and the public presence of Muslims in Scottish politics have been cited as captivating the imagination of many young Muslims, revealing that Scottish electoral politics and Scottish issues are a political concern for young Muslims. The politicisation of the Scottish public that is considered to have occurred over recent years, and especially the politicisation of Scottish young people, is not limited to the White majority population, but incorporates sections of the young Muslim population. Scottish institutional electoral politics, then, is a significant and important aspect of young Muslims' political participation in Scotland.

SOCIAL MOVEMENTS AND ACTIVISM

Moving on from institutionalised and electoral political engagement, we now look at less conventional forms of political involvement, analysing the role of social movements and activism in the political participation of young Muslims. Social movements and activism are generally considered to be groupings of people or organisations that campaign about political issues outside mainstream electoral institutions (Deela Porta and Tarrow, 2005). In recent decades, there has been an increase in social movements, with growing struggles around issues such as feminism, the environment, globalisation, anti-racism, refugees and immigration, to name but a few (Oslender, 2004). Social movements can range from local grassroots groupings to international networks, and they generally incorporate forms and practices of protesting, demonstrating and awareness raising (Oslender, 2004). Social movements are part of what O'Toole and Gale term 'new grammars of political action' (2013), and they resonate with Beck's notion of 'subpolitics', which is a politics 'outside and beyond the representative institutions of the political system of nation-states' (Beck, 1996: 18). As a result of their non-institutionalised form, social movements and activism are considered a key way in which young people engage with politics, providing an alternative to the mainstream parties that many young people are frequently reported to feel disillusioned with (O'Toole and Gale, 2013).

For a number of young Muslims in our research, social movements and activism were a salient feature of their political engagement. Although not limited to a certain demographic of the Muslim population, we argue that social movements and activism were particularly important for those who were not born in Scotland, but had arrived as migrants, asylum seekers and refugees. For example, Fvodo, a twenty-six-year-old man who lived in Glasgow and had migrated to Scotland from Azerbaijan, engages with a number of different social movements and forms of political activism:

> I just like interviewing people and tried to do it in Glasgow, like a 'Humans of New York' project, and that pushed me to the more journalism part and I started to get involved in activism. Since then, I have been strongly engaged with activism in Scotland. I mainly work with refugees, well that's probably what I'm mainly known for, but I wouldn't say I only do refugee stuff, but I do mainly work with refugees, immigration topics, I'm a strong supporter of human rights and disability rights. I'm very much anti-Trident, anti-nuclear. As a result, I started to do convoys [trips to support refugees in France and Greece] as well, I just broadened my horizons. On 15 September 2015 in Glasgow, an event happened regarding Alan Kurdi, the child who unfortunately drowned near Syria. My friend said, let us make an event about that, and that went viral, like, global viral. We gathered 12,000 people in Glasgow and overall forty cities participated, with about two million people demonstrating. That is when I became really known as an activist.

Fvodo engages with a wide repertoire of social movements, incorporating global/transnational and local issues. The plight of refugees and immigration is one of his core political concerns. He engages with these issues on the local scale through volunteering with campaign groups such as the Glasgow Campaign to Welcome Refugees and, on the international scale, he has visited France and Greece to volunteer and provide aid to refugee camps. Moreover, he has jointly organised events in Glasgow to raise awareness about Syrian refugees and the deaths of many refugee children during their journeys to Europe. Demonstrating, volunteering and raising awareness with regards to refugees were salient forms of political engagement for many of the politically active young Muslims we spoke to, and this was especially apparent for those who had experiences of migration and asylum themselves. Experiences of seeking asylum – such as being held in a detention centre – would appear to engender solidarity with new arrivals, resulting in political activism in a range of social movements and campaign groups. However, unlike narratives that assert that young Muslims are primarily concerned with global politics, many of those that campaign about global issues were also active and concerned with local Scottish issues. For example, during an interview with Linzi, who is a political activist, she talked about how she had both an interest in, and campaigned about, international politics and national Scottish politics. Linzi, aged eighteen was born in Scotland and lived in Glasgow. Her international political activism has incorporated demonstrating about the war in Iraq, the conflict in Gaza and raising awareness about the Arab Spring, while, since the independence referendum in 2014, she has campaigned about Scottish independence and Trident nuclear weapons, and has joined the SNP. Linzi considers this engagement with both national and international politics as important for young Muslims:

> With regard to British politics, I think there is also a narrative there that is missing, where Muslims are normally seen as only being concerned about when it is international politics. Like we are not really seen as people who engage within British politics, I think. Obviously, like, obviously we are now getting more into it, where you have got your first Muslim mayor, the first Muslim NUS president, stuff like that. You know ... we are getting a bit more heard and seen.

For Linzi, young Muslims' engagement with national politics, both through social movements and institutional politics, assists in countering narratives of young Muslims only being concerned with international politics. Linzi believes that through engaging with national and local politics, along with international matters, young Muslims can rerepresent themselves and their communities positively and demonstrate an involvement in local affairs. During the interview, Linzi highlighted that the independence referendum in 2014 was the key event that sparked her interest in Scottish politics and affairs; prior to that, her political activism was mainly related to international affairs. Again, this demonstrates that distinctive features of Scotland's political geography can engender youthful Muslim political engagement, especially with regard to national and local issues in Scotland.

What Linzi and a number of other participants have demonstrated is that political activism through social movements does not necessarily mean a complete disengagement with institutional politics. Rather, the young Muslims whom we spoke to frequently combine political activism in social movements with moments of participating in institutional and mainstream politics. For example, as highlighted previously, Linzi engages in social activism around international and Scottish issues such as Trident and the Palestine–Israel conflict, but she is also a member of the SNP, and campaigned and voted for Scottish independence, demonstrating an engagement with mainstream Scottish politics.

Many of the politically engaged young Muslims in our research have a wide repertoire of political participation, and were not limited to either global/local issues or conventional/unconventional politics. This is not to say that there is no disillusionment with institutional politics – clearly there is, for some – but Scottish political processes still often attract the attention and participation of politically engaged young Muslims, and the binary separation between social movement activist and institutional politics does not clearly resonate with the young Muslims in the research. Finally, a useful way of describing the way in which young Muslims engage politically with social movements in Scotland is 'glocal' activism. 'Glocalisation' is the term used to describe the simultaneous occurrence of global and local tendencies in economic, cultural and political processes (Robertson, 1997), concurring with the activism described in this section, as it incorporates global and local political issues and issues that are the result of the interplay of both the global and the local.

VOLUNTEERING AND CHARITY WORK

A final form of political participation that we shall discuss, one that can intersect with social movements and institutional politics, is volunteering and charity work. For O'Toole and Gale (2013), charity work, volunteering and community groups can function as an alternative public sphere of political participation and contribute to new and emerging patterns of young people's political actions. They highlight that it can function as a form of Beck's notion of 'subpolitical' activism, as it is a way to engage politically outside of the mainstream political institutions. For the young Muslims in the research, volunteering and charity work were often something that they engaged in, but how conscious they were that it was a form of political engagement varied. As charity is one of the five pillars of Islam, volunteering and community engagement can be seen by some as more of a religious act than a political one. Shakir, a twenty-seven-year-old young man who was born in Pakistan and lives in Dundee, is a member of a Muslim youth association, and during an interview he talked about how the group participated in charity and community work:

> So the young community do a lot of charity work, we do a lot of clean ups working with the local community, that's what we try and do, a lot of sports. Basically, we try to engage the younger generations from six onwards. So, for instance, we did a clean-up on New Year's Day, which was in Glasgow and Dundee at the same time, so do you know Dundee Law [a key hillside landmark in Dundee]? It's sort of the peak point in Dundee, so we went there, did a lot of cleaning up there, and in Glasgow we did a clean-up, and that was done all over the UK, not just in Scotland ... The main aim is to get the youth involved, because until they understand the importance of these things, working with the community, trying to help your local community, they won't understand the concept of Islam. Islam is a very inclusive religion, and that is what we try to instil in our youngsters.

In addition to the community and charity work highlighted in the quote, Shakir stated that the youth group organised 5km 'fun runs' and collections for charities such as Yorkhill Children's Hospital (a Glasgow children's hospital), Children's Hospice Association Scotland, the ARCHIE foundation (for sick children) and Humanity First (charity aid for developing countries). Community work and charity fundraising is therefore a core part of the youth group's activities. However, as alluded to in the quote above, these activities are primarily considered as religious acts and part of their religious duty. Shakir stated later in the interview that the youth group was apolitical and did not align itself with a specific political party or social/political movement and, if members did participate politically, it was often done in an individual way through voting and so on. For the youth group, community and charity work is considered more as a civic engagement based on religious ideas and duties than overtly political. As discussed in much literature (Wilson and Janoski, 1995; Smidt, 2003), faith communities are considered to be at the 'vanguard of charitable initiatives' (Stepick et al., 2009: 3), engaging in a wide array of civic issues, and this is clearly demonstrated by the youth group. The political nature of religious civic engagement will vary between groups, with some conveying overt political motivations and opinions, while others shy away from political dialogue.

This therefore raises questions about what religious civic engagement is political. Does the religious group need to be consciously political for it to count as political participation? Or is the act of civic engagement inherently political, even without a clear political motivation or ideology? In this instance, if we consider that young Muslim identities are highly politicised by political and media discourses, then the charity and community work of the Muslim youth group can be seen to have a political effect and message. It provides a narrative of young Muslims' community participation, countering the narratives of disengagement and lack of integration. Although Shakir does not consider these activities to be political, he is aware that charity and community work fosters good community relations and helps to counter negative stereotypes. Therefore, although religious civic engagement may not always be a conscious political act, it can feed into and alter political and media discourses, making it function as a form of political engagement.

Other participants, however, engaged in volunteering and charity work and were more conscious and welcoming of its political nature. Raza, a twenty-one-year-old young Muslim man who was born and brought up in Glasgow, noted:

> There is something we do called Radio Ramadan. So like Ramadan is coming up in a couple of weeks' time. And throughout that month we have a radio station set-up. So we will talk charity issues on that as well. So, like, I am one of the co-hosts on that station as well, and kind of a lot of young Muslims get together and volunteer during that as well. So it is a radio station set up for Muslims, obviously, but we try to talk about issues in the community and what we can do to sort of combat them. So, one of them was that there are people in the community who are actually starving right now, don't have anywhere to live. So we should be trying to help them along as well.

Raza's volunteering on a radio show during Ramadan demonstrates a clear interplay between religious civic duty and political engagement and concern. On the radio show, he engages in fundraising for numerous charities and raises awareness about key political issues such as poverty, refugees, homelessness and marginalisation. In comparison to the work of the Muslim youth group discussed above, Raza's volunteering involves a more explicit awareness-raising campaign, incorporating both local and global issues. Similar to what Linzi stated earlier in this chapter, Raza asserted the importance of local and global charity work. He believes that it demonstrates an engagement and concern with Scottish society, which is often missing from mainstream narratives about young Muslims. Raza, then, is consciously aware of the political nature of his religious volunteering and that it is a way to participate politically and contribute to political debates.

In addition to those who volunteered through religious movements and associations, there were also participants who had volunteered in more ostensibly secular organisations such as Shelter, the housing and homeless charity, the Stand up to Racism campaigning group and Amnesty International. There is therefore a diversity of charity associations and forms of volunteering that participants have been involved in, ranging from those clearly based on religious beliefs and those emanating from a more secular viewpoint. All these varied forms, to some degree, function as a form of 'subpolitical' participation in which young Muslims engage with politics and political discourses outside of mainstream politics. Moreover, as young Muslim identities are often politicised by political and media discourses, volunteering and charity work can inadvertently convey a political message, even for those who do not consciously see it as a political act.

CONCLUSION

This chapter has opened out and analysed the way that young Muslims in Scotland engage with politics, highlighting a variety of political concerns and participation. Contributing to understandings surrounding 'new grammars of political action' (O'Toole and Gale, 2013), we have highlighted that many young Muslim people in the research were highly active political agents, engaging with political issues through mainstream Scottish politics, social movements and charity/volunteer work. We now make three final concluding points about the political participation highlighted.

First, there is a diversity of ways in which the young Muslims in our research engaged with politics, incorporating both conventional and non-conventional forms. Through the variety of political participation, young Muslims in our research demonstrated political concerns and interest with both global and local issues. Although young Muslims are primarily seen to be concerned with global politics and international events, this chapter shows a wider variety of political concerns, with a clear engagement in national and local affairs in Scotland. This engagement with Scottish affairs is carried out though participation in both mainstream Scottish politics and less conventional forms, such as social movements/activism and charity/volunteering work.

In their political repertoires, most participants incorporated both conventional and non-conventional forms of participation, challenging the notion that these forms of engagement are in binary opposition. In addition to Scottish affairs, global events and how global events impact on the local were frequently incorporated into political activities. Issues such as the refugee crisis, the war in Syria and the Palestine–Israel conflict were often part of the awareness raising and campaigning carried out by a number of participants. Thus, both Scottish affairs and global events and how these two scales intersect have been frequently highlighted as capturing the attention of the young Muslims discussed in the chapter.

Second, specific features of Scotland's political geography have engendered young Muslims' political participation, especially with regard to institutionalised mainstream Scottish politics. Political processes and events such as the rise in Scottish nationalism, the increased popularity of the SNP, the independence referendum in 2014 and the presence of Scottish Muslim politicians have captured the imagination of many young Muslims in the research, engendering an interest and participation in Scottish electoral politics. Scottish nationalism is perceived by a number of participants as inclusive and progressive, and the SNP is often considered to provide an alternative style of politics to the other parties, which can appeal to young Muslims and motivate them to engage in politics. This highlights, then, the fact that specific political contexts can produce distinctive forms of Muslim and minority political participation.

Third, the political participation of young Muslims is partly in response to the way that young Muslim identities are often politicised by media and political discourses. A number of respondents were aware of the need to provide alternative narratives, and engaging with politics was considered as a way of doing so. Participating in local Scottish affairs and charity/volunteer work were regarded as ways for young Muslims to counter negative representations and rerepresent themselves in a more positive light. However, there is also a feeling that young Muslims may be put off engaging with politics for fear of being branded as extremists. Again, this is due to external discourses and global events that frequently cast Muslim identities as potentially radicalised and extreme, especially with regard to political viewpoints. Political participation for young Muslims was perceived by some as a resource to challenge stereotypes and negative representations, but, for others, political expression is seen as a potentially dangerous act, in light of the suspicion that Muslim identities are under. Symptomatic of the way that youthful Muslim identities are externally politicised by discourses, political participation will often take on more weight than for other identities, providing both opportunities and challenges.

REFERENCES

Anwar, M. (2015). 'Foreword'. In T. Peace (ed.), *Muslims and Political Participation in Britain*. London: Routledge.

Bang, H. (2005). 'Among everyday makers and and expert citizens'. In J. Newman (ed.), *Remaking Governance: People, Politics and the Public Sphere*. Bristol: Policy Press.

Baxter, G., Tait, E., McLaverty, P. and MacLeod, I. (2015). 'The independence referendum shows that young people can be mobilised politically given the right circumstances'. *Democratic Audit Scotland*, available at www.demo craticauditscotland.com/the-independence-referendum-shows-that-young-pe ople-can-be-mobilized-politically-given-the-right-circumstances

Beck, U. (1996). 'World risk society as cosmopolitan society?: Ecological questions in a framework of manufactured uncertainties'. *Theory, Culture and Society*, 13(4), 1–32.

Brookes, R. and Hodkinson, P. (2008). 'Introduction – young people, new technologies and political engagement'. *Journal of Youth Studies*, 111(5), 473–9.

Deela Porta, D. and Tarrow, S. (2005). 'Transnational processes and social activism: An introduction'. In D. Deela Porta and S. Tarrow (eds), *Transnational Protest and Global Activism*. Oxford: Rowman and Littlefield.

Farthing, R. (2010). 'The politics of youthful antipolitics: Representing the "issue" of youth participation in politics'. *Journal of Youth Studies*, 13(2), 181–95.

Henn, M. and Foard, N. (2014). 'Social differentiation in young people's political partcipation: The impact of social and educational factors on youth political engagement in Britain'. *Journal of Youth Studies*, 17(3), 360–80.

Hopkins, P. (2007). 'Global events, national politics, local lives: Young Muslim men in Scotland'. *Environment and Planning A*, 39, 1119–33.

Hopkins, P. (2015). 'Young people and the Scottish Independence Referendum'. *Political Geography*, 46, 91–2.

Kimberlee, R. H. (2002). 'Why don't British young people vote at general elections'. *Journal of Youth Studies*, 5(1), 86–98.

McAngus, C. (2015). 'The election has transformed Scottish politics, and created a context where another referendum is possible'. *Democratic Audit UK*, available at: www.democraticaudit.com/2015/05/08/the-election-has-transformed-scottish-politics-and-created-a-context-where-another-referend um-is-possible

Mooney, G. (2013). *Scotland: An Increasingly Distinctive Society*, available at www.open.edu/openlearn/society/politics-policy-people/politics/scotland-increasingly-distinctive-society

Mustafa, A. (2015). *Identity and Political Partcipation among Young British Muslims: Believing and Belonging.* Basingstoke: Palgrave Macmillan.

National Records of Scotland (2011). *Scotland's Census 2011 – Religion by Sex and Age*, available at www.scotlandscensus.gov.uk/ods-analyser/jsf/ tableView/tableView.xhtml

National Records of Scotland (2013). *Briefing Paper 2011 Census – Release 2A – Results for Glasgow City*, available at www.glasgow.gov.uk/chttphandler. ashx?id=16943

Oslender, U. (2004). 'Fleshing out the geographies of social movemnets: Colombia's Pacific coast black communities and the "aquatic space"', *Political Geography*, 23, 957–85.

O'Toole, T. and Gale, R. (2013). *Political Engagement amongst Ethnic Minority Young People.* Basingstoke: Palgrave Macmillan.

Pilkington, H. and Pollock, G. (2015). '"Politics are bollocks": Youth, politics and activism in contemporary Europe'. *Sociological Review*, 63(S2), 1–35.

Poole, E. (2011). 'Change and continuity in the representation of British Muslims before and after 9/11: The UK context'. *Global Media Journal – Canadian edn*, 4(2), 49–62.

Robertson, R. (1997). 'Glocalization: Time-space and homogeneity-heterogeneity'. In M. Featherstone, S. Lash and R. Robertson (eds), *Global Modernities*. London: Sage.

Rosie, M. (2015). 'Scotland: All change?' *Scottish Affairs*, 24(4), 383–8.

Smidt, C. (ed.) (2003). *Religion as Social Capital: Producing the Common Good.* Waco, TX: Baylour University Press.

Stepick, A., Rey, T. and Mahler, S. J. (eds) (2009). *Churches and Charity in the Immigrant City: Religion, Immigration and Civic Engagement in Miami.* London: Rutgers University Press.

Wilson, J. and Janoski, T. (1995). 'The contribution of religion to volunteer work'. *Sociology of Religion*, 56(2), 137–52.

5

GENDER AND MIGRATION
The Role of the 'Other' Woman in Shaping the Subjectivities of Recent Muslim Migrant Women to Scotland

Rebecca Syswerda

INTRODUCTION

While much of the literature about Muslim identities has tended to focus on British-born Muslims in densely populated 'Muslim' localities, the experiences of Muslim migrants living outside such localities have been largely overlooked. This leaves unanswered questions about the role of 'other' women – that is, women from diverse religious, cultural and ethnic backgrounds – in shaping Muslim migrant women's sense of self and their attitudes towards post-migration life. This chapter seeks to address this oversight by exploring the ways in which recent Muslim migrant women to Scotland construct new identities in relation to the 'other' women whom they encounter in their post-migration, everyday lives, including friends, neighbours and local community members. Thus, this chapter steps off from what is now a 'relatively widespread understanding of the self as a relational achievement' (Conradson and McKay, 2007: 167).

While acknowledging the dangers of juxtaposing the over-determined categories of 'Muslim' and 'non-Muslim' women in this chapter, this distinction, I argue (perhaps ironically), is necessary to illuminate aspects of *sameness* between Muslim migrant women and the 'other' women. In so doing, I follow Nagel (2005: 13), who suggests, in discussions of Muslim migrants' assimilation in the West, the importance of identifying 'commonalities' between Muslims and non-Muslims 'rather than only difference and otherness'. Indeed, this chapter seeks to challenge mounting public and political rhetoric about the incompatibility of Muslim women's subject positions, particularly concerning motherhood and work, with life in the West. Drawing on a feminist ethnographic methodology, the analysis and discussion illustrate the relational nature of Muslim migrant women's gendered identities and subjectivities, which are not pre-determined by culture, religion or ethnicity but are always in flux, influenced by an array of *new* social encounters in day-to-day life. In presenting these insights, this chapter highlights the ongoing negotiation and thus the fluidity of Muslim migrant women's subject positions in a post-migration context.

SETTING THE SCENE: MUSLIM WOMEN, GENDER AND MIGRATION

Over the last fifteen years, a considerable body of work has advanced understandings of Muslim gender relations. In so doing, scholars have sought to undermine the 'cultural model', which until recently attributed the high incidence of Muslim women's socioeconomic exclusion in the UK to patriarchal family practices and gender inequality (Dwyer, 1999: 7; see also Ahmad and Sardar, 2012; Aitchison et al., 2007; Hopkins and Gale, 2009). The starting point for this work is that gender identities are not predetermined according to biological sex, but are socially constructed and reinforced through repetition (that is, performance); seen in this way, what it means to be a woman or a man changes in different situations, places and times (Butler, 1990; Hopkins, 2009). This conceptualisation of gender asks us to consider the relational nature of gender identities and subjectivities: not only are femininities constructed both *in relation to* and *against* masculinities, and vice versa, but also (and crucially within the context of this chapter) women's gendered identities and sense of self are relational to other *women* (Hopkins, 2009).

A pause is necessary here in order to note the difference between identity and subjectivity, the former of which has been the primary focus in existing work on Muslim gender relations, whereas the latter has received less attention overall. As Silvey (2004: 498) notes in her scholarship on migrant women, 'Current concern with migrants' subjectivities is distinct from the concern with identities, though the two are often conflated.' She continues, 'Attention to subjectivity connotes a more Foucauldian view of the migrant self, a view that attends less to human agency than does the concept of identity' (ibid.). Thus, Silvey, along with other scholars (see, for example, Lawson, 2000; Silvey and Lawson, 1999), emphasises the discursive fields and social forces that influence a person's sense of self, implying wider power relations at work. Relevant to this study, Mohammad (2005: 180) suggests that Muslim women's 'subjectivities are produced across a matrix of discourses – Western liberal, secular, consumerist, as well as Islamist'.

A range of research exemplifies Mohammad's (2005) claims, bringing to light the discursive influences on Muslim men's and women's subjectivities. The evidence pinpoints racialised, gendered discourses in excluding Muslim women from employment. For example, Bowlby and Lloyd-Evans (2009) discuss employers' intolerance of Muslims in the workplace, citing the need to pray five times a day and religious dress as sources of frustration for employers. Hopkins and Smith (2008) found that anti-Muslim narratives following the events of 11 September 2001 prompted young Muslim men to withdraw from the public and seek refuge in the home space. Such findings show how wider discourses define Muslim men and women's 'proper places' and influence their sense of self (Silvey, 2004: 499).

Notwithstanding these important contributions, prevailing studies emphasise Muslim social relations – parents, elders, aunts and siblings – in reproducing patriarchal and gendered discourses that re-inscribe more 'traditional' notions of womanhood among young Muslim women. For instance, both Ehrkamp (2013) and Wright (2014) highlight other Muslim women in monitoring Muslim migrants and defining appropriate gendered comportment in the host community. Dwyer (1999, 2000) considers young Muslim women's resistance to patriarchal constraints on their life choices by adopting religious dress and drawing on the teachings of the Qur'an to emphasise their religious subjectivities. Mohammad (2005) deliberates the reproduction of patriarchal discourses through transnational families – discourses that place spatial and temporal constraints on young British Muslim women, thereby limiting their sense of independence. Thus, there is evidence of the ways in which Muslim women's subjectivities are shaped in relation to other Muslims, some of whom push them towards a particularly narrow sense of self and limit their possibilities as subjects.

In light of this, scholars have examined the role of institutions – schools, mosques, community-based organisations and neighbourhood groups – in exposing Muslim women to an array of subjectivities from which they can construct an alternative identity (Dwyer, 1999, 2000; Ehrkamp, 2005, 2007, 2013; Gale, 2007; Green and Singleton, 2007; Kong, 2009). However, much of this scholarship focuses on non-secular 'Muslim' institutions, and there is less known about the importance of secular institutions in shaping women's subject positions by providing a space for social interactions between diverse groups of women (but see Dwyer, 1999).

The emphasis on Muslim-based social relations and Muslim spaces in existing scholarship has resulted in a relative silence on the ways in which Muslim women's identities and their senses of self are formed in relation to their encounters with women from diverse religious, cultural and ethnic backgrounds. Specifically, there is little 'known' about the ways in which relations with friends, colleagues, neighbours or local community members illustrate alternative notions of womanhood to Muslim women. This silence is problematic, because it implies that Muslim migrant women's subject positions are either static or change only in relation to Muslim social relations or Islamic discourses. Such oversight leaves unchallenged the policy and media narratives that depict Muslim migrant women as the 'main importers of "backwards" practices', and 'at odds' with life in the West (Kofman et al., 2013: 1).

To address this relative silence, this chapter explores the extent to which migration, which brings Muslim migrant women into contact with a diverse range of women, extends the array of possible subject positions from which they can renegotiate their identities. In seeking to illuminate the fluidity of Muslim women's subject positions, the analysis and discussion in this chapter draws on a growing body of work on subjectivity and migration. This body of work asserts migration as a major life course event that disrupts everyday life, resulting in the possibility of resubjectification (Conradson and McKay, 2007; Datta et al., 2009; Ley and Tse, 2013; Sheller and Urry, 2006; Silvey, 2004). The underlying premise of such assertions is that, once again, the self is a relational concept: subjectivity is attained through a web of social connections, personal histories, events, discourses and images (Conradson and McKay, 2007) and, as such, migration exposes people to a range of possible subjectivities from which they can 'try on' alternative identities. In the following section, I outline the methodology of the study before presenting and discussing the evidence.

RESEARCH CONTEXT AND METHODOLOGY

The emphasis on personal Muslim spaces, outlined above, reflects a methodological privileging of densely populated 'Muslim' localities in existing research: North Yorkshire, Birmingham, London and the M4 corridor, in England; and Glasgow, in Scotland. In contrast, this chapter examines the divergent experiences of Muslim migrant women who live outside such localities, in predominantly 'White' Scottish neighbourhoods, with few or no existing friends and family nearby. The evidence presented and discussed in this chapter was gathered as part of doctoral fieldwork conducted between 2011 and 2013 in Dundee, a medium-sized post-industrial Scottish city. Dundee is quickly becoming more ethnically and religiously diverse with the arrival of migrants from sub-Saharan East and West Africa, Eastern Europe, and West and Central Asia, who complement a substantial South Asian presence established in the 1960s. Using a feminist ethnographic methodology, the project explored Muslim women's subjective experiences of migration to Scotland and the role of a secular community-based organisation in supporting their socioeconomic integration. This chapter draws predominantly on the life narratives of seven Muslim migrant women between the ages of twenty-seven and forty-five. Ethnographic evidence gathered through four focus groups with nineteen participants, and three key actor interviews complements the women's accounts. All focus groups, life narratives and interviews were conducted in English, voice recorded and transcribed. The research participants' names have been changed to protect their anonymity.

Relative to British-born Muslim women, the voices of first-generation migrants remain marginalised in existing scholarship; thus, this chapter seeks to address this gap. A feminist methodology, which strives to 'add in' previously marginalised voices (McDowell, 1992: 403), was key to achieving this aim. That is not to say that such voices represent a universal 'truth'; rather, feminist approaches emphasise the socially constructed nature of knowledge, highlighting the power relations that underpin social research (Staeheli and Lawson, 1995).

The study took place at a community-based organisation for migrant women in Scotland for which I volunteered as a classroom assistant. Volunteering held three advantages for the study. First, it enabled regular encounters with Muslim migrant women to build relationships, learn from them and earn their trust; second, the community-based organisation also provided a bounded space for observing how women with diverse cultural, religious and ethnic backgrounds interacted in a mostly informal setting; third, cognisant of increasing calls for social researchers to improve the lives of the people and communities with whom they engage (Cloke, 2002), volunteering felt like the right thing to do while undertaking research with marginalised women. Nonetheless, as a volunteer-researcher, a 'White' English woman, non-Muslim and a Christian, my positionality in relation to the participants was in flux. I do not seek to resolve this issue here, but you should keep in mind the potential for such fluctuating, and at times conflicting, identities to influence participants' accounts, as well as my interpretation of them.

In seeking to minimise the researcher-researched dichotomy, loosely structured ethnographic methods were used to gather evidence about the participants' lives. Focus group discussions aimed to explore participants' priorities and aspirations for life in Scotland, as well as their struggles to fulfil their aspirations. Building on this, life narratives were used to understand more about how these issues related to participants' personal histories and the extent to which their migration experiences had resulted in new forms of subjectivity. Through participant observation, I noted in a field diary conversations, body language and the use of space at the community centre. This enabled me to tease out the subtle ways in which interactions with other women, or simply the presence of other women in this space, influenced the participants' subject positions.

Participants were recruited through direct contact at the community centre, using initially purposive sampling and latterly convenience sampling. The participants were mostly unemployed and mostly mothers, who had migrated either with their husbands and children or alone as transnational marriage migrants to a Scottish city in which they had no (or very few) existing social or family connections.

In the absence of extended family and friends, research participants talked about the presence of other women in their lives, some of whom they interacted with, others whom they simply noticed or watched in passing or from a distance. Through the participants' narratives, focus group discussions and my own observations at the community organisation, it emerged that the presence of such women had a profound impact on the participants' subjectivities. This evidence is presented and discussed in the following section.

NEIGHBOURS AND STRANGERS

Perhaps because they had few friends or family members living nearby, participants spoke extensively of encounters with neighbours and strangers in the local area. All of the participants described living in predominantly 'White' Scottish neighbourhoods, and some women talked about encounters with neighbours that had influenced their self-perceptions and shaped their hopes for the future.

Zaira migrated to the UK from southern Africa when her family arranged for her to marry a British national. Zaira explained that she was so excited to move to the UK with hopes of continuing her education or finding work. However, she told me that, with her relatives living in England, she found Scotland a lonely place. To make matters worse, she is now a single mother and is estranged from her husband. Zaira spoke of feeling trapped as a full-time single mother, unable to pursue her desire to work outside of the home. However, her friendship with her 'White' Scottish neighbour, as well as her observation of other mothers at her children's school, seemed to illuminate the possibility of occupying multiple subject positions, as a mother, employed and thus the breadwinner for her family. Zaira said:

> One was a chemist, a pharmacist, then Gina was a nurse. They were always working; it was nice. I always wished I could even get out of the house and go and work and get back in the afternoon, you know, that type of life … Gina's got two kids and she's split [from her husband] as well, so she had to move out, but luckily now she's moved back into her house and she's going to pay the rest of the mortgage herself … I see this lady at school sometimes, one of the other mums, and she's divorced and she's a midwife, and I think that's what I want to do! But you know, her mum lives here and so she can get the kids from school when she's working, so she can do it.

It seems that these 'other' women have exposed Zaira to an alternative gendered subjectivity; that is, what it means to be a woman. Thus, in shifting the focus to Muslim migrant women living outside densely populated Muslim localities and considering the role of the 'other' woman in shaping their subjectivities, the findings diverge from existing studies that emphasise patriarchal discourses in shaping Muslim women's subjectivities and gendered identities (Dwyer, 1999, 2000; Ehrkamp, 2013; Mohammad, 2005, 2013). Instead, they highlight the matriarchal discourses that have opened up new ways for Zaira to think and feel about herself and her possibilities for the future.

Matriarchal discourses abound in the city of Dundee. High levels of female employment in the jute mills prevailed through the late nineteenth and early twentieth centuries, and the city became colloquially known as 'She Town', characterised by female breadwinners (Wright, 2014). While the jute mills have closed and Dundee has undergone significant economic restructuring since the 1970s, this colloquialism is still used today, reflecting the continued high numbers of female breadwinners and female-headed households throughout the city. In light of this, place-based identities emerge as important, lending support to Nayak (2003), who demonstrates the importance of regional economies and local nuances in shaping 'White' masculinities in post-industrial northern England.

Despite the importance of place-based identities, Zaira was seemingly torn between the multiple subject positions of mother, nurturer and breadwinner, and drew on religious discourses to explain her conflicting desires to stay at home and care for the children, and to work outside the home:

See, you know with me, with the kids – Islam says men are here to work; men are the breadwinners [and] mothers are to do the education and caring, so I want to help them … If I do too much, I won't be able to concentrate on the kids and this is their age to learn and to study, and I need to be there for them, yeah.

It would seem, then, that while migration has exposed Zaira to new social relations and thereby new ways of understanding herself, she is equally influenced by religious and patriarchal discourses more in keeping with her pre-migration life in her home country. As such, Zaira's experiences illustrate the multiple, and at times conflicting, discursive influences on migrant women's subjectivities. This finding is supported by Conradson and McKay (2007: 168), who claim that, for migrants, 'In the process [of migration], their selves will be shaped by new relations in the destination setting, as well as through the distance obtained from those that characterise the sending context.'

Another participant, Nabila, is also caring for her children alone in Scotland, although she remains happily married. Nabila's husband stayed in central Africa for his job, leaving Nabila as temporary head of the household until he can afford to join them. In contrast to Zaira's positive experiences outlined above, Nabila discussed the conflict that she had with her neighbour: a younger, professional Scottish woman who lived with her partner. Recalling the conflict and how much it had upset her, Nabila talked about occasions when she and her children had performed, or imagined performing, 'acts of kindness' towards neighbours and local community members:

The lady who lives in the flat downstairs, well she was shouting at me and at my daughter, I think she was drunk … but, you know, we keep the entrance to our house clean and my daughters help the shopkeeper across the street, not for money, but to teach them to be good kids and such. Then I see this man in a wheelchair out from my window, and I think I should go push him, take him to the shops and things, you know?

Nabila went on to say:

Sometimes things that come up in the media regarding Islam affect me, it does affect me … what is happening has got nothing to do with me because I'm just a Muslim, and I've been told the neighbour is your first relative, be good, treat them well, the way you want to be treated; teach your kids the same thing; do not lie, do not steal, no abusing whether you're a Christian or Hindu or Muslim. We are all one.

Situating her narrative against the backdrop of negative media attention on Muslims, it may be inferred that Nabila wanted to represent herself as a 'good migrant' and a worthy community member compared to her 'drunk' and disruptive Scottish neighbour. I would suggest, therefore, that Nabila intentionally positioned herself in opposition to her neighbour to justify her rightful place in the local community and Scotland more generally. This resonates with Dyck and McLaren's (2004) findings that Korean family migrants to Canada emphasise certain subjectivities, for example caring neighbours and upstanding, hard-working migrants, to position themselves as 'ideal' immigrants. Further, by drawing on religious discourses to do so, there is some resonance between Nabila's account and Levitt's (2003) findings that transnational migrants believe that their faith provides a moral framework for being exemplary neighbours and community members in the host society. Certainly, Nabila's recollection is illustrative of the relational nature of subjectivities and the complex webs of power through which Muslim migrant women come to understand themselves and their place in the host society.

ENCOUNTERING THE 'OTHER' WOMAN IN COMMUNITY-BASED ORGANISATIONS

Largely because of the lack of local social relations in terms of nearby family members and friends, many of the participants explained that the community centre had been their primary (or in some cases only) source of social interaction since arriving in the city. One of the staff members, Dariya, spoke with pride about their diverse membership:

> I think that's the beauty of this place ... we have women who speak over sixty different languages ...[it] is so diverse and I think it provides such good learning for these women, it gives them such a great opportunity because they are being exposed to different cultures, religions, languages.

Speaking specifically of the Muslim migrant women who attend the centre, another staff member, Katy, elaborated on the benefits of bringing them together with women from diverse cultural, religious and ethnic backgrounds:

> I think that the vast majority of the women we work with are kind of negotiating between two very complex cultures and that negotiation is very often about normalities. It's about what's normal for me, what's normal for that person. You come in with your own ideas and normality and you're challenged, not in a kind of aggressive in-your-face way, but just in an everyday osmosis all around; you kind of suck it in, you learn through looking, hearing, seeing, feeling, asking questions, which is hugely encouraged.

Katy's remarks echo Lawson's (2000: 174) claim that 'migrancy creates especially fluid forms of subject position', a 'state of between-ness' and it is interesting that Katy seems to think that the community centre is a space for challenging subjectivities. Alicia expanded on this, detailing the important role of other women in encouraging individuals to think differently about themselves and their possibilities for self-transformation. Alicia explained:

> We have a series of springboard classes, such as sewing classes or cooking classes, and it's very much aimed at women who come in and say, 'Oh no, I couldn't do an educational class. I don't know how to read in my own language, but oh cooking, I can do cooking, I do that every day.' So they come in and they join the class, make friends, build confidence, build self-esteem, see other women doing other things, and they say, 'I know that woman, maybe I know that woman and I'm friends with her, maybe I can join that.'

One of the study participants, Mehreen, confirmed both Katy's and Alicia's sentiments. Mehreen is a transnational marriage migrant, having migrated to Scotland from Pakistan to marry a British citizen. Raised in a conservative Muslim family, Mehreen explained that she did not realise her potential before coming to the centre because of restrictive 'family values'. She went on to say:

> The communication, different people of different location come here ... Now I have become clever since I'm coming to the centre. I didn't know what potentials I had [before], what I can do because in our family values a woman doesn't go out after marriage, we can't work ... Now I can do anything! ... Yeah, because of the centre I have come to know what our values are ...

Inference can be made from Mehreen's words that this new way of seeing herself and her possibilities stemmed from her interaction with 'different people of different location' at the centre. Thus, Mehreen's narrative highlights the importance of the 'other' woman in shaping her sense of self and feelings about her future.

Other participants spoke about their encounters with women that helped them to sustain a more positive outlook towards their daily lives in Scotland, which was an otherwise lonely and isolating existence. For example, Zaira commented on how she would relive her encounters with different women at the community centre when she returned home, which helped her to overcome feelings of sadness. She said:

> I used to meet mums here, speak to other women and go[ing] back home I used to have them in my mind – thinking about their life, imagining their

life, imagining their living it used to make me feel better. Otherwise, I felt sad most of the time, and I used to feel low low low.

For Zaira, it seems that at this point in her life she is only able to 'imagine' an alternative life. In contrast, Aalimah has reclaimed her subjectivity by becoming a volunteer. Aalimah met her husband – a British national – through a chance encounter during a family holiday. She described their encounter as love at first sight. Educated to degree level in Iraq, Aalimah was excited to leave Iraq for Scotland, not only to be with her husband but also because the war had destroyed the economy and diminished her chances of finding a job. With hopes of pursing her PhD and becoming a teacher in Scotland, Aalimah was shocked on arrival by her in-laws' expectations that she conform to more traditional Muslim constructions of femininity, which contrasted sharply with her more conventional upbringing in Iraq. Aalimah said:

> I shocked when you thought you go to heaven and you finding nothing, because I don't think it is like this here ... and his family say... do you think you can have a Masters or a PhD just like that? No ... it's not like that ... you can't do that, this is too big for you, you can't do that now you're a mum and you have husband, family, house – that's it.

With tears running down her face in the interview, Aalimah described the six years of mental ill health that she experienced because she felt trapped in the house as a wife and mother, unable to realise her dreams for life in Scotland. More recently, she began volunteering at the community centre. In so doing, she has reclaimed her subjectivity that she had lost through migration. She said:

> I say to my kids, 'Mum has to go to work now' ... Before volunteering I am thinking, I am feeling I am just wife and mother, but now I am feeling I am back, yes, Aalimah is back!

Aalimah's account illuminates the importance of a 'third space' for enabling Muslim migrant women to experiment with alternative gendered subjectivities and express new identities, as found by Dwyer in her study with young British Muslim schoolgirls (1999). Further, the women's narratives support Green and Singleton's (2007: 109–21) findings that leisure spaces provide Muslim women with the opportunity to 'be', 'become' or 'resist'.

Another staff member at the centre, Erina, elaborated on the tangible impacts of women's shifting subjectivities in their daily lives:

> Some of them [women] have come back [to the organisation] and volunteered, and are now actually teaching less confident women, so that's a huge

confidence boost for them to be able to do that, but for others it's opening up other doors, because they're able to see other things that they can join in outwith [outside] the centre, other organisations that some have gone to because they feel 'right if I do this here, I can also do it in a different setting and in a different place'. So I'd say it's opening up a lot of doors for them … It's opened the door for jobs as well [for] women who have never worked before, even if it's just part time or a volunteering placement. And then we've had some who have gone off to university or college to get a qualification.

To understand how this self-transformation that Erina talks about takes place, I turn to consider Hana's story. Hana was born in Nigeria and migrated to the UK on a temporary family (dependents) visa with her husband and four children. Having married at a young age, Hana's education was incomplete, and she had never worked outside of the home. On arrival in Scotland, Hana spoke and read only a very basic level of English. When I first met Hana, she was attending English language and IT classes at the centre. Having shown an aptitude for IT, Hana was invited to volunteer as a class tutor. In her life narrative, Hana explained that she had never imagined that this was possible until she began attending the centre and had seen other women volunteering and working. Hana told me that she now wants to teach IT to women in Nigeria when she and her family eventually return there. This big change for Hana highlights the importance of new experiences and social encounters, brought about through migration, in challenging her sense of who she is and her capabilities, as well as showcasing new possibilities for her future.

Hana's desire to secure work in the future was not exceptional, as all of the participants spoke of the importance of finding work at some point in their future. However, questions arise over the extent to which participants' emphases on volunteering and work reflect the privileging of neo-liberal government agendas by the third sector over the last decade (Martin, 2010; Trudeau and Veronis, 2009; Williams et al., 2012). I do not intend to delve any further into that discussion in this chapter, but I raise it here simply to reiterate the ways in which Muslim women's subjectivities are formed in relation to a wide range of discourses available in diverse settings.

The evidence presented here illustrates the importance of the 'other' woman in this space (whether she be a staff member, a fellow volunteer or a class member) in making new subjectivities available to Muslim migrant women. This supports Conradson and McKay (2007: 168), who suggest that exposure to new social relations and experiences through migration 'provides opportunities for new forms of subjectivity

... to emerge'. Furthermore, the community centre itself, with its diverse mix of women, emerges as an important space in which participants have been able to experiment with alternative subjectivities, as found by Dwyer in relation to Muslim young women in British state schools (1999). However, in keeping with Zaira's remarks above, some participants seemed only able to imagine a different life, because they faced significant barriers to re-enacting new subjectivities and experimenting with new identities in their everyday lives. This will be discussed in the penultimate section below.

THE REALITIES OF LIFE IN SCOTLAND

As Zaira alludes to earlier, the absence of extended family nearby means that, for some of the women in this study, the ability to transform their sense of self and experiment with new identities, for example to become a working mother, was a source of conflict and frustration, because they had no one to help them with childcare. Lamah, for example, had to quit teacher training because of the strain of caring for four children with no extended family in the city to help her:

> I couldn't do it, the placements were killing me, the placements were just so hard with the baby, so when I come in the house, think about it, I have to prepare something for the kids; its already three kids in the house, prepare food and everything and the time I sit down to do my lesson plans and everything, that was like around 6 or maybe after 7, and then sometimes I'm just so tired, but I have to prepare this lesson ... in the morning I have to drop her at the childminder at 8 o'clock, it means I wouldn't be able to be at school early, so I put her behind my back in the night just try to do what I have to do ... at that time I lose weight completely, from size 16 to size 10, so I said no, I'm going to die here, so there is no point continue so I said no ... so that's how I stopped ... It's so hard here; it's not what I thought.

In highlighting the difficulty that some participants experienced in balancing childcare and the desire to work, it is necessary to acknowledge that this experience is not necessarily unique to the women as Muslim migrant women; rather, it is a challenge for all women who seek to balance childcare and working without extended family (namely grandparents) nearby to help with childcare. Of note, scholars examining the impact of internal migration – that is, migration within the UK – on individual family members have highlighted the caring responsibilities as a key factor in explaining migrant women's high levels of unemployment (Cooke, 2001; Halfacree, 1995; Michielin et al., 2008). In making this point, I seek to show that for many women it is the patriarchal structuring of society, rather than their families, religion or culture, that makes realising certain subjectivities difficult or, in some cases, impossible.

In keeping with this, Kofman et al. (2013) claim that political and media narratives tend to overlook the structural inequalities that limit Muslim migrant women's socioeconomic participation, emphasising instead cultural and religious constraints on their lifestyles. Yet scholars stress the gendered and racialised discourses that complicate Muslim women's access to work and education, as discussed earlier (Bowlby and Lloyd-Evans, 2009; Dwyer and Shah, 2009). Likewise, there is a significant literature that details the structural inequalities faced by female family migrants, specifically migrant wives (for reviews see Boyle and Halfacree, 1999; Kofman et al., 2000; Willis and Yeoh, 2000). Of note, this work finds that migrant wives, or 'trailing spouses', have high rates of unemployment or under-employment; that is, working in jobs for which they are overqualified, and employers typically devalue or fail to recognise their existing skills and education, known as de-skilling. Thus, Muslim migrant women are triply discriminated against – as women, as migrants and as Muslims (Hart-Dyke and James, 2009). In view of this, it is unsurprising that participants spoke regretfully of being unable to find paid work or be taken seriously by potential employers. For example, Lamah said:

> Moving here, I was feeling like, okay, when we first move I will get a job, but I was already pregnant four months. So I start looking for a job constantly, but nothing. I got one interview in the end, but they didn't take me. It was just for administration, all you need to do is scan when people send their stuff to you, then enter it on the system, it's not difficult to do! They wanted a French speaker and I speak French – I have a degree in French!

Lamah's account suggests that her pregnancy stopped her from getting a job for which she was more than qualified when she arrived in Scotland. If this was the case, then it highlights gendered structural inequalities in preventing her from finding work. In addition, some participants' accounts inferred racialised discourses that prevented them from finding work. For instance, Mehrnaz said:

> I was head of my university department in Pakistan, but here I can't even get a job in Debenhams! ... I think with the hijab that there is a blockage in some places ... I went to apply at Debenhams and I can see the reaction of the lady; she was like, no, we don't want your CV, but still I'm like, no please, take it, please take it ... I think maybe my scarf is the reason, because if I go to some store like Next or something, or as I told you for Debenhams, maybe they

are right, because they want someone trendy for this kind of shop assistant, I think. But that's fine, what can I say? It's their country.

Referring to Scotland as 'their country', Mehrnaz seems resigned to unemployment and she later remarked that if she couldn't find work, she would 'just have a baby'. Silvey argues, 'Migrant subjectivities are formed through discursive fields that push migrants to develop specific views of themselves'(2004: 498). Mehrnaz's remarks support this, and her narrative illustrates the power of gendered and racialised discourses in pushing Muslim women towards a narrow view of themselves, either as unemployable or as 'just' wives and mothers, thereby reducing the range of possible subject positions from which women can choose in experimenting with their identities. Thus, while the evidence in this chapter supports Conradson and Latham's (2007: 237) claims that exposure to new social relations through migration 'expands the repertoire of possible subject positions', the findings also highlight the challenges that some women have experienced in seeking to re-enact these subject positions in their everyday lives.

CONCLUSION

As outlined in the introduction to this chapter, empirical bias in existing studies towards densely populated Muslim localities, as well as British Muslim women, has resulted in a relative silence about the experiences of first-generation Muslim migrants to Scotland who have no nearby kin. As such, in focusing on a small group of migrants living outside densely populated 'Muslim' areas, what this chapter sacrifices in terms of generalisable evidence is made up for by its unique insights into the role of the 'other' woman – women from diverse religious, cultural and ethnic backgrounds – in Muslim migrant women's subject formation. Nonetheless, it is important to reiterate that, in focusing on this small sample, the evidence presented and discussed in this chapter is intended to be illustrative, rather than representative of Muslim women's migration experiences.

Participants' accounts illustrate the significance of encounters with the 'other' woman in shaping their identities and their sense of self. The findings also show that these encounters are underpinned by multiple discourses that influence how women feel about themselves and the aspects of their identities that they chose to emphasise in their accounts. Of note, there is some evidence of the matriarchal discourses that shape women's subjectivities, thus undermining the emphasis on patriarchal discourses in re-inscribing 'traditional' Muslim gender roles in existing studies, as well as in political and media narratives concerning Muslims in the West.

The community centre provides a space for participants to meet, observe and learn from women from diverse ethnic, religious and cultural backgrounds who occupy multiple subjectivities. It is in this space that participants can experience new, or reclaim previously held, subjectivities. This resonates with Dwyer's (1999) findings that schools provide a 'third space' for young Muslim women to experiment with alternative subjectivities. However, the evidence also raises the possibility that social relations in the community centre reflect wider neo-liberal discourses around paid work and self-sufficiency. Accordingly, questions arise over the extent to which women are subjected to a 'normalising ideal' in this space (Butler, 2004), which pushes them towards a specific view of themselves as neo-liberal subjects.

The penultimate section of this chapter offers insights into the wider structural inequalities that make it difficult, if not impossible, for Muslim migrant women to sustain certain subjectivities and express new identities outside the community centre. Specifically, the challenges in balancing caring responsibilities with work meant that some participants gave up their dreams of becoming 'working mothers'. While this is not necessarily exclusive to Muslim women, migration emerges here as an important factor in limiting women's access to work, because of the lack of family members nearby to share the burden of care. This is important, as it gives further credence to those who suggest that Muslim women are unfairly depicted as irrationally prioritising childcare over paid employment (Hart-Dyke and James, 2009; Moosa and Woodroffe, 2009). In a similar vein, participants also spoke about job rejections, and their perception that such rejection stemmed from their religious and gendered identities. If this is the case, then the evidence presented in this chapter illustrates the pervasive power of wider racialised and gendered discourses in shaping Muslim migrant women's possibilities in Scotland.

ACKNOWLEDGEMENTS

I am indebted to the Muslim migrant women who took part in this study and the staff members at the community centre that formed the field site for this research. Additionally, I would like to extend my thanks to my doctoral supervisors, Dr Emilia Ferraro and Dr Louise Reid, from the School of Geography and Geosciences at the University of St Andrews, for their comments on my doctoral thesis, which formed the basis of this chapter.

REFERENCES

Ahmad, W. and Sardar, Z. (2012). *Muslims in Britain: Making Social and Political Space*. Abingdon: Routledge.

Aitchison, C., Hopkins, P. E. and Kwan, M. P. (2007). *Geographies of Muslim Identities: Diaspora, Gender and Belonging*. Aldershot: Ashgate.

Bowlby, S. and Lloyd-Evans, S. (2009).'"You seem very Westernised to me": Place, identity and othering of Muslim workers in the UK labour market'. In P. Hopkins and R. Gale (eds), *Muslims in Britain: Race, Place and Identities*, pp. 37–54. Edinburgh: Edinburgh University Press.

Boyle, P. and Halfacree, K. (1999). *Migration and Gender in the Developed World*. London: Routledge.

Butler, J. (1990). *Gender Trouble: Feminism and the Subversion of Identity*. New York: Routledge.

Butler, J. (2004). *Undoing Gender*. New York: Routledge.

Cloke, P. (2002). 'Deliver us from evil? Prospects for living ethically and acting politically in human geography'. *Progress in Human Geography*, 2(5), 587–604.

Conradson, D. and Latham, A. (2007). 'The affective possibilities of London: Antipodean transnationals and the overseas experience'. *Mobilities*, 2(2), 231–54.

Conradson, D. and McKay, D. (2007). 'Translocal subjectivities: Mobility, connection, emotion'. *Mobilities*, 2(2), 167–74.

Cooke, T. J. (2001). '"Trailing wife" or "trailing mother"? The effect of parental status on the relationship between family migration and the labor-market participation of married women'. *Environment and Planning A*, 33(3), 419–30.

Datta, K., McIlwaine, C., Herbert, J., Evans, Y., May, J. and Wills, J. (2009). 'Men on the move: Narratives of migration and work among low-paid migrant men in London'. *Social and Cultural Geography*, 10(8), 853–73.

Dwyer, C. (1999). 'Veiled meanings: Young British Muslim women and the negotiation of differences'. *Gender, Place and Culture: A Journal of Feminist Geography*, 6(1), 5–26.

Dwyer, C. (2000). 'Negotiating diasporic identities: Young British South Asian Muslim women'. *Women's Studies International Forum*, 23(4), 475–86.

Dwyer, C. and Shah, B. (2009). 'Rethinking the identities of young British Pakistani Muslim women: Educational experiences and aspirations'. In P. Hopkins and R. Gale (eds), *Muslims in Britain: Race, Place and Identities*, pp. 55–73. Edinburgh: Edinburgh University Press.

Dyck, I. and McLaren, A. T. (2004). 'Telling it like it is? Constructing accounts of settlement with immigrant and refugee women in Canada'. *Gender, Place and Culture: A Journal of Feminist Geography*, 11(4), 513–34.

Ehrkamp, P. (2005). 'Placing identities: Transnational practices and local attachments of Turkish immigrants in Germany'. *Journal of Ethnic and Migration Studies*, 31(2), 345–64.

Ehrkamp, P. (2007). 'Beyond the mosque: Turkish immigrants and the practice and politics of Islam in Duisburg-Marxloh, Germany'. In C. Aitchison, P. Hopkins and M. P. Kwan (eds), *Geographies of Muslim Identities: Diaspora, Gender and Belonging*, pp. 11–28. Aldershot: Ashgate.

Ehrkamp, P. (2013). '"I've had it with them!" Younger migrant women's spatial practices of conformity and resistance'. *Gender, Place and Culture: A Journal of Feminist Geography*, 20(1), 19–36.

Gale, R. (2007). 'The place of Islam in the geography of religion: Trends and intersections'. *Geography Compass*, 1(5), 1015–36.

Green, E. and Singleton, C. (2007). 'Safe and risky spaces: Gender, ethnicity, and culture in the leisure lives of young South Asian women'. In C. Aitchison, P. Hopkins and M. P. Kwan (eds), *Geographies of Muslim Identities: Diaspora, Gender and Belonging*, pp. 109–24. Aldershot: Ashgate.

Halfacree, K. H. (1995). 'Household migration and the structuration of patriarchy: evidence from the USA'. *Progress in Human Geography*, 19(2), 159–82.

Hart-Dyke, J. and James, L. (2009). *Immigrant, Muslim, Female: Triple paralysis?* Quilliam, available at www.quilliamfoundation.org/wp/wp-content/uploads/publications/free/immigrant-muslim-female-triple-paralysis.pdf

Hopkins, P. (2009). 'Women, men, positionalities and emotion: Doing feminist geographies of religion'. *ACME: An International E-Journal for Critical Geographies*, 8(1), 1–17.

Hopkins, P. and Gale, R. (eds) (2009). *Muslims in Britain: Race, Place and Identities*. Edinburgh: Edinburgh University Press.

Hopkins, P. E. and Smith, S. J. (2008). 'Scaling segregation; Racialising fear'. In R. Pain and S. Smith (eds), *Fear: Critical Geopolitics and Everyday Life*, pp. 103–16. Aldershot: Hampshire.

Kofman, E., Phizacklea, A., Raghuram, P. and Sales, R. (2000). *Gender and International Migration in Europe: Employment, Welfare and Politics*. London: Routledge.

Kofman, E, Saharso. S. and Vacchelli, E. (2013). 'Gendered perspectives on integration discourses and measures'. *International Migration*, 53(4), 77–89.

Kong, L. (2009). 'Situating Muslim geographies'. In P. Hopkins and R. Gale (eds), *Muslims in Britain: Race, Place and Identities*, pp. 171–92. Edinburgh: Edinburgh University Press.

Lawson, V. A. (2000). 'Arguments within geographies of movement: The theoretical potential of migrants' stories'. *Progress in Human Geography*, 24(2), 173–89.

Levitt, P. (2003). '"You know, Abraham was really the first immigrant": Religion and transnational migration'. *International Migration Review*, 37(3), 847–73.

Ley, D. and Tse, J. (2013). '*Homo religiosus?* Religion and immigrant subjectivities'. In E. Olson, P. Hopkins and L. Kong (eds), *Religion and Place: Identity, Community, and Territory*, pp. 149–65. New York: Springer.

Martin, N. (2010). 'The crisis of social reproduction among migrant workers: Interrogating the role of migrant civil society'. *Antipode*, 42(1), 127–51.

McDowell, L. (1992). 'Doing gender: Feminism, feminists and research methods in human geography'. *Transactions of the Institute of British Geographers*, 17(4), 399–416.

Michielin, F., Mulder, C. H. and Zorlu, A. (2008). 'Distance to parents and geographical mobility'. *Population, Space and Place*, 14(4), 327–45.

Mohammad, R. (2005). 'Negotiating spaces of the home, the education system and the labour market'. In G. Falah and C. Nagel (eds), *Geographies of Muslim Women: Gender, Religion and Space*, pp. 178–202. New York: Guilford Press.

Mohammad, R. (2013). 'Making gender ma(r)king place: Youthful British Pakistani Muslim women's narratives of urban space'. *Environment and Planning A*, 45(8), 1802–22.

Moosa, Z. and Woodroffe, J. (2009). *Poverty Pathways: Ethnic Minority Women's Livelihoods*. Fawcett Society and Oxfam GB, available at www.womens.cusu.cam.ac.uk/campaigns/bem/fawcett_ethnicminoritywomen.pdf

Nagel, C. (2005). 'Introduction'. In G. W. Falah and C. Nagel (eds), *Geographies of Muslim Women: Gender, Religion and Space*, pp. 1–15. New York: Guilford Press.

Nayak, A. (2003). 'Last of the real Geordies? White masculinities and the subcultural response to deindustrialisation'. *Environment and Planning D*, 21(1), 7–26.

Sheller, M. and Urry, J. (2006). 'The new mobilities paradigm'. *Environment and Planning A*, 38(2), 207–26.

Silvey, R. (2004). 'Power, difference and mobility: Feminist advances in migration studies'. *Progress in Human Geography*, 28(4), 490–506.

Silvey, R. and Lawson, V. (1999). 'Placing the migrant'. *Annals of the Association of American Geographers*, 89(1), 121–32.

Staeheli, L. A. and Lawson, V. A. (1995). 'Feminism, praxis, and human geography'. *Geographical Analysis*, 27(4), 321–38.

Trudeau, D. and Veronis, L. (2009). 'Enacting state restructuring: NGOs as "translation mechanisms"'. *Environment and Planning D*, 27(6), 1117–34.

Williams, A., Cloke, P. and Thomas, S. (2012). 'Co-constituting neoliberalism: Faith-based organisations, co-option, and resistance in the UK'. *Environment and Planning A*, 44(6), 1479–501.

Willis, K. and Yeoh, B. S. A. (2000). *Gender and Migration*. Cheltenham and Northampton: Edward Elgar.

Wright, T. (2014). 'Managing gendered expectations upon resettlement: The experiences of Iraqi Kurdish Muslim women in the UK'. *Gender, Place and Culture*, 21(6), 733–49.

6

SEXUALITY
Scottish Muslim Gay Men and the Troubling
Intersection of Sexuality and Religion

Asifa Siraj

INTRODUCTION

This chapter explores how three Scottish Muslim gay men struggle to integrate their sexual and religious identities as they navigate their sexual orientation within an existing condemnatory religious, social and cultural context. The present study illuminates the heterogeneity and diversity of experiences within the lesbian, gay, bisexual and transgender (LGBT) population. It further raises the importance of providing a nuanced portrayal of the lives of men, who do not necessarily incorporate Western discourses into making sense of their identity as gay men (Rahman, 2015).

Perusing the literature on the subject of sexuality and religion, we find that the existence of gay Muslim men in Scotland has been neither recorded nor studied. To my knowledge, no academic literature has focused specifically on Muslim men from the LGBT 'community' in Scotland. Their stories remain hidden and their existence ignored. I aim in this chapter to expose some of the issues that emanate from their multiple identities, to consider the intersection of the men's gay and religious identity and to explore the interplay of oppression that they experience. The chapter begins by highlighting the very limited research carried out on the lives of gay people in Scotland. This is followed by an overview of the theory of intersectionality in order to understand and situate how sexuality is not a separate entity of one's identity, but is interconnected to other parts. Adopting an intersectional framework allows us to appreciate how gay men experience different forms of oppression in relation to their race/ethnicity and sexuality in ways that are distinct from their White counterparts and/or heterosexual men (cf. Crenshaw, 1996). It is also pertinent to discuss previous research undertaken on the lives of gay Muslims to position the findings of the present study. The final part of the chapter identifies the themes emerging from the narratives of the three participants and their experiences as Scottish gay Muslim men.

THE SCOTTISH GAY SCENE

The Rainbow Europe Index 2015, which evaluates progress in European countries on LGBT equality, declared Scotland to be the 'best country in Europe for LGBT legal equality'. Scotland met 92% of the International Lesbian, Gay, Bisexual and Trans and Intersex Association (ILGA) Europe's criteria, compared to 86% for the UK as a whole. Yet, despite the sociopolitical transformations that have led to Scotland becoming a haven for the LGBT population, only a very few publications have documented the life experiences of LGBT individuals who have lived in Scotland for at least part of their lives (Galford and Wilson, 2006). Many of the research studies focusing on Britain have continued to neglect Scotland, and continue to do so (Meek, 2015: 2). Meek (2015) acknowledges that very little has been 'written about Scotland's queer history, which is the result not of a lack of interest but of the difficulty in finding the necessary sources from which to chart the nation's queer past' (Meek, 2015: 13). While Meek (2015) bemoans the lack of sources available to chronicle the lives of Scottish gays in the past, the situation in the present is just as dire. With the exception of *Footsteps and Witnesses: Lesbian and Gay Life-stories from Scotland* (Cant, 1993), which provides an historical account of the lives of LGBT people in Scotland, to date scholarship in Scotland has been limited. While statistical data is difficult to come by, there are approximately 300,000 gay people in Scotland: 6% of the population. We are unable, however, to quantify the number of minority ethnic gay men and lesbians, or their religious affiliation, given the dearth of information, as very little has been devoted to charting the lives of LGBT people from a minority ethnic background (cf. Cowen et al., 2009). The 'Everyone In', Minority Ethnic (ME) LGBT Research Project (2009) undertaken by the Equality Network in Edinburgh was an attempt to redress the neglect of the ME/LGBT community in Scotland, and to suggest areas for future research, since 'no previous research has been undertaken in Scotland that has examined the intersection of race with sexual orientation or gender identity' (Cowen et al., 2009: 195). The project was also a springboard to introduce new policies, because there are 'no dedicated Scottish services or organisations for people who are ME/LGBT' (Cowen et al., 2009:

16). However, since the project report was published in 2009, the issue continues to be overlooked and largely ignored in academic research. In Scotland, for instance, minority ethnic gay men, and I would add Muslim gay men and lesbians, remain fixed in a state of invisibility, complicating the process of understanding the issues that they face in their lives (Siraj, 2011, 2012).

INTERSECTIONALITY

The theory of intersectionality acknowledges that people's multiple identities and membership of different groups create overlapping systems of oppression. By adopting an intersectional lens we are able to examine the way that race, gender, sexual orientation and class influence the experiences of gay men of colour who are from a faith-based 'community'. In the present study, it helps to situate religion in an intersectional framework, exposing the unique set of experiences of Muslim gay men and how it shapes the construction of their sexual identity, but also how it simultaneously disempowers and creates oppression. Intersectionality promotes an understanding of how race, gender and sexuality, among other aspects of one's identity, impact upon an individual's experience of multiple forms of discrimination. Rahman (2010), for instance, advises that intersectionality is employed to study gay Muslims, because they 'occupy an intersectional social location between political and social cultures, and ... they suffer oppression through this position' (Rahman, 2010: 945). Sexuality should not be viewed in isolation; rather race, religion and class impact upon identity-making and meaning (Crenshaw, 1996; Collins, 2000). Gay Muslim 'identities and experiences are located at the intersection of these apparently exclusive cultures. They are properly understood as theoretically "queer intersectional identities"' (Rahman, 2010). The theory of intersectionality is especially relevant in examining LGBT lives, as their sexual identities are intersectional, since they encounter discrimination as people of colour and of faith, among other aspects of their identity. Yip (2015) articulates that the intersection of religion and sexuality essentially leads to conflict and tension, and is expressed in 'individuals' deference to religious institutional and community diktats, exacting high psychological and social costs for those who do not fall within the rigid and narrow definition of acceptable sexual and gender expression, namely (heterosexual) sex only within marriage' (Yip, 2015: 119). As members of a sexual, ethnic and religious minority, gay Muslims often experience multiple layers of oppression, not only in relation to their sexual orientation but also as a result of racial prejudice in society, and 'hostility and intolerance from within their own ethno-religious cultural community' (Siraj, 2014: 199). Gay Muslims then suffer from oppression through occupying an intersectional social location (Rahman, 2010). For Muslim gay men in particular, the intersection between sexuality and religion is more pronounced, given their strong underlying relationship with their faith (Jaspal, 2012: 767). Thus, we find that for gay men from a faith-based 'community', the intersection between religious, sexual and gender identities can be unstable. This is because religion is regarded an essentially restrictive force, regulating sexual and gendered subjectivities and practices (Yip, 2012).

ISLAM AND MUSLIM GAY IDENTITIES

The Qur'an, revered as the infallible word of Allah, addresses the issue of homosexuality through the parable of Prophet Lut (Qur'an 7: 80–4). The story restricts homosexuality to the practice of male sodomy, with scholars condemning same-sex sexuality as being contrary to the prescription of Islam (Yahya, 2000; Zafeeruddin, 1996: Doi, 1984). Prophet Lut was instructed by God to forewarn the people from committing same-sex sexual acts. However, as a result of his warnings being ignored, the people were punished through a shower of brimstone. Homosexuality is considered a violation of nature and a criminal act (Duran, 1993), punishable by death (cf. Bouhdiba, 1985; Doi, 1989). However, a number of scholars are reinterpreting the Lut story by demonstrating the ambiguity that exists because of the contextual nature of the interpretations of the Qur'an (Rouhani, 2007). In the Qur'an, for instance, there is no explicit or implicit statement that death is the appropriate punishment for being homosexual (Siraj, 2009). Kugle (2003), for example, states that the Qur'an is grounded on the principles of equality and justice, and by emphasising these elements he calls for more understanding, compassion and consideration to be shown towards Muslim homosexuals in order to uphold the Prophet's ethics of care. According to Kugle (2003), then, Muslim homosexuals should adopt their religious and sexual identities with courage and optimism.

Being gay and Muslim is no longer considered an oxymoron, as a result of the growing global cacophony of 'dissenting' LGBT Muslim voices. Nevertheless, there are myriad internal, as well as external, pressures and forces that continue to oppress this population. Momin Rahman, a gay academic who was born within the Muslim faith, describes these pressures well, inhabiting mutually exclusive, jarring social and cultural worlds: 'I have chosen that sin, chosen to come out and live as a gay man, an identity that has pushed me away from a Bengali and Muslim community both geographically and culturally ...' (Rahman, 2014: 11). His view is shaped by his frustration at the constraints imposed by orthodox Islam, which inhibits non-heterosexual-identifying Muslims to lay claim to their Islamic heritage. Acquiring any form of theological support as a gay Muslim is made difficult, because of an uncompromising, rigid interpretation of Islamic texts that largely condemns homosexuality (Siraj, 2006). However, gay Muslims are seeking to unify their two seemingly incompatible identities by forming strategies to manage the conflict between faith and sexuality. A number of studies that are based on the lives of gay Muslims articulate the possibility of embracing hyphenated identities (gay and Muslim). According to Rahman (2015), research on LGBT Muslims residing in the West highlights four important issues: the perception of negative reactions from familial ethnic communities to declaring a public homosexual identity; the related perception of public homosexual identity as 'Western'; individual reinterpretations of Islamic texts to accommodate homosexuality; and the absence of any visible community. LGBT Muslims are addressing these four issues, as well as assuaging the tension between faith and sexuality through their involvement in gay-affirming religious organisations and groups.

One of the very first studies focused on the lives of six gay Muslim activists from Al-Fatiha (an LGBT support group founded in North America), and how they constructed a progressive gay identity (Minwalla et al., 2005). Their participants were able to reclaim and redefine their conceptualisation of what it means to be a Muslim in a religious context. They achieved this through a reinterpretation of religious texts, simultaneously promoting the message of tolerance (pivotal to Islamic thought and practice). In a study that unveiled the complexities of holding seemingly incompatible religious and sexual identities, Siraj's (2006) study on seven gay Muslim men traced their endeavour to integrate their Muslim and (homo)sexual identities. Participants who had come out to their family described the rejection and intolerance that they had experienced. However, through their membership of Al-Fatiha and adhering to a queer-friendly interpretation of Islamic text, they had overcome the struggle that they experienced as men on the fringes of mainstream Muslim society.

British Pakistani gay men are more inclined to perceive their gay identity as a negative aspect of their self-identity (Jaspal, 2012; Yip, 2004). Jaspal's (2012) comparative study of British Indian and British Pakistani gay men, all of whom self-identified as members of their religious communities, suggests that the intersection between religion and sexuality is more significant for British Pakistani gay men. In contrast, for British Indian gay men, the intersection between ethnicity and sexuality was far more pronounced. For the former cohort, homosexuality was psychologically and socially problematic; that is, gay Muslim men were not able to establish feelings of coherence and compatibility between their Muslim and gay identities, which they perceived as being interconnected (Jaspal, 2012: 768). In this way, British Pakistani gay men struggle with the conflict between their religious and sexual identities at a psychological level. Resolving the conflict between faith and sexuality often leads to gay men rejecting their religious identity in order to accept and celebrate their (homo)sexual identity (Yip, 2007). The aforementioned research studies are testament to the growing interest in the lives of gay Muslims in Britain. While acknowledging the enormous value that these studies have generated with respect to raising awareness of the consequences of oppression gay Muslims experience, the lives of gay Muslims in Scotland are almost completely ignored and woefully under-represented in academic literature.

METHODOLOGY

The difficulty in obtaining participants from the minority ethnic/Muslim gay/lesbian population in Scotland presents an arduous task (Siraj, 2011, 2014). As in the present study, the relatively small sample size is a reflection of the challenge in accessing a 'hidden population' of men who remain stigmatised and marginalised. I acknowledge, therefore, that the small sample size will not support any generalisable conclusions. However, it is hoped that the study provides the reader with a greater understanding and appreciation of the intricacies of the men's lived experiences.

My search for participants began in 2009, I placed several flyers at two universities in Glasgow, stating the aim and purpose of the study and that I was seeking gay, Scottish Muslim men to participate. The resident artist at a Glasgow art gallery emailed me to request help in finding LGBT Muslims to contribute to an exhibition project. The exhibition was based on celebrating the lives of LGBT people from different faiths. I was invited to the exhibition and introduced to Qaiser, a young art student from Dundee, and, after discussing the research with him, he agreed to participate in the study. The research was also publicised in the Equality Network's LGBT newsletter and the Imaan website (a Muslim LGBT support group). However, I received no response from this advertisement. I was invited to the EveryOne IN report launch, an exhaustive study to promote inclusion of the needs and aspirations of minority ethnic/LGBT people in Scotland. The launch afforded me the opportunity to talk about my research with professional individuals and organisations working with the LGBT 'community' in Scotland, which may have led to gaining potential participants. A large majority of the people whom I spoke to stated that they were unaware of any gay Muslims within their professional or social circle. There were a few instances at which I was given the contact details of potential participants who failed to respond, or who showed an initial interest but subsequently chose not to participate. I also created a profile on Gaydar (the online gay dating site), under the username 'ree_searcher' and sent around fifteen messages to gay Muslims based in Scotland. This elicited two responses, both of whom conversed with me via the website's chat service. Not unexpectedly, they sought assurances and wished to secure their anonymity. I alleviated their concerns by discussing my previous research on the topic, and emphasised that both the interview and their identity would be anonymous and confidential. One of the men asked to read my previous research to gauge my credibility as a researcher. Both (Tariq and Saif) agreed to participate. Saif, on my behalf, contacted twelve men through Gaydar. However, he was unable to produce any real interest.

In the present study, data was gained via a qualitative, in-depth interview with each participant that was tape recorded and subsequently transcribed verbatim for analysis. An information sheet was given to each participant, stating the study's aim and purpose. Written informed consent was obtained prior to the interview. The semi-structured interviews consisted of open-ended questions on the men's Muslim identity, the importance of their faith, how it shaped their understanding of their sexual orientation, coming out, and how they managed and negotiated with the difficulty that arose from being gay and Muslim. The demographic details of each participant were obtained via a questionnaire prior to the interview. To analyse the data gained, I used two types of coding: manifest and latent. Manifest coding identifies themes, which involves creating categories in the text using the themes identified, while latent coding entails highlighting meanings that become apparent though reading the text (Sarantakos, 2005: 303). Interviews with the participants took place in Dundee (Qaiser) and Glasgow (Tariq and Saif), between 2009 and 2010. All the men were given a pseudonym to protect their identity and to ensure confidentiality. All three men were born and raised in Scotland, self-identified as Muslim and were of a

Pakistani background. Qaiser, who lived in Dundee, was a nineteen-year-old university student and lived with his parents and sister. Saif was a twenty-one-year-old college student who had recently separated from his partner; he lived in Glasgow with his parents and brother. Finally, Tariq, a thirty-six-year-old medical doctor, lived on his own, and had also recently separated from his partner of three years. In the following section, I make extensive use of the participant's 'voice' to illustrate the sense of social emasculation that they experienced because of their situatedness at the intersection of sexuality and religion, which creates multiple form of oppression.

COMING OUT ... STAYING IN

Coming out, or the process of an individual publicly acknowledging their homosexual identity, empowers them to carve out a new/true 'version' of themselves. By gaining more visibility in public they are able in turn to heighten a call for recognition and rights. Indeed, coming out is both emancipatory and liberatory for those choosing to declare their sexual orientation openly. Qaiser was the only participant to have disclosed his sexual orientation to his family, but his decision to 'come out' did not result in support or affirmation of his sexuality:

> I remember coming out to my mum while doing my Standard Grades, because I couldn't take the pressure and I wanted to be open with them about it, also I wanted them to hear from me first before hearing from anyone else. My mum couldn't take it, so she called my dad straight away – I thought this would be aggressive and the whole situation would be total abuse – but it was the opposite. However, they blamed my lack of religious attention and practice, and hanging around with girls rather than boys, and also the music and fashion I was into, too. I think they're in denial – they do know – I don't understand, they're so liberal and so free about everything else. However, they are open with me having relationships with girls, they've been coaxing me to go out or bring girls home and stuff ... and they ask me about marriage ... they do know, they just don't accept it, and they hope I just carry on and play along with them.

According to Qaiser, who came from a middle-class background, his parents were 'not from your average Asian family, they're definitely not your traditional practising Islamic family'. They were both born and bred in Scotland, fell in love and had a love marriage rather than the customary arranged marriage. He characterised them as 'really liberal', although both came from a very traditional family background. Qaiser felt increasingly estranged from his family post-disclosure and, despite their liberal attitude, they failed to extend their tolerance to him as a gay man. Ryan (2001) explains that disclosing one's gay identity to parents may lead to a family crisis. He asserts that parents face a multi-stage coming-out process through which they mourn

> [the] loss of their child's heterosexual identity and ultimately reframe negative social sanctions and lost expectations into positive experiences of lesbian and gay lives. This process is lengthy; for some parents, it is not achievable, and they will never be able to accept their child as lesbian or gay. (Ryan, 2001: 235–6)

Despite declaring that he was happy at home with his family, he admitted that 'arguments I have with my parents and especially my sister come from my sexuality, not directly, but the issue, it's there in the background'.

Saif and Tariq were both 'in the closet' and stated that they would not consider coming out. Saif relays a conversation that he had with his mother, who he described as being traditional, but 'Islamic':

> The TV programme on gay Muslims on Channel 4 was on, and she was like 'Oh my God! These Muslims are trying to make other Muslims bad, trying to accept the situation that it's OK to be gay, when it's not!' I realised that, 'oh my God, I cannot come out to my mother', she is really aggressive towards gay people; as for my Dad, he would never accept it.

LGBT Muslims hide their sexual identities from their families to maintain family honour, given that Muslims, in general, exhibit a strong adherence to a collectivist cultural orientation (Jaspal, 2014), in which interdependence and group solidarity are essential to one's identity. With this in mind, it 'is inconceivable that homosexuality could be thought of as a form of sexual selfhood given the importance of marriage, children and family in Islam' (Siraj, 2009: 44). For Pakistani gay men in particular, familial expectations to marry and have children perpetuate the tension between ethnic background and sexual identity (McKeown et al., 2010). Tariq, who came from a relatively affluent family and was privately educated, faced immense pressure to marry. He described the methods he employed to resist this stress:

> I'm meant to be at two weddings today, one just now and another one this evening. I've used work as an excuse actually, I said, 'Look, I'm just going to be busy and I'm not going to be able to make it'. Generally, I will avoid them, because it's just the pressure. I'm well past that age where I should be married ... so many people have said to me, 'You tick all the boxes, you're born in Scotland, you're a doctor, you've got your own place, so what's

going on?' When I qualified [as a doctor] at 22, they [parents] said, 'Now that you've graduated, you've got to work out the way to start thinking about getting married'.

Withstanding parental pressure to get married was influenced by Tariq's belief that his family would not be able to understand his sexual orientation. He acknowledged: 'it's probably less hurtful for them to do this [avoid marriage] than to actually come out and say I'm gay'. There are a number of factors at play here. Heteronormativity portrays heterosexual marriage as a cultural obligation which, in turn, depicts homosexuality as an aberration and antithetical to marriage. Awareness of these representations creates lower psychological well-being among gays (Jaspal, 2014: 444). These attitudes shape gay men's unwillingness or conscious inability to come out and declare their sexual orientation to their family. Being 'in the closet' requires discretion and secrecy, but also creates fear and risk. Tariq, who was 'in the closet', managed his identity as a gay man through meeting and dating men on Gaydar, allowing him to remain invisible yet to socialise with a certain degree of selectivity:

> I've never understood this cruising thing, it's just not something I get at all … So yeah, mainly through Gaydar for me, I probably go for White men because I perceive that as being safer … with Asian gay men I do worry, what if I know who they are or they know me?

By dating White men, Tariq was able to protect himself from the potential scrutiny and intrusion that he may encounter with other gay Asian men. He dissuaded himself from dating/meeting someone with an Asian or Muslim background to deflect unnecessary attention and avoid the possibility of involuntary disclosure. There was therefore an active resistance to forming relationships with other gay men, due to fear of admission (cf. Jaspal and Cinnirella, 2012). Despite being raised in a Western society, the men confronted difficulties within the gay scene as a result of their religion and race. Qaiser and Saif were especially contemptuous about the wider LGBT community; they avoided participating in the gay scene and were not able to identify with the White gay 'community':

> I want to steer away from the LGBT community, I find it very closed and it's a stereotype … I feel it limits me. If I do go gay clubbing, it's with White people, because I don't have Asian friends to go with, but I wish I did, I'd feel more comfortable and secure. I don't know why, but in gay clubs I feel under threat, nowhere else in any other clubs but gay clubs. I feel as if my skin colour matters, because everyone in there essentially wants to hook up

and fuck. Sometimes I do feel lost and I feel I have no community to turn to, because LGBT communities really suck, gay clubs and scenes and all that. (Qaiser, 19)

Because they [White gay people] think there's nothing wrong with being gay, they think you've only got one life, you might as well live how you want, there's no rules present. They're so brainwashed by that idea, enjoy your life, they think you can't have regrets. I don't think like that ... (Saif, 21)

Qaiser's and Saif's comments portray the White gay scene as morally bankrupt. The importance seems to be less on 'community' and more on the pursuit of sex. Saif, in particular, imposes and reinforces the discourse of being openly gay as an aberration. Qaiser's sense of isolation and lack of belonging to the gay scene were formed by his ethnic identity; he adjudged the scene critically as frivolous and fake. The gay club was a distinct social space; not inherently liberatory, it was a 'space' that holds particular privilege for the gay White man. Jaspal and Cinnirella (2010) note that interpersonal contact in gay bars, meeting groups and nightclubs may present further psychological and social problems to British gay Muslim men. For instance, there is a real risk of exposing one's sexual orientation through socialising with White British gay men, who were held to be 'too' open about their sexual identities. This increases their vulnerability in terms of being excluded and rejected by other men on account of their religious/ethnic identity. Qaiser found it difficult to develop a sense of gay social consciousness and to negotiate his sexual identity in spaces where ethnicity prevailed over sexuality. The isolation and depression that this created made him feel impotent as an agent of change within his own life:

I've just hit 19 and already I'm severely depressed. I'd like to live on my own so I can express myself and my sexuality; when I can't do things that may offend or upset my family, this upsets me. If I lived on my own I'd have more personal/sexual relations with men. I'm not happy with my physical state or mental state.

Qaiser endured years of bullying at school as a result of his multiple identities (gay, Asian and Muslim), and the ostracism made him feel not only alienated from the Asian/Muslim 'community', but also

shunned by the gay community here – a gay Muslim on the scene, it's something they really don't like. I'm lost, up here in Scotland. I've never encountered a gay Muslim in my life, and so I feel really alone. I mean, in Scotland, a young teen, I am supposed to be having fun and enjoying life. But instead I am depressed.

However, he was able to overcome the isolation, to a degree, through connecting with other gays and lesbians who provided him with the support that he lacked at home. While this contributed to a positive sense of self-worth, the psychological damage caused by bullying continued to have an impact on his life. Qaiser's struggle was strongly connected with his need for recognition and acceptance. He sought social independence, but felt stifled and geographically isolated by living in Scotland, as well as residing in a small Asian 'community'.

MANAGING ONE'S MUSLIM IDENTITY

The stigma associated with homosexuality in Islam critically contributes to negative feelings among the gay Muslim population (Siraj, 2006; Jaspal and Siraj, 2011). The adverse consequences of Muslim homophobia, through vocal opposition to being homosexual and Muslim (cf. Siraj, 2009), render the lives of gay Muslims invisible and unimportant. The intersection between religion and sexuality is riddled with tension, as many Muslim gay men suffer from identity conflict. Sexuality and religion are perceived as essential components of the self, yet there is an underlying and potent belief that homosexuality is incompatible with Islam (Jaspal and Cinnirella, 2010). This influences the decision of gay Muslim men to stay 'in the closet' (Jaspal and Siraj, 2011). Qaiser, Saif and Tariq all accepted that Islamic scriptures prohibit homosexuality and, while they all wrestled with their faith and its stance on homosexuality, Saif suffered considerably more, given his strong commitment to his faith. Grappling with his sexuality remained a continual, if not constant, feature of his life. Saif's ideas on homosexuality were rigidly situated within a religious discourse of condemnation, He considered homosexuality with a great deal of disapproval: 'if you are a homosexual, then that's a fault'. As a result of this belief, he was uninterested in resolving the conflict between faith and sexuality. Nevertheless, he believed that he could, despite being a homosexual, navigate through life as a God-fearing Muslim:

> Just because I'm a homosexual, I'm not going to stop praying/fasting/reading the Qur'an. Every human being commits sins, but you see the good thing I find in myself is that, as long as I feel guilty doing it, the guilt makes me a strong person, because when you are guilty at least you are aware of it. Imagine if you are going to eat *haram* [forbidden], but you go around saying this isn't *haram*, that's them satisfying their brain that this is right and I will go ahead with it. Guilt is what makes us do the right thing in life ... guilt is to make you realise that you are going on the wrong path.

While this contributed to a feeling of dejection for Saif, it did relieve some of the emotional pain that he experienced. Feelings of guilt and regret acted as a moral safeguard to prevent him from committing further sin. Saif's Muslim identity was deemed as virtuous, but his homosexual identity was portrayed as immoral and 'wrong ... I'm not happy about being a homosexual, but I've just learned to adapt to it, but there's always guilt there'. He suffered from 'internalised homophobia'; that is, levelling antigay social attitudes toward the self, causing internal struggles, devaluing the self, leading to low self-regard (Meyer and Dean, 1998). A strong religious commitment has been shown to predict internalised homophobia among sexual minority individuals (Herek, 1987). The vast disconnect between religion and sexuality was an unbridgeable gap. Nevertheless, Saif still sought comfort in his faith to lessen the stress and anxiety that he experienced about his sexual orientation:

> Sometimes I feel that maybe if I go to *Hajj* [pilgrimage] and make a *dua* [supplication], maybe that will change me. I believe in miracles and maybe who knows ... God obviously has seen everything, He's seen how I've struggled with it and how I've coped with it. It's *farz* [obligatory] to read *namaz* [pray]. There are a lot of *farz* – as long as I keep to my *farz*, obviously we're human after all; even heterosexuals commit sins.

The conflict between being gay and Muslim is maintained because of the lack of theological support in Islam. As a consequence, many gay Muslims tend to negate their Islamic identity (Jaspal and Cinnirella, 2010; Siraj, 2006). Tariq, who was single and lived on his own, spoke about a particular incident that highlighted the difficulty in carving a place as a gay man within the wider Muslim 'community':

> I remember vividly, it was about seven or eight years ago, going to the mosque for *Eid* prayers ... I got there quite early and the Imam was talking about liberal Islam, he was saying there are all these people saying that we should be less conservative and that we should accept people even if they're not doing all the things that the Qur'an said we should do. He said, 'recently I was in San Francisco and there was a march going', and it was obviously Gay Pride and that he saw a banner and gay Muslims ... and how he saw these people and how they looked like Muslims and some of the women were wearing headscarves, and then there was a pause. And just at that minute I was thinking, this is really bizarre, I didn't expect to come and hear this from a *Hafiz* at the mosque, and there was a pause and then he just kind of bellowed 'THEY ARE NOT MUSLIMS!' I just went through the motions for the rest of that prayer. I didn't actually say it with my heart. I guess, at that point in my life, I just accepted it. I said, 'if he's telling me I'm not a Muslim, then I'm not'.

The episode is an example of how ostracised gay Muslims are made to feel. While Tariq did not undergo a crisis of faith, he was left with the stark realisation that his sexual orientation was inherently sinful in the eyes of Muslims. The mosque was not a place of solace, but one of condemnation of people like Tariq. Another incident accentuated his alienation and weakened his Muslim identity:

> Allah can tell me if I am or not a Muslim, but over the years I've heard other things as well. One of my cousins got married and they were reading the Nikah [marriage ceremony], and the Imam was talking about marriage and its importance and saying, 'you parents out there that have children who aren't married or if you're not married, then remember what the Qur'an says, you're only half a Muslim, you're only 50% Muslim'. I remember standing there thinking, 'God, I'm not married, I'm gay, I don't drink but you know I will occasionally have a drink, and I will have meat that's not halal', and I remember thinking I must be in single figures [laughs]. I'll be lucky if I'm 10% Muslim!

Tariq recognised that only God would be able to judge him as a Muslim, however the Imam's message was one of exclusion. The ideal, 'preferred' Muslim, according to the Imam and the Qur'an, is one who is married. Those who are not are deemed deficient ('only 50 per cent Muslim'). There is no recognition of individuality, and those who are 'different' are marked as less worthy and marginalised. The incident illustrates the intersections of identity that lead to gay men being excluded on the basis of their sexuality and stigmatised as a result of their religion. Tariq's admission that he occasionally drank alcohol and consumed non-halal meat served to amplify this sense of being outside the realm of Islam. Qaiser, equally, felt shunned by the wider Muslim/Asian 'community', yet the pull of his Muslim identity remained strong:

> There are days where I am like, 'there is no God, religion sucks', but when my identity or Islam/Muslims are attacked I feel I should be a part of that and I'm proud to be Muslim. I want to be religious or at least a good Muslim, but my sexuality gets in the way. If I get involved with religion or if I attempt to be religious, people judge and say I can't be both and that my own people will kill me – if I advance too much towards the gay side, I feel really bad and guilty sometimes. But I'm a strong believer in God, although sometimes I'll lose my faith in such a deity from time to time, such as a time just now.

Being a Muslim and belonging to a faith that Qaiser believed rejected homosexuality prompted a strong sense of dejection and disenfranchisement. It had a damaging impact on his identity as a gay man; his sexuality was an obstacle that impeded his affirming and celebrating his Muslim identity, and vice versa. His identity as a Muslim was also dominated by the reaction and response he received from his local 'community', as well as the prejudice and mistreatment that he suffered. Qaiser's visibility and seeming self-confidence at being open about his sexuality incensed others, and coming out had implications for his psychological well-being. That is, he 'faced a bi-dimensional homophobia from ethno-religious in-group members and the general population ...' (Jaspal and Siraj, 2011: 183):

> People began to get used to the fact of me being gay and it wasn't a problem so much ... The Muslim boys at school couldn't take it, and this is when it started to leak out into the Asian/Muslim community, when I turned up at mosque for the first time in years it was the most awkward moment of my life, the youths were pointing and staring and it then became a proper witch hunt. Our town is so small that when I walked past an Asian/Muslim person my heart would jump, I'd feel sick and I became paranoid. At this point I wasn't religious, but after hearing about how much LGBT Muslims suffer ... I decided to drop religion and become an out gay man. The advice I used to get from fellow 'brothers' was to give up religion. An Arab girl at school told me to stop fasting and stop being a Muslim. That's great religious advice there, who's the sinner now? Isn't that a whole lot worse?

Religious identity, practice and spaces have been colonised and appropriated by heterosexual Muslims, and the intersection between faith and sexuality resulted in a sense of involuntary excommunication from the wider Muslim/Asian 'community'. This inevitably led to a sense of powerlessness for Qaiser, whose quiet battle for respect and acceptance was made difficult as a result of the homophobia from within his own religious and ethnic community. An incident that affected Saif's Muslim identity was his first same-sex sexual experience. This episode in his life compounded feelings of emotional distress and undermined his Muslim identity:

> When I was nineteen, he was a Turkish man from Middlesbrough, that was like really hard because I was a virgin, I hadn't even kissed anyone. We were chatting online and speaking on the phone for about a year. He kept on telling me he's fallen in love with me, it was just about a month later. I was, like, you hardly know me. But as we spoke on the phone I began feeling the same ... because on the phone he was really caring, compassionate. That's what attracted me towards him. I thought maybe if I was to go with someone, maybe this is the person I should. I felt really guilty, but then he turned out to be a jerk as well. He was such a liar, he brainwashed me right into it. I was, like, if you wanted to experience it you could have experienced it with someone else, why ruin my life?! I had been controlling myself since

puberty, I went out of control when I met the Turkish guy, when I actually felt love for someone everything went blind to me, religion, everything went blind ... that's what made me commit adultery with a guy. [When I returned to Glasgow] I just cried and said *tawba* [repented] and I'm like, God, I know what I'm doing is not right but it's just so hard. Maybe at the end of the day God understands what I'm going through. He knows how hard I'm trying, everyone sins OK, as long as your *niyya* [intention] is *saaf* [clean] ... you'll get *ajar* [rewarded] for your *niyya* as well, that's how I feel that God knows at least I'm trying. It's so hard to control, it's like keeping your feelings in a cage, it's like an animal in a cage ...

For all three men, there was no seamless integration between their ethnic, religious and/or sexual identities. Therefore, there was no attempt to transform or reconstitute the Islamic frame of thought to alleviate the conflict between being gay and Muslim. This was largely because there was an explicit acceptance that to be gay and to put those feelings into physical practice was wrong, according to Islam.

CONCLUSION

The chapter examined how the negativity surrounding homosexuality in Islam impacts on the lives of three Scottish gay men, as well as their perception and attitudes towards their own sexual identity. The men inhabit a social reality that operates behind a shroud of secrecy. As a consequence, they remain largely unaffected by the legal and social changes in Scottish civic society that protect the rights of gay men. Qaiser was the only participant to have disclosed his sexual orientation. Nevertheless, life as an openly gay man continued to be problematic. He continued to feel marginalised, ignored, silenced and invisible as a result of his intersecting identities. Tariq and Saif, on the other hand, felt insecure in 'coming out'. They therefore had to sacrifice openness and honesty as well as to exercise a constant policing of their behaviour. Staying 'in the closet' and not acknowledging their sexual orientation prevented them from forming an authentic sense of selfhood. The men, as gay Muslims, faced unique challenges in their lives. For Qaiser, living in a close-knit Pakistani 'community' led to being marginalised. He found it immensely difficult to channel his energy into constructing a gay identity, because of his powerlessness at mitigating the effects of outside oppression. As an openly gay man, he did not have access to a support-ive and nurturing network, be that his own family, his faith 'community' or his ethnic group. Whether the message of religious condemnation was implicitly or explicitly accepted, it continued to define and shape the men's religious and sexual identities. Saif, unlike Qaiser and Tariq, judged homosexuality as something abnormal and wrong. The tension between religion and sexuality was particularly pronounced for him, and the inner turmoil that he experienced led him to distance himself from his identity as a gay man. Saif's understanding of his sexual orientation was based on the strictures of Islam, a religious framework that condemns homosexuality. Qaiser and Tariq also accepted this position, but they felt a forcible sense of disconnect from Islam and disentangled themselves somewhat from Islam. Specific to Tariq's experience was the pressure of marriage, which he felt to be constrictive, yet he believed that this was a far better solution than coming out to his parents and family.

The Scottish gay Muslim population lacks both a visible face and presence in Scotland, and more explicit attention to the diversity of the LGBT 'community' is essential to understand the distinctly different cultural discourse around their sexual identity. At present, the struggle of gay men from faith-based communities in Scotland has yet to be understood and contextualised within an academic framework. While there has been exponential growth in recent years in research on Muslim gay men (Siraj, 2006; Jaspal and Siraj, 2011; Jaspal and Cinnirella, 2010, 2012, 2014) and lesbians (Siraj, 2012, 2016), much of this research has centred on the lives of gays and lesbians who are based, or were born or raised in England (cf. Cowen et al., 2009). The lives of the three men as sketched here demonstrates that research needs to be conducted on the lives of gay Muslims in Scotland to expand our understanding of how they negotiate their sexual identities using the lens of intersectionality, but also how their multiple identities interconnect to create different aspects of oppression.

REFERENCES

Bouhdiba, A. (1985). *Sexuality in Islam* (trans. A. Sheridan). London: Routledge and Kegan Paul.

Cant, B. (ed.) (1993). *Footsteps and Witnesses: Lesbian and Gay Life Stories from Scotland.* Edinburgh: Polygon.

Collins, P. H. (2000). *Black Feminist Thought: Knowledge, Consciousness, and the Politics of Empowerment* (2nd edn). New York: Routledge.

Cowen, T, Rankin, S. A., Stoakes, P. and Parnez, T. (2009). *Everyone In: Minority Ethnic LGBT Project Scotland*, available at www.equality-net work.org/Equality/website.nsf/webpages/9352D823321F8004802575C100 5E2EBF

Crenshaw, K. W. (1996). 'Mapping the margins: Intersectionality, identity politics, and violence against women of color'. In K. W. Crenshaw, N. Gotanda, G. Peller and K. Thomas (eds), *Critical Race Theory: The Key Writings that Formed the Movement*, pp. 357–83. New York: New Press.

Doi, A. R. I. (1989). *Woman in Shari'ah, Islamic law*. London: Ta-Ha.

Duran, K. (1993). 'Homosexuality in Islam'. In A. Swidler (ed.), *Homosexuality and World Religions*. Harrisburg, PA: Trinity Press International.

Galford, E. and Wilson, K. (2006). *Rainbow City: Stories from Lesbian, Gay, Bisexual and Transgender Edinburgh*. Edinburgh: Word Power Books.

Herek, G. M. (1987). 'Religious orientation and prejudice: A comparison of racial and sexual attitudes'. *Personality and Social Psychological Bulletin*, 13, 56–65.

Jaspal, R. (2014). 'Arranged marriage, identity and psychological wellbeing among British Asian gay men'. *Journal of GLBT Family Studies*, 10(5), 425–48.

Jaspal, R. (2012). '"I never faced up to being gay": Sexual, religious and ethnic identities among British South Asian gay men'. *Culture, Health and Sexuality: An International Journal for Research, Intervention and Care*, 14(7), 767–80.

Jaspal, R. and Cinnirella, M. (2010). 'Coping with potentially incompatible identities: accounts of religious, ethnic and sexual identities from British Pakistani men who identify as Muslim and gay'. *British Journal of Social Psychology*, 49(4), 849–70.

Jaspal, R. and Cinnirella, M. (2012). 'Identity processes, threat and interpersonal relations: Accounts from British Muslim gay men'. *Journal of Homosexuality*, 59, 215–40.

Jaspal, R. and Cinnirella, M. (2014). 'Hyper-affiliation to the religious in-group among British Pakistani Muslim gay men'. *Journal of Community and Applied Social Psychology*, 24, 265–77.

Jaspal, R. and Siraj, A. (2011). 'Perceptions of "coming out" among British Muslim gay men'. *Psychology and Sexuality*, 2(3), 183–97.

Kugle, S. S. (2003). 'Sexuality, diversity and ethics'. In O. Safi (ed.), *The Agenda of Progressive Muslims on Gender, Justice and Pluralism*. Oxford: Oneworld Publications.

McKeown, E., Nelson, S., Anderson, J., Lowd, N. and Elford, J. (2010). 'Disclosure, discrimination and desire: Experiences of Black and South Asian gay men in Britain'. *Culture, Health and Sexuality*, 12(7), 843–56.

Meek, J. (2015). *Queer Voices in Post-War Scotland: Male Homosexuality, Religion and Society*. Basingstoke: Palgrave Macmillan.

Meyer, I. H. and Dean, L. (1998). 'Internalized homophobia, intimacy, and sexual behavior among gay and bisexual men'. In G. M. Herek (ed.), *Stigma and Sexual Orientation: Understanding Prejudice against Lesbians, Gay Men, and Bisexuals*, pp. 160–86. Thousand Oaks, CA: Sage.

Minwalla, O., Rosser, B. R. S., Feldman, J. and Varga, C. (2005). 'Identity experience among progressive gay Muslims in North America: A qualitative study within Al-Fatiha'. *Culture, Health and Sexuality*, 7(2), 113–28.

Rahman, M. (2010). 'Queer as intersectionality: Theorizing gay Muslim identities'. *Sociology*, 44(5), 944–61.

Rahman, M. (2014). *Homosexualities, Muslim Cultures and Modernity*. Basingstoke: Palgrave Macmillan.

Rahman, M. (2015). *The Politics of LGBT Muslim Identities, E-International Relations*, 2 April, available at www.e-ir.info/2015/04/02/the-politics-of-lgbt-muslim-identities

Rouhani, F. (2007). 'Religion, identity, and activism among transnational Queer Muslims'. In G. Brown, K. Browne, and J. Lim (eds), *Geographies of Sexualities: Theory, Practices and Politics*. Aldershot: Ashgate.

Ryan, C. (2001). 'Counseling lesbian, gay, and bisexual youths'. In A. R. D'augelli and C. Patterson (eds), *Lesbian, Gay, and Bisexual Identities and Youth: Psychological Perspectives*, pp. 224–51. Oxford: Oxford University Press.

Sarantakos, S. (2005). *Social Research*. Basingstoke: Palgrave Macmillan.

Siraj, A. (2006). 'On being homosexual and Muslim: Conflicts and challenges'. In L. Ouzgane (ed.), *Islamic Masculinities*, pp. 202–16. London: Zed Books.

Siraj, A. (2009). 'The construction of the homosexual "other" by Muslim heterosexuals'. *Contemporary Islam: Dynamics of Muslim Life*, 3(1), 41–57.

Siraj, A. (2011). 'Isolated, invisible and in the closet: The life story of a Scottish Muslim lesbian'. *Journal of Lesbian Studies*, 15(1), 99–121.

Siraj, A. (2012). '"I don't want to taint the name of Islam": The influence of religion on the lives of Muslim lesbians'. *Journal of Lesbian Studies*, 16(4), 449–67.

Siraj, A. (2014). 'Islam, homosexuality and gay Muslims: Bridging the gap between faith and sexuality'. In Y. Taylor and R. Snowdon (eds), *Queering Religion, Religious Queers*, pp. 194–210. New York: Routledge.

Siraj, A. (2016). 'British Muslim lesbians: Reclaiming Islam and reconfiguring religious identity'. *Contemporary Islam: Dynamics of Muslim Life*, 10(2), 185–200.

Yahya, H. (2000). *Perished Nations*, 3rd edn. London: Ta-Ha.

Yip, A. K. T. (2004). 'Embracing Allah and sexuality? South Asian non-hetero sexual Muslims in Britain'. In K. A. Jacobsen and P. P. Kumar (eds), *South Asians in the Diaspora*, pp. 294–310. Leiden: Brill.

Yip, A. K. T. (2007). 'Sexual orientation discrimination in religious communities'. In M. V. L. Badgett and J. Frank (eds), *Sexual Orientation Discrimination: An International Perspective*. London: Routledge.

Yip, A. K. T. (2012). 'Homophobia and ethnic minority communities in the United Kingdom'. In L. Trappolin, A. Gasparini and R. Wintemute (eds), *Confronting Homophobia in Europe*, pp. 107–30. Oxford: Hart.

Yip, A. K. T. (2015). 'When religion meets sexuality: Two tales of intersection'. In P. D. Young, H. Shipley and T. J. Trothen (eds), *Religion and Sexuality*, pp. 119–40. Vancouver: University of British Columbia Press.

Zafeeruddin, M. M. (1996). *Islam on Homo-Sexuality* (trans. S. Azhar Ali Zaidi). Karachi: Darul Ishaat.

7

YOUNG PEOPLE
Muslim Youth in Scotland: Politics, Identity and Multicultural Citizenship

Katherine Botterill, Gurchathen Sanghera and Peter Hopkins

INTRODUCTION

Until recently, much academic and policy research about Muslim youth and politics tended to focus on issues of radicalisation and extremism (Bakker, 2006; Hemmingsen and Andreasen, 2007; Kuhle and Lindekilde, 2010; Spalek and McDonald, 2011), mirroring the political and policy landscape on this issue. While some of these studies attempt to disrupt popular conceptions of the link between Muslim youth and radicalisation, others have assisted in fuelling perceptions of Muslim youth as taking a more politicised stance on religious belief than their parents (Policy Exchange, 2007, cited in Field, 2011: 160). Furthermore, some have attempted to categorise Muslim youth into those who are 'moderate', 'apartist' and 'alienated' (Field, 2011) and, while painting a more complex picture, remain rather rigid and do little to challenge homogenised representations of Muslim youth. Media representation of Muslim youth as either politically apathetic, radicalised or vulnerable to radicalisation further contributes to misconceptions about young Muslim identities and their political agency. Such representations are gendered and embodied, for example with Muslim young men being read as the Asian 'new folk devils' (Alexander, 2000), as 'militant and aggressive' (Archer, 2003: 81) or as academic and effeminate (Hopkins, 2006).

Recent scholarship on the political participation of young Muslims in Britain has shown that young Muslims are politically engaged and developing new political subjectivities in diverse ways (O'Toole and Gale, 2013). Significantly, political engagement can lead to a sense of belonging and inclusion in Britain (Mustafa, 2015). Hopkins (2007) has explored the ways in which young Muslim men in Scotland engage with mainstream politics and their understanding of how the political system operates. Rather than being apathetic, disengaged and inert, the young men involved in this study in the early 2000s were recognised as possessing a range of carefully considered political opinions, particularly on matters relating to global politics. Building upon this earlier work, we discuss the political participation of young Muslims in Scotland, particularly in the context of the 2014 Scottish independence referendum. In doing so, we challenge problematic assumptions that see young Muslims as apolitical or that having political agency suggests vulnerability to radicalisation. We then report on youth perspectives of politics in the media, focusing on the impact of media representations of geopolitics on young Muslims' everyday lives. Finally, we discuss how youth political subjectivities have been animated by narratives of multicultural nationalism in Scotland. More broadly, we argue for greater recognition of the diversity and hybridity of youth identities in media and policy landscapes.

THE STUDY

This study engaged with 382 young people from across Scotland from diverse ethnic and religious minority backgrounds. A three-year project, funded by the Arts and Humanities Research Council, aimed to (1) examine how Muslim and non-Muslim (i.e. those who 'look' Muslim) young people experience and respond to Islamophobia, and (2) explore how international, national and local events (geopolitics) impact on such experiences. For the purposes of this chapter, we focus on the data collected from twelve focus groups and forty-five individual interviews with young Muslims living in Scotland.

The focus groups took place in Glasgow, East Renfrewshire and Fife, while the interviews were conducted in a range of places across Scotland including Edinburgh, Dundee, Glasgow, Aberdeen, East Renfrewshire, Inverness, Dumfries and Fife. Participants were recruited from secondary schools, colleges, universities, youth groups, community groups, voluntary organisations, religious groups and places of worship. We analysed the data using thematic coding through NVivo software. Those who participated in the research were given a gift voucher as a token of our appreciation for giving up their time to participate in the research. One school, however, preferred a donation to the school's hardship fund to individual vouchers for those pupils who volunteered to take part in the research. When we have used direct quotations from respondents in this paper, we use self-selected pseudonyms to protect their anonymity.

Therefore, the pseudonyms used do not necessarily correspond to the ethnic background or religious affiliation of the participants.

YOUNG MUSLIMS AND POLITICAL PARTICIPATION IN SCOTLAND

There has been much academic discussion about the supposed political apathy of young people across the UK (Kimberlee, 2002; Henn and Foard, 2014). In response, scholars have explored new forms of political engagement and participation among young people from more traditional (i.e. electoral, party politics) to newer (less formalised) forms of politics (activism, protest, boycotts, blogging, e-activism) (Brookes and Hodkinson, 2008; O'Toole and Gale, 2013). Our research was conducted prior to and just after the 2014 Scottish independence referendum. As such, this event stimulated politically charged discussions among the young people interviewed. The referendum marked an opportunity for young people, in that for the first time in Scotland sixteen- and seventeen-year-olds were given the right to vote. For many, the inclusion of youth voices in decision making at the national level was a positive and empowering opportunity, as a Muslim pupil from Glasgow suggests here:

> this shows the development of society, like they are relying on younger minds as well ... not just people who are older. (Male, 16–18, Muslim focus group, Glasgow)

While not all young Muslims felt fully engaged in the debate, most expressed an intention to vote and a voting preference. Many felt that extending the right to vote was an important step in Scotland's future, garnering a sense of responsibility for deciding Scotland's future:

> I think that's a really good idea because obviously it's our future, it's the teens' future that's going to after like twenty-odd years, we're going to be the adults, and stuff like that ... since it's our future, I guess we should be making a decision about what we want to do with our lives. (Maalik, Pakistani Muslim refugee, male, 16–18, Fife)

Maalik's reference to 'our future' echoes some of the rhetoric on both sides of the Scottish referendum campaign. Throughout the campaign, those promoting a 'Yes' vote stressed the inclusion of the youth voice in the debate in Scotland's constitutional future. Much of their narrative for independence spoke, for example, of putting young people at the 'heart of the debate' and pledged 'opportunities' for young people through various schemes, such as the European Youth Guarantee (BBC

News, 2014a). 'Generation Yes', a youth movement supporting independence, also claimed to be the 'largest youth movement Scotland has ever seen' (*The Herald*, 2014). There were also a number of events, such as the 'Big, Big Debate' at Glasgow's Hydro Arena, aimed at encouraging young people's engagement in the debate, particularly first-time voters (BBC, 2014b). Similarly, the 'No' campaign stressed the importance of preserving the Union for the sake of the 'life chances' of 'future generations' (BBC, 2014c).

Sayeed, a young Pakistani Muslim man from East Renfrewshire, also saw the vote as a duty for young people to claim their stake in society at a key historical moment:

> At the end of the day, we need to recognise that young people are a vital part in society. They are the future and they are the leaders of today and not just tomorrow. By that, meaning, yes they will lead us in the future, but they are also able to lead us today and we need to empower them to do that; one way to do that is by giving them the vote. (Sayeed, Scottish-Pakistani Muslim, male, 19–21, East Renfrewshire)

Despite some of these positive engagements around the referendum vote, young Muslims were not always clear on how to access politics and influence change. Levels of political engagement varied, with some expressing a disinterest, lack of awareness and mistrust of mainstream political parties:

> I don't think people have a say in general politics. I think this is there, I would like to say I am disappointed, but I would actually say that I am not surprised. (Tariq, Muslim, male, 22–25, Aberdeen)

> I've never voted before, because I've never really, I never got a letter or anything saying that I need to vote, so I don't know whether I'm supposed to go somewhere to sign up for it. (Nuz, Scottish-Pakistani Muslim, female, 19–21, Dundee)

A lack of information on the practical aspects of voter registration was cited as an issue for some young Muslims, particularly first-time voters who expressed lower confidence levels due to a perceived lack of knowledge:

> I think it's been more directed to older people. I think even though young people are allowed to vote, I think they've just sort of dismissed them, in a way. So I think more information should have went to them first, and then sort of went to older people. 'Cause then, the younger people were sort of, they were a bit confused. (Qasim, British-Pakistani, male, 16–18, Inverness)

> I think there should be a law against voting without knowing ... I do think they need to simplify it and they do, and if they've widened the vote to sixteen-year-olds you need to start targeting them. (Rahielah, Scottish-Asian Muslim, female, 16–18, Glasgow)

The language used and strategies employed to engage Muslim communities in politics, such as visits to mosques and community centres by politicians, were also criticised by some young people as tokenistic, disingenuous and elitist:

> I don't know how inclusive they have been of sixteen-year-olds generally, and especially of the Muslims, because I am not sure if they are feeling very ... I don't know, it is a tough crowd, it is a tough crowd. But an important crowd, I think, to get on board ... I would say that not enough Muslims care, not enough Muslims are aware. (Afia, Scottish Muslim, female, 16–18, Glasgow)

Here, Afia refers to a range of reasons for non-participation in politics among Muslim youth, citing a lack of awareness and a lack of care. She links political apathy to the absence of knowledge and lack of inclusion. For others, too, disinterest in politics appeared to be linked to feeling disconnected or lacking confidence in mainstream politics. Low membership of political parties also demonstrated weak association with Scottish/British national politics beyond the referendum campaign and low levels of trust in mainstream politicians and political parties:

> I don't know, 'cause even if you do go about it the right way and go through Parliament and stuff, like, the people higher up are always going to have the ultimate say. (Betty, British Muslim, female, 22–25, Edinburgh)

Furthermore, the growing media presence of right-wing or 'racist' parties, such as UKIP, put some people off engaging with party politics, though this was seen as more of an issue in England than in Scotland, as Flynn suggests here:

> I don't think there is a lot of right-wing politics in Scotland. I mean I think the SNP, now they are, they're quite big on social justice and equality ... I did read about Conservatives in England focusing less on ethnic minorities, and focusing more on trying to obtain the voters that vote for UKIP, so more of the right-wing people. That's kind of disheartening. When you know that more ethnic minorities are being, kinda, shoved to the side so that they can get more of the votes from people who are a bit, you know, a bit shady. (Flynn, Palestinian Muslim, male, 16–18, Fife)

Flynn sees Scotland as having a different political character to England, emphasising values of social justice and equality associated with Scottish politics. Others also cited particular policies, such as the Forced Marriage

Bill, to demonstrate that Scotland was 'further ahead' than England in terms of promoting and managing multiculturalism. This echoes what Breeze et al. (2015: 429) found: that 'the young people ... offer[ed] more grounded and hopeful accounts ... inspired not by "raving" or "romantic" nationalism, but by a desire for a just and equal Scotland'.

Young Muslims engaged in politics through a range of mediums. For example, higher education student associations, such as Islamic societies, were important spaces of political expression and student activism, particularly for Muslim international students living in Scotland. Youth political involvement in local organisations also fostered a sense of integration or inclusion among some young people, as Azlan reflects here while talking about his activities with local trade union:

> I think the trade union activity has really had, like, just in knowing more, because I didn't ... I wasn't born here, so still sometimes I feel like an outsider. But I think getting involved with the trade union activity, meeting all these politicians and, you know, speaking at conferences and events and all that – that has really helped me become part of the society. (Azlan, Pakistani Muslim, male, 22–25, Dundee)

Many young Muslims who expressed interest in politics often referred to issue-based international politics that they were involved with. Some international students and non-British Muslims tended to refer to the politics of their home countries or regions. Interest in Middle Eastern politics was highly variable, with some expressing views on issues such as the Palestinian-Israeli conflict, and others having little awareness of geopolitical events in these areas.

> The Palestine issue is something that I always like to have debates about. And also people have a lot of stereotypes about the Middle East that I tend to like to challenge a lot. (Esti, Sudanese-British Muslim, female, 19–21, Edinburgh)

For some, however, and in particular Muslim refugees and asylum seekers, there was intentional disengagement from home country politics through fear of upset:

> I'm mostly interested in politics but there is some problems in Turkey lately. So I'm gettin' too much deep into politics, so I'd rather like leave it. 'Cause it, it changes people, you know, you can argue with your best friend an' everything for just, just for politics. (Nabi, Turkish Muslim, male, 22–25, Inverness)

Similarly, some young Muslims expressed reluctance to discuss international politics with British or Scottish friends at school or university, as Nabila discusses here:

I think people knew I was Libyan so they didn't really know what to say to me. So I tried to keep it like so I didn't really mention it at all. I didn't really get involved in all the debates [about the Libyan conflict]. But it is weird when people are debating certain things when it involves your country. So they were like, 'Oh no it is just because of the oil' or 'I don't think America should go into ...' and 'I don't think Britain should get involved ...' Whereas I felt like they should ... it stopped it by doing the no-fly zone and stuff ... people kind of knew, but they were that age where they didn't ... like most of my friends are quite in a bubble, I feel. They are ... they are really nice, like I love them and stuff, but I just feel sometimes, oh god. You just bring up like current events and they are like 'Oh I didn't realise that was happening' and you are like 'OK ...', ha ha ... yeah, I avoid, definitely avoid. Like I would speak to my Arab friends maybe, Muslim friends, just because they could identify a bit more ... But not really, not really with my British friends. (Nabila, British-Libyan Muslim, female, 19–21, Dundee)

Nabila reflects on the discomfort of talking openly about Libyan politics with her friends, suggesting that they do not 'identify' as closely with her own experience. So she deploys a strategy of self-silencing in order to negotiate this discomfort. This 'discursive insecurity' around current affairs places limits on engagement and reduces possibilities for meaningful youth dialogue on a range of important political issues (Botterill et al., 2016). Similarly, Parveen also sees having a political voice on international issues as a 'risk', in Scotland:

It would be different if I was in Pakistan. I would be like very much into the debates and everything, but here I am just like, no. Let's not risk it. Because you never know what is going to happen. It is not like ... I don't know, it is just better to be safe than sorry. (Parveen, Pakistani Muslim, female, international student, 19–21, Dundee)

Despite such reservations, the level of young people's engagement in the referendum has had what McLaverty et al. (2015) describe as the 'referendum effect' on young voters. In other words, young people from all different backgrounds seem to be more engaged in politics. As a result, on 18 June 2015, the right to vote in Scottish elections was extended by MSPs to sixteen- and seventeen-year-olds. Supported by the SNP government, the Scottish Election (Reduction of Voting Age) Bill lowered the voting age, with eighty-six MSPs across parties voting in favour of the bill and eight against.

YOUTH PERSPECTIVES ON POLITICS IN THE MEDIA

Most of the young people interviewed engaged with some form of media as their source of information about politics. Within the critical literature on media representation of Muslims is a widespread perception among scholars and commentators that there is a link between media-propelled representations of Islam and Muslims and the everyday Islamophobia experienced in communities (Ansari, 2002; Alexander, 2000; Gardner et al., 2008; Poole, 2002; Saeed, 2007). Some have argued that Muslims, particularly young Muslims, have been pathologised in media discourse as the 'new folk devil' (Shain, 2011; see also Poynting et al., 2004; Alexander, 2000). In our study, young people frequently criticised the mainstream media for associating Muslims with a discourse of threat and violence:

> I think everything, anything a Muslim does [in the news] – even if they've just got a Muslim-sounding name. Like, these people that killed Lee Rigby. I don't know what kind of Islam they were following – 99.9% people would say that's wrong ... people are bound to look at you in a different way if they know you're Muslim and then they're reading all this in the news every day. (Azlan, Pakistani Muslim, male, 22–25, Dundee)

> Some people misunderstand [Islam] for, like, terrorism and in Somali where we are from, pirates. There is pirates and terrorists, so they take it too far and say, 'Haha, look at you, pirate.' And it is not like that. (Amir, Somali Muslim refugee, male, 12–15, Glasgow)

In December 2015, Humza Yousaf, Scotland's Minister for International Development and MSP for the SNP, noted that:

> [f]rom my perspective this is as concerning as it felt in the days after 9/11. There was a tangible feeling of fear and it was very tense for the Muslim community. I've not felt that since – even after 7/7 it still didn't feel as tense.

For him, today racism and Islamophobia have become less pernicious and subtle; instead, they are more obvious and direct. We found that, for young people, media representation impacted directly on their everyday experiences of racism and Islamophobia. While the intensity of these experiences were contingent on age, gender, nationality and place, young Muslims reported a universal experience of feeling targeted and misrecognised as a threat, as the following extract shows:

> No matter how nice you are, they are sometimes, just because you are Muslim and you came from another country. They said we are terrorists, but we are not terrorists! (Female, 12–15, Muslim focus group, Glasgow)

Many of the young people we interviewed, however, were hopeful about the capacity of the general public to see beyond simplistic stereotypes of Muslim communities. Some highlighted that people understood that the media representation of Islam did not accurately reflect the reality, particularly those who had experienced multicultural interactions and encounters in local communities:

> I kind of understand from their point of view, watching that like in the news or whatever and everything, and their family believing the same thing, that can have a strong impact on them believing the same thing. But I think with going to school with Muslim people and they should know our personalities, and we are not like that. They should understand that is not the case, and grow up about it really. To start to think for themselves and don't really believe anything they hear. (Male, 16–18, Muslim focus group, Glasgow)

> So, yeah, something like that gets reported, it gets put all over the news, this guy's Muslim, he's just killed a British soldier, get them. It has a big effect, you know it has a lasting effect. But you just hope that people kind of have the capacity to learn that that's not the truth. (Adam, White Scottish Muslim convert, male, 19–21, Inverness)

Young Muslims are active in disrupting media stereotypes of Islam, whether through educating others about the meaning of Islam in everyday conversations or through activist networks that challenge Islamophobic discourse. For example, AMINA, a Muslim women's resource centre in Dundee, has developed campaigns to promote understanding of Muslim women in schools, working against media stereotyping. Indeed, similar to other scholars (e.g. Afshar et al., 2005; Sanghera and Thapar-Bjorkert, 2012), we found that young Muslim women who wear the headscarf also talked about how they respond with resilience to racism and Islamophobia, using dress as a performative act to disrupt assumptions about Muslim women as 'oppressed':

> I think, well, I'm wearing this hijab, yeah, as I mentioned previously, it's made me focus on why I want to wear it more and it's to defeat all these stereotypes which have been created from all these 9/11 bombs and everything like that. (Amber, Scottish Muslim, female, 16–18, Dumfries)

These acts of resistance have worked to neutralise young people's experiences of racism in some local spaces, yet there remains a troubling pressure on the part of young people to be resilient and let racism 'bounce off'. While many felt there was less racism and more understanding of Muslim communities in Scotland than in England, most reported experiencing some form of racism growing up in Scotland, ranging from relatively innocuous 'banter' to the more aggressive forms of physical violence. Equally, young people's responses to racism varied, depending on the context and intensity. For example, in a senior Muslim boys focus group in Glasgow, one participant reflected:

> Some people don't even know they are doing something bad or saying something bad. Like, I mean, if someone says to me like, calls me Paki I wouldn't really mind it sometimes. (Male, 16–18, Muslim focus group, Glasgow)

For others, too, racism is acknowledged as 'there', but not as bad as in other places. In the following narrative, Afia, a Scottish Muslim from Glasgow, remarks on the shifting emotional landscape of media-fuelled racism in Scotland. While Scotland is perceived as a more welcoming space, it is not immune to media-fuelled racism:

> I think, thankfully, in Scotland I have not perceived this whole idea that wearing a headscarf is an oppressive thing ... But it is there, unfortunately, it is there. It doesn't really make sense for us, I suppose, but obviously media and all the rest of it. You know, I know a lady that she used to just veil a little bit, she had cigarette butts burnt into her in Glasgow ... Maryhill, but you know I don't think – a lady at Central Station got the headscarf ripped off her ... There was a man that made comments to me about 'oh you know ...' He was looking at me and was like 'oh, is that a woman?'. These kind of silly remarks. I mean, for me obviously it just bounces off ... I have been in the subway sometimes and there is a feeling you get. That is what I say, on the whole, that my Scottish experience has been fantastic, but there is a feeling you get definitely of, they are looking at me in a way that they shouldn't be looking at me because I am dressed like this ... You tend to find that you are always in a position where you have to be apologising. You are meant to be uncomfortable ... it is always in the back of my mind. You always aware of it, you know ... And the media feeds it. (Afia, Scottish Muslim, female, 16–18, Glasgow)

Afia's narrative darts from revealing a deplorable act of racism that she has witnessed to her own experiences and resilient responses to everyday 'comments'. And while she praises Scotland in one sense, she also tells of the underlying discomfort in everyday interactions and public spaces. The negotiations that Afia is discussing suggest, as Humza Yousaf has observed, that racial and religious tensions are 'felt' by young Muslims and they deploy a range of resilient strategies to cope.

YOUTH POLITICAL IDENTITIES

Many of the young people in the study expressed resistance to Islamophobia through national identity. When asked, 'What does it mean to be Scottish?', young people reflected positively on their affiliation with Scotland and Scottishness, irrespective of ethnic or religious heritage:

> I think I would use Scottish Muslim on my Instagram actually [both laugh], yeah, I would say I'm proud to be Scottish and Muslim at the same time. So if I go to England I'm automatically the minority and doesn't matter if I'm Muslim or not, I'm still Scottish. (Amber, Scottish Muslim, female, 16–18, Dumfries)

Many felt that Scottishness related to 'fairness' and 'diversity', making direct comparisons with English people as money-oriented and exclusionary, as these two extracts reveal:

> We are less driven by money, whereas I think that England and especially London, everything is to do with money. And nothing is to do with what is right and what is morally right. Whereas I think Scotland is a more just society. (Male, Senior Muslim focus group, Edinburgh)

> We live in Scotland and there's a community, you talk to all different types of people, Sikhs, Hindus you can even talk to some atheists, you talk to everybody and that's what I like about being Scottish. We're very diverse ... (Malcolm, Scottish Pakistani Muslim, male, 16–18, Glasgow)

While the discourse of Scotland being a fair and equal society was a key theme in many of the interviews, it nevertheless has been problematised (Morton, 2011). For example, the Social Mobility and Child Poverty Commission (2015: 1) highlighted that 'the top of Scottish society is significantly unrepresentative of the Scottish population – though less so than the top of British society'. Indeed, there is a 'glass ceiling' that locks people out from less advantaged backgrounds.

The extent to which Scottish nationalism has penetrated the political identities of young Muslims is not clear from this research. Few of those interviewed explicitly called themselves Scottish nationalists. However, the association of the SNP with a 'fair' and 'just' society was evident from many of the narratives. In particular, young people who participated in focus groups referred to free healthcare, free education and race equality as key policies that enhance Scottish society:

> Scottish nationalism, the one that Alex Salmond and that lot are selling, is a nationalism based on inclusion, civic nationalism. His argument is regardless of your race, your religion, your class, there is a Scottish identity. The thing about the nationalism that Nigel Farage is talking about is a nationalism based on difference. So surely, in an independent Scotland, then, would be a bit more attractive, this inclusive nationalism where everyone has a place

regardless of your skin colour and your race and your ethnicity and your religion. (Mohammad, Scottish-Bangladeshi Muslim, male, 16–18, Dundee)

Single-issue campaigns, like the referendum, were more likely to gain interest among young people than broader party politics. Scottish Government 'No Racism' campaigns, for example, were referred to on a number of occasions as fostering a sense of inclusion and national belonging among young Muslims:

> Whenever I think of a Scottish flag I think 'No Racism', because it's always been like that. There was just in the past few years you see it on TV, 'No Racism', then you see it on billboards and posters outside like, promoting 'No Racism'. (Nuz, Scottish Muslim, female 19–21, Dundee)

The association between Scottish nationalism and anti-racism was also referred to in discussions about nationalism more broadly. Here, Betty and Tariq talk about the differences between Scottish and British variants of nationalism, marking out the racialised nature of British nationalism:

> what I would consider someone being Scottish and I said heritage, I think SNP's more like that, where they don't, it's not race, it's just being proud of being Scottish, regardless of how you look and all that sort of stuff. Whereas BNP you've got, when you think of BNP ... you have a vivid image of what that BNP guy looks like, maybe not for a girl, but you know, that guy with the skinhead and the tattoos walking down the street, like, very cockney accent, I don't know whether, obviously it's a very stereotypical view, but when you look at the marches, a lot of them look like that. And that's the kind of thing they want ... they just want jobs for like the English and put like no one coming across the border type thing. (Betty, British Muslim, female, 22–5, Edinburgh)

> SNP is a lot more ... based on people, their values, whereas the BNP are based on opinions, I would say extreme opinions ... Obviously the wrong reasons I would say because they ... I think SNP have actually got something credible, like could possibly be able to run a government, it could possibly look after its people, whereas BNP I don't think really at all. (Tariq, Muslim, male, 22–25, Aberdeen)

In an analysis of White Scottish youth responses to the 'One Scotland, many cultures' campaign, Ross et al. (2008) found that for many White Scottish young people Scottishness is perceived as an inclusive category. The research also found, however, that although young people were positive about multiculturalism in Scotland, some racial tensions arose in the local community context, particularly relating to anxiety over asylum seekers and refugees among those living in recently mixed areas.

Furthermore, an Ipsos Mori poll of attitudes to Muslim integration in Scotland found that, while most majority non-Muslim respondents (of all ages) felt that Muslims were integrated in Scotland (58% generally and 69% of 18–24-year-olds), 26% of these agreed with a statement that more Muslim settlement would dilute Scottish identity. This undermines the notion of 'One Scotland, many cultures' and the achievement of 'multicultural nationalism' (Arshad, 2010). Hopkins (2004: 265) asserts that young Scottish Muslims navigate and negotiate different markers of Scottishness, 'simultaneously includ[ing] themselves in the perimeters of Scottishness, while also excluding themselves from belonging completely within the boundaries of Scottishness'. While characteristics like place of birth, accent and schooling give young Muslims a sense of Scottishness and inclusion in the nation, non-participation in perceived Scottish cultural practices, such as drinking and clubbing, are more likely to generate a feeling of exclusion. Similarly, in this study, Scottishness was frequently referred to as a means of validating national belonging. This was reproduced through young people's encounters with formal institutions and the rights afforded to them by the state. Betty discusses the civic dimensions of her 'connection' to Scotland:

> Having lived most of my life here, I've got quite a connection with Scotland, so and being able to like, 'cause I've got the right to vote here, my tuition fees, they were paid for by the Scottish government and, like, yeah Scotland has helped me, I've lived like, I've gone into uni [university] in Scotland, I've just got quite a, yeah, I think I would connect myself to being Scottish more than anything else. (Betty, British Muslim, female, 22–25, Edinburgh)

Betty links being Scottish to civic participation that is formed around distinct opportunities in Scotland for her, compared with that of her home country. Similarly, for other refugees, asylum seekers and some international students from Commonwealth countries, gaining the right to vote in the Scottish independence referendum fostered feelings of inclusion and national belonging. This, coupled with the pro-migration policies of the SNP, symbolised a politics of hope for many of those seeking greater rights and recognition for migrants in Scotland. Az, an Arab asylum seeker living in Glasgow, refers here to her experience when registering to vote:

> I ... remember asking them that 'you know, we are asylum seekers and you know our nationality is still Indian' and they're like, 'but you are living here, you're a Scot, you're from the Commonwealth, you are Scottish'. And that made me realise, somebody else, I didn't have to say it, somebody else said it and we signed in, and we go to elections and stuff. (Az, Arab Muslim asylum seeker, female, 22–25, Glasgow)

These examples suggest that mainstream political participation is one route to integration, yet there are limitations placed on non-EU and non-Commonwealth migrants to political participation in this context. As such, those positioned at the boundaries of electoral participation are excluded from the national conversation, resulting in a segregated political debate. Furthermore, the everyday misconceptions over who is and is not 'foreign' undermine state-sanctioned inclusion strategies:

> I think of myself as [Scottish], I would say, if someone asks me. I got this a lot when I was travelling actually, like, 'where are you from?'. And I would say Scotland, and they would say no, but where are you really from. (Flynn, Palestinian Muslim, male, 16–18, Fife)

This seemingly banal and commonplace question – 'Where are you from?' – has more serious implications when seen as a form of 'identity denial' (Cheryan and Monin, 2005). Despite its intentions, being questioned in this way serves as an interrogation of one's location, mobilities and histories, and its undertone – often fuelled either by intrigue of the exotic or suspicion of difference – leaves one feeling out of place, outcast as 'stranger' or 'foreign'. Going further, questions regarding accents, dress and the duration of their residency in Scotland were all mentioned by young people in discussions of the barriers to inclusion. In a focus group with Pakistani Muslim young people, for example, the different aspects of prejudice are made clear:

> I think they don't have a problem straight away with most things, but still in their heart or something they don't accept ... we are not like Scottish, you know Scottish have got their own tartan names, and they have got their own clan, as they say. Like we are classed as different, like we are outsiders. Like some people ... even English people say 'how long have you been here?'... 'you have got quite a Scottish accent'. It is a bit ... like, obviously at the end of the day the youngsters, how are the youngsters going to learn? And if they hear Paki and all this, they say I am going to the Paki shop for a packet of fags. I am going to the Chinkis for a Chinese ... Yeah, just the way they categorise. (Male, Pakistani Muslim focus group, Fife)

The assumption that non-White equals non-national also affected young Muslims' expressions of nationalism in Scotland. Malcolm, a Muslim 'Yes' voter and self-identified 'nationalist', experienced racism on social media after tweeting a pro-nationalist message. An older man responded, arguing against his right to 'be a nationalist' because of his skin colour and 'foreign' name:

> 'Cause I'm a Nationalist, some people might be like, oh, 'cause I'm brown I can't be a Nationalist ... Even if somebody's not from here, OK if they

call Scotland their home they have a right to be here as well. People have rights as much as we do, you can't just say to that person they didn't have a right because they've got a different skin colour. That's not right. (Malcolm, Scottish Pakistani Muslim, male, 16–18, Glasgow)

Affiliations and associations with Scottish national identity shape youth engagements with Scottish politics. These narratives show that such engagements are also affected by the attitudes and behaviours of others – the everyday encounters that make young people feel out of place, unwelcome or devalued in spaces of national politics and society more generally. Many have bypassed such hostile atmospheres and express 'pride' 'in being Scottish. For others, there was more reluctance to identify as Scottish and relinquish another national identity, as Talia says here:

> I've been here for like nearly 15 years, everything like whatever, but I wouldn't say I was Scottish. Like I speak the language, I go to school, to uni and stuff, but I wouldn't say I was Scottish. I was born in Kosovo and, see, if Kosovo was good, I'd be living there. The only reason I moved here was because war. (Talia, Kosovan Muslim, female, 19–21, Glasgow)

Political exclusion in Kosovo through war has left Talia in a liminal political space, unsure of where to practise her political agency, feeling a connection to her home country but with rights neither there nor, given her refugee status, in Scotland. Her interest in politics, however, is not muted by the limits of her migration status.

As discussed, many young people engaged in international politics, particularly those who held loyalties to more than one nation state. These interests most often reflected transnational heritages and were reworked to form hybrid or transnational political subjectivities. Moreover, faith and language also played a role, intersecting with national identity to shape young people's sense of belonging and political beliefs:

> Obviously, living with my parents who are very strong with their Pakistani heritage, who watch Pakistani television and, you know, so have hung onto their Asian heritage. And then it's like when I go to school, OK, you could say I feel Scottish with my friends and, you know, the way we talk. Soon as I come back home, speaking in Urdu and, you know, it's like I'm back in Pakistan, just speaking casually to my parents in Urdu and stuff like that. (Maalik, Pakistani Muslim refugee, male, 16–18, Fife)

> because our religion have very, very big impact ... Muslim follow their religion very strictly ... That make a Muslim different from a Scottish people, but if you put the religion aside then, yes, I do feel like a very much a Scottish, like a long lie on a Sunday, going out on weekends and all these kinds of

things, and going on a, in summer enjoying, especially barbeque and stuff, all these kind of stuff you know. (Nadeem, Muslim international student, male, 22–25, Glasgow)

These narratives show that young people negotiate their Scottishness according to different contexts. Being Scottish, for them, is a fluid category relating to specific times, places and activities. This is affected not only by symbols of national identity, but also the social relationships and practices that make up particular communities.

CONCLUSION

This chapter has explored the political participation and identities of young Muslims in Scotland in the context of the 2014 Scottish independence referendum. We have reflected upon qualitative data collected from 100 young Muslims in Scotland in twelve focus groups and forty-five interviews. This sample is diverse and includes Muslim youth with Scottish Pakistani heritage, as well as international students, asylum seekers and refugees. We have demonstrated that the referendum, coupled with the vote for sixteen- and seventeen-year-olds, provided a platform for some young Muslims to take an active role and interest in political issues. Student associations – such as student Islamic societies – were important places for engendering an interest in political matters. Moreover, a number of young Muslims were particularly interested in global political issues. However, others articulated a lack of trust in politics and politicians and felt uncertain about the possibility that any engagement with politics would make a difference. More broadly, a lack of information and ineffective communication on the details and impacts of the referendum for young Muslims meant that, while many were hopeful for change, they were unclear on how exactly their lives would be affected by such change.

Muslim young people have diverse multi-ethnic and multi-heritage backgrounds and their political agency and participation is contingent on a range of factors and context specific. The broader political narrative of 'multicultural nationalism' in Scotland has been effective to some degree in cultivating a sense of inclusion for young Muslims, but young people are also acutely aware of the barriers to participation. Everyday racism and Islamophobia continue to undermine young Muslims' political agency in complex ways. Young people felt that their entitlement to participate in politics was, in some cases, denied through a process of 'othering'. We also found political disengagement due to a fear of misrecognition or misunderstandings, brought about by anti-Muslim political discourse in the media and everyday experiences of discursive and embodied insecurity.

REFERENCES

Afshar, H., Aitken, R. and Franks, M. (2005). 'Feminisms, Islamophobia and identities'. *Political Studies*, 53(2), 262–83.

Alexander, C. E. (2000). *The Asian Gang: Ethnicity, Identity, Masculinity*. London: Berg.

Ansari, H. (2002). *Muslims in Britain*. London: Minority Rights Group International Report.

Archer, L. (2003). 'Muslim brothers, black lads, traditional Asians. British Muslim young men's constructions of race, religion and masculinity'. *Feminism and Psychology*, 11, 79–105.

Arshad, R. (2010). 'Foreword'. In A. Homes, C. McLean and L. Murray (eds), *Muslim Integration in Scotland*. Edinburgh: Ipsos Mori.

Bakker, E. (2006). *Jihadi Terrorists in Europe: Their Characteristics and the Circumstances in Which they Joined the Jihad: An Exploratory Study*. The Hague: Netherlands Institute of International Relations.

BBC News (2014a). 'Scottish Independence: "Yes" vote is "opportunity for young", says Salmond'. *BBC News*, 20 June, available at www.bbc.co.uk/news/uk-scotland-scotland-politics-27939816

BBC News (2014b). 'What 7000 teenagers talked about during the Big, Big Debate'. *BBC News*, 11September, available at www.bbc.co.uk/news/uk-scotland-scotland-politics-29157668

BBC News (2014c). 'Scottish independence: Alistair Darling calls on young people to vote "no"'. *BBC News*, 16 January, available at www.bbc.co.uk/news/uk-scotland-scotland-politics-25751939

Botterill, K., Hopkins, P., Sanghera, G. and Arshad, R. (2016). 'Securing disunion: Young people's nationalism, identities and (in)securities in the campaign for an independent Scotland'. *Political Geography*, 55, 124–34.

Breeze, M, Gorringe, H., Jamieson, L. and Rosie, R. (2015). '"Everybody's Scottish at the end of the day": Nationalism and social justice among "yes" voters'. *Scottish Affairs*, 24(4), 419–31.

Brookes, R. and Hodkinson, P. (2008). 'Introduction – Young people, new technologies and political engagement'. *Journal of Youth Studies*, 111(5), 473–9.

Cheryan, S. and Monin, B. (2005). '"Where are you *really* from?": Asian Americans and identity denial'. *Journal of Personality and Social Psychology*, 89(5), 717–30.

Field, C. D. (2011). 'Young British Muslims since 9/11: A composite attitudinal profile'. *Religion, State and Society*, 39(2–3), 159–75.

Gardner, R., Karakaolus, Y. and Luchtenberg, S. (2008). 'Islamophobia in the media: A response from multicultural education'. *Intercultural Education*, 19(2), 119–36.

Gilliat-Ray, S. (2010). *Muslims in Britain: An Introduction*. New York: Cambridge University Press.

Hemmingsen, A. S. and Andreasen, S. J. (2007). *Radicalisation in Europe. A Post-9/11 Perspective*. Copenhagen: DIIS Brief.

Henn, M. and Foard, N. (2014). 'Social differentiation in young people's political participation: The impact of social and educational factors on youth political engagement in Britain'. *Journal of Youth Studies*, 17(3), 360–80.

Herald Scotland (2014). 'Generation "Yes": New group launched to persuade Scotland's young to vote for independence'. *Herald Scotland*, 29 March, available at www.heraldscotland.com/news/13152962.Generation_Yes__new_group_launched_to_persuade_Scotland_s_young_to_vote_for_independence

Hopkins, P. (2004). 'Young Muslim men in Scotland: Inclusions and exclusions'. *Children's Geographies*, 2(2), 257–72.

Hopkins, P. (2006). 'Youthful Muslim masculinities: Gender and generational relations'. *Transactions of the Institute of British Geographers*, 31(3), 337–52.

Hopkins, P. (2007). 'Global events, national politics, local lives: Young Muslim men in Scotland'. *Environment and Planning A*, 39(5), 1119–33.

Hopkins, P. and Gale, R. (2009) (eds). *Muslims in Britain: Race, Place and Identities*. Edinburgh: Edinburgh University Press.

Kimberlee, R. H. (2002). 'Why don't British young people vote in general elections?' *Journal of Youth Studies*, 5(1), 86–98.

Kuhle, L. and Lindekilde, L. (2010). *Radicalization among Young Muslims in Aarhus*. Research report for the Centre for Studies in Islamism and Radicalisation (CIR). Denmark: Aarhus University.

McLaverty, P., Baxter, G., McLeod, I., Tait, E., Göker, A. and Heron, M. (2015). *New Radicals: Digital Political Engagement in Post-referendum Scotland*, Working Papers of Communities and Culture Network +. Aberdeen: Robert Gordon University, available at www.communitiesandculture.org/files/2013/01/New-Radicals-Final-Report.pdf

Morton, R. (2011). 'Class in a "classless" society: The paradox of Scottish egalitarianism'. *Scottish Affairs*, 75, 83–99.

Mustafa, A. (2015). *Identity and Political Partcipation Among Young British Muslims: Believing and Belonging*. Basingstoke: Palgrave Macmillan.

O'Toole, T. and Gale, R. (2013). *Political Engagement amongst Ethnic Minority Young People: Making a Difference*. Basingstoke: Palgrave Macmillan.

Poole, E. (2002). *Reporting Islam: Media Representations of British Muslims*. London: I. B. Tauris.

Poynting, S. and Mason, V. (2007). 'The resistible rise of Islamophobia: Anti-Muslim racism in the UK and Australia before 11 September 2001'. *Journal of Sociology*, 43, 61–86.

Poynting, S., Noble, G., Tadar, P. and Collins, J. (2004). *Bin Laden in the Suburbs: Criminalising the Arab Other*. Sydney: Sydney Institute of Criminology.

Ross, N. J., Hill, M. and Shelton, A. (2008). '"One Scotland. Many cultures": The views of young people from White ethnic backgrounds on multiculturalism in Scotland'. *Scottish Affairs*, 64, 97–116.

Saeed, A. (2007). 'Media, racism and Islamophobia: The representation of Islam and Muslims in the media'. *Sociology Compass*, 1, 1–20.

Sanghera, G. and Thapar-Bjorkert, S. (2012). '"Let's talk about … men": Young British Pakistani Muslim women's narratives about co-ethnic men in "postcolonial" Bradford'. *Interventions*, 14(4), 591–612.

Shain, F. (2011). *The New Folk Devils: Muslim Boys and Education*. London: Trentham Books.

Social Mobility and Child Poverty Commission (2015). *Elitist Scotland?* London: Social Mobility and Child Poverty Commission with the Hume Institute.

Spalek, B. and McDonald, L. Z. (2011). *Preventing Religio-Political Extremism Amongst Muslim Youth: A Study Exploring Police-Community Partnership*. AHRC Research Report, University of Birmingham, available at: www.religion andsociety.org.uk/uploads/docs/2011_04/1302685819_preventing-religio-political-extremism-spalek-april2011.pdf

8

GENERATIONAL RELATIONS
Gender and Generational Relations for Muslim Women in Scotland

Hengameh Ashraf-Emami

INTRODUCTION

Researchers have paid attention to the significance of intergenerational research for several years (see Maxey, 2006; Punch, 2002; Skelton, 2000; Tucker, 2003; Valentine, 2003). Some important scholarly works have focused on intergenerationality and identities, particularly using intersectionality to understand people's multiple identities (Crenshaw, 1993; Brah and Phoenix, 2004; Dwyer, 1999; Nayak, 2003; McDowell, 2003; Hopkins, 2006). Pain et al. (2001: 141) argue that 'age is a social construction' and Hopkins et al. (2011) draw attention to the complexity of intergenerationality and its functions in the everyday lives of younger and older generations by examining the experiences of Christian families in Scotland. There are some influential scholarly works on the intergenerational identity of Scottish Muslim men (e.g. Hopkins, 2006), but there is still a dearth of intergenerational research on Scottish Muslim women's identities. By intergenerational research, I mean the study of the differences and similarities – and the transformation between generations – in the Muslim community. This phenomenon is most evident in the dynamic relationship between mothers and daughters, but the interactions between other family members are also important.

Indeed, generational characteristics are not a static phenomenon, but dynamic (see Hopkins and Pain, 2007). The multidimensional benefits of intergenerational research lie in the importance of building a positive connected society. Intergenerational knowledge may possibly help society to build bridges between generations. As a result, it allows us to anticipate changes that may occur in society, and the best ways to deal with these in the future. I believe it is crucial to expand the academic knowledge of intergenerational experiences, as this could lead to a future society more attuned to its diverse communities and could possibly address potential tensions and conflict in order to develop solutions.

My research focuses on Muslim women in order to shed light on the changes and transformations that occur between generations. Intergenerational research of this kind may provide a platform to discuss social integration and equality issues.

Understanding intergenerational relations for Muslim women in Scotland is important, as it allows us to explore the complexity of identities and how these change or not over time. It is also important because demographic changes in Muslim communities – particularly given the more recent arrival of diverse Muslim communities to Scotland – may alter intergenerational relationships. Also, the transformations of the family through gender and generational dynamics (including possible tensions, conflicts, strengths and women's agency) are important considerations.

This research has an important contribution to make to the exploration of Scottish Muslim women's agency in the family, and their contribution to the construction and reconstruction of their identity in future generations. It reveals the dynamics of gender relations in these families, including the dynamic relationship between parents and daughters. This study provides some insight into the lives and concerns of Scottish Muslim women, and fills many of the gaps that currently exist in intergenerational research in this area. I explore the process of constructing and reconstructing identity across generations of Scottish Muslim women and their agency, in part through practices of veiling and unveiling. This feature of some Muslim women's lives makes them uniquely visible; however, it is also a focus for negative stereotypes about their perceived lack of agency. The chapter refers to the intergenerational dynamic through the degree of visibility of these women's religion. It details how my research participants reconstructed their identities in different ways and how they demonstrated agency within society, family and as individuals. The themes of identity are examined as they intersect with ethnicity, gender and religion. The accounts of Scottish Muslim women in this study reveal that the construction and reconstruction of identity is worked and reworked as an active dynamic process through multiple forms of agency in various arenas of their lives. This is achieved through interaction and involvement with family and society in a variety of situations, for instance various social and political engagements. I argue that, while these women have similarities in their experiences of veiling and unveiling, they have their own personal strategies for negotiating their religious and gendered identities. For example, Muslim women are taking the lead by negotiating and enforcing changes in various environments, including within their families, as well as in social situations such as the mosque, in order to express their own identities through multiple expressions of agency. This dynamic phenomenon is explored through the narratives of my research participants concerning their experiences of wearing the veil.

In this research, the term 'veil' is used to refer to various forms of head covering worn by Muslim women, such as the headscarf, jilbab and niqab. In the case of the niqab or burka, I make it clear if the face is covered.

THE STUDY

This research highlights and discusses the findings of my study regarding the significance of Muslim women's construction and reconstruction of their identity, by focusing on gender dynamics and women's agency through several generations. The research participants had diverse backgrounds in terms of education, class and ethnicity, as well as sect, such as Sunni or Shia. The question of the contextual and situational aspects of veiling within the family and intergenerational relations are discussed through the voices of Muslim women in order to reveal their multiple identities. Their accounts also show that their agency is constructed and reconstructed in multiple ways. They may encounter multiple opportunities and challenges because of these intersecting identities, which makes their identity construction very complex. These multiple identities are sometimes related to the multi-ethnic nature of this group of women, and are also connected to the intersection of gender, religion and ethnicity; this, in turn, causes them to face multiple stereotyping.

This generational research is a critical examination of family cohorts. I explore some of the themes regarding intergenerational relations that emerge from interviews and participant observations in various settings. The interviewees were from three generations and were racially and ethnically diverse. In fifteen interviews, there were seven Pakistanis, of whom one was first generation; two Turkish, both first generation; one with Egyptian heritage from the second generation; two with Libyan heritage of the second generation; one second-generation Muslim from Dubai; and two White English converts. However, during my participant observation, I was also able to interact with wider groups of more ethnically diverse Muslim women. By using the term 'first generation', I am referring to those who were born and brought up in their country of origin. The term 'second generation' is used to identify those born and brought up in the UK, or who immigrated to the UK at a young age.

It is important to avoid essentialising ethnicity and Muslimness: therefore, we cannot ignore the dynamic relationship between ethnicity and religion, which is connected to social and geopolitical conditions. Indeed, this study attempts to take a positive step towards a better understanding and welcoming of diversity, as well as opening up a positive dialogue across generations that may counteract bias in the understanding of gender, religion and culture. Moreover, acknowledging these differences, my research explores the agency of women who take a role in interpreting and reinterpreting their religion and cultural practices. In this way, my research participants create a dynamic dialogue that explains how they have transformed and retransformed some of the cultural and religious beliefs and practices in an intergenerational context through their effective agency.

The first section of this chapter describes and explores the research method, including positionality and reflexivity. The second section interprets the intergenerational negotiation of identities and gender dynamics in the family. The third section examines generational challenges. The fourth section explores some of the intergenerational issues in the family. Finally, the conclusion shows how Scottish Muslim women negotiate their identity in the family through the dynamic of their agency, and how this relates to the intersections of gender, ethnicity and religion.

In total, fifteen interviews took place with Scottish Muslim women in Glasgow from a variety of backgrounds and with variations in age, ethnicity, career and education. Some areas of Glasgow, such as the suburb of Pollokshields, are particularly identified with the Muslim population of the city (see Census, 2011). However, my research is not confined to this area, and several interviews revealed that Muslim geographical patterns have changed over time; for this reason, my research was open to Muslim women from all areas of the city. Muslims now live in many areas in Glasgow, although many participants told me that they had lived in Pollokshields when they first arrived.

I sought participants among Scottish Muslim women over the age of eighteen who had been living in the UK for at least ten years. I interviewed all volunteers who met the criteria and were interested in participating. The number of volunteers was beyond my expectation, and I found it very encouraging that, after my original publicity for participant recruitment, many participants introduced friends and relations who were keen to take part. Because the vast majority of Muslims living in Glasgow are of Asian ethnicity, it was convenient to recruit

participants from this ethnic group. However, my study aimed to maximise the diversity and depth of the research findings and to reflect as
wide a range of ethnicities as possible. In order to protect the confidentiality of my research participants, all names are pseudonyms.

The research adopted snowballing and gatekeeper methods of recruiting participants. The locations of interviews varied, and included participants' homes, university student unions, mosques, cafés and community
centres. Most interviews took about an hour; the shortest lasted half an
hour. Participants' passion and enthusiasm to participate in the research
were evident. As part of my research fieldwork, I attended several celebrations during Eid, several weddings and several less formal social
gatherings. All interviews were conducted in English, apart from one
in which the participant's daughter translated for her mother. Informal
conversations with the participants before and after the interviews produced further knowledge and understanding that enhance the results of
the study.

It is noteworthy that, in contrast to the experience of Ryan et al.
(2011), but similar to Hopkins' (2009) study, my research participants
were keen to know about my ethnic background, when I came to the
UK and whether or not I was married. As in the experience of Hopkins
(2006), participants' questions sometimes threatened to divert the interview from its purpose, and I had to redirect the conversation and clarify
my position as a researcher. Because I wear the hijab, they tended to
assume that I was Muslim. However, I was surprised that they did not
ask if I was Sunni or Shia; was this because, knowing that I was from
Iran, they assumed that I was Shia? It is important to bear in mind that
researcher positionality is not a fixed phenomenon (see Hopkins, 2006;
Mohammad, 2001). My position moved between that of insider and
outsider. A researcher might be seen as an outsider by their research
participants and, as a first-generation immigrant, I am to some degree an
outsider to the second generation of my research participants. However,
as a visibly Muslim woman, I worked on the assumption that I was
also considered an insider by all the participants in my study, given
my religious identity. This had a significant impact on the recruitment
of research participants in Glasgow: I believe it made potential participants more willing to speak freely, feeling safe in the knowledge that,
as another Muslim woman, I would be sensitive to their concerns and
cultural parameters. This was an obvious advantage during my research.

As a visibly Muslim woman, it was not hard for me to build a rapport
with my participants. My interviews empowered the interviewees and
gave them confidence, as I was able to build trust with them. I do not

suggest that this close connection, through gender and religion, broke down all the barriers between myself and my participants. I acknowledge that there was still a power imbalance of a different kind, since my position was not fixed and static (see Hopkins, 2006). In terms of positionality, Collins (2000: 258) talks about 'connected knowers'; this defines my position as a woman, born in Iran during the reign of the last Shah, living through the upheaval of the Islamic revolution of 1979, and the completely different society that followed it, and then coming to live in the UK and becoming a British citizen. These experiences allowed me to connect with my research participants and granted me a deeper understanding of many of the challenges they face. My position as a researcher who shares some similarities with my research participants has led me to have, as identified by Collins (2000: 258), 'empathy and compassion' with them.

INTERGENERATIONAL NEGOTIATION OF IDENTITIES IN THE FAMILY

As the smallest unit of society, the family has a significant place in the life of Muslims (see Joly, 1987). My participants were asked about various aspects of family behaviour, such as freedom of choice in marriage, relations between parents and children, and the relevance of gender roles. The answers to these questions were often discussed in relation to the customs and manners of Western culture. In general, it was evident that the vast majority of those family rules and regulations were observed in order to promote respect, dignity and protection among family members (see Hopkins, 2006).

The dynamic relationships in the family, especially those between mothers and daughters, are explored in this chapter. For instance, Nasim, who was born in 1967 in Glasgow and has Pakistani heritage, explains that her fourteen-year-old daughter believes that she has been forced by Nasim to wear the hijab, but she attempts to prove, by referring to her younger daughter, that this is not the case. During the interview, Nasim strives to contest her elder daughter's claim by referring to her younger daughter's freedom of choice. Nasim said, 'So I told her [the elder daughter] to take it off, but my twelve-year-old wants to wear it, you know.' She feels the need to defend herself in the matter of her daughters' veiling and unveiling. She is conscious of her relationship with her daughter and of her own influence on her daughter. In her narrative, the veil is employed as an effective medium to assess and describe the situation. Her account explicitly and implicitly explains that motherhood roles are significant social tools in influencing daughters' attitudes, choices and behaviour, as well as demonstrating that both mother and daughter are conscious of these. Thus, Nasim emphasises her agency as a mother who provides or withholds the choice of veiling to her daughters. It is striking how she employs her multiple positions, first as a mother to explore her identity, then connecting this with her experience of being a daughter. She explains her own trajectory of wearing the veil, saying that when she was younger, she wore it only occasionally. She herself believes that wearing the hijab increases her confidence in her daily life.

One aspect of women's agency relates to how critical they are about the sociopolitical situation, both in their community and in the wider society. Drawing on her observations about gender inequalities in some Muslim societies, Nasim made a comparison between Western culture and that in Muslim countries, and criticised some of the latter for not providing equal opportunities for women. Hence, Nasim explores her authority and agency in interpreting her religion, and is critical of some social-political situations, particularly gender inequality. In addition, she observes that women's rights in some Muslim countries are often limited to theoretical recommendations, based on theological arguments, while actual implementation of equal rights between the genders is overlooked. She explores her agency in interpreting her religion without reference to institutional or patriarchal interpretation, and illustrates her standpoint as a Muslim woman who questions social injustice in Muslim countries. On this point, Nasim makes a comparison between her perception of gender positions in the West and Muslim customs outside Western borders. She believes that Western women are privileged because of their opportunities for following their own desires in life. Nasim articulates:

I think the positive thing I can say from the Western culture is that they give everybody a chance and they give women a chance, whereas, see, in the Muslim countries, no matter how much, because a lot of the time you will find that they start explaining the Qur'an to you that women have rights, that women have these rights, but they don't get them. In the Muslim countries, it's, basically, they know women have rights, women have every right, but the men don't give it to them. Rights, up here, it's like, fine, OK, you want to do everything the Muslim way but there's nothing stopping you, you know, you can live it like properly, so like, I think, I think personally, girls and women have a bigger chance of doing stuff when they are in the Western countries, as long as you don't forget your culture and your religion. (Nasim, Glasgow, 2012)

Nasim's narrative illustrates her belief about her identity as transnational, and she explores a sense of adhering to both Western culture and her religious values, since she emphasises the importance of not leaving behind cultural roots and elements of heritage, such as religion; this also illustrates the construction of a hybrid identity. Nasim is conscious that some negative attitudes towards women's education, seen as essentially Muslim, are derived from rigid beliefs and practices that have no actual basis in the Qur'an. She calls these unacceptable attitudes 'unwritten culture' and explains that they have had an adverse influence on the chances of many women in Pakistan to obtain an education. In this way, Nasim interprets her religion as a tool to empower women rather than limiting them:

> The religion doesn't stop you really … they don't have the same chance, there's unwritten cultures that they go by, because … in Pakistan that there are some people that think that girls don't even have to be educated, which, if you look at the Qur'an, if you look at the religion, girls have every right to education.

She intends to defend women's rights to education through their religious rights (Afshar, 2012). In this way, she explores her agency (Collins, 2000) through her interpretation of her religion, and constructs it through her knowledge and interpretation of her religion, in a similar way to some of the other participants. In doing so, she empowers herself. In fact, by illustrating transnational Muslim identity, in this quote Nasim explores generational attitudes in the family towards her daughters, which she believes are based on a lack of deep reflection on religious knowledge, linked with patriarchal power. Hence, she emphasises her interpretive and critical agency in the family, and contests gender inequality in education among those with the same cultural heritage. Nasim explains:

> When my dad wasn't religious, it was a case of, you don't do this, you don't do that, you're not going here, you're not going there, but then now, after he became religious, the others didn't have those restrictions, you know, they had kind of a different lifestyle.

It is striking that Nasim's father realised that many of the restrictions that he imposed on his family were based on personal attitudes rather than religious doctrine. An increasing knowledge of religion made him become more liberal in terms of how he treated his children.

This section has illustrated how – through the experiences of Nasim – a Scottish Muslim woman understands her multiple identities as a woman, mother and daughter, constructing and transforming her transnational Muslim identity. Through her interpretative and critical agency, she has challenged some dogmatic social issues. The next section will explore the dynamics of intergenerational identity through a discussion of marriage and family among Scottish Muslims.

GENDER, GENERATION AND MUSLIM WOMEN'S AGENCY

Points similar to those made by Nasim emerged from Aseif, a young Masters student of Pakistani heritage who contests some of the cultural challenges in the Pakistani community in relation to family and marriage: 'Yeah, there is a cultural barrier between me and my parents … There is a difference between our thinking and the older generation's thinking.' It is very powerful and significant that her identity, and the way in which she constructs it, differs from that of her parents. I argue that women's agency is a powerful explanatory factor for exploring various aspects of my research participants' identities across generations.

The narratives indicate that gender dynamics have societal functions, and reveal that some transformations occur through Muslim women's agency. Aseif was also asserting her identity through intergenerational comparisons, which she does not intend to hand on passively to the next generation. She emphasises her determination to transform some practices for the next generation of British Muslim women with a Pakistani heritage, such as restrictions on inter-ethnic marriage. Thus, she illustrates the dynamic of her agency in transforming cultural practices in the family. Aseif said: 'Once I'm gonna get married and then I'll obviously have my own children, I think, some of the cultural things won't be there.' This quote indicates that the construction and reconstruction of cultural identities among third-generation Muslim women, especially those with Pakistani heritage, are in process and are progressing within their families.

According to the Office for National Statistics (2014), the 2011 census provides information about inter-ethnic relationships that reveals that such relationships have increased in Britain compared to 2001 (2012–13). While the census does not indicate the impact of religion on inter-ethnic relationships, it nevertheless illustrates this change. My research data indicates that this phenomenon will also increase among the next generation of Muslim women. South Asian couples from Bangladesh, Pakistan and India were the least likely of the four ethnicities to be in inter-ethnic relationships, at 7%, 9% and 12% respectively. However, my interviews and observations reveal that the inter-ethnic marriages of participants from Turkey and Iran were mostly contracted with White

British people, and they had not encountered any barriers, because this kind of ethnic restriction is not emphasised. This illustrates the dynamics of intercultural relationships among Scottish Muslim women.

It is notable that my research participants discussed intergenerational dynamics in marriage, as well as gender roles in Muslim families. For instance, Intesar, who was in the second-generation cohort and of Libyan heritage, was born in 1989 to highly educated and professional parents. She explains that her family moved to the UK after living in Canada for a year. She had an unsettled childhood, in which she moved between London and Greece with her mother in order to visit her affluent grandparents, who had been an important influence in constructing her identity. She says that her parents' marriage – although it had taken place over thirty years previously in Libya – was not arranged. This was the case for many first-generation non-Asian participants in my study. However, the element of class and the higher education associated with socioeconomic status cannot be disregarded in the construction and reconstruction of identity and lifestyle, and intergenerational experiences varied considerably, as described in more detail below.

When discussing gender roles, Intesar explains that her mother had most of the authority in the family and made most of the decisions. Her description of how tasks were allocated between her parents illustrates that the gender roles are not fixed in the traditional way – her father did most of the housework. I was struck by the fact that Intesar was non-prescriptive about the ethnicity of her future husband, and illustrated a non-biased Muslim culture. She describes the specific criteria for her future marriage, in which the practice of faith was the most important factor. She explains that this commitment to religion, apart from its overt expressions such as religious ritual (for example attending the mosque and praying five times a day), has to be demonstrated by the practice of the social and political requirements of Islam, including voluntary work and involvement in the community. However, she also exhibits some materialist attitudes in her choice of husband, since she mentions the importance of a secure job. This is probably because the experience of her parents' marriage has given her an expectation of a similar lifestyle. Hence, generational dynamics in marriage patterns are demonstrated. Intesar also says that good looks are the least important criterion when choosing the right marriage partner. This example reveals the complexity of marriage for the second and third generations of British Muslim women. Intesar is conscious of power relations after marriage, and believes that men think their wives will conform to their requirements after marriage.

Thus, here she employs her agency to challenge the possible hierarchical power in the family.

In my study, I found many examples of second- and third-generation Muslim women being more conscientious about their religion than their parents who had immigrated to Britain. Intesar describes herself as being stricter in her religious observance than her parents; she is also concerned about her younger siblings, who are influenced by celebrity culture. This is not what might be expected. It might be thought that with each generation there would be a blurring of the differences between the original cultural background and that of the UK, in the context of secularisation theory, but it does not seem to apply to non-Western societies or in communities of non-Western cultural heritage. Intesar senses a lack of knowledge among non-Muslims about Muslim women, and expresses her frustration with the focus on differences, mainly exemplified by the veil. Instead, she prefers to emphasise the commonality between women of all backgrounds, such as an interest in fashion and dressing up.

The dynamic relationship between some participants and their fathers was striking. In some cases, their relationships with their fathers are described as being stronger than those with their mothers. For instance, Massika has Algerian heritage. Her father had a doctorate and her mother was a teacher. She emphasises the importance of the moral values that she received from both parents, based on their religious beliefs. However, she also explains that her relationship with her father is stronger than the one that she has with her mother. As she explains, she was able to have deeper and more interesting discussions with her father, and received his support in respect of her decision to go to university. By contrast, she describes her mother as being less open-minded than her father. This example illustrates that the perceived patriarchal nature of the Muslim family is not universal but varies between individual families, possibly connected to the level of education. More research into links between education level, gender and disposition to stay within, or see past, traditional cultural boundaries would enrich this discussion. The patriarchal nature of Massika's family, in which the father, not the mother, is the one who demonstrates knowledge and intellectual generosity, means that he is the parent who can share these elements with his daughters.

It is striking that power equality between parents is emphasised by most of my research participants. They did not perceive an issue with gender power in their families. For instance, Massika's description of the power relationship in her family indicates a connection between her mother's career and her equality of power in the family. This may show that there is a link between education, gender equality and gender power balance, as illustrated:

> Well, my mum and dad both are equal, er like, in my eyes they're equal and I'm sure they both see each other as equal in their eyes. Erm, I don't think my dad's got more power than my mum or anything like that, but my mum does go out and work where my dad doesn't, but I don't see any power in both of them, I think, I don't think power is an issue in the family, so I don't think that's a problem.

Like several other participants in the study, Massika's parents, although first generation, did not have an arranged marriage, since they met at university. This meant that they did not see the need to arrange a marriage for her, either. However, she acknowledges that her parents had lived in the UK for many years and their attitudes were different to those of her father's family in Algeria.

It must be borne in mind that this integration may not happen at the same level in communities with different ethnicities. Ethnicity is a significant factor in the likelihood of an arranged marriage. It was more prevalent among the participants with an Asian background, regardless of educational level. Even here, there were exceptions. For example Azza, a forty-three-year-old second-generation Pakistani woman, says that although she does not mind if her son marries a non-Pakistani girl, her husband was insisting that he should, and that he should have an arranged marriage.

The interviews with some of the mothers and daughters revealed several concerns about the marriages of Muslim women. While most of the first generation had married in their home country (this was especially evident in the Asian community), the second and third generations revealed different attitudes and expectations. While my research participants are still strongly committed to marrying within their faith, they also want a spouse who has been brought up in the UK and who will have similar cultural experiences of living in the West. This scenario was different in the Iranian and Turkish communities, since there was only occasionally any issue with marrying outside the ethnic group, but this was not the case in the Pakistani and Bangladeshi communities. My research reveals that this pattern is changing, and that inter-ethnic marriage is increasing among the latter group.

Most of my research participants had a serious commitment to their religion, and consequently it is challenging to find partners who share the same level of commitment. Furthermore, these young women's lifestyles limit the opportunities for contact that are available to most non-Muslims, and their insistence that their marriage partners meet specific criteria further limits their choice. However, the mothers definitely expected their daughters to marry, as they actually promised to invite me to attend the weddings when they took place. Here, we see that there is a dynamic relationship between young Muslim women and their parents that is influenced by intersections of ethnicity, class, religion and education. I now discuss some of the intergenerational challenges negotiated by my research participants.

NEGOTIATING TENSIONS WITHIN INTERGENERATIONAL RELATIONS

My participants also faced challenges in terms of how they negotiated their relationships with their parents. The evidence here supports previous research by Dwyer (2008) that Muslim women face a double challenge from within and from outside their communities. Afshar (2012: 5) argues that, nowadays, Muslim women are aware of their rights in Islam and 'have a better understanding of their faith than their partners'. During my study, generational tensions were discussed to some extent by the research participants. Some young Muslim women reported tension between their own views and their parents' opinions about wearing the veil, and said that they find a lack of support in this from their parents. Mashel, a twenty-three-year-old Masters student of Pakistani heritage, living in Glasgow, illustrates these challenges:

> I think, mostly, challenges come from within your own family ... I think people who think that hijab isn't compulsory or isn't regarded as a good thing, erm, because they've got lack of knowledge or don't understand. I think also they've got insecurity about hijab because maybe they don't wear it or something like that, so they're more harsher or maybe like quite critical of you, I think that was a challenge. (Mashel, Glasgow)

It appears that some young Muslim women resist the ideals of their parents with respect to the interpretation of religious prescriptions, as well as patriarchy in the community (Jacobson, 1997). My study showed that they use religion to advance gender equality. In terms of women's agency and empowerment, religion gives them authority concerning decision making within the family, and a powerful role with which to establish a solid platform and control over their bodies.

Surprisingly, some of the older generation of Muslims are more critical of certain aspects of religious practice, and this leads younger Muslims to become involved in intellectual debates to challenge them. Mashel demonstrates her own understanding of Islam, and disagrees with her parents' views on the hijab. She is very assertive about wearing it, and criticises the older generation for being anxious and doubtful about it. This creates a clash in interpreting religion from intergenerational viewpoints. Mashel articulates this as follows:

> I think the main problem that sometimes you feel you have got is that you are kind of expected to be one thing from non-Muslims, that you've got challenges from non-Muslims to be more like them. Then in your own kind of community there's, I think especially for the younger generation, there is pressure from the older people to be more in touch with your culture, but then you feel like that it maybe clashes with your religion, especially when it comes to specific religious things when the older generation don't agree.

During my research, several young Muslim women demonstrated the double challenges that emerged from both within and outside their community (see Dwyer, 1999). Their narratives demonstrate how they have created a framework in which they act and negotiate their multiple identities within patriarchal constraints, while simultaneously challenging them. In this way, they strive to contest the multiple challenges created by the intersectionality of gender, ethnicity and religion. It is fair to say that their determination to contest these multiple challenges creates an emancipation movement that turns the visibility of their voice, through their agency in decision-making and interpreting faith, including practices such as veiling in diverse styles and colours, into a positive factor.

The narratives in this section explore the intergenerational gender dynamics of Scottish Muslim women's agency in the family, showing the complexity of their identities. It shows how ethnicity has been a significant factor in constructing and reconstructing these identities, especially in marriage patterns. This is very evident among first-generation Pakistanis, who mostly expected to marry within their ethnicity. However, this characteristic has decreased among the second generation, and is being questioned and challenged by the third. This decrease might be expected to continue in subsequent generations until it resembles that of other ethnicities.

CONCLUSION

The chapter has shown the dynamic intergenerational relationship between mothers and daughters, as well as fathers and daughters, among my research participants. The participants' agency was illustrated in various ways, through the employment of their authority and their empowerment through decision making in the family. Moreover, they employ their interpretive agency through their engagement with theology and relate it to sociopolitical issues. The discussion shows that, while common values and beliefs exist between generations, the participants from the second and third generations acknowledged and appreciated intergenerational differences. The analysis indicates that ethnicity is an important factor in constructing an intergenerational identity among Scottish Muslim women. The intersection of gender, ethnicity and religion is undeniably influenced by class and educational background, as well as length of residence in the West.

The narratives indicate that women's transnational identities are significantly marked in the second and third generations, and illustrate their interpretive and critical agency through their identifying some individual dogmatic attitudes, as opposed to genuine religious strictures. The multidimensional identities of Scottish Muslim women across the generations are influenced by various elements of sociopolitical and sociocultural phenomena. In this study, it was evident that intergenerational dynamics and differences in cultural background are complex and multidimensional. That there is growing personal female authority in Muslim families is one of the characteristics of the generational phenomenon. Cultural continuity exists in cross-cultural generations, suggesting that the core culture of family is widely embedded. It remains to be seen if future research, conducted among Muslim women from a less middle-class and well-educated background, obtains similar results.

REFERENCES

Afshar, H. (2012). *Women and Fluid Identities: Strategic and Practical Pathways Selected by Women*. London: Palgrave Macmillan.

Brah, A. and Phoenix, A. (2004). '"Ain't I a woman?" Revisiting intersectionality'. *Journal of International Women's Studies*, 5(3), 75–86.

Bryman, A. (2008). 'Why do researchers integrate/combine/mesh/blend/mix/merge/fuse quantitative and qualitative research?'. In M. M. Bergman (ed.), *Advances in Mixed Methods Research*, pp. 87–100. London: Sage.

Cesari, J. (2004). *When Islam and Democracy Meet: Muslims in Europe and in the United States*. New York: Palgrave Macmillan.

Collins, P. H. (2000). *Black Feminist Thought: Knowledge, Consciousness, and the Politics of Empowerment*. Boston, MA: Unwin Hyman/ Routledge.

Crenshaw, K. (1993). 'Mapping the margins: Intersectionality, identity politics, and violence against women of color'. *Stanford Law Review*, 43(6), 1241–76.

Dwyer, C. (1999). 'Contradictions of community: Questions of identity for young British Muslim women'. *Environment and Planning A*, 31(1), 53–68.

Dwyer, C. (2008). 'The geographies of veiling: Muslim women in Britain'. *Geography*, 93 (3), 140–7.

Hopkins, P. (2006). 'Youthful Muslim masculinities: Gender and generational relations'. *Transactions of the Institute of British Geographers*, 31(3), 337–52.

Hopkins, P. (2009). 'Women, men, positionalities and emotion: Doing feminist geographies of religion'. *ACME: An International E-Journal for Critical Geographies*, 8(1), 1–17.

Hopkins, P., Olson, E., Pain, R. and Vincett, G. (2011). 'Mapping intergenerationalities: The formation of youthful religiosities'. *Transactions of the Institute of British Geographers*, 36(2), 314–27.

Hopkins, P. and Pain, R. (2007). 'Geographies of age: Thinking relationally'. *Area*, 39(3), 287–94.

Jacobson, J. (1997). 'Religion and ethnicity: Dual and alternative sources of identity among young British Pakistanis'. *Ethnic and Racial Studies*, 20(2), 238–56.

Joly, D. (1987). *Making a Place for Islam in British Society: Muslims in Birmingham*. Centre for Research in Ethnic Relations. Research papers in Ethnic Relations, no. 4. London: Economic and Social Research Council.

Maxey, L. (2006). 'Playing with age: Performativity and participation within children's geographies'. Unpublished paper, University of Swansea.

McDowell L. (2003). *Redundant Masculinities: Employment Change and White Working-Class Youth*. Oxford: Blackwell.

Nayak, A. (2003). 'Last of the "real Geordies"? White masculinities and the subcultural response to deindustrialisation'. *Environment and Planning D: Society and Space*, 21(1), 7–25.

Pain, R., Barke, M., Gough, J., Fuller, D., MacFarlane, R. and Mowl, G. (2001). *Introducing Social Geographies*. London: Arnold.

Punch, S. (2002). 'Youth transitions and interdependent adult-child relationships in rural Bolivia'. *Journal of Rural Studies*, 18, 123–33.

Ryan, L., Kofman, E. and Aaron, P. (2011). 'Insiders and outsiders: Working with peer researchers in researching Muslim communities'. *International Journal of Social Research Methodology*, 14(1), 4.

Skelton, T. (2000). '"Nothing to do, nowhere to go?": Teenage girls and "public" space in the Rhondda Valleys, South Wales'. In S. L. Holloway and G. Valentine (eds), *Children's Geographies: Playing, Living, Learning*, pp. 80–99. London: Routledge.

Tucker, F. (2003). 'Sameness or difference? Exploring girls' use of recreational spaces'. *Children's Geographies*, 1(1), 111–24.

Valentine, G. (2003). 'Boundary crossings: Transitions from childhood to adulthood'. *Children's Geographies*, 1(1), 37–52.

9

HERITAGE
Feeling Scottish and Being Muslim: Findings from the Colourful Heritage Project

Omar Shaikh and Stefano Bonino

INTRODUCTION

The Colourful Heritage Project (CHP) is the first community heritage-focused charitable initiative in Scotland aiming to preserve and to celebrate the contributions of early South Asian and Muslim migrants to Scotland. It has successfully collated a considerable number of oral stories to create an online video archive, providing first-hand accounts of the personal journeys and emotions of the arrival of the earliest generation of these migrants in Scotland and highlighting the inspiring lessons that can be learnt from them.

The CHP's aims are first to capture these stories, second to celebrate the community's achievements, and third to inspire present and future South Asian, Muslim and Scottish generations. It is a community-led charitable project that has been actively documenting a collection of inspirational stories and personal accounts, uniquely told by the protagonists themselves, describing at first hand their stories and adventures. These range all the way from the time of partition itself to resettling in Pakistan, and then to their final accounts of arriving in Scotland. The video footage enables the public to see their facial expressions, feel their emotions and hear their voices, creating poignant memories of these great men and women, and helping to gain a better understanding of the South Asian and Muslim community's earliest days in Scotland.

The website contains nearly seventy oral stories, captured with digital media as short films, all easily accessible and available to view online at www.colourfulheritage.com. No other such project or data sample exists in Scotland. The interviews encompass men and women, the English, Urdu and Punjabi languages, and people from all different walks of life, covering Glasgow, Edinburgh and Dundee. These stories have been preserved for current and future generations of Scottish Asians and anyone else who has an interest in the evolution of the Scottish Muslim community.

In addition, the CHP, together with Glasgow Life, has launched a dedicated physical archive based at the Mitchell Library in Glasgow. The archive, named after Mr Bashir Maan, a leading political figure in the Scottish South Asian community, contains photographs and documents from as far back as the 1930s. The archive gives many useful insights into the lives of these first brave explorers and the CHP seeks to continue to gather stories, personal accounts, anecdotes and any other documents or photographs that could be added to build the archive further so it achieves its full potential. The archive has also been referenced in the analytical observations relating to hybrid identities, as set out later in this chapter. The core theme of this chapter draws on the oral stories as a form of social-scientific data to reflect on feelings of 'Scottish-ness' and 'Muslim-ness' among the older generation that constitute the data sample.

WHAT MAKES SCOTLAND SPECIAL?

At the outset, it is worth noting some unique characteristics of Scotland's Muslim community that make this analysis different from its equivalent counterpart based on an England-only data set. Indeed, it is very relevant in the current geopolitically tense climate for migrants and the rise in anti-Muslim discrimination.

The Scottish Muslim community has been characterised as being very well organised and visionary (Maan, 2014), as well as better integrated than the English Muslim community (Hussain and Miller, 2006). It has been the first to pioneer many major first-time achievements within the United Kingdom. By way of example, Scotland produced Britain's first Muslim Justice of the Peace in 1968 and Britain's first Muslim elected as a councillor in 1970, in Mr Bashir Maan. Moreover, Scotland has Britain's first Muslim Member of Parliament (MP), Mr Mohammed Sarwar, who was elected in 1997 to represent Glasgow Govan as a Labour candidate and later, in 2013, became Britain's first Governor of the Punjab in Pakistan. The unique story of Mr Mohammed Sarwar is narrated in his recently published autobiography (Sarwar, 2016). The growing political participation of Muslims in Scottish politics is further demonstrated by the positions held by Member of the Scottish Parliament (MSP) Humza Yousaf, as junior minister in the Scottish Government (currently as Minister for Transport and the Islands and formerly as Minister for Europe and International Development), MSP Anas Sarwar and former MSPs Hanzala Malik and the late Bashir Ahmad (the first ethnic minority MSP, elected in 2007).

Muslims in Scotland have not just made their mark politically, but have also been major contributors to the economic landscape of Scotland in the form of successful entrepreneurship. One such person was Haji Sher Mohammed, who came to Glasgow in 1936, starting as a door-to-door salesman. He was among one of the first members of the Asian community to come to Glasgow and he, along with his brothers and other members of the Sher family, established the Sher Brothers' empire. This consisted of several cash-and-carries, including Scotland's largest, Sher Bros Ltd, at Stromness Street in 1970, as well as Bonnypack and House of Sher. Today the Sher Brothers' empire has successfully diversified and has established itself in all major areas of wholesaling and in 2016 opened Scotland's first Asian shopping mall.

Successful entrepreneurship was also demonstrated by the late Mr Yaqub Ali, owner of the largest Castle cash-and-carry in Europe. In recognition of his distinguished services to trade and industry, he became the proud recipient of an OBE, awarded by the Queen in 1984. He came to Scotland from Pakistan in 1952 as an illiterate nineteen-year-old with only a couple of pounds in his pocket. His success in business helped him to become a millionaire by the early 1980s. Another such entrepreneur is Mr Maqbool Rasool, who created the Global Video empire, the second largest video rental company in the UK, which at its peak had more than 250 stores.

A testimony of the largely positive relationships between Islam and other faiths in Scotland is the memorable event of October 1991: a repentance service for the first Gulf War attended by both Muslims and Christians, held at St Giles' Cathedral in Edinburgh. This is remembered as a unique event and perhaps a first in the history of Christian–Muslim relations within the UK. Muslims performed their prayers next to the altar of the cathedral amidst a Christian congregation of over a thousand, with the call to prayer being made from the pulpit (Maan, 2014). In the words of Bashir Maan, 'such an unprecedented humanitarian gesture could only have happened in Scotland, where tolerance and benevolence in society always exceed expectations' (Maan, 2014: 82).

These successes beg the question, 'Why Scotland?', as Scotland is home to one of the smallest populations of Muslims in the UK, at 1.4% as compared to 4.8% in England and Wales. The Muslim community of Scotland has a distinct combination of factors, such as a relatively smooth settlement, a predominantly self-employed Pakistani section in the community (Maan, 1992, 2008, 2014) and a sense of historical oppression that is shared with the Scottish majority, which enabled these immigrants to produce pioneering political figures and successful entrepreneurs. The following sections explore identity, focusing on Scottish Asian Muslims, and will ultimately seek to analyse some of the reasons why Scotland's influence has been so different from that of England.

'BECOMING' SCOTTISH: THE EXPERIENCE OF EARLY SOUTH ASIAN AND MUSLIM MIGRANTS IN SCOTLAND

This section draws from evidence that has been taken from more than fifty CHP interviews, along with documents and pictures from the 'Bashir Maan' archive. First, the results of the oral interviews are quantified and presented to show how the interviewees responded to questions on identity and self-categorised themselves by extracting key terms revolving around nationality, religion and a hybrid of both. The interviewees' explanation of the sequencing order of their identity is also presented by selected quotes that help to illustrate their mindset, experience and perception of life in Scotland. Second, analysis of historic archive pictures dating back to the 1950s is presented to observe any clothing styles prevalent, as well as clues from other objects present in the pictures to reflect on expressions of identity. Third, analysis of historic archive documents has been undertaken to illustrate the titles and terminology used and identify evolutionary trends in these.

In terms of methodology, the analysis on identity presented in this chapter is unique as it is based on first-hand accounts of how the largest ethnic minority community of Muslims felt when they first migrated to Scotland. They were asked how their perception has changed over the many years, how they have come to accept Scotland as home and how 'feeling Scottish' has evolved through the decades into the new millennium.

Over a period of three years, nearly seventy participants were interviewed, of which fifty-six were selected for relevance to this study. The CHP has aimed to interview a broad sample of men and women representing both first- and second-generation individuals who typically migrated between, respectively, 1947 and 1965, and 1960 and 1979. Different lifestyles and careers have been reflected, not just those of commercially successful individuals, and data from multiple Scottish cities was used, including Glasgow, Edinburgh and Dundee, in order to provide geographical variation, thereby offering more significance to the results. Academic research that has been recently conducted with

Table 9.1 The different generations of Scotland's Muslims

1920s–1947	Early migrants/settlers/pioneers	Mainly Muslims as well as Hindus and Sikhs from pre-partition India
c. 1947–1965	First generation	Those who migrated to the UK from India or Pakistan, of working age and seeking employment, and eventually gained citizenship.
c. 1960s–1970s	Second generation	Those who either came to Britain at a very young age (pre-employment) and gained citizenship or were born to first-generation settlers
c. 1965–1980s	Third generation	Children born in the UK to second-generation parents
1990s–2000 onwards	Fourth generation	Children born in the UK to third-generation parents

third- and fourth-generation Muslims in Scotland (see Bonino, 2015a, 2015b, 2016; Hopkins 2004a, 2004b, 2007) broadly reflects the findings of this chapter.

The characterisation of the various generations used in this chapter is described in Table 9.1.

These timescales are not in continuation of date, but overlap in order to reflect the range of dates of arrival to the UK or dates of birth. For the purposes of this chapter, we examined the complete, unedited interviews, which differ from the edited versions that are available online. The key themes explored during the interviews are migration, entrepreneurship, family life, identity and religion. The term 'Asian' is intermittently used to reflect Pakistani, Bangladeshi and/or Indian ethnicities. However, all interviewees are Muslim, although they may follow different schools of thought and they may practise Islam in different ways.

From the fifty-six interviews conducted, forty relayed answers specifically about identity as follows: twenty-seven out of forty participants (68%) felt that they had a Scottish or 'Scottish hybrid' identity and thirteen out of forty participants (32%) stated an 'other' identity (such as Pakistani or British). The results show a clear indication of 'Scottish' identity emerging in two-thirds of the interviewees who all migrated initially from South Asia mainly from Pakistan and India.

The results from the last Scottish census, held in 2011, showed that, specifically within the Pakistani ethnic group in Scotland, exactly 50% felt a Scottish identity either on its own or coupled with another identity (National Records of Scotland, 2013). Although our sample set is far smaller and focused on the older generation, our results show a higher degree of feeling Scottish. This is by no means an unusual finding; comparative academic research has shown that Scottish Muslims have stronger national sentiments towards Scotland than English Muslims have towards England (Kidd and Jamieson, 2011). Evidence from interviews, pictures and documentary sources further reinforces these findings. Shown below is a general schematic of the types and evolution of identity responses that were given by the 68% of participants who had by now assumed either a 'Scottish hybrid' or simply a 'Scottish' identity.

Pakistani → Pakistani Scottish   → Glaswegian
            Scottish Pakistani   Scottish
            Pakistani Scottish Muslim   Scottish Muslim
            Scottish Pakistani Muslim
            Muslim Pakistani Scottish

From the above identities, it can be seen that the participants mostly used a variety of two or three words in a varying order to self-categorise their 'hybrid' identity. Participants used no single term to define themselves and seem to display dynamic and often multi-layered identities. The layout above also serves to show the evolution of their identity, initially starting with the Pakistani nationality that would have been on their passports, through to a variety of 'Pakistani-Scottish hybrid' identities and further evolving and refining themselves into variants of the 'hybrid Muslim' identity. The evidence is very clear: South Asians' self-expressed identity does not seem to be defined by a single term. It appears to comprise multi-layered ethnic, national and religious affiliations.

From the fifty-six CHP interviews selected, over 90% of participants felt comfortable giving their interviews in the English language, with some even using a Scottish dialect. Most of them told us that they could not speak, read or write the English language at the time of their arrival in the UK. This, in itself, is a testament to the fact that nearly forty years later they have become fluent enough in English to be able to express and communicate their emotions and feelings comfortably in their newly learned tongue, and further evidences linguistic and cultural integration, which is subsequently expressed by a declared 'Scottish hybrid' identity.

By highlighting their hybrid identity, which in some cases includes their ethnic nationality of being Pakistani and/or their religious identity of being Muslim, the interviewees are confirming their affiliation and links to their ethnic heritage and/or religious roots from their parents. In this chapter, we have used the term 'Pakistani' because the majority of the interviewees identified themselves as such. However, they also identify as and 'feel Scottish', which shows the extent to which they are comfortable in Scotland and see it as being their home.

Some participants were quite particular in the sequence of the terms used to describe their identity, followed by various justifications as to why they chose to self-categorise in this manner. A second-generation man who arrived in the Gorbals area of Glasgow at a very young age identifies not just himself but his extended family as being solely 'Scottish', saying:

> We have been here since we were very, very young in school. This is our country and we know more of this country than anywhere else, so anywhere we go, this is home ... I would consider myself and my brothers and sisters and my kids and my grandchildren as Scottish, we will always be Scottish and we are Scottish. This is our home ... The Scottish people, I don't think you can get anywhere. Scottish people, the way they treat foreigners, they accept people here ... And we have been fully accepted. I think our host nation, Scottish people, they are the best.

Similarly, another man who came to the UK at the age of twelve calls himself solely 'Scottish', and goes on to say:

> I consider myself more Scottish than Pakistani as I have lived and spent most of my time here. My kids and grandkids are here. We are all Scottish.

Another prominent businessman who came to England before finally settling in Scotland described himself specifically as a 'Scottish Pakistani'. He went on to quickly justify his identity and, in particular, the specific sequence of it, saying:

> Scottish first, because I have spent most of my life in Scotland, and Pakistani second, because I was born there, therefore I cannot forget my roots.

A man in his early sixties, who was born in Scotland to a Scottish mother and a Pakistani father, also considered himself 'Scottish Pakistani', although for completely different reasons, which he goes on to explain as follows:

> Scottish, as I was born in Scotland and through my Scottish mother, I have her heritage, and at the same time I am Pakistani, due to my Pakistani father and his heritage.

He felt that both identities had an equal weighting, and did not specify a particular order as he enjoys aspects of both countries equally, including family and friends. His views are particularly poignant, as his family was the first Asian family to reside in the tenements in Pollokshields, Glasgow, which today has the highest concentration of Asians in Scotland. He feels loved, welcomed and comfortable with both identities. With this in mind, he went on to say that he had 'never felt like a "fish out of water" in both Scotland or Pakistan'. In terms of integration, he thought that people from an ethnic minority group should try to go that extra mile, perhaps giving a larger tip when in a taxi or at a restaurant, being polite and being helpful to older people. He explained that his Muslim faith teaches him to do this, and it is far from an isolated concept. This attitude also gives out a clear message to Scottish people that different faith groups can live together side by side with considerable engagement.

A woman who migrated to Scotland at primary school age described herself as a 'Scottish Muslim'. She spoke of her school experience, which helped her to develop an understanding of Scotland, and said:

> My identity has never really changed, because for me this is still home. And I believe where you live, you need to love that place, you have to because this place has given me so much, this country has given me so much, right. I know I'm a Muslim.

A professional woman who migrated to Scotland at the age of twenty-five with her husband also described herself as a 'Scottish Muslim'. Originally, she came from India to England in 1965, then to Scotland in 1969, and she went on to describe herself as follows:

> I'm Scottish now, because I'm here more. I came here to this country at the age of twenty-five, now I am seventy-three, so for forty-eight years I am here. I've lived twice of my life in Scotland than in India, so I'm mostly Scottish now, than Indian.

She further described her observations of the English compared with the Scottish people and said:

> We came to Glasgow, we found the people were much more friendly here. We used to travel in train, you know an English man or English person will just newspaper in front of you and keep on reading and won't even notice you, but the Scottish people will chat to you and see where you are going and where you're coming from and what you are doing and everything. Considerable difference between the English and Scottish people.

Another man who arrived in the late 1950s at a very young age identified himself as a 'Muslim Scottish Pakistani'. He went on to specify that he does not feel that he is either British or English, and that being Muslim is his first identity; he gives no particular order and equal weighting to the next two terms in his hybrid identity of being 'Scottish and Pakistani'.

This idea of identity is related to cultural integration within the wider society, which is one of the key factors in these people feeling Scottish. Other factors, such as language barriers, social acceptance, sense of inclusion in a community and, most importantly, job opportunities, have all shaped the integration and identity of South Asian immigrants. The most important factor that they all associate with 'feeling Scottish' is working and integrating well with the Scottish indigenous population. Some Pakistanis were able to do this better, because they had their primary or secondary education in Scotland, while others, once better established in their shops and warehouses, used innovative approaches, such as employing Scots who were then able to earn a living. In turn, the Pakistanis gained security from having a Scottish workforce and managed to engage not only the Pakistani community, but other Scots, as customers. They also used this as an advantage in overcoming any language or dialect problems (Maan, 1992).

Naturally, there were still challenges. One participant recalled:

> I employed a Ghanaian boxer at the shop. People were afraid of him, so there was no trouble in my Maryhill shop.

One participant commented that Pakistanis have added to the Scottish culture and economy by adding 'corner shops' that provide not just a service but employment, and have influenced the Scottish palate by introducing the Scots to South Asian cuisine. He further explained how he felt that there has been a slow and gradual impact on the Scottish environment through the Pakistanis quietly contributing in turn by their positive characteristics and values. He went on to say that Scottish people 'are being influenced by us and in turn teaching us to be good citizens. It's a two-way learning process', and compared it to water seeping under a rug. As such, the first and second generation developed a symbiotic relationship with the indigenous Scottish community. Some even went on to draw parallels between the Scottish and Pakistanis in terms of being 'caring, friendly and having extremely good host qualities'.

In Scotland, the early South Asians either took up jobs that were rejected by the native workforce, or became innovative and created their own peddling jobs (Maan, 1992, 2008). They called at door after door to sell their goods out of a suitcase, thus providing a much-needed and convenient mobile shopping service for the locals. They were given training on a few words and phrases that they could use, with the rest being picked up through interaction with their customers. They would travel far and wide out of Glasgow, often on buses, where they were also exposed to a variety of people from the local Scottish community, unlike their English counterparts who worked in the mills and factories in the Midlands and Yorkshire, often without being exposed to many people other than their fellow workers.

After gaining experience, they moved into jobs within the transport system, starting off as bus conductors and eventually becoming bus drivers. They offered to work all the available overtime and frugally saved up their hard-earned money to fund both their families back home and their domestic aspirations to become their own boss. Eventually, they bought their own shops, transforming these into bigger premises, further expanding into warehouses and cash-and-carries, as well as opening takeaways and restaurants. Thus, the trend of self-employment set by the pioneering pedlars was as strong as ever (Maan, 2014).

Being self-employed presented Scottish Asians with a greater chance to interact confidently with and understand the community in which they were living. This, in turn, enabled them to integrate better into host communities and understand the local customs, while at the same time allowing their own cultural and religious diversity to flourish. With certainty, it can be concluded that the 'Pakistani nationality' with which these people initially associated themselves when they first came to Britain slowly evolved over time to take on the 'Scottish identity'. Perhaps this was initially due to necessity and circumstances but, with the passage of time, self-discovery, greater self-confidence and social acceptance were certainly contributing factors. Other factors may have been place of birth, faith, length of time spent in Scotland and a friendly political system.

These first- and second-generation interviewees, whether they were young or old when they originally came from Pakistan, would have possessed a Pakistani nationality only. In their mind, most of them went to Scotland with a view to work for a few years, make their fortune and then return to their homeland to their loved ones whom they had left behind (Maan, 1992, 2014). However, after working in Scotland for a number of years, followed by their families arriving to settle, they found themselves beginning to integrate better into the Scottish environment. This, in turn, influenced them to settle permanently in Scotland.

Yet heritage has not been completely lost. Several participants stressed the importance of not forgetting their past, where they came from and how they came here. They said that important lessons and lifelong skills and attitudes should be learned from previous generations. One interviewee noted that if you do not remember your past, it is difficult to appreciate the future. The identity of the future generations is also a matter of great importance. One respondent raised concerns of identity among present and future generations. He argued that the youth from minority groups felt that they needed to prove something. They had the drive to promote Scotland and were focused on wanting to achieve things, but he warned that this drive could leave them frustrated if they were not supported in their efforts. He went on to say:

> The identity of the next generation will be a challenge. Most young say 'we are Scots'. This in his words is not identity – this is recognition of nationality, where you live and work, but not identity. Yes, we are Scots but we have a code of conduct in life. Youngsters need to understand identity in the fullest sense. Age makes you find balance between two extremes of identity. Need to live with challenge of living in Scotland.

Another interviewee raised the issue that the vast majority of young people today are confused about their identity and whether they are Muslim, Scottish or Pakistani. He believes that this is due to a failure in our communities, with a lack of positive role models and not enough of a visible presence of Muslim professionals involved in society at a community level for youngsters, who can be inspired by their work, life and religious balance. He went on to say:

> A generation gap, which is an artificially created concept, has been created which is both dangerous and destructive. This gap of misunderstanding creates a vacuum whereby elders don't understand the youth and vice versa. This vacuum has to be bridged.

This vacuum is also encapsulated by the lack of connection with Scotland expressed by thirteen out of forty interviewees (32%) who were specifically asked about their own identity. Out of these thirteen people, four respondents (31%) felt either a 'British' or a 'British hybrid' identity. These respondents identified themselves as British, because they had lived in both England and Scotland, or they had British passports and therefore felt more British. Nine people (62%) identified as 'Pakistani', 'Bangladeshi' or 'Muslim'. These could indicate the struggles of a minority of the community to integrate well into wider society due to language barriers or remote locations of residence, as in the case of people living in Dundee. Further, some of the female participants actively strived to uphold their Pakistani identity among their family unit by continuing to speak Urdu/Punjabi at home as well as following the national dress code after school and at weekends. One respondent (7%) identified as Muslim only.

THE EVOLUTION OF HYBRID IDENTITIES IN HISTORICAL CONTEXT

Another phenomenon that was noticed was the evolution of hybrid identities and the emergence of religious identities. This, of course, is not new and is part of a wider gradual move towards a dual Scottish-Muslim identity that has become more markedly evident among third and fourth generations and has been documented in various pieces of academic research (Bonino, 2015, 2016; Hopkins et al., 2015; Hopkins, 2004a, 2007). Hopkins (2007) pioneered the study of Scottish Muslim identity and, as far back as the early 2000s, started documenting how young Scottish Pakistanis manage to uphold dual Scottish and Muslim identities without any apparent contradiction. This finding also speaks of a slow shift from ethnic to religious identities (Archer, 2001) that can be extended to a large portion of Britain. Already in the early 1990s, research conducted by Knott and Khokher (1993) showed that young Muslim women in Yorkshire demarcated religion and ethnicity. In the same decade, British academic scholarship further captured the emergence of Muslim identities that transcend strict ethno-national boundaries (Jacobson, 1997). The Fourth National Survey of Ethnic Minorities in Britain further strengthened this idea, demonstrating that South Asians in Britain tended to self-identify through religion rather than ethnicity alone (Modood et al., 1997).

In the specific case of the CHP, it was found that: fourteen out of forty (35%) of participants assumed a 'hybrid Muslim' identity (that is, Scottish/Pakistani/Bangladeshi Muslim) while twenty-six out of forty (65%) felt a mono or dual national identity.

The general scheme shown below illustrates the evolution of Muslims' religious identities and demonstrates that the term 'Muslim' is either attached to one or two other national identities or, in one case, is a single identity:

Pakistani → Pakistani Muslim → Scottish Muslim
                Bangladeshi Muslim   Scottish Muslim Pakistani
                                         Scottish Pakistani Muslim
                                         Muslim Pakistani Scottish
                                         British Muslim
                                         Muslim

Overall, the levels of 'feeling Scottish' appear to be on the rise, while ethnic identities seem to be on a downward trend. At the same time, although their religious identity would always have been present, only recently have our interviewees felt confident enough to openly express being a Muslim. This was particularly visible from the clothing and head coverings that the interviewees were wearing during the interviews.

Several pictures collected by the CHP demonstrate that, from as early as 1953 through to 1967, a strong national connection was at the forefront in terms of writing messages on display boards in Urdu, with some hints of clothing worn showing adaptation to wider society. Religion also played a part in early settlement in the form of an Islamic school. Pictures from the archive in 1953 show a group of Pakistani and Indian peddlers gathered outside the warehouse owned by Messrs Tanda and Ashrif to see Mr Ashrif off to Pakistan. All the men are dressed in suits with ties, and even overcoats and hats (Fig. 9.1).

Figure 9.2 from 1959 Pakistan Day celebrations also shows all five Pakistani men wearing suits with ties. At such a nationalistic event, there is no visible Pakistani or religious attire to be seen in any of these photos.

This shows that, upon their arrival, Pakistani migrants adopted the British style of shirts, ties and trousers (CHP interviewee). They would have had to give up their national two-piece dress of long shirt and loose trousers, known as *shalwar kameez*, or a one-piece loose sarong called a *dhotti*, which they all would have been comfortable with and accustomed to in Pakistan. This demonstrates that they had an open- minded, adaptable and proactive attitude and embraced their new British identity.

Figure 9.1 Pedlars gather to wish Mr Ashrif well as he travels back to Pakistan

Figure 9.2 Pakistan Day celebrations, 1959

Figure 9.3 A desire to belong to Britain

A picture of Pakistan Independence Day 1963 shows the Pakistani flag and the British flag hanging in equal reign in the background, with male participants, Pakistani or non-Pakistani, wearing suits with shirts and ties in a British manner, and even the children wearing Western dresses or shorts with shirts and bow ties. There was no sign yet of a specific Scottish identity presence. However, the desire to belong to Britain is visible in both the participants' clothes and the presence of the Union Jack flag at a Glasgow event (Fig. 9.3).

Figure 9.4 Gendered experiences of integration

A picture from the Colourful Heritage 'Bashir Maan' archive of a weekend Islamic School from 1967 shows both the organisers and the visiting Pakistani minister, Abdul Qayyum Khan, wearing suits. Interestingly, even the young boys are wearing suits with shirts and ties, with a few wearing shorts, as opposed to *shalwar kameez* or religious Arabic dress consisting of a long white shirt called a *joba* or *thoub*. However, the young girls all appear to be wearing traditional *shalwar kameez*, pointing to a different integration experience among female members of the community (Fig. 9.4).

Another picture from 1961 shows teachers and organisers holding a blackboard with the words 'Muslim School, Glasgow' written on it, although this is in Urdu, the national language of Pakistan, as opposed to English. As confirmed by one female interviewee, this highlights that the earlier Islamic Schools taught Islam in the national language of Urdu and that these classes were also used by children and teachers to practise their Urdu. It is interesting to note that both adults and children are wearing Western clothing, rather than national or religious dress (Fig. 9.5).

One of the interviewees recalled that, when he was a child, older men wore suits and trousers during the day for work purposes while wearing their traditional dress underneath. Upon arrival at the mosque later in the evening after work, where they would gather socially and to fulfil their religious duties of prayer, they would take off their work clothes, revealing their Pakistani national dress beneath. From both the documents and the pictures as well as comments in interviews, it is evident that, deep down, they were clear in their understanding of being Pakistani. However, in order to fit in with society at large, they

Figure 9.5 Adults and children at the Muslim School, Glasgow, wearing Western clothing

were wary of manifesting this identity in their choice of clothes, keeping up outward appearances by wearing British clothes in their usual daily lives. This is in stark contrast to the present day, when at an Eid gathering at the mosque or in children's Islamic classes, the children and the Imams have a tendency to wear religious costume of the *thoub* (traditionally worn in the Gulf states, thus associated with the dress code of the Prophet Muhammad who was born and lived in present day Saudia Arabia), even more so than the *shalwar kameez* of Pakistan. This demonstrates that the children of the new generation and their teachers are very comfortable in expressing their religious identity through their clothes, perhaps as a result of more acceptance and tolerance of other cultures by the Scottish population and newly found self-confidence.

Yet, historical ties to Pakistan are well encapsulated in the documentary evidence collected by the CHP. Documents from the archive include an invitation to the Pakistan Independence Day celebrations in 1962 (Fig. 9.6). Its title is: 'The Glasgow Pakistan Students Union, The Pakistan Social and Cultural Society and the Moslem Mission (Glasgow).'

The front of the invitation shows two Pakistan flags crossing over one another. No Scottish flag is visible. The first two societies mentioned are clearly Pakistani dominated. The most interesting element is that organisers had invited the Muslim Mission to this celebration, with the event starting with the recitation of the Holy Qur'an. People in 1962 were aware of their religious identity although, as their name is placed at the end of the title, it suggests that the former two societies were the more prominent and dominant at this event. The programme also shows

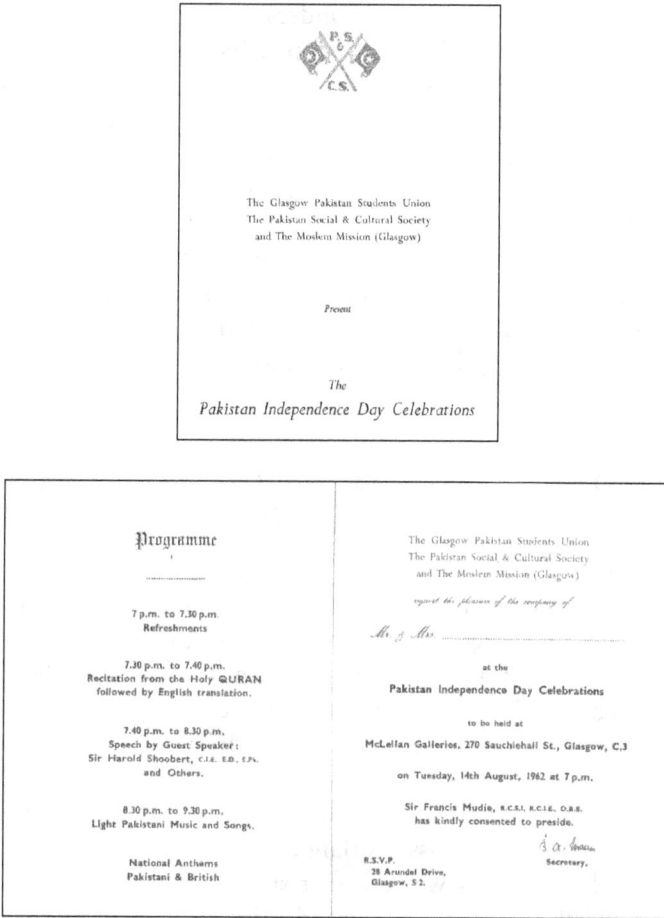

Figure 9.6 Invitation to Pakistan Independence Day celebrations, 1962

both the Pakistani and British anthems being played, as opposed to any Scottish national song.

The recitation of the Holy Qur'an being followed by its English translation so that all present could understand, as well as both anthems being played to finish off the event, is evidence of a gradual integration into wider society. The celebration of Pakistan's Independence Day, on the actual day of Tuesday 14 August itself, is also a testament to their feeling very Pakistani while sitting thousands of miles from their original homeland. Nowadays, such events are rarely celebrated apart from at the Pakistan consulate.

Later, in 1982, the Scottish Pakistani Association (SPA) was formed and actively engaged in promoting and fostering cultural and social activities in order to develop greater understanding between the Pakistani community and all other Scottish people. Its membership was drawn from the Scottish and Pakistani communities in almost equal numbers, with its activities reflecting the cultures of both communities. The name of the association itself, with the word 'Scottish' taking the lead in the name 'Scottish Pakistani Association', demonstrates that the Pakistani community started to take on a Scottish identity and was beginning to feel Scottish. An interesting observation worthy of note is that the Scottish and religious identity among the Pakistani community seemed to be emerging in parallel with the construction of Central Mosque in Glasgow being completed in 1984 and playing an important role in this respect.

VISIBLE TESTAMENTS OF ISLAM IN SCOTLAND: JAMIAT ITTEHAD UL MUSLIMIN AND GLASGOW CENTRAL MOSQUE

When the early migrants from the British Indian subcontinent arrived, before the partition of Pakistan and India, this very small and well-organised community set up the Jamiat ul Muslimin in 1933. This was done by Mr Atta Mohammed Ashrif in Glasgow and sowed the seeds for what has been described as 'perhaps the first unintentional step towards Muslim settlement in Scotland' (Maan, 2014: 26). This later developed into the organisation called Jamiat Ittehad ul Muslimin (the Muslim Mission). To date, it has been a template for the foundation of more than sixty associations across Scotland.

The arrival of families was the first step to settling in Scotland; the next step towards their forming their identity began with the acquisition of a property in Oxford Street in the Gorbals area of Glasgow, which was converted into Scotland's first mosque in 1944–5. Every weekend children would be taught the Qur'an and Islamic studies in Urdu there. This first mosque was set up thanks to donations of £100 each made by seven members of the Jamiat committee. These committee members were not only generous, but also had a sense of responsibility and a strong commitment of faith for the welfare of their growing community. They planted the roots of the presently flourishing Muslim community in Scotland.

Scotland was also the first to pilot a project in the early 1970s involving a Muslim youth movement for the UK Islamic Mission under the supervision of Hanzala Malik, now a retired MSP. The purpose of this youth group was to provide a platform for Muslim youth to learn their religion and engage in positive social activities, including sports. At the time, these fluent English-speaking Muslim youth were struggling to engage with the mosques dominated by Urdu-speaking elders. Its immense success meant that it was then rolled out nationally to other Islamic institutions around Britain known as 'Young Muslims'.

The growth of the Muslim community in Scotland has been gradual, as were the important changes in Muslims' attitudes to settling down and making Scotland their home. A fine example and testament of the faith of the Muslim community within Scotland was the construction of the first purpose-built and magnificent Glasgow Central Mosque (GCM) in 1984. Muslims steadily outgrew their existing places of prayer, progressing from Oxford Street through to Carlton Place, which was generously donated by the late Mr Tufail Shaheen. The GCM finally ended up at the present four-acre site at 1 Mosque Avenue, which was built at a cost of over £3m and was officially opened to the public on 18 May 1984.

At the time, some elders in the community were against the construction of a purpose-built mosque and preferred acquiring and converting another larger building. However, a few of the younger Jamiat committee members put forward their case for a new purpose-built building that would combine traditional Islamic architecture and the large glass panels typical of Scottish public buildings (The Economist, 2015), which future generations could feel proud of. Their wisdom and farsightedness was able to predict the needs of the growing Muslim community in Glasgow. They started with meagre resources, yet they set high ideals such as the construction quality of the GCM, supplementary schools for religious education and the planning of Muslim burial grounds (Maan, 2014).

One respondent described the role that the mosque played in the early days for the Pakistani community, as follows:

> The mosque was a centre point for everyone and it brought people together. Any problems you had, you turned to the mosque, which was controlled by the community leaders, for help and advice and to approach the authorities and help each other.

He went on to talk about the immensity of the achievement and his doubts that it could be repeated by today's generation:

> Glasgow Central Mosque was a major project for the community. If you consider in the level of 2012 GCM is worth £20 million nowadays, and if I think, could the Muslim community collect that kind of money today to build such a mosque? I find it hard to believe that this would be possible nowadays.

The GCM is a symbolic reflection of the identity of the new Scots, and occupies a landmark position in Glasgow in terms of its location being the Gorbals area, where the majority of the Asian Muslims from Pakistan and India initially resided in the early 1930s through to the late 1960s before branching out to the more affluent areas of Pollokshields and the West End. It was there that they lived in substandard conditions while they worked to open their shops and build their warehouses. During the regeneration of this area, the GCM plans were finally approved and the mosque eventually built along the southern banks of the River Clyde, to a scale and design that the Muslims, and indeed all people of Glasgow, are proud of. It has since been expanded, now housing a new bigger community hall for the growing generation. Today, the GCM is the largest mosque in Scotland and can host around 2,500 worshippers.

The increased number of mosques in Scotland demonstrates the religious needs of a community that, over the decades, has collectively embraced Islam and nurtured a strong Muslim identity. Another important sign of the gradual move to a religious rather than strictly ethnic identity among Scottish Muslims is exemplified by the abolition of community Urdu schools, whose roles have slowly been taken over by mosques and community centres with a focus on the Qur'an and Islamic study classes, which are mainly taught in English. Overall, Scotland is generally acknowledged as having a relatively egalitarian society where an awakened Muslim consciousness has the potential to flourish (Bonino, 2015a). The specifics of the Scottish environment are the focus of the next section.

MUSLIMS AND SCOTLAND: A STORY OF INTEGRATION

The relatively positive relationship between the Muslim and non-Muslim communities in Scotland has facilitated the integration of Muslims in society and the process of shaping dual Scottish-Muslim identities. A lack of competing jobs and housing and, in turn, little related hostility from the local population, have helped the community to settle in a comparatively smoother fashion than their English counterparts. Had it not been for these migrants, the Glasgow transport system would have struggled to operate full services. These men's attitude towards hard work ensured that they always remained within a work environment rather than relying on state benefits and becoming a social burden. Since most of them initially rented their homes then bought them outright, they also avoided competition for housing (Maan, 1992, 2008, 2014). The women also adopted a supportive role in caring for the children and running the home. They engaged in integration by assisting in the family business, sharing food and making local friends, and helping older Scottish neighbours (Morrison, 2011).

All these factors helped to promote a positive image of Pakistanis within Scotland, giving them a sense of inclusion, respect and tolerance. Other factors that helped integration in Scotland were having access to education and health, as well as learning the language and cultural knowledge. This came about thanks to interaction on a daily basis with customers while peddling, on buses, in shops, or with other parents and teachers at the children's schools.

The Scottish sociocultural environment has also been posited as being conducive to the integration of minorities. While a lack of Scottish ancestry can still be an obstacle to Muslims' claims to Scottish identity, Scotland nevertheless seems to offer a relatively 'low entry tariff' to national claims of 'Scottishness' and, certainly, a more benign disposition to minorities than England. Whereas being white is identified as a key factor in being English, this is less the case when it comes to having Scottish identity (Bonino, 2016).

Certain Scottish cultural characteristics such as socialising, language, cultural knowledge and having enmity towards the English are often adopted by Scottish Asian Muslims. Nowadays, Muslims and non-Muslims are better integrated than before due to the lack of a language barrier and, from a cultural point of view, both communities enjoy one another's cuisine and accept mixed Eastern and Western clothing.

The Pakistanis were a smaller community in Scotland than in England. The majority of migrants to Scotland, as reflected in the CHP interviewees, were from the Jalandhar and Ludhiana regions within Punjab, or from villages such as Kot around Faisalabad, Pakistan. The fact that they came from nearby villages meant that the people formed a close-knit community and therefore encouraged their friends and relatives to move to Scotland through a special support system that they developed. Punjabis are very sociable and therefore formed good relations with fellow Punjabis, as well as with the indigenous Scottish population. In addition, the Pakistanis in Scotland were not entirely 'segregated' from the rest of the community as a whole and pushed into specific neighbourhoods, as they were in other parts of Britain. In England, ethnic communities are often grouped together within certain areas of a city, such as in Bradford or Rochdale. The majority of Pakistanis in England are from Mirpur in Kashmir and tend to have particularly strong extended family units. This situation has arguably created an unintentional ethnic 'self-segregation', not just from other, non-Mirpuri

Pakistanis but also from the non-Muslim population. These areas are often stigmatised under the Pakistani and Muslim banner by the English and face serious problems of discrimination and racism, as well as unemployment and resultant poverty. In Scotland, Muslims spread out as far north as Stornoway and the Shetland Islands, as well as in and around all the major Scottish cities. With the exception of Govanhill and Pollokshields in Glasgow (National Records of Scotland, 2013), there are no areas largely populated by Muslims, thus demonstrating that the small community has scattered across Scotland and has integrated with the wider non-Muslim society.

Many Muslims view Scotland as a fairly open and porous society that can accommodate diversity (Bonino, 2016). On the whole, Scottish people are perceived to be friendly, sociable and tolerant (Homes et al., 2010). Several interviewees reported that, on their arrival in Scotland, they were helped by bus drivers and taxi drivers who went beyond their normal duty to make sure their newly arrived Pakistani passengers reached their destinations safely.

The anglophobic attitudes of Scottish people may also have been a contributing factor, as Scottish people are more likely to accept 'anyone but the English' (Hussain and Miller, 2006). In Scotland, Muslim minority communities have been given space to express themselves and practise Islam. In 2013 in Aberdeen, St John's Church allowed the Muslim community to use their chapel up to five times a day due to the overcrowding of the nearby mosque at *Jumu'ah* (Friday) prayers. This was the only place in the UK where followers of both Islam and Christianity shared a religious place of worship. With both religions working together and with such special relationships forming, this can serve as a model for both faiths for the future.

While both discrimination against Muslims in the country (Bonino, 2015b, 2016; Hopkins 2004a, 2004b; Hopkins and Smith, 2008) and the deep involvement of Scotland in the British Empire (Devine, 2012) have been well documented, Scotland is perceived to be less Islamophobic than England (Hussain and Miller, 2006). The proposed explanations are factors related to the settlement and development of Muslim communities in Scotland, specific features of Scottish geography, and social as well as political attitudes towards diversity. The smaller Muslim population in Scotland is composed of many Pakistani self-employed businessmen and entrepreneurs (National Records of Scotland, 2013) compared to Muslims in England who are more often unskilled labourers. The higher employment rates among Pakistanis in Scotland (Weedon et al., 2013), compared to Pakistanis in some English regions, have helped too. Moreover, it is important to note that Islamophobia is 'much more closely tied to English nationalism within England than Scottish nationalism within Scotland' (Hussain and Miller, 2006: 65).

Scotland is a country where freedom of expression is valued and multiculturalism has been promoted through the Scottish Government's political manifesto in 2007 of 'One Scotland, many cultures' (today known as 'One Scotland'). This campaign had a very clear message, with advertisements showing the words 'racism' and 'discrimination' appearing in graffiti style on a blue painted wall, sprayed over by a large white cross. This was a very powerful image sending out an important message to the nation. Along with the Scottish Government's Race Equality Statement, published in 2008, this shows a commitment to improving the evidence base regarding issues of race, faith, equality and discrimination, to assist with policy development at both national and local level. In turn, this helps to understand and respond to the needs of the people of Scotland. The political reaction of the then Scottish First Minister, Alex Salmond, on the day after the 2007 Glasgow airport attack, is particularly striking. Mr Salmond proceeded to Glasgow Central Mosque to stand alongside Scottish Muslims to make his statement to condemn the attack and give the firm message that this was not representative of Scotland's Muslim community.

More recently, in 2015, the Scottish Government welcomed nearly one-third of Britain's total number of Syrian refugees, which testifies to the work of the special taskforce that was set up, along with local authorities and other organisations (Addley and Pidd, 2016). Careful preparations for their arrival were made months in advance to help them to settle and feel welcome in Scotland. It is this attitude that has made Muslims feel safer and more appreciated in Scotland, and has helped them to feel like one of the threads in the tartan fabric of Scottish society.

The first Asian Muslim MSP for the Scottish National Party (SNP) in Holyrood was the late Mr Bashir Ahmed, who was elected in 2007. He wanted to see Scotland as an independent country, as 'he could see the potential of this country'. He took it upon himself to setup 'Scots Asians for Independence' in the 1990s. This event was significant, as the Asian community makes a considerable, positive contribution to the Scottish economy, yet there was no Asian representation until that point in the Holyrood Parliament. Mr Ahmed arrived at the Scottish Parliament wearing his traditional Pakistani *shalwar kameez* and *sherwani* overcoat, rather than his suit and tie, to take his oath before being sworn into the Scottish Parliament. His son, Dr Atif Bashir, said of him:

A wonderful example of how one can actually integrate into a community or into a society that you don't come from, but still maintain your identity from the previous one. So often people think it's one or the other, but actually it can be both and it was very much both. He then took the oath in Urdu first of all, and then he took the oath in English.

He went on to say, of his father's legacy: 'My father would often say, "It does not matter where you come from, what matters is where we are going as a nation", and also described how a Scottish Asian person should 'add value to Scotland, embrace it and want to make this country a better place'. The 2014 independence referendum was very important to the majority of the population, with nearly 85% of the nation voting. It managed to engage and excite both young and old across a diverse range of backgrounds. Traditional Labour Party Muslim voters appeared to be swinging to the SNP after what was seen as Labour's decision to go to war in Iraq in 2003. The foreign policy of Westminster remains a concern to many people in Scotland, particularly ethnic minorities, and independence is arguably seen as a solution to it under a relatively pacifist SNP government. A survey of sixty-four people conducted in the year of the referendum by Scotland's leading Asian radio station, Awaaz FM, in Glasgow, showed that two-thirds of respondents voted 'Yes' and a third voted 'No' on independence (Duffy, 2014). While such a small sample is by no means representative of the wider community, there is anecdotal evidence that Scottish Muslims may advocate independence at higher levels than non-Muslim Scots (Hussain and Miller, 2006; The Economist, 2009). Overall, it demonstrates that Muslims have taken a keen interest in the political future of Scotland, evidencing a sense of belonging to the country that has evolved and strengthened since the pioneers started settling in Scotland.

CONCLUSION

Various factors have influenced participants of the CHP in how they feel both Muslim and Scottish as part of their multi-faceted hybrid identity. These factors also help to explain why the experience for Scotland's minorities is so markedly different and why this small community of migrants achieved so much and have so many 'firsts' to their name. In today's world, the two major, yet very distinct, challenges that face European governments relate to: (1) dealing with migrants, integrating existing minority communities and addressing anti-Muslim discrimination, often fuelled by far-right politics; and (2) tackling domestic and international religious extremism.

Scotland, relative to its European counterparts, has navigated the above challenges with success. There are lessons for both migrant communities and host societies to be learned from the people of Scotland. Many of these can be gleaned from the life experiences of CHP interviewees.

Muslims in Scotland have flourished and prospered, due not only to their hard- working, innovative and adaptable qualities but also to the positive social and political atmosphere in Scotland, which was reflected in the voting pattern of the Brexit referendum and in the country's largely pro-European Union stance. This positive atmosphere has allowed Muslims to grow and progress and to confidently identify as both Scottish and Muslim in their everyday life experiences.

ACKNOWLEDGEMENTS

The CHP would like to thank Dr Saqib Razzaq for her support in the writing of this chapter. The contribution of Dr Stefano Bonino is limited to co-authoring this chapter and does not extend to the wider work conducted by the CHP.

REFERENCES

Addley, E. and Pidd, H. (2016). 'Scotland has taken in more than a third of all UK's Syrian refugees'. *The Guardian*, 27 May, available at www.the guardian.com/world/2016/may/27/scotland-welcomes-third-of-uk-syrian-refugees-resettlement

Archer, L. (2001). '"Muslim brothers, black lads, traditional Asians": British Muslim young men's constructions of race, religion and masculinity'. *Feminism and Psychology*, 11(1), 79–105.

Bonino, S. (2015a). 'Scottish Muslims through a decade of change: Wounded by the stigma, healed by Islam, rescued by Scotland'. *Scottish Affairs*, 24(1), 78–105.

Bonino, S. (2015b). 'Visible Muslimness: Between discrimination and integration'. *Patterns of Prejudice*, 49(4), 367–91.

Bonino, S. (2016). *Muslims in Scotland: The Making of Community in a Post-9/11 World*. Edinburgh: Edinburgh University Press.

Devine, T. (2012). *The Scottish Nation: A Modern History*. London: Penguin.

Duffy, J. (2014). '"I may be Muslim but I identify myself as Scottish": The indyref battle for the Scottish Asian vote'. *Herald Scotland*, 16 February, available at www.heraldscotland.com/news/13145999._I_may_be_Muslim_but_I_identify_myself_as_Scottish___the_indyref_battle_for_the_Scottish_Asian_vote

The Economist (2009). 'Islam in tartan'. *The Economist*, 7 May, available at www.economist.com/node/ 13611699

The Economist (2015), 'The thistle and the crescent'. *The Economist*, 15 August, available at www.economist.com/news/britain/21661000-muslims-seem-happier-identify-scottish-english-thistle-and-crescent?zid=315andah=e e087c5cc3198fc82970cd65083f5281

Homes, A., McLean, C. and Murray, L. (2010). *Muslim Integration in Scotland*. Edinburgh: Ipsos Mori.

Hopkins, P. (2004a). 'Everyday racism in Scotland: A case study of East Pollokshields'. *Scottish Affairs*, 49(Autumn), 88–103.

Hopkins, P. (2004b). 'Young Muslim men in Scotland: Inclusions and exclusions'. *Children's Geographies*, 2(2), 257–72.

Hopkins, P. (2007). '"Blue squares", "proper" Muslims and transnational networks: Narratives of national and religious identities amongst young Muslim men living in Scotland'. *Ethnicities*, 7(1), 61–81.

Hopkins, P., Botterill, K., Sanghera, G. and Arshad, R. (2015). *Faith, Ethnicity, Place: Young People's Everyday Geopolitics in Scotland*. Newcastle-upon-Tyne: Newcastle University.

Hopkins, P. and Smith, S. (2008). 'Scaling segregation: Racialising fear'. In R. Pain and S. Smith (eds), *Fear: Critical Geopolitics and Everyday Life*, pp. 103–16. Aldershot: Ashgate.

Hussain, A. and Miller, W. (2006). *Multicultural Nationalism: Islamophobia, Anglophobia, and Devolution*, Oxford: Oxford University Press.

Jacobson, J. (1997). 'Perceptions of Britishness'. *Nations and Nationalism*, 3(2), 181–99.

Kidd, S. and Jamieson, L. (2011). *Experiences of Muslims Living in Scotland*. Edinburgh: Scottish Executive.

Knott, K. and Khokher, S. (1993). 'Religious and ethnic identity among young Muslim women in Bradford'. *New Community*, 19(4), 593–610.

Maan, B. (1992). *The New Scots: The Story of Asians in Scotland*. Edinburgh: John Donald.

Maan, B. (2008). *The Thistle and the Crescent*. Glendaruel: Argyll Publishing.

Maan, B. (2014). *Muslims in Scotland*. Glendaruel: Argyll Publishing.

Modood, T., Berthoud, R., Lakey, J., Nazroo, J., Smith, P, Virdee, S. and Beishon, S. (1997). *The 4th National Survey of Ethnic Minorities in Britain: Diversity and Disadvantage*. London: Policy Studies Institute.

Morrison, S. (2011). *She Settles in the Shields: Untold Stories of Migrant Women in Pollokshields*. Glasgow: Glasgow Women's Library.

National Records of Scotland (2013). *2011 Census: Key Results on Population, Ethnicity, Identity, Language, Religion, Health, Housing and Accommodation in Scotland – Release 2A*. Edinburgh: National Records of Scotland.

Palmer, M. and Nigel, P. (2000). *The Spiritual Traveler: England, Scotland, Wales. The guide to Sacred Sites and Pilgrim Routes in Britain*. Mahwah, NJ: Hidden Spring.

Sarwar, M. (2016). *My Remarkable Journey: The Autobiography of Britain's First Muslim MP*. Edinburgh: Birlinn.

Weedon, E., Riddell, S., McCluskey, G. and Konstantoni, K. (2013). *Muslim Families' Educational Experiences in England and Scotland*. Edinburgh: University of Edinburgh, Centre for Research in Education Inclusion and Diversity.

10

MULTICULTURALISM
Multiculturalism and Scotland:
'Bringing the Outside into the Middle'

Nasar Meer

INTRODUCTION

The purpose of this chapter is to locate the discussion about Muslims in Scotland in relation to questions of national identity and multicultural citizenship. While the former has certainly been a prominent feature of public and policy debate, the latter has largely been overshadowed by constitutional questions raised by devolution and the referenda on independence. This means that, while we have undoubtedly progressed since MacEwen (1980) characterised the treatment of 'race-relations' in Scotland as a matter either of 'ignorance or apathy', the issue of where ethnic, racial and religious minorities rest in the contemporary landscape remains unsettled.

One of the core arguments of this chapter is that these issues are all interrelated, and that the present and future status of Muslims in Scotland is tied up with wider debates about the 'national question'. Hitherto, however, study of national identity in Scotland has often (though not always) been discussed in relation to the national identities of England, Wales and Britain as a whole. In this respect, national identity debates in Scotland have not predominantly been about how Muslim and other non-Christian religious minorities might remake common membership. As such we do not really know whether – in the late Stuart Hall's terms – Scotland has 're-written the margin into the centre, bringing the outside into the middle' (Hall, 2005: 31). This is an unfortunate omission that this collection will help to redress. One of the conclusions of this chapter is that Muslims, as the largest non-Christian minority, can help to remake not only Scottish identities but also the identity of Scotland.

To explore this we need to take a step back and consider what the 'national question' comprises, in order that the rest of this collection can squarely focus on the contemporary status of Muslims in Scotland.

SCOTLAND, 'SUB-STATE' NATIONALISM AND MULTICULTURALISM

It is common to refer to Scotland as a 'stateless nation' (or, in David McCrone's term (2002), an 'understated' nation). Since the 1707 Acts of Union moved the Parliament to Westminster, Scotland has not had a sovereign or centralised administrative bureaucracy. This union, however, was only ever partial in that 'it did not take away from Scotland any of the major institutions of civic life' (Patterson, 2000: 46). It did not dissolve civil society, or the independence of the Church of Scotland, systems of law, education or local governance. It was, instead, 'an amalgamation of Parliaments ... not an absorption of Scotland into England' (ibid.) (cf. Pittock, 2012: 13). This is why the characterisation of Scotland as a 'stateless nation' was always more contentious than might be implied. In either case, through processes of legal and political devolution facilitated through the Scotland Act (1998), which re-established a Scottish parliament, 'after almost 300 years [it] means that Scotland is no longer stateless' (McCrone, 2001: 1).

This begins to explain why citizenship in Scotland has typically been studied through a focus on multi-level governance, constitutional devolution and federalism, rather than identity and belonging, religious or otherwise. The tension relevant for this chapter concerns how this can relate to multiculturalist perspectives. The latter, though understood differently across varying contexts, has more broadly been focused on the accommodation and integration of migrant and post-migrant groups, typically termed 'ethnic minorities'. To confuse matters, multiculturalism has also taken in multinational questions; for instance, multiculturalist Canada focused from the outset on constitutional and land issues, too. We might therefore summarise that multiculturalism can simultaneously describe the political accommodation by the state and/or a dominant group of all minority cultures, defined first and foremost by reference to race or ethnicity and, additionally but more controversially, by reference to other group-defining characteristics such as nationality, aboriginality or, latterly, religion (Modood and Meer, 2013: 113).

As a set of political positions, the tension *between* sub-state nations and multiculturalism turns on how, 'for minority nations, the sustainability of their projects in the context of growing immigration depends on immigrants making a conscious choice to affiliate themselves with that national project' (Kymlicka, 2011: 294). Some try to overcome the tension by stating that multinational and multicultural perspectives can be mutually reinforcing, with each perspective contesting notions of monocultural nation-states, and encouraging cultural minority for- mation 'linking these to social equality and protection from discrimi- nation' (Castles, 2000: 5). Thus, several accounts understand the two approaches as co-constituting, insofar as one creates space for the other (Crick, 2008, 2009); perhaps this is illustrated in Britain by the ways in which 'present immigrant minorities easily fit into ... the diversity of its four nations' (Parekh, 2009: 37). Yet, in a number of cases, these perspectives have not come together as predicted or have come to imply problematic hierarchies within federal settlements where established *nations* set the terms of inclusion for more recent *ethnic minorities* (Foweraker and Landman, 2000).

Signalling a revision of an earlier hypothesis, that multinationalism and multiculturalism would indeed come together, Kymlicka (2011: 289) has recognised that 'countries with an inherited ethos of accom- modation in relation to old minorities are *not predestined to be inclusive of new minorities* – there is no inherent tendency for the former to spill over to the latter' (emphasis added). Indeed, he continues, in many cases we are finding that 'practices of multinational citizenship are privileged over, and preclude, the fair inclusion of immigrants' (ibid.).

Is Scotland a possible exception to Kymlicka's reading? While undoubtedly affected by the 'advancing and receding tides of British multiculturalism' (Hussain and Miller, 2006: 31), what remains under- explored from a multiculturalist perspective is 'the extent to which eth- nicity continues to shape their own view of Scottish nationalism and national identity' (Mycock, 2012: 65). Even though questions of mul- tinationalism and multiculturalism in Scotland 'have managed to fire past each other' (McCrone, 2002: 304), there is a prevailing assump- tion that a 'civic' and inclusive 'big tent' national identity is a prevailing aspiration (Keating, 2009; cf. Hepburn and Rosie, 2014).

Yet it remains to be ascertained where newer religious minorities might come to rest in debates about nationalist politics, identity and contemporary nationhood more broadly. It has been argued that this may result from the comparatively smaller presence of such groups in Scotland, or that such minorities have not become politicised in a manner comparable to England (McCrone, 2001: 171), and certainly that they have not been racialised in the same way (Miles, 1986). Since 'all civic and democratic cultures are inevitably embedded into specific ethno-national and religious histories' (Bader, 2005: 169), however,

Scotland cannot rely on the view that, in merely promoting itself as 'impeccably civic' (Keating, 2009: 217), it will be able to secure a future in which such minorities are included.

Bridging literatures on migration-related minority 'difference' (i.e., multiculturalism) with those concerning nationalism and drawing on primary research interviews with Scottish politicians from across the spectrum, this chapter elaborates on the ways in which ideas of a Scottish nationhood are being configured according to various agendas. These include multicultural citizenship, specifically equality and non-discrimination, existing church settlements, prevailing notions of 'civic' participation and inclusion, and implicit norms of 'legitimate' and 'illegitimate' religious minority claims-making, among other things. Before proceeding, however, a fuller methodological rationale needs to be set out, and this is what we turn to next.

WHY POLITICAL ELITES IN SCOTLAND?

It is said that, since devolution, 'a distinct Scottish political class has emerged, with its own career trajectory separate from the UK one' (Keating and Cairney, 2006: 56). Interestingly, in their study Keating and Cairney find that this does not so much mark a radical break with what has gone before; rather, 'devolution has accelerated the trend towards professional middle-class leadership' (ibid.). Leith and Soule (2012), too, explore the emergence of an elite political class in Scotland. They observe, for example, that while elite political actors 'present an inclusive sense of identity that is not predicated on any sense of birth, ethnicity or history' (ibid.: 148), this contrasts with the mass perception which conceives the 'Scottish nation as having much firmer and more distinct boundaries in terms of membership' (ibid.: 149).

The nature and extent of this possible divergence is explored further below. What is important to register here is that, with the exception of these few accounts, the study of elite political actors in Scotland is relatively sparse, but is otherwise consistent with a broader tendency in which social and political scientists 'too rarely "study up"' (Ostrander, 1995: 133). There are important methodological reasons for this, not least obstacles centring on researcher access, yet the notion that elites matter is commonplace within the social and political sciences, and insofar as 'their undeniable influence' warrants consideration (Leith and Soule, 2012: 122), empirical inquiry might draw on at least two rich veins of literature in democratic theory (Plamenatz, 1973) and nationalism studies (Gellner, 1983). While neither is a perfect fit, we might search for an idea of institutional opportunities among those typically associated with behaviourist traditions; something that flourished for a period in North American political sociology. This saw both Dahl's (1961) *Who Governs?* and Mill's *The Power Elite* employ methods that focused on the behaviour of a relatively small number of actors in particular political situations. While these authors profoundly disagreed in their understanding and analyses of political systems, they had in common the view that 'the politically active elites in a modern democracy are … only the tip of what appears in national parliaments' (Goodwin, 1987: 226). The wider body of elites in their account was populated by 'politics facilitating occupations' (King, 1980, quoted in Keating and Cairney, 2006: 45). These elites include journalists, lobbyists, barristers and financiers, among others, and are precisely some of those who emerge in more diffuse conceptions envisaged in the nationalism studies literature, some of which maintains that 'cultures and politics are forged by small minorities, usually by one kind of elites or other' (Smith, 2008: 6). Were we to assess the normative premises of such views, we would inevitably encounter a dense literature elaborating the continuing disputes over the creation of nations, national identities and their relationship to each other, as well as to non-rational 'intuitive' and 'emotional' pulls of ancestries and cultures, and so forth. Chief among these are whether or not 'nations' are social and political formations that developed in the proliferation of modern states from the seventeenth and eighteenth centuries onwards, or whether they are tied to historical formations – or 'core ethnies' – bearing an older pedigree that may be obscured by a modernist focus.

These tensions are relevant because, while the current focus is a more future- oriented one, 'the debris of history [remains] a source of building materials for discretionary construction by current history making entrepreneurs' (Hussain and Miller, 2006: 121). Indeed, we know that 'elites in Scotland are … trying to harness an already significant level of national attachment' (Leith and Soule, 2012: 122), and we are precisely interested in the ways in which some political elites are imagining Scottish nationhood vis-à-vis ethnic and racial minorities. Here, Leith and Soule (2012: 121–2) take the view that political elites in Scotland 'invite the masses into history' (Nairn, 1997: 340), and they maintain that elites do so in a language that connects elite and mass ideas of what the 'nation' is. 'In contemporary Scotland', they continue, 'everyday politics is a situation of contending elites who seek to construct a specific sense of national identity' (Leith and Soule, 2012: 121–2).

It is important, however, not to overstate this, for we should reject the assumption that national identities in Scotland are marshalled in a purely party-political fashion. McCrone and Bechhofer (2010) have repeatedly established that there is no linear relationship (running in either direction) between self-identification as Scottish and an aspiration for greater national self-determination (either in terms of constitutional arrangements for greater devolution or, indeed, independence). Hence, if 'one does the survey equivalent of hitting people over the head with a blunt instrument and forces them to choose just one national identity' (Bechhofer and McCrone, 2009: 9), it still remains the case that we encounter only a 'weak' association between national identity and devolution, a tendency that remains true of those deemed 'exclusive Scots' (who self-define as Scottish, not British). These findings are reiterated in Bond and Rosie's (2010) conclusion that, although the prioritisations of one or other national identities can be related to likely electoral choices, the tendency is one of a 'non-alignment' (ibid.: 96).

We might further add that, since the Scottish Nationalist Party (SNP) has been in power, the appeal of full independence has not prevailed. Of course, this was no longer a theoretical question. The SNP's victory allowed it to honour its manifesto pledge to negotiate with Westminster to hold an independence referendum. This took place on 18 September 2014 and showed that electoral support (expressed in voting patterns) for the SNP was not matched by support for the constitutional independence of Scotland. With an electoral turnout of nearly 85% (the highest in any election in the UK since the 1950s), over 55% voted against independence. While post-referendum analyses are still being undertaken, a Lord Ashcroft opinion poll carried out on 18 and 19 September is useful indicator of preferences. What is especially relevant for our discussion is that, with a sample of over 2,000 respondents, it showed that 20% of SNP supporters were unlikely to vote for independence. This reiterates why we should avoid the category error of trying either to equate Scottish nationalism with – or principally understand it through – the premier nationalist party. Moreover, the campaign in favour of independence has had the support of another party represented in the Scottish Parliament, the Scottish Greens, as well as all of the independent members (the late Margo MacDonald, Jean Urquhart, John Finnie and Bill Walker).

While this is not to deny that 'nationalists are [most] successful when they capture the "nation" for their own political project' (McCrone, 2001: 177), in the case of Scotland it does not need to be about independence alone. It is precisely because political elites of all hues are reaching for some ownership of nationalism in Scotland that the topic is especially interesting (the unionist parties in Scotland are thus named *Scottish* Labour, *Scottish* Conservatives, *Scottish* Liberal Democrats and so on). The tendency, of course, is to assume that the independents are the only nationalists, and so to ignore how all have appropriated the nation and configure Scottishness to their respective policy projects.

In the next sections, I outline three political themes that emerge from the interview data with Scottish MSPs. In total, twenty-one interviews were undertaken with members of the Scottish Parliament (out of a possible 129 members), between March and November 2012 in their Parliamentary offices in Holyrood. As outlined in Table 10.1, a gender balance was sought and achieved for the two parties with the largest number of Parliamentarians: four male and four female each for the SNP and Scottish Labour, out of a total number of sixty-five and thirty-seven respectively. This was less successful with the two Conservative respondents (two males out of a possible fifteen), two male Liberal Democrat respondents (out of a possible five) and one Green respondent (out of a possible two) (here the gender of the interviewee is not cited, as it would easily identify the respondent since there is a single male and a single female Scottish Green Party representative in the Scottish Parliament) (see Table 10.1).

As a sample, the number of interviewees are just short of a fifth, and an additional set of interviews (eleven in total) was conducted with journalists, civil society actors and intellectuals deemed to be in 'politics-facilitating occupations' (King, 1980, quoted in Keating and Cairney, 2006: 45). The latter were especially instructive during the early stages of the research, and the discussion here is principally focused on the parliamentary elites who remain understudied in the literature on minorities and nationhood in Scotland. It is important to bear in mind that these are not intended to be a statistically representative number, but instead a

Table 10.1 Interview participants by political party and gender

Political Party	Male	Female	Total
Scottish Labour Party	4	4	8
Scottish National Party	4	4	8
Scottish Conservative Party	2	1	3
Scottish Liberal Democrats	2	0	2
Scottish Green Party	*	*	1
Total	12	9	22

* For reasons of confidentiality, the gender of the one Green Party supporter has not been specified.

Table 10.2 Interview participants by 'political facilitating occupations' and gender

Occupation	Male	Female	Total
Academic	2	1	3
Civil servant	1	1	2
Civil society actor	1	2	3
Journalist	2	1	3
Total	6	5	11

meaningful inclusion of people who have featured in debates about and/ or are relevant to the topic more broadly (see Table 10.2).

AN ASPIRATIONAL PLURALISM

The historian Tom Devine has proposed that we can understand the incremental self-confidence expressed by political elites in Scotland as an 'aspirational nationalism' (quoted in Goursoyanni, 2012: 63). This, he allies to a broader social transformation and cultural renaissance that has accompanied both devolution and the shift to a service-based economy. A key question for our discussion is whether this also includes an aspiration for pluralism. Here, there is evidence of a consensus across unionists and nationalists that a project of diverse nation building is underway. Below are four expressions of this, two from unionist (Scottish Labour and Scottish Liberal Democrats) and two from nationalist (Scottish National Party and Scottish Greens) parliamentarians. Two frames are especially evident. The first gains purchase from Scotland's historical multinational diversity and is expressed in the following two quotations:

> If you're in Scotland, or you're in Wales, you know, it's abundantly clear. Because you're in a small part of Britain, the smaller nations within Britain, it's very clear that Britain is a union of nations. It's inherently a multinational, multi-ethnic, multilingual, multicultural entity. It can't be anything else. (Scottish Green Party MSP [H1])

> If you read down through Scotland's history we have a fairly, I think, proud tradition of assimilating waves of different groups in a way that has sustained a population in many communities. And I think that's led to a far more diverse and vibrant and interesting cultural mix ... (Scottish Liberal Democrat MSP [M1])

The second frame is more active insofar as Scottish nationalism, it is claimed by both nationalist and unionist political elites, has been cast in an inclusive mould, not least by these MSP's respective parties:

> I suppose, without patting ourselves on the back too much, this is to the credit of the Scottish Parliament. And, I mean, I say Labour and SNP, I'm not actually saying that the other parties have dissented from this, but they dominate Scottish politics to such an extent that it's what they do that's been decisive in these areas. So, you know, that probably sounds a bit complacent, but I do think that we've had a more positive record than, you know, both Labour and Conservative in England. (Scottish Labour Party MSP [T1])

> So, we've captured nationalism and made it something positive, and made it civic, so that's been, you know, eight decades worth of work. It doesn't happen overnight ... If you don't have this alternative nationalism, national movement, national political party that a nationalist might be civic, then the EDLs [English Defence League] of the world, and the BNPs [British National Party] and the National Fronts, they fill that void ... (Scottish National Party MSP [E1])

Each testimony illustrates the nebulous ways in which elite political actors understand the function of nationhood. Beginning with the first, to place Scotland's diversity within a historical register of multinationalism assumes that this has served as a sort of prophylactic against exclusivity. This is a hypothesis that can be partially tested. Surveying the attitudes of Scottish majorities to claims-making by minorities on nationhood in Scotland, McCrone and Bechhofer (2010: 922, 937) point to a small but consistent 'ethnic penalty' that reveals itself as *marginally* more in Scotland than in England, such that 'Scottish' is possibly more likely to equate to 'being White'. As they discuss, residence in Scotland is deemed a weak claim on national identity, but when markers such as accent are added, 'between 50 per cent and 60 per cent of people accept the claim, but introducing parentage, which implies a blood link, produces a further big increase in acceptance' (McCrone and Bechhofer, 2010: 937). What should we make of this? It certainly challenges the prevalent view among political elites that 'there's not a sort of idea among Scottish people that you have to be White and, you know, in order to be Scottish' (Conservative MSP [P2]).

While the marginally higher rejection rates towards non-White in Scotland than in England is concerning, the authors argue that it is important not to exceptionalise Scottish attitudes for, while they are slightly more exclusionary than English attitudes, they are not radically so. Interestingly, in their follow-up study, Bechhofer and McCrone

(2012: 1364) found a closer pattern between England and Scotland when they looked to see whether national identity 'discriminates in terms of *judging claims*', something statistically affected by levels of education or and age. Either way, these findings need to be understood alongside ways in which minorities in Scotland are more likely than their counterparts in England to appropriate hyphenating self-defined identity categories, for instance Scottish-Pakistani. This is a well-established trend that political elites sometimes bring in to support their view that Scottishness is an open identity. One respondent describes this in the following terms:

> there's something in that Scottishness, and a separate Scottish identity, or nationalism [that] is not about choosing one identity over the other, and maybe identity can be multi-layered, can be fluid, and can exist cohesively, rather than be juxtaposed, and constantly in conflict with one another. (SNP MSP [A1])

This is a well-established trend in self-identification, our understanding of which was profoundly deepened in Hussain and Miller's (2006: 168) work. The latter observe that '[b]ecause spatial [territorial] identities are not the primary identities for a majority of [Scottish] Pakistanis; they find it easier to adopt a Scottish identity'. Just as Scottish identities change over time, so do Muslim identities.

As Bonino (2016) has recently shown quite clearly, what has emerged alongside 'religious' Muslim identities in Scotland are political 'associational' national identities, where increasing self-identification of Muslims in Scotland *as Muslims* reflects a story of socialisation in Scotland. This is a sociological dynamic that is not unique to Scotland and was first shown by Knott and Khokher (1993) in how young Muslim women in Yorkshire drew a distinction between 'religion' and 'ethnicity' in rejecting their parents' subscription to traditions that the young women thought were less consistent with the aspirations of those young people themselves. Jacobson (1997) later referred to this development as a 'religion-ethnic culture distinction' and contrasted it with a 'religion-ethnic origin distinction'. While the former involves a perception of identity in terms of one's attachment to a place, the latter point to one's identity as a Muslim in a manner that denotes belonging to a global community, which transcends ethnic boundaries. The striking observation is that, in Scotland, this includes national identities, too. Other, smaller-scale studies open up lines of inquiry that broadly show continuities in this trajectory, which is partly why McCrone and Bechhofer (2010: 926) have argued that 'being Scottish may be thought of as an inclusive club with a low entry tariff', a kind of '"big tent" Scottishness' where 'every-one living in the country has a claim'. The important aspect here is the subjective confidence and willingness among minorities to stake such a claim.

What, however, of the second view that political elites have *actively* steered Scottish nationhood in a more inclusive direction, what Reicher and Hopkins (2001: 92) quote one SNP Member of Parliament as naming: 'a *tartan* in which so many different, brightly coloured parts of the whole merge together as a pattern'? We might here point to political speeches; for instance, Alex Salmond has previously stated, and subsequently reinforced, that 'Scotland is not Quebec ... the lin-guistic and ethnic basis [of Quebec] nationalism is a two-edged sword ... we [in Scotland] follow that path of civic nationalism' (Salmond, 1995, quoted in Brubaker, 2004: 135). Or we might highlight policy references, not to 'Scottish people' but to 'all the people of Scotland'. Indeed, the White Paper *Scotland's Future* (2013), which set out the Scottish Government's case for independence, insists that 'a commit-ment to multicultural Scotland will be a cornerstone of the nation on independence' (ibid.: 271).

In many respects, what is most interesting is that this is a self-conscious goal among political elites, because it distinguishes Scotland from com-parable autonomy-seeking nations. Of course, there is an instrumental political logic at play, insofar as political elites 'have a powerful incen-tive to recruit immigrants to their national projects, both to disprove charges of ethnic exclusion and to build internal consensus' (Kymlicka, 2011: 294). This would seem self-evident. 'Better in terms of *realpolitik* to draw the boundary around as many as possible; better to have them inside the tent than out of it if one was trying to govern the kingdom' (McCrone, 2001: 178). Yet some other minority nations have shown a marked inability among elite political actors to overcome this. As one puts it:

> If you live and work in Scotland, you're a Scot, and if you want to be ...
> You need to want to be part of it. We can't bully people into being Scottish
> if they don't want to be, you know? (SNP MSP [L1])

Scottish political elites therefore express their nationalism as a 'politi-cal' and not 'social' matter, and certainly not as a matter of blood and soil. While the distinction between 'civic' and 'ethnic' nationalism has already been identified as problematic, it makes sense that the late Bashir Ahmed, Scotland's first ethnic minority MSP, could confidently state: 'it isn't important where you come from, what matters is where we are going together as a nation' (quoted in Salmond, 2009). Either way, historical experience self-evidently casts a shadow over contemporary expressions of nationhood in nearly all cases, and it is to this in relation to Scotland that we now turn.

EXPEDITIONARY PROTEOPHILIA

Scottish political elites frequently invoke experiences of empire, allied but also parallel to the history of Scotland as an emigrant-sending nation in their discussion of pluralism. The relevant question for our discussion is how these narratives are assembled. Tom Devine, for example, has complained that 'between 1936 and 2003, there was no academic analysis of Scotland's role in the British Empire' (quoted in Goursoyanni, 2012: 61). As a consequence, he maintains, Scottish public discourse has 'suffered from amnesia on that' (ibid.: 61). This a view shared by a prominent intellectual, who points to 'victimhood works' that have created a 'chip on the shoulder, you know, Scotland as victim ... because the nation's history was not really taught in schools, or at least [not] until very recently' (Academic [K1]).

In putting it in these terms, the respondent is making the significant point that the Scottish story, just like the British one, is 'bursting with skeletons' (Marquand, 2009). Throughout various cycles of British expansionism, the sons and daughters of Scotland made up its military and civilian ranks in copious number. Devine (2003: 251) has set himself the task of elaborating how, in the most profitable parts of the East Indian Trading Company, roughly half of the accountants and officer cadets were Scottish. In the words of the third Earl of Rosebery, this relationship 'Scotticised India and orientalised Scotland' (quoted in Devine, 2010: 126). Indeed, from the middle of the nineteenth century, the British Raj system was created under a Scottish Governor (General James Dalhousie), while elsewhere the Scot Charles James Napier effectively annexed the Sind province (a large part of modern Pakistan). By the mid-nineteenth century, when one in ten of the British population was Scottish, one-third to a quarter of the civil service elite grade of the East India Company was Scottish. '[A]s late as 1928, the Chief of the Imperial and Indian General Staffs were both Scots' (Pittock, 2008: 9), while the hymns of war 'Scotland the Brave' and later 'Flower of Scotland' were appropriated as popular national anthems (McCrone, 2001: 158).

What is especially interesting for our discussion is the tension that Mycock (2010: 351) describes over the ways in which 'national narratives must remain largely positive and not dwell on the imperial sins of the past'. How, then, is Scotland's role in the empire, and the historical impact this has had upon various interconnected spheres, negotiated by Scottish elites? One prevailing trope is what we could describe as an *expeditionary proteophilia* – by this, I mean an appetite for diversity born of searching it out over the centuries. This is demonstrated in the following two quotations from unionist and nationalist political actors respectively:

> I mean, we've always been an outward looking society; Scots have traditionally had no inhibitions about setting forth usually to the, kind of, wettest, windiest parts of the world ... The Hudson Bay Company exploration, North West Passage, the Antarctic Whaling Fleet, none of those would have happened or been sustained without Orcadians very much in the mix. I think the more outward- looking you are, the more prepared you are to go out and experience different cultures and societies; the more receptive probably your community is to that reverse process. (Liberal Democrat MSP [O1])

> Scottish people have a recognition of their part in the British Empire, and that when you have been part of an Empire, and part of the Commonwealth as well, that you are part of a world society, and that you have a responsibility for history. So we don't see people, certainly not in the biggest population which would be the Pakistani population, we don't see them as being different to us other than, you know, they're all part of the Commonwealth. (SNP MSP [Q1])

It is evident that each focuses on the positive inheritance of empire, much as Mycock predicts, yet it is also intriguing to note that neither unionist nor nationalist MSP refuses ownership of empire. There is, moreover, a persistently ambiguous tendency for recalling empire and decolonisation in Scottish politics, for it is something that taps into a sociological contradiction. This is reported by Hussain and Miller (2006: 16), in that it is common to hear Scottish ethnic minorities maintain that 'Scots understand colonialism – from their past history they understand what ethnic minorities feel'. It is reminiscent of the late Bernie Grant MP, one of the first ethnic minority candidates elected to the post-war Parliament, who insisted that he would refer to himself as British because 'it includes other oppressed peoples, like the Welsh or the Scots. It would stick in my throat to call myself English' (quoted in Paxman, 1999: 74). Yet the ambiguities of recalling empire are so multiform that they can service the argument of the SNP's Angus Robertson MP (2010: 22), who uses a post-colonial framing in arguing that

> there was a time when Australia, Canada, Ireland, and United States were all run from London. They are all now wealthier per person than the

economically centralised UK. And none of these nations would let London decide what is best for them today.

In this reading, *partners* in empire become the *objects* of empire.

It is a tension that has not gone unnoticed among critics who complain that 'nationalists declare themselves victims of colonialism, conveniently forgetting how many of them strutted around the colonies barking orders at the natives and relishing their sundowners' (Alibhai-Brown, 2002: 45). So there is certainly something in how empire 'complicates post-colonial dimensions of secessionist nationalist discourses' (Mycock, 2010: 350), specifically in highlighting a 'common imperial experience' (ibid.: 350). What is especially interesting is how this can harness imperial history to make a pro-immigration account:

> Do we want to be part of the world? Absolutely. Is our outlook international? Yes, it should be. That's very much, I think, Britain's approach to these things too. Good gosh, you can't have Britain's history and not be that. So why have very restrictive immigration policies in that, particularly in that kind of area? (Liberal Democrat [R1])

In different ways, then, such readings are competing to select 'from all that has gone before that which is distinctive, "truly ours", and thereby to mark out a unique, shared destiny' (Smith, 1998: 43). While this is in part a historical activity, it has observable contemporary implications, and it is to this that we now turn.

BOUNDARIES FOR INTEGRATION

Kymlicka (2011: 284) has argued that multinational settlements are often 'provisional' in their accommodation of ethnic minority claims, and suggests that there is often a dissonance between the reasonable aspiration of minorities and the degree of willing accommodation by states. There is a tangible expression of this tension in Scotland. Political elites frequently point to a number of boundaries for ensuring integration and pursuing unity. Two examples include the question of multilingualism and multi-faithism. Taking the issue of language first, the national languages of Scotland include Scottish Gaelic, of which there are approximately 60,000 speakers and which has seen important advances in its recognition. This includes the Gaelic Language (Scotland) Act 2005 which created the *Bòrd na Gàidhlig*, a body charged with 'securing the status of the Gaelic language as an official language of Scotland commanding equal respect to the English language'. Among other rationales put forward is that 'Gaelic is ... an element of Scottishness because it's not spoken anywhere else' (Academic [U1]). Despite this recognition, it is clear that, in contrast to other nations, 'the language tariff which people have to pay to be "Scots" has been low to the point of non-existent' (McCrone, 2001: 177), and so allows Scottish nationalism to be more than 'protecting a cultural past under threat' (ibid.: 50, cf. Bechhofer and McCrone, 2014). Yet when the question is raised of bringing other languages into the fold, which are more frequently spoken and appear to be taking on distinctive Scottish forms in terms of content and dialect, there is a consensus among respondents that Scottish Urdu and Scottish Punjabi could not warrant a status as one of Scotland's national languages. A typical summation, one that actually shares much with nationalist responses, is put forward by a Conservative MSP:

> Gaelic has a privileged position because of the heritage and the desire to preserve the culture and the language so it's always going to get special treatment. As far as the rest is concerned I, by and large, think that we should be looking to integrate. Let's not get into this situation where there are sectioned-off communities who can't communicate with people outwith their own immediate society, I think that's very dangerous. (Conservative MSP [V1])

In this assessment, historical multilingualism is a feature of the national identity, whereas migrant languages are potentially, but not necessarily, fragmentary. This does not need to be illustrated further, as there was a consistency (though softer language was used by other respondents). Whether or not political elites favoured or opposed the recognition of Gaelic (some respondents argued it was *a* and not *the* national language), there was a view that recognising further languages could be divisive. Of course this is precisely what some authors argue will leave minorities feeling 'left out [when] the majority understand the polity as an expression of their nation, or agreed purpose, whatever it may be' (Taylor, 2001: 123).

A more charged illustration, however, concerns the prospects for religious pluralism, especially corporate recognition, anything up to how 'the Irish Catholics secured various gains as part of a settlement' (Academic [U1]). The settlement being referred to emerges through a period of Catholic emancipation in Scotland, most clearly symbolised by the restoration in 1878 of the hierarchy of the Catholic Church in Scotland (McCrone, 2001). A synopsis of responses are quoted here, centring on the issue of parity for the state funding of faith schools to minority religions, in addition to Protestant and Catholic groups. While at a general level, the question did ask specifically about Muslim school-ing, and in this respect the answers are striking :

> That's a bit of a controversial topic, actually. I personally don't think it's a great thing ... I just don't think they're particularly helpful in this day and age. (SNP MSP [A1])

> I think the scars of the, kind of, sectarian divide we've had are there and probably more of the focus of attention in terms of things that we need to resolve. (Liberal Democrat MSP [R1])

> I think it would be extremely depressing to think that in fifty or sixty years' time, Muslims were no more integrated than that. There remain serious problems in terms of sectarianism and attitudes and prejudices against the Catholic community and between the Catholic community and what you might call Protestants, but if we repeated those mistakes in terms of other ethnic groups and other religions, I think that would be very depressing. (Green [H1])

> But I'm not keen on that, you know ... I still don't like too much separation because I think you need to respect each other while talking to each other and being engaged with each other, so I suppose in that sense I'm not really an enthusiast for Catholic schools, but yet I'm not going to stand up and try and abolish them because ... (Labour [U1])

There are some very good reasons to be cautious about seeking to mirror one religious settlement in the present with something from the past, and it must be stressed that all respondents were positive (often very positive) about the fact of religious pluralism in Scotland. What is interesting in these responses, however, is how each frames the question of formally recognising religious pluralism – as opposed to the fact of religious pluralism at large – within a register of sectarianism. There is a lively debate over the form and scale of sectarianism in Scotland (Raab and Holligan, 2012), but in most instances this has centred on enmity and discrimination between Scottish Protestants and Scottish Catholics, something that has given rise to recent Government initiatives through legislation, such as the Offensive Behaviour at Football and Threatening Communications (Scotland) Act 2012.

The danger is that newer religious minorities being asked to integrate into existing configurations reproduces certain hierarchies, something recognised by Hussain and Miller's (2006) observation that 'faith-based schooling has many critics, but they [critics] are at once reluctant to dis-mantle the existing system of Catholic schools yet reluctant to set up a system of Muslim schools'. The clear danger for newer religious minority claims-making, such as Muslim parents seeking Muslim schools, is that it is framed by political elites within a register of historical sectarianism, rather than according to its own dynamics. The latter would preferably occur within a 'democratic discourse, which makes explicit the grounds on which proposals are linked to identities and hence opens up space for debate and alternatives' (Reicher et al., 2005: 636). In many respects, then, this returns to tension between multinationalism and multiculturalism discussed at the outset, insofar as there is a danger that the sustainability of minority national projects in conditions of ethnic diversity places the two diversities into a hierarchy that is limiting for the latter.

CONCLUSION

Ernest Barker (1948: 14) once insisted that 'nations [have] long dreamt for their national unity in some common fund of religious ideas'. Linda Colley's (1992: 362) characterisation of an earlier Britain as 'a protestant Israel' and Geoff Levey's (2009) reminder that despite its wall of separation, the US has always remained 'One Nation Under God' are both well-known affirmations of Barker's earlier observation. Going further, in his *Chosen People: Anglo-American Myths and Reality*, Longley (2002: 10) insists that 'we are never going to reach the bottom of issues of national identity until we delve into the religious dimension and give it its proper weight'.

In this chapter, we have considered how elite political actors are locating minorities within projects of nation building under conditions of multinationalism and multiculturalism. Taken together, it shows how these actors can play a vital role in ensuring that appeals to nationhood in Scotland can be meaningfully calibrated to include minorities too. At a time when all Scottish political parties are jockeying over a vision for the nation, the chapter uses original empirical data to show the emergence of the three predominant clusters: an aspirational pluralism; a multiform appropriation of empire; and potential limitations in minority claims-making and recognition. While it is certainly the case, as Kymlicka (2011: 289) recognises, that 'countries with an inherited ethos of accommodation in relation to old minorities are not predestined to be inclusive of new minorities', Scotland is not a textbook expression of this. Not only is the tension less stark than in some other cases, but what is especially interesting is that there is also a strong and unambiguous trend not only among majorities, but among ethnic minorities, in identifying themselves with the nation (either as Scottish only, or Scottish-British, or Scottish plus something else). The question that this leaves unanswered is whether it revises how Scottish identity is imagined by the majority, too, something that points to a gap between the official identity of Scotland as a nation and people's Scottish national identities.

ACKNOWLEDGEMENTS

This chapter draws on materials from Meer, N. (2015) 'Looking up in Scotland? Multinationalism, multiculturalism and political elites', *Ethnic and Racial Studies*, 38(9), 1477–96. I gratefully acknowledge Routledge in allowing me to reproduce these here.

REFERENCES

Alibhai-Brown, Y. (2002). 'The excluded majority: What about the English?' In P. Griffith and M. Leanard (eds), *Reclaiming Britishness*. London: Foreign Policy Centre.

Bader, V. (2005). 'Ethnic and religious state neutrality: Utopia or myth'. In H. G. Sicakkan and Y. Lithman (eds), *Changing the Basis of Citizenship in the Modern State*. Lewiston, NY: Edwin Mellen.

Bechhofer, F. and McCrone, D. (2009). 'Stating the obvious: Ten truths about national identity'. *Scottish Affairs*, 67, 7–22.

Bechhofer, F. and McCrone, D. (2012). 'Changing claims in context: National identity revisited'. *Ethnic and Racial Studies*, 37(8), 1350–70.

Bechhofer, F. and McCrone, D. (2014). 'What makes a Gael? Identity, language and ancestry in the Scottish *Gàidhealtachd*'. *Identities*, 21(2), 113–33.

Bond, R., and Rosie, M. (2010). 'National identities and attitudes to constitutional change in post-devolution UK: a four territories comparison'. *Regional and Federal Studies* 20(1): 83–105.

Bonino, S. (2016). *Muslims in Scotland: The Making of a Community after 9/11*. Edinburgh: Edinburgh University Press.

Brubaker, R. (2004). 'Beyond "identity"'. In R. Brubaker (ed.), *Ethnicity Without Groups*. Cambridge, MA: Harvard University Press.

Castles, S. (2000). *Ethnicity and Globalization: From Migrant Worker to Transnational Citizen*. London: Sage.

Colley, L. (1992). *Britons*. New Haven, CT: Yale University Press.

Crick, B. (2008). 'Four nations: interrelations'. *Political Quarterly*, 79, 71–9.

Crick, B. (2009). 'Do we really need Britannia?' *Political Quarterly*, 78, 149–58.

Dahl, R. H. (1961). *Who Governs?: Democracy and Power in an American City*. New Haven, CT: Yale University Press.

Foweraker, J. and Landman, T. (2000). *Citizenship Rights and Social Movements*. Oxford: Oxford University Press.

Gellner, E. (1983). *Nations and Nationalism*. Oxford: Blackwell.

Goodwin, B. (1987). *Using Political Ideas*. Chichester: John Wiley.

Goursoyanni, P. (2012). 'An historical moment'. *Holyrood*, Summer, 61–4.

Hall, S. (2005). 'Whose heritage? Un-settling "the heritage", re-imagining the post-nation'. In J. Littler and R. Naidoo (eds), *The Politics of Heritage: The Legacies of Race*. London: Routledge.

Hepburn, E. and Rosie, M. (2014). 'Immigration, nationalism and politics in Scotland'. In E. Hepburn and R. Zapata-Barrero (eds), *The Politics of Immigration in Multilevel States*. Basingstoke: Palgrave Macmillan.

Hussain, A. and Miller, W. (2006). *Multicultural Nationalism*. Oxford: Oxford University Press.

Jacobson, J. (1997). 'Perceptions of Britishness'. *Nations and Nationalism*, 3(2), 165–79.

Keating, M. (2009). 'Nationalist movements in a comparative perspective'. In G. Hassan (ed.), *The Modern SNP: From Protest to Power*. Edinburgh: Edinburgh University Press.

Keating, M. and Cairney, P. (2006). 'A new elite? Politicians and civil servants in Scotland after devolution'. *Parliamentary Affairs*, 59(1), 43–59.

Knott, K. and Khokher, S. (1993). 'Religious and ethnic identity among young Muslim women in Bradford'. *New Community*, 19, 593–610.

Kymlicka, W. (2011). 'Multicultural citizenship within multination states'. *Ethnicities*, 11(3), 281–302.

Leith, M. S. and Soule, D. P. J. (2012). *Political Discourse and National Identity in Scotland*. Edinburgh: Edinburgh University Press.

Longley, C. (2002). *Chosen People: Anglo-American Myth and Reality*. London: Hodder and Stoughton.

Marquand, D. (2009). '"Bursting with skeletons" – Britishness after Empire'. In A. Gamble and T. Wright (eds), *Britishness – Perspectives on the British Question*. Chichester: Wiley-Blackwell.

MacEwen, M. (1980). 'Race relations in Scotland: Ignorance or apathy?' *Journal of Ethnic and Migration Studies*, 8(3), 266–74.

McCrone, D. (2001). *Understanding Scotland*. London: Routledge.

McCrone, D. (2002). 'Who do you say you are?' *Ethnicities*, 2(3), 301–20.

McCrone, D. and Bechhofer, F. (2010). 'Claiming national identity'. *Ethnic and Racial Studies*, 33(6), 421–98.

Modood, T. and Meer, N. (2013). 'Multiculturalism'. In *The Oxford Companion to Comparative Politics*. Oxford: Oxford University Press.

Mycock, A. (2010). 'British citizenship and the legacy of Empire'. *Parliamentary Affairs*, 63(2), 339–55.

Mycock, A. (2012). 'SNP, identity and citizenship: Re-imaging state and nation'. *National Identities*, 14(1), 53–69.

Ostrander, S. (1995). 'Surely you're not in this just to be helpful: Access, rapport, and interviews on three studies of elites'. In R. Hertz and J. Imber (eds), *Studying Elites Using Qualitative Methods*. Thousand Oaks, CA: Sage.

Parekh, B. (2009). 'Being British'. In A. Gamble and T. Wright (eds), *Britishness: Perspectives on the British Question*. Oxford: Blackwell.

Patterson, L. (2000). 'Scottish democracy and Scottish utopias'. *Scottish Affairs*, 33, 45–61.

Paxman, J. (1999). *The English: Portrait of a People*. London: Penguin.

Peleg, I. (2007). *Democratizing the Hegemonic State*. Cambridge: Cambridge University Press.

Pittock, M. (2008). *The Road to Independence*. London: Reakton.

Pittock, M. (2012). 'Scottish sovereignty and the union of 1707: Then and now'. *National Identities*, 14(1), 11–21.

Plamenatz, J. (1973). *Democracy and Illusion: An Examination of Certain Aspects of Modern Democratic Theory*. New Haven, CT: Prentice Hall.

Raab, G. and Holligan, C. (2012). 'Sectarianism: Myth or social reality?' *Ethnic and Racial Studies*, 35(11), 1934–54.

Reicher, S. D. and Hopkins, N. (2001). *Self and Nation*. London: Sage.

Reicher, S. D., Hopkins, N., Levine, M. and Rath, R. (2005). 'Entrepreneurs of hate and entrepreneurs of solidarity: social identity as a basis for mass communication'. *International Review of the Red Cross*, 87: 621–37.

Robertson, A. (2010). *Why Vote SNP*. London: Biteback Publishing.

Shirin, R. M. (2000). *International Perspective on Gender and Governance*. Basingstoke: Palgrave Macmillan.

Smith, A. D. (1998). *Nationalism and Modernism: A Critical Survey of Recent Theories of Nations and Nationalism*. London: Routledge.

Smith, A. D. (2008). *The Cultural Foundations of Nations*. Oxford: Blackwell.

Taylor, C. (2001). 'Multiculturalism and political identity'. *Ethnicities*, 1, 122–8.

11

MEDIA
Muslim Engagement with the Mainstream Media in a Scottish Context

Michael B. Munnik

INTRODUCTION

Muslims are a subsidiary concern for religion reporting in Scotland's news media. If journalists must cover religion, issues pertaining to Christian sectarianism still occupy a central focus, although, as more Scots identify with no religion, news reports take on a memorialising tone, marking religion's decline. Sometimes these storylines merge, as was the case with the biggest religion story in the news during my research about Muslims and the news media in Scotland: the revelation of the sexual abuse of several priests by Cardinal Keith O'Brien (Deveney, 2013). The dominant Scottish story overall was the preparation for the referendum on independence. Muslims played a humble part in coverage of the second story and no part at all in the first.

Muslims are not ignored by the Scottish media, however. The relationship is characterised by a kind of benign neglect. By this, I do not mean that Muslims are neglected by the media in a way that allows them to flourish through a lack of interference. Journalists often report 'bad news' (Glasgow University Media Group, 1976), and being off the front page or the evening line-up certainly means that fewer bad things are said about you. In that sense, as the adage goes, no news is good news. But to be neglected by the media is not necessarily a positive or helpful state: scholars note the pervasive presence of media in our modern world – a presence sometimes described as 'mediatisation' (Hjavard, 2013; Deacon and Stanyer, 2014). At a conceptual level, the priorities of the media can leak into other fields. In a more practical sense, coverage in the media can help your organisation achieve its goals, and publicity carries currency – Pierre Bourdieu (1986) uses the term 'capital' to describe not only economic but social and cultural qualities that can be usefully converted into specific advantages. In this sense, the fact of being someone whom journalists turn to for information for the news confers social capital on the person or the institution that becomes a source. Taken together, we can say that if you are not 'in' the media, then you are not 'in' society in a particular and important way. Nick Couldry (2012) takes this further, talking of the 'hidden injuries' of media representation, by which people determine themselves powerless before an all-encompassing media world. In this sense, to be neglected by the news media, even if it means they are not saying bad things about you, is not necessarily a good thing.

If there is neglect, there is also a benign approach. The vociferous hostility toward Muslims that scholars and lay observers have identified in some elements of the British press is quite muted in media organisations based in Scotland that serve an exclusively or primarily Scottish audience. Politically and socially, Muslims fare relatively well north of the Scottish/English border (Miles and Dunlop, 1986; Hussain and Miller, 2006; Meer, 2015), and this extends to their encounters with the news media. Perhaps, then, it is not so much benign neglect as benign and neglectful coverage that Muslims receive.

I should immediately qualify this reflection, which is not derived from hard statistics: there is no qualitative or quantitative content study of religion in general, or Islam in particular, as covered in the Scottish media. Scotland is notionally bundled with the UK as a whole but, given that major news studies tend to focus on the national press based in London, their geographic and social pertinence for the nation is limited (Law, 2001; Rosie et al., 2004). To the extent that the Scottish news media are singled out for analysis, such treatment concerns Scotland's regional or national distinctiveness in relation to the UK (Hetherington, 1989; MacInnes, 1992, 1993; though, for a concrete study of political reporting in isolation, see Schlesinger et al., 2001). Religion is not examined directly in Neil Blain and David Hutchison's volume *The Media in Scotland* (2008), though Anthea Irwin's chapter on race and ethnicity (Irwin, 2008) discusses stories that might also be characterised as 'Muslim' stories.

In lieu of concrete, quantitative studies of Scottish news content, we must determine the relation of Muslims to the media in Scotland by other means. Media studies can be roughly broken down into three areas of focus: production, content and reception (Philo, 2007). The first examines news workers and news organisations, considering the conditions in which journalism is constructed. These studies can also include the transmission of information from source groups. These studies tend to be qualitative and ethnographic. Content studies, as referred to above, examine news texts themselves. Such studies can be quantitative, counting frequencies of terms or ideas, or qualitative, interpreting the meaning that certain words and frames might convey. Reception studies turn to audiences, asking or intuiting what people think of the news that they encounter and what effect it might have on their opinions and decisions. An interesting example of such a study in a Scottish context is from a team of Edinburgh researchers comparing claims of national identity with the choice of whether to read British or Scottish newspapers (Kiely et al., 2006). Greg Philo, part of the original Glasgow University Media Group and, since 1980, the group's research director, says that the most effective studies encompass all three foci, though he acknowledges this to be 'a complex task' (Philo, 2007: 195).

From August 2012 to March 2014, I examined the relationships of journalists and Muslim sources in Glasgow to observe some of their interactions and understand their conceptions of each other. As such, it was a production study focused on a specific issue. The bulk of the study consisted of thirty semi-structured interviews with a purposive sample of journalists and sources who either identify as Muslim or have contributed to coverage of Muslims; the sample can be notionally divided in two, with twelve news workers and eighteen news sources, though the boundary between these categories is porous. I also conducted observation in both newsroom and source group settings, analysed relevant documents and incorporated in a reflexive manner my prior experience as a journalist in Ottawa, Canada, building relationships with Muslim communities in that city (Munnik, 2015). These are the sources of my data; they provide an insight into Muslims and media relations in Scotland that can initiate further reflection. A purpose-built 'Scotland-only' content study would be welcome in terms of providing numbers, but is not necessary in order to achieve a sense of the interpenetration of these communities.

SCOTLAND'S MEDIA AND RELIGIOUS LANDSCAPE

I have described Muslims as a subsidiary concern for the Scottish media – a comment that I intend with reference to reporting on religion. Scotland is, historically, a Christian nation, and a specifically Presbyterian one, though Callum Brown declares that 'religious Scotland was dead' by the last decade of the twentieth century (Brown, 1997: 2). Steve Sutcliffe, examining religious identities in a recently devolved Scotland, writes of a 'post-Presbyterian culture' (2004: 99). Nonetheless, the residue of

Presbyterianism and its entanglement with Catholicism still holds some purchase on the Scottish imagination, and the news media are one site that nurtures this. Scholars of Scottish religion and culture doubt that Christian sectarianism is as salient a social force as journalists would suggest (Bruce et al., 2004; Rosie, 2004); even they concede, however, that it remains a media fixation, and this chimed with responses from participants in my study. Often, the frame of reference that journalists used for understanding how religion worked, such as its authority structure, was a Christian one.

Sutcliffe writes that the post-Presbyterian Scotland occupies a 'liminal space' in which 'no one group commands sufficient support across the Scottish population to define a national identity' (2004: 89). Among the groups staking a claim on Scotland's religious landscape are Muslims: he suggests that Muslim communities supply 'cultural and ethnological resistance to the popular market' version of Scottishness, and, five years into a politically devolved Scotland, he foresaw that 'the possibility of joint mobilisation on selected moral issues with other such minorities ... is likely to grow rather than diminish as the Parliament beds in' (2004: 91). The 'minorities' that Sutcliffe intended in his comment were ethnic (which should not be so easily conflated with 'Muslim'), but we saw alliances with what one could term a religious majority when Muslim groups and individuals aligned with Catholic and evangelical groups to campaign against equal marriage legislation. This common purpose was noted in the news (BBC Scotland, 2013; Duffy, 2013). Sutcliffe imagined Muslims as a force on 'selected moral issues', but this limitation overlooks ways in which Scottish Muslims have contributed to justice issues, such as airport profiling (Naysmith, 2015; Smith, 2012; cf. Blackwood et al., 2013), in which they have also served as a catalyst for wider group interests.

The question of where to position Muslims in Scotland – as a religious group, as a minority religious group, in relation to ethnic groups – shows the slipperiness with which the term is applied. In wider examinations of Muslims in society, scholars have grappled with the like-for-like sensible comparison that restricts Islam to religious matters on the one hand, and a recognition that social lives are not so neatly compartmentalised on the other. This is so for religious subjects *tout court*, but it is acutely so for Muslims. It is in recognition of this that Nasar Meer designates 'Muslim' as a 'quasi-ethnic sociological formation' that encompasses, but is not limited by, religious qualities (2008: 66). What this means for a discussion of Muslims in the media is that religion ought not to be the exclusive frame through which such coverage is represented.

JOURNALISTS – THEIR KNOWLEDGE OF MUSLIMS

Journalists in my sample exhibited some tension in describing when they applied the label 'Muslim' to sources and stories. Some emphatically stated that they would prefer not to use the word in their news copy unless the story pertained to religious affairs. What counted as religious, of course, was largely determined through their familiarity with the mechanics of Christianity, tempered by an expectation of increasing privatisation of religion in a secular public sphere. Nonetheless, and in keeping with the broader frame that I endorse above, many of the story ideas we discussed are what I classify as ethnic or social in focus rather than religious. For example, the story of a group of 'Asian businessmen' buying a local cinema has little to recommend itself as a 'Muslim' story, but the fact that Sue, a journalist, mentioned it in our interview reveals the associations that she makes about the 'Asian' community (this is a pseudonym, and all names are replaced by pseudonyms throughout the chapter). The idea of terrorism, as a more salient example, is so strongly associated in the news with Muslims (Said, 1997) that they are hard to decouple, nor is it a straightforward task to delimit terrorism from an association with religion. On this point, however, journalists were quick to disturb the association of Muslims with terrorism without any prompting from my questions.

The journalists whom I spoke with showed a general goodwill to Muslims and a curiosity about what might make Muslims in Scotland particular and unique. None of them were 'out to get' Muslims, in either a professional or a personal capacity. They demonstrated familiarity through their usage of terms and concepts associated with Islam. For example, Abigail, a broadcast journalist, showed a nuanced understanding of *fatwa* – first, that it was a legal ruling rather than simply a 'death sentence', as some journalists imagine (Vultee, 2006), and, second, that it can be contested: another jurist might issue a competing ruling, and lay Muslims may or may not adhere to the *fatwa* for a variety of reasons. Derrick, another broadcast journalist, articulated a desire to clarify terms, saying that the word 'Muslim' on its own was often insufficient to locate the subject properly, making it vulnerable to various associations. Other descriptors might be required, such as 'Shia' or 'Sunni' to indicate the sectarian orientation, or qualifying phrases such as 'an extremist branch of', which align the subject with political trends. Scholars have noted the harmful effects of associating the word 'extremist' with 'Muslims' in media or other public discourses (e.g., Moore et al., 2008; Nickels et al., 2012; Baker et al., 2013), but Derrick defended the practice, saying it demonstrated diversity by implying that not all Muslims shared such views or endorsed such activities. He was less supportive of the term 'Islamist': he said that it sounded too much like 'Islamish', and therefore the activity or the subject cleaved too closely to Islam as a whole; moreover, he said that there was little consensus among journalists about what the word actually meant and so it was vague and slippery, and prone to misuse by journalists and misunderstanding by audiences.

This desire to distinguish subjects and be precise with descriptors connects to the journalistic value of accuracy. However, other elements of journalistic practice can work against such fine-tuning, including conventions of language, ideological leanings and the collective nature of journalism. Ivor Shapiro (2009) notes a strong emphasis on style and presentation in evaluating journalism, which balances against qualities such as rigour in reporting. News favours writing that is clear, simple, expressive and free of jargon. News workers also face practical challenges specific to each medium: of space (for print); time (for broadcast); and available images (for television). Satisfying these requirements can interfere with the impulse to be as specific as possible about the subject of coverage. Cumbersome phrases that specify which particular Muslims the journalist means, the ways in which they differentiate themselves or their claims to be either representative or not representative of Muslims can be smoothed into easy but less precise terms. Finally, house styles, or the preferred stylistic choices of particular news organisations, can direct word choice, trumping the desires of individual journalists. For example, a journalist, after talking with several sources, may prefer to use the word 'Daesh' to describe the insurgent group in Iraq and Syria, but the organisation that the journalist works for may insist, as a rule, on referring to the group as 'Islamic State'.

The performance of an ideological stance is also a factor – overtly for the print media and, as the Glasgow University Media Group (1976) alleges, more subtly for the ostensibly neutral broadcasters. The critical tone that many news outlets employ in coverage of Muslims has led observers to accuse them of Islamophobia: this critique dates back to the Runnymede Trust's original report on Islamophobia (1997) and, although it has potentially more force with regard to the tabloid press (Muir et al., 2011), scholars have found ample material to criticise in the broadsheet press (Baker et al., 2013; Richardson, 2004). It is helpful here to note that journalism in Scotland does not all originate from Scotland. The relatively benign social and political approach to Muslims in Scotland that I indicated above was echoed in comments from journalists. I asked them whether they recognised the critique from Muslims – that the media produce and reproduce Islamophobic content – in their organisations' output. The majority said that it did not happen in Scottish news organisations; a few denied it of the organisations that they worked for but suggested that 'other' media might make such associations. Only one participant, who writes for a tabloid, said that her publication sometimes took a negative ideological line concerning Muslims. The kick against an exposed and celebratory Islamophobic discourse was one way in which Scottish journalists (and Scots in general) distinguished themselves from English co-unionists.

This distinction can itself be a performance, as with the 17 November 2015 front page of *The National*, a pro-independence daily newspaper that had only begun publishing a year previously. At a time when the UK national media were debating the admittance of refugees from Syria, balancing ethics against security with an undercurrent of Islamophobia, the newspaper printed a picture of Eilean Donan Castle, with a rowing boat in the foreground and a Highland mountain range as the backdrop. Above the scene, the headline ran as follows: 'To the first refugees fleeing war-torn Syria who will arrive at Glasgow Airport today, we'd just like to say: WELCOME TO SCOTLAND'. The front page conveyed the message that Scotland was different – its media covered differently a political frame that was itself different from the rest of the UK. Scotland as a polity took a greater proportion of Britain's incoming refugees than its demographic share would demand. The cover also, however, served as an editorial response to a Scottish Defence League rally in Ayrshire two days before, near a hotel where some of the refugees were to be housed (Schmid, 2015). This rally was itself met by a pro-refugee rally, which enjoyed greater numbers. The purpose here is not to manipulate numbers into some metric to determine whether Scotland is more or less Islamophobic than its neighbours, but merely to demonstrate that media rhetoric that is friendly to Muslims responds not only to trends in England but also to developments north of the border.

Ideological shading of news texts is not necessarily the result of a choice from the individual journalist writing the piece. As former *Daily Star* reporter Richard Peppiatt said in his testimony to the Leveson Inquiry (Peppiatt, 2011), pressure from superiors can determine what gets printed, regardless of whether it is true, let alone responsibly presented. Even if journalists writing the original copy are sensitive and cautious in the language that they use, this may be cut by subeditors on the article's march towards publication. During fieldwork, I watched on-the-fly editing of television news copy with minutes to go before the evening news broadcast went to air, and phrases were being clipped, cut and reworked because the text was 'heavy' and the programme was liable to overrun. These decisions were made without the journalist present to defend particular word choices or offer palatable alternatives. Unlike the examples that Peppiatt referred to, these changes were not done for ideological but for practical reasons. The overriding concern for the editor – and indeed for the entire production team – was that the programme did not 'go over'. Other edits may have a negative impact on the story without being directly ideological: for example, 'a work might be "in context" by the time a reporter is finished arranging its content and structure, but taken out of context by its presentation with a poorly chosen headline' (Shapiro, 2009: 158). Therefore, it is helpful to think of journalism as a collective achievement rather than the work of particular, individual journalists.

This is not to say that the agency of individual journalists is irrelevant, nor that the collective character of journalistic production necessarily leads to a negative or, at least, a less satisfying outcome. Journalists work with more or less shared understandings of both the final story and the processes that bring that story about. Sue told me of a story that she had written concerning forced marriage, which was anchored by a feature interview with a young Glaswegian woman who shared her personal experience of forced marriage. When Sue turned her copy over to the subeditors, she was able to monitor its progress electronically, and the subeditors and editors checked with her through the various changes. They wanted to make sure that they were not misrepresenting the source's story or using words in a harmful way out of ignorance. When they put the headline together – and it was, as she put it, a 'screaming headline': large text with dramatic language for a tabloid front page – they asked her if it was acceptable to her and her source. She was invited to call the source to run it past her before they sent it to print. Sue described this as 'best practice' and attributed it to the culture of that newsroom, the tone of which was set by the editor: 'our editor ... is very receptive to balanced reporting. He's not – he's unwilling to [pause] stick the knife in, for want of a better phrase'. She suggested that not all the organisations that make up Glasgow's media ecosystem would treat this story with the same sensitivity.

In this example, the collective character of the journalistic enterprise, the benign ideology of the journalists and their organisation, and even the conventions of language conspired to produce what this reporter deemed exemplary coverage of Muslims in Glasgow. It would be cumbersome to follow this practice for every story that goes to print and, in some cases, such as accountability stories, it would be inappropriate. But the example, to adopt terms from anthropologist Clifford Geertz (1973: 93), serves as both a 'model of' coverage of Muslims in Scotland in which journalistic practices did not counter a sense of social responsibility to the subject, and a 'model for' coverage that can foster trust and encourage Muslims to engage with the Scottish media.

JOURNALISTS – LIMITS TO THEIR KNOWLEDGE

Alongside demonstrations of knowledge, journalists discussed the limits of their knowledge concerning Islam and Muslims. This reflexive practice concerned both the concepts that govern Islam, such as the distinction between Shia and Sunni, and, more importantly for this discussion, the lived experience of Muslims, near and far. Authority and representative status were vexing questions for some of the journalists in my study, a problem that goes to the root of what journalists do. Herbert Gans (1980), in his ethnography of US national newsrooms in the 1970s, found that 'considerations' concerning source selection were the most important in determining the resulting news stories. Those whom reporters spoke to had a significant influence on the shape of the story, and he noted that some of the salient considerations for sources included their authority – their perceived power to make things happen in society – and their proximity, or the degree to which the journalist was likely to encounter, identify with or be able to access the source.

Confusion about the relative authority of Muslims in Glasgow was a prominent theme in my interviews. Several journalists spoke dismissively of 'other' journalists who go to 'the mosque' and speak with 'the Imam' when they are covering issues related to Islam. The inverted commas indicate their emphasis on the dubious aim and the insufficiency of this practice. They knew that 'the mosque' did not represent all Muslims, nor was 'the Imam' authorised to speak on their behalf in the same way that, for example, a spokesman from the Catholic archdiocese can provide the official Roman Catholic view on a matter (and, relative to the argument of this chapter, that was the direct comparison that these journalists made). Notionally, 'the mosque', in their statements, stands for the Glasgow Central Mosque, but the generality with which they spoke implied that they were extending the critique to other journalists and other mosques in other places, or even an ideal type of journalistic practice that is not empirically to be found anywhere, but serves as a foil for their specific good practice.

However general this critique might have been intended, it is also the case that journalists in the mainstream media in Glasgow may lack the social proximity to Muslims that Gans identified as important, when considering news sources. Myriam, a broadcast journalist who identified as Muslim, described herself as something of an ambassador for her faith in the newsroom, encountering and countering bad information from her colleagues. It can be difficult for journalists unfamiliar with the nuances of lived Islam to branch out from a limited range of sources – 'official' organisations such as the mosque, or the Muslim Council of Scotland, or the 'usual suspects' to whom journalists have already turned. As Ian, a broadsheet reporter, put it to me, 'I get the impression that a lot of the people we go to as Muslim leaders are not viewed as such by lots of Muslims. That makes it hard. So it's not always easy to know who to go to.' This reflexive and humble statement was welcome, though it was accompanied by the concession that, if it is hard to find a good source, he might just do the easy thing and turn to other stories instead. He has, he said, no shortage of groups willing to share ideas that fit with his beat or area of speciality.

Ian did not want to give up on stories from Glasgow's Muslims, however, and he turned some of the work of establishing authority and representative status over to Muslims themselves: 'that's something that would probably help journalists, if it was made a bit more clear' who the acceptable leaders were. His statement included an invitation for Muslims to engage with him and share stories. It nonetheless betrays an essentialising or homogenising impulse: if not this leader, then which one? Underlying this sentiment, there remains the idea that someone could speak 'for' Muslims, which sits awkwardly with a devolved religion such as Islam, even in a small and concentrated population such as Scotland.

SOURCES – A RANGE OF VOICES

Though sources and authority remain a problem for journalists, there are an increasing number and range of people in Scotland's Muslim communities who are available to speak and share stories. Notwithstanding vague references to 'the Imam' from journalists, in Scotland's history it is typically politicians who were 'the spokesmen' for 'the Muslims'. Early figures such as Bashir Maan and Mohammad Sarwar took on a connective role, representing immigrants with poor English and low social capital to various institutions, such as the police, the council and the media. Maan showed me clippings of stories, such as a 1958 article in the *Scottish Sunday Express* with the headline 'The Quiet Strangers Work and Pray'. It was an orientalist but largely positive feature on South Asian immigrants, and Maan had been the interlocutor, showing the journalist around the neighbourhood, introducing him to people and speaking representatively for others. His community service was formalised when Maan was named Justice of the Peace, and, two years later, he was elected to Glasgow council for Labour – both roles a first for Muslims in Britain. Sarwar was later elected to council and, in 1997, he became the first Muslim MP elected to Westminster, joining Tony Blair's New Labour sweep to power.

These men mediated the engagement of Muslims with journalists, and their social prominence and authority gave them a fair degree of clout. Moreover, they were accessible to journalists who had any questions regarding Muslims. To the degree that journalists had such questions, they had key spokespeople to turn to, thus facilitating coverage. This meant, however, that the representation of a diverse identifiable group was, by and large, managed by a small number of people with similar profiles: men from Pakistan who were affiliated to the Labour Party and politically quietist.

Since the attacks of 11 September 2001, this has opened up: more people (and, significantly, younger people) wanted to speak out at a time when more journalists wanted to listen. Myriam described being called in to sit with a senior editor in her organisation the day after 9/11 and build a list of Muslim contacts. She observed an appetite for names and groups, and she was able to provide links to a wider range of Muslim voices than her organisation had hitherto allowed to speak. Having started her media work at an entry level, she appreciated this opportunity to contribute in a substantial way: 'It actually helped me a lot in my career.' She has maintained this function, and although she jokes about being 'the unofficial Muslim helpline' for her colleagues, she is glad to be asked: 'I would rather they contact me and get proper information.'

Meanwhile, several source participants referred to a meeting in Glasgow about a fortnight after the attacks: Muslim community leaders gathered to discuss how 'the community' ought to respond. Participants said that the prevailing opinion among the elders was to keep a low profile. As Ahmed, who was a student activist at the time, put it, 'the best hope that we had was to keep quiet, to just sit in the corner, hope that no one noticed us, and we could possibly ride it out'. For him and others of his cohort, whom he distinguished less by age than by place of birth – those born in Britain versus those who had emigrated here – the assessment instead was 'that this had to be a moment where we seek to explain ourselves, we seek to build bridges between ourselves and other communities, and more than ever we need to speak'. These people described various ways of engaging more directly with journalists, to the point of turning up at the Glasgow office of a daily broadsheet and offering to do media monitoring specific to the subject of Muslims. Some of these figures remain active in media relations nearly fifteen years later, in fields such as law, politics and journalism.

Moreover, this new cohort of sources projects a more diffuse and connective model of authority, rejecting singular authority and an assumed spokespersonship. They insist that they do not speak 'for' Islam and they are happy to direct journalists to other voices from among Scotland's Muslims who might be more appropriate for the subject of the particular story. For example, Mohammed told of being contacted by a reporter to talk about women wearing the niqab in a court of law; this was for a feature in a weekend broadsheet providing a local Scottish angle to a story from London's Blackfriars Crown Court about a woman insisting on wearing her niqab while giving evidence as a witness. The journalist had called people on her contact list, and this source was a lawyer and therefore familiar with the courtroom setting and its issues, as well as being a prominent and outspoken source for journalists. He told her, 'You need to speak with women [who wear the niqab] themselves. Not people like me and community leaders.' Though he did not take credit in our interview for supplying the journalist with names, the story that she published included four original Scottish voices – three of them women, one of whom sometimes wears the niqab.

By acting as a conduit, sources enlarge and enrich not only the stories that journalists report but the range of Muslims who participate in these reports. This is a hidden contribution of sources: if they are not quoted themselves, these bridging sources do not appear in the published news text. Their involvement, though, has a significant influence on the content of that text. Moreover, it shows a greater degree of engagement and contact between journalists and Muslims than conventional wisdom would suggest, which is why it is important to study news production rather than restricting our analytical focus to the product.

SOURCES – BARRIERS TO ENGAGEMENT

Nonetheless, sources who identify as Muslim still described barriers to media access. Sometimes this was a matter of not understanding journalistic needs, priorities or schedules; but it was also the case that these sources did understand those needs, yet such knowledge did not help them to secure the coverage that they wanted. AMINA-Muslim Women's Resource Centre (hereafter Amina), which I examined as a case study, had invested time in media training in the summer of 2012, in advance of a new campaign on the public perception of Muslim women in Scotland. This campaign generated a marked increase in coverage, and it initiated what Amina's staff and volunteers hoped would be an ongoing and reciprocal relationship with journalists.

What they found was that, in the wake of that campaign, they were successful in being contacted by journalists, but unsuccessful at contacting these journalists and converting that contact into stories. We can distinguish these categories as 'reactive' versus 'active' media relations. For example, the centre was invited to contribute to a broadcast discussion about changes to the government's 'Life in the UK' test, which is used to secure citizenship or long-term residency – a subject that is, at best, marginal to the centre's work of supporting Muslim women with counselling and skills development. (At worst, it reiterates the status of Muslims in Scotland as foreign, undermining Amina's efforts to project an indigenous Scottish Islam practised by people with long roots in the nation.) The director did take part, however, to help the journalists, nurture the centre's media relations and extend its public profile. In other instances, Amina staff have used their network to find 'real people' – ordinary Scottish Muslims who might fit the profile for a particular journalistic request. Centres such as Amina function as an identifiable conduit to Muslim sources, and members have told me that they are happy to serve in that role.

However, their own attempts to interest journalists in a second campaign – this one focused on violence against women – were met with silence. They described applying all the lessons from their media training, which had served them so well with the first campaign, and yet there was no response from journalists. Their generic press releases and targeted pitches – like a press release but tailored to specific, individual journalists and referencing prior contact and coverage – were sent out in November 2012, and they heard no expressions of interest until the period between Christmas and New Year, when the rape and murder of a woman in Delhi made international headlines. In an effort to localise a global story, journalists were now calling Amina for comment, only the staff and volunteers were away from the office over the holiday break and unable to respond.

More than merely a failure brought on by bad timing, Amina members described this as an illustration of a lack of reciprocity with journalists. Throughout our interviews, they referred to 'the peg', an

'insider' journalistic term that they absorbed during their media training. It refers to current events or predictable occasions, such as public
holidays or political elections, through which sources can frame their
pitch to journalists, and journalists can frame their story to audiences.
Science journalist Andrew Revkin writes of 'the tyranny of the peg'
(2006: 224–5), and this is what Amina members encountered: no matter
how compelling they believed their story to be, they felt that they could
not capture the attention of journalists until something else made the
journalists care – in this case, a horrific event half a world away. This
contributed to a kind of fatalism on their part, in that they needed to
enact media relations but had no guarantee that their efforts would be
rewarded with success. Recalling the discussion in the introduction to
this chapter concerning mediatisation and Couldry's 'hidden injuries'
relating to participation and representation, we see in Amina a source
group in thrall to media processes without the ability to control them.
The training that members received and the positive exposure of their
first campaign gave them some capital, but they were unable to convert
it in a way that satisfied their organisational needs. Muslim sources
in my study, in line with other media sources (Davis, 2002), want a
measure of agency in sharing their stories; they do not wish merely to
be available for the occasions when journalists choose to pick up the
telephone.

CONCLUSION

Muslims who are active in media relations with journalists in Scotland
desire more of an appetite from the media for stories about Muslims.
They want a wider range of stories presented, including stories of everyday life, and a wider range of people represented in the media. They are
contributing to this by contacting journalists and by sharing details of
alternate sources so as to spread the pool wider. In the decade and a
half since 9/11, we have seen a proliferation of sources who identify as
Muslim and, in their diversity, challenge the suggestion that Muslims
comprise a monolithic bloc.

Journalists, for their part, seem reasonably well informed about Islam
and reflexive about their lack of knowledge. The participants in my
study displayed no hostility to Muslims, but neither were they ambitious
about forging stronger connections with communities. Some journalistic
participants, including two editors, said they did not want stories about
Muslims to get 'out of balance', implying that the representations in
their coverage need to reflect the whole community that they report

on, of which Muslims are just a small sliver. Even in Glasgow, site of
the densest concentration of Muslims in Scotland and also the nation's
'media capital' (Reid, 2006: xiv), Muslims account for only 3% of the
population. In terms of the audience that these journalists imagine their
particular news organisation captures, that percentage is lower still. As
a relevant part of the journalists' audience, workforce and subject of
coverage, Muslims in Scotland remain a subsidiary concern.

We know, however, that Muslims punch above their demographic
weight when it comes to news coverage (Moore et al., 2008; Baker et
al., 2013). Whether that has developed for reasons that Muslims would
welcome, nonetheless they comprise a newsworthy group. Foreign
stories, terrorism and ruptures with so-called British values tend to drive
that newsworthiness. But Scotland hosts people who are willing to share
stories that widen that range and, with a willing ear, journalists could
make use of the current newsworthiness of Muslims to direct attention to
other places, events, people and narratives. Scotland could be a trailblazer,
as it has been in other aspects of Muslims participating in public life.

REFERENCES

Baker, P., Gabrielatos, C. and McEnery, T. (2013). *Discourse Analysis and
Media Attitudes: The Representation of Islam in the British Press*. Cambridge:
Cambridge University Press.

BBC Scotland (2013). 'MSPs hear from two sides of same-sex marriage debate'.
5 September, available at www.bbc.co.uk/news/uk-scotland-scotland-poli
tics-23970370

Blackwood, L., Hopkins, N. and Reicher, S. (2013). '"I know who I am, but
who do they think I am?" Muslim perspectives on encounters with airport
authorities'. *Ethnic and Racial Studies*, 36(6), 1090–108.

Blain, N. and Hutchison, D. (2008). *The Media in Scotland*. Edinburgh:
Edinburgh University Press.

Bourdieu, P. (1986). 'The forms of capital'. In J. G. Richardson (ed.), *The
Handbook of Theory and Research for the Sociology of Education*, pp.
241–58. New York: Greenwood.

Brown, C. G. (1997). *Religion and Society in Scotland since 1707*. Edinburgh:
Edinburgh University Press.

Bruce, S., Glendinning, T., Paterson, I. and Rosie, M. (2004). *Sectarianism in
Scotland*. Edinburgh: Edinburgh University Press.

Commission on British Muslims and Islamophobia, (1997). *Islamophobia: A
Challenge for Us All*. London: Runnymede Trust.

Couldry, N. (2012). *Media, Society, World: Social Theory and Digital Media
Practice*. Cambridge: Polity.

Davis, A. (2002). *Public Relations Democracy: Politics, Public Relations and the Mass Media in Britain*. Manchester: Manchester University Press.

Deacon, D. and Stanyer, J. (2014). 'Mediatization: Key concept or conceptual bandwagon?' *Media, Culture and Society*, 36(7), 1032–44.

Deveney, C. (2013). 'UK's top cardinal accused of "inappropriate acts" by priests'. *The Guardian*, 23 February, available at www.theguardian.com/world/2013/feb/23/cardinal-keith-o-brien-accused-inappropriate

Duffy, J. (2013). 'Scotland's Muslim leaders to target politicians over same-sex marriage'. *The Herald*, 17 February, available at www.heraldscotland.com/news/13092569.Scotland_s_Muslim_leaders_to_target_politicians_over_sa me_sex_marriage

Gans, H. J. (1980). *Deciding What's News: A Study of CBS Evening News, NBC Nightly News, Newsweek, and* Time. London: Vintage Books.

Geertz, C. (1973). *The Interpretation of Cultures: Selected Essays*. London: Basic Books.

Glasgow University Media Group (1976). 'Bad news', *Bad News*, vol. 1. London: Routledge and Kegan Paul.

Hetherington, A. (1989). *News in the Regions: Plymouth Sound to Moray Firth*, Basingstoke: Macmillan.

Hjavard, S. (2013). *The Mediatization of Culture and Society*. London: Routledge.

Hussain, A. and Miller, W. (2006). *Multicultural Nationalism: Islamophobia, Anglophobia, and Devolution*. Oxford: Oxford University Press.

Irwin, A. (2008). 'Race and ethnicity in the media'. In N. Blain and D. Hutchison (eds), *The Media in Scotland*, pp. 199–212. Edinburgh: Edinburgh University Press.

Kiely, R., McCrone, D. and Bechhofer, F. (2006). 'Reading between the lines: National identity and attitudes to the media in Scotland'. *Nations and Nationalism*, 12(3), 473–92.

Law, A. (2001). 'Near and far: Banal national identity and the press in Scotland'. *Media, Culture and Society*, 23(3), 299–317.

MacInnes, J. (1992). 'The press in Scotland'. *Scottish Affairs*, 1, 137–49.

MacInnes, J. (1993). 'The broadcast media in Scotland'. *Scottish Affairs*, 2, 84–98.

Meer, N. (2008). 'The politics of voluntary and involuntary identities: Are Muslims in Britain an ethnic, racial or religious minority?'. *Patterns of Prejudice*, 42(1), 61–81.

Meer, N. (2015). 'Looking up in Scotland? Multinationalism, multiculturalism and political elites'. *Ethnic and Racial Studies*, 38(9), 1–20.

Miles, R. and Dunlop, A. (1986). 'The racialization of politics in Britain: Why Scotland is different'. *Patterns of Prejudice*, 20(1), 23–33.

Moore, K., Mason, P. and Lewis, J. (2008). *Images of Islam in the UK: The Representation of British Muslims in the National Print Media 2000–2008*, Cardiff: Cardiff School of Journalism, Media and Cultural Studies, available at www.cardiff.ac.uk/jomec/resources/08channel4-dispatches.pdf

Muir, H., Petley, J. and Smith, L. (2011). 'Political correctness gone mad'. In J. Petley and R. Richardson (eds), *Pointing the Finger: Islam and Muslims in the British Media*, pp. 66–99. Oxford: Oneworld Publications.

Munnik, M. B. (2015). 'When you can't rely on public or private: Using the ethnographic self as resource'. In C. Paterson, D. Lee, A. Saha and A. Zoellner (eds), *Advancing Media Production Research: Shifting Sites, Methods, and Politics*, pp. 147–60. Basingstoke: Palgrave Macmillan.

Naysmith, S. (2015). 'Airport security undermining race relations, report warns'. *The Herald*, 17 August, available at www.heraldscotland.com/news/13600608.Airport_security_undermining_race_relations__report_warns

Nickels, H. C., Thomas, L., Hickman, M. J. and Silvestri, S. (2012). 'Constructing "suspect" communities and Britishness: Mapping British press coverage of Irish and Muslim communities 1974–2007'. *European Journal of Communication*, 27(2), 135–51.

Peppiatt, R. (2011). 'Witness statement of Richard Peppiatt'. *Leveson Inquiry: Culture, Practice and Ethics of the Press*, available at www.levesoninquiry.org.uk/wp-content/uploads/2011/11/Witness-Statement-of-Richard-Peppiatt.pdf

Philo, G. (2007). 'Can discourse analysis successfully explain the content of media and journalistic practice?'. *Journalism Studies*, 8(2), 175–96.

Reid, H. (2006). *Deadline: The Story of the Scottish Press*. Edinburgh: Saint Andrew Press.

Revkin, A. C. (2006). 'The environment'. In D. Blum, M. Knudson and R. M. Henig (eds), *A Field Guide for Science Writers*, 2nd edn, pp. 222–8. Oxford: Oxford University Press.

Richardson, J. E. (2004). *(Mis)Representing Islam: The Racism and Rhetoric of the British Broadsheet Newspapers*. Amsterdam: John Benjamins.

Rosie, M. (2004). *The Sectarian Myth in Scotland: Of Bitter Memory and Bigotry*. Basingstoke: Palgrave Macmillan.

Rosie, M., MacInnes, J., Petersoo, P., Condor, S. and Kennedy, J. (2004). 'Nation speaking unto nation? Newspapers and national identity in the devolved UK'. *Sociological Review*, 52(4), 437–58.

Said, E. W. (1997). *Covering Islam: How the Media and the Experts Determine How We See the Rest of the World*, revised edn. London: Vintage.

Schlesinger, P., Dinan, W. and Miller, D. (2001). *Open Scotland? Journalists, Spin Doctors and Lobbyists*. Edinburgh: Polygon.

Schmid, S. (2015). 'Scottish Defence League bring protest to Monkton but anti-refugee group are easily outnumbered'. *The National*, 16 November, available at www.thenational.scot/news/scottish-defence-league-bring-protest-to-monkton-but-anti-refugee-group-are-easily-outnumbered.10042

Shapiro, I. (2009). 'Evaluating journalism'. *Journalism Practice*, 4(2), 143–62.

Smith, E. (2012). 'Muslim MSP Humza Yousaf's fury at "random" airport check'. *Daily Record*, 1 July, available at www.dailyrecord.co.uk/news/politics/muslim-msp-humza-yousafs-fury-1109338

Sutcliffe, S. (2004). 'Unfinished business – devolving Scotland/devolving religion'. In S. Coleman and P. Collins (eds), *Religion, Identity and Change: Perspectives on Global Transformations*, pp. 84–106. Aldershot: Ashgate.

Vultee, F. (2006). '"Fatwa on the Bunny": News language and the creation of meaning about the Middle East'. *Journal of Communication Inquiry*, 30(4), 319–36.

12

REPRESENTATION
Representing Islam at the Edinburgh International Book Festival

Fayaz S. Alibhai

INTRODUCTION

The year 2013 saw the thirtieth Edinburgh International Book Festival (EIBF), where it was expected that 200,000 people would be in attendance over the course of 17 days for some 700 events involving '[m]ore than 800 authors from around the world' (BBC, 2013). Despite its size, the festival, set in Charlotte Square Gardens, manages to feel like a tented village community. Children laugh and loll about on a low wooden dais, eating ice cream from the stall inside the gardens, their parents sitting beside them. It is usually too wet to sit on the grass, so there is often a polite scramble for the deckchairs, appropriately emblazoned with literary aphorisms, strewn around the square under the shade of umbrellas. The sun is not particularly out in full force during this time of the year, so there is not as much a pull to orient the deckchairs to its rays. But people are enjoying the intermittent sunshine, reading the papers, listening to music through headphones or speaking to others on their mobiles. Some sit on plastic chairs around a table or two, talking, poring over the festival programme. Others kick back on the benches, reading their newly signed books. Yet others are simply people watching. It is quiet, but certainly not silent. The steady hum of conversations in the square mingles occasionally with a child's plaintive cry or the clink of glasses. Clapping and laughter in equal measure erupt intermittently from inside the tents. Playful yet serious, expansive yet intimate, the festival's garden setting is idyllic, a veritable Eden pregnant with the promise of delight and knowledge.

Gardens in Islam are quintessential representations of heaven on earth. Mirroring the gardens of paradise, where the righteous are promised flowing rivers of water, milk, honey and wine (Qur'an, 47: 15), these earthly manifestations of almost Platonic forms of beauty and order provide relief, entertainment and sanctuary. Above all, they are spaces for contemplation. The parallel with the literary festival at Charlotte Square Gardens, 'the biggest in the world' according to its director Nick Barley (2011) is, therefore, particularly salient. As a public space for the production of ideas and their dissemination, this home of the EIBF plays a major role in not only influencing but also defining wider debates about art, science, governance, social justice and religion. This may be surprising in a globalised context, in which much traditional media cycles relentlessly through the triumvirate of reality TV, the cult of celebrity, and coverage of conflict and violence. But, as Barley (2011) goes on to note:

> literary festivals have become some of the most vibrant forums for public discussion of the early 21st century. For anyone who thinks that the book is dead, the literary festival boom is clear evidence that reading, writing and ideas are anything but.

This is especially significant for discourses about Islam and Muslims. Daily, it seems, the public is assaulted afresh by yet another incomprehensible narrative of irrationality and lawlessness. The intractable threat of terror that results from this coverage also feeds it, contributing to populist debates about the 'problem with Islam' among both Muslims (Manji, 2003) and non-Muslims (Geller, 2011). In all, they evoke the emotions precisely opposite to the idea of the Islamic garden – a widespread sense of the chaos rather than the order, the ugliness rather than the beauty (Abou El Fadl, 2006), the barbarity rather than the civilisation associated with Islam and Muslims.

Much analysis of this phenomenon, particularly within the specialism of Muslims in Britain, has revolved primarily around representation in the media (Poole, 2002; Petley and Richardson, 2011). There is, of course, a long and established history of analysis on the representation of Islam and Muslims. Epitomised by classic treatments such as Edward Said's *Orientalism* (1978), these works remain salient against the backdrop of contemporary policy and academic debates about the extent and dangers of not only radicalisation among Muslims but also Islamophobia.

This study draws from ethnographic fieldwork conducted between 2011 and 2013 and focuses on Edinburgh, where comparatively little research on Muslims has so far been undertaken. In doing so, it explores the representation of Islam within the confines of one of Britain's most widely acclaimed literary festivals, the EIBF. It begins by examining the festival as a public square. It then discusses the festival's production of an 'Islamicate' space. Finally, it analyses how the festival may be conceived as a representation of Islamicate space.

THE FESTIVAL AS A PUBLIC SQUARE

Ever since the invention of Gutenberg's printing press in around 1455, reading and writing in the Western context have been private, if not predominantly solitary, acts. Now, reading out loud as a public act is limited perhaps only to baby and toddler parenting and spousal allocutions from the weekend papers that are received rather more absent-mindedly. While book and poetry readings may constitute counter-examples of such public performance, they tend to be considerably limited in time, and often form only part of a larger discourse. In this context, the festival's celebration of books is paradoxically less about the individual act of reading and writing per se than it is about the collective creation of a new conversation. As Barley noted for the festival in 2014, historic for the Scottish referendum on independence, it had:

> been a breathtakingly vibrant year ... The atmosphere among audiences has ranged from exuberant to deeply thoughtful, with a real sense that Scotland is on the cusp of an epoch-defining decision. True to the spirit of dialogue that ran through this year's programme, authors and audiences alike engaged in conversations that were intelligent and often incredibly perceptive. Public democracy is alive and kicking in Charlotte Square Gardens. (quoted in EIBF, 2014)

Like the genre of the novel, the public square is a site of formation as well as encounter (Hirschkop, 1990: 71). For some, it is different, however, from civic spaces, 'the discursive spaces of the life of the state, where the individual speaks as a *citizen*, and so enters "world-history" through his state membership' (Hirschkop, 1990: 72). Being a citizen requires giving up a 'differentiating, local identity in favour of [an] abstract equality' (Hirschkop, 1990: 72). In this sense, the public square is not constituted of the particular, but as a collective for 'the formulation of all values as distinct "points of view"' (Hirschkop, 1990: 71). Here, groups come together 'to "make history" ... which requires ... a change in form, from private world to "world-view", from personal passion to public ... argument' (Hirschkop, 1990: 72).

This coming together of a variety of points of view, of difference, for wider social ends, is often referred to as civil society. A particular kind of public space, civil society is an 'aesthetic form of the public square'

(Hirschkop, 1990: 72). In that 'intermediate realm of public interests and activities', it is, according to Bakhtin, semi-official: 'at once public yet not official, concerned with a range of social identities between those imposed by the state and the economy' (Hirschkop, 1990: 72–3). In this regard, the EIBF may be seen as an 'institution of civil society', and thereby 'capable of being both public and meaningful, which is to say that [it] offer[s] quasi-aesthetic, rather than strictly political or economic rewards' (Hirschkop, 1990: 73). As such, it is an arena of what Habermas would call 'public communicative action, thereby distinct from both "private life" and the public yet rationalised domains of state bureaucracy and economy' (Hirschkop, 1990: 73).

Light and Smith (1998: 2) provide a striking image for the idea of the public square:

> Picture an open plaza overlooked by a regal balcony. In the plaza stand the people, for the moment listening; on the balcony stands the ruler, for the moment pronouncing. The people assembled in the square become a public once they are able to debate among themselves and respond to the pronouncements of the state with rational protests and formal petitions. In other words, if the balcony is taken as a metonymy of the state speaking to the people, the public square is a metonymy of the people talking among themselves and, perhaps more importantly, talking back to the state.

Together with being 'an aesthetic form of the public square', such pronouncement and debate is an integral part of the experience of the EIBF, and the festival's numerous spaces, both open and enclosed, are key to this exchange. In its execution the festival is, unsurprisingly, tightly regulated and nowhere is this more manifest than in its set-up of individual events. The organisers are almost militant about start and end times. Every year, festival-goers complain about not being let in to events because they were only seconds late. These complaints are aired over social media as well as in person, overheard at the entrances to tents, or narrated to others in queues for alternative events. For its part, the festival sticks to its guns, citing not only its clearly printed policy about late arrivals on the festival programme, website and tickets, but also its specific recommendations on all these media that people should be aware that buying tickets for back-to-back events can sometimes be risky. Box office staff at the returns queue are in radio contact with ushers at the tents' entrances who confirm whether people can still come in or not. Once the event has started, however, it is all but impossible to get the doors opened, and late arrivals are politely, but firmly, turned away. Only once in the course of three years of fieldwork did I observe that the time limit for an event was violated. But this was for 'Eskenderella, Music from Tahrir Square', who succeeded in carrying on with their musical performance past the allotted time only because of a combination of the audience's insistence for an encore, the chair's implicit go-ahead and the late hour, it being the last and rousing event of the evening in the tent. Even then, the irritation of the technical staff at the back of the tent was clear to see.

Depending on the event, there are between two and four people on the stage. There are rarely more, unless it is a music group, or similar, like Eskenderella above. A moderator or chair usually sits across from the author, facing the audience. Some authors have interpreters in attendance. If there is more than one author, the moderator or chair will take centre stage with an author on either side. Besides introducing the author and asking some key questions, the moderator will field questions from the audience towards the end of the event. For more high-profile events, the chair will be joined by the Festival Director, who will give a 'meta' introduction and then either sit with the audience or proceed to double duty as chair/moderator. The introduction is followed by an author reading, lecture or speech, sometimes supplemented by a film clip or two. Less often, authors might choose to give a PowerPoint presentation to which they will speak directly. But even here, ironically, the slides are led primarily by images and little text. Much of the actual event is constituted as a précis of the book in question, with moderators making reference to specific incidents and passages, striking turns of phrase, and the relevance and impact of the work beyond the book itself. There is frequently a compelling backstory, often humorous, sometimes shocking, presented variously as anecdotes that formed the genesis of a book, including specific and extraordinary biographical incidents constituting the bulk of a memoir or other kinds of personal experience or material that did not make it into the book. The parallel, then, of the set-up of the festival with the plaza and the balcony referenced earlier is evident.

The intimacy of this narration, the opportunity for interaction and the limits of time make for great storytelling. Indeed, it has elements that are almost revelatory – unfolding, minute-by-minute access to insights unavailable to most others, moments of resolute curiosity and questioning followed by an 'aha!' profundity and a most satisfying, if not stimulating, admixture of amazement, despair, hope, sadness and laughter. Similarly, the tented space, its close and tiered seating, level of lighting and quality of sound, make a great *space* for storytelling. And from the discreet efficiency in being ushered in and out of the festival tents, to the availability of refreshments, the layout of the bookshops, and the book-signing tables and stands, little hubs for people to meet their favourite authors up close and personal at regular intervals throughout the day, the festival makes a great *business* of storytelling. In this way, the EIBF is not only a valuable site for a study of the public square but also, as argued below, a remarkable and novel illustration of the production as well as representation of 'Islamicate' space.

THE PRODUCTION OF (ISLAMICATE) SPACE

In discussing the terms 'representation', 'Islamicate' and 'space', this section aims to meld elements from the field of human geography with that of Islamic studies. Specifically, it draws upon Henri Lefebvre's *The Production of Space* (1991), a seminal theoretical framework that has remained largely unexplored in the context of Islam and Muslims. In doing so, it references Lefebvre's triadic framework, namely, spatial practice, the representation of space and, finally, the space of representation (sometimes termed 'representational spaces'), as it applies to knowledge about Islam and Muslims.

The term 'Islamicate' comes from Marshall Hodgson's also seminal three-volume work, *The Venture of Islam: Conscience and History in a World Civilization* (1977). Hodgson cautions against the scholarly tendency 'to use the terms "Islam" and "Islamic" too casually both for what we may call religion and for the overall society and culture associated historically with the religion' (1977: 57). Over the years since he published this work, this tendency to conflate the particularity of the properly religious with the generality of the widely cultural has only gained momentum, becoming entrenched in media representations and popular discourse, among not just non-Muslims but also Muslims themselves.

Although it has not caught on as much as Hodgson had hoped, the term 'Islamicate' helps to distinguish these two related, but nonetheless different, analytical concepts. Hodgson uses 'Islamicate' to refer to the '*culture*, centred on a lettered tradition, which has been historically distinctive of Islamdom the *society*, and which has been naturally shared in by both Muslims and non-Muslims who participate at all fully in the society of Islamdom' (1997: 58). Hodgson concedes that even though the additional neologism 'Islamdom' might not be adopted widely, its obvious analogy with 'Christendom' might render it less easily dismissed. He also points out that one could use Islamicate in the form 'of the culture of Islamdom', but that this is periphrasal and ultimately clumsy in style. He thought it far better, instead, to use the neologism explicitly and pedagogically (Hodgson, 1977: 59).

The term Christendom is admittedly dated in an increasingly sec-ularised Western context, so 'Islamdom' may be seen as even more antiquated, if not wholly alien. Furthermore, it carries a potentially hegemonic connotation that Islamophobics would perhaps perversely relish, especially when tied to contemporary discourses that present Islam, the religion and associated practice in areas of law, justice, gender relations and so on as medieval.

Notwithstanding these challenges, the use of 'Islamicate', at least, cer-tainly remains warranted. Importantly, Hodgson sees it being 'used for *the milieu of a whole society* and not simply for the body of all Muslims, for the Ummah' (1977: 58). The term 'Islamic', then, he restricts to its adjectival sense, '"of or pertaining to" Islam *in the proper, the reli-gious, sense*' (1977: 59). So, Hodgson continues, '"Islamicate" would refer not directly to the religion, Islam, itself, but to the social and cul-tural complex historically associated with Islam and the Muslims, both among Muslims themselves and even when found among non-Muslims' (1977: 59). Having outlined the scope of the term 'Islamicate', as articu-lated by Hodgson, the chapter turns now to a wider discussion of how key elements of Lefebvre's notions of the production of space may be understood in the context of the EIBF, and particularly as it applies to the production of an Islamicate space.

For Henri Lefebvre, representations of space refer to 'conceptualized space, the space of scientists, planners, urbanists, technocratic subdivid-ers and social engineers, as of a certain type of artist with a scientific bent' (1991: 38). It is, he continues, 'the dominant space in any society (or mode of production)', tending 'towards a system of verbal (and therefore intellectually worked out) signs' (1991: 38–9). In other words, representations of space are 'conceived' (Lefebvre, 1991: 40).

In its inaugural year in 1983, the EIBF was the first of its kind in Scotland and only the third in the rest of the UK. Now there are over 300 such events (BBC, 2013). According to Jenny Brown, the festival's first director, 'it was conceived of as being a big, one-off celebration of books and the written word at the Edinburgh Festival, which had every other art form represented but nothing on literature' (quoted in BBC, 2013). As the 'biggest and best-respected festival of books in the world' (Barley, 2013: 2), the EIBF not only draws out the world by bringing attention to the diversity of authors and genres, but also maps it by organising them thematically and in the light of contemporary conver-sations. Crucially, in so doing, it actively produces a social space which is 'tied', as Lefebvre would put it, 'to relations of production and to the "order" which those relations impose, and hence to knowledge, to signs, to codes, and to "frontal" relations' (1991: 33). As such, it is not just the content of the books, the reading and writing of which, as we have already seen, is a largely solitary affair, but the idea of books and what they stand for – what might be called their performance in the public square – that is at play here.

Furthermore, the representation of space is 'in thrall to both knowledge and power' (Lefebvre, 1991: 50). In Lefebvrian terms, therefore, authors, moderators, chairs, panellists and interpreters who are invited by the festival's programmers all 'identify what is lived and what is perceived with what is conceived' (Lefebvre, 1991: 38). As such, they represent particular kinds of spaces by engaging in a series of conversations that are of both contemporary and historical relevance. The quality of those conversations as expressed in on-stage readings, presentations and question-and-answer sessions, together with reputational capital from authors' previous appearances and their overall fame – all these elements provide a sense of the place of these books and the spaces that they produce, often even before they have been purchased, let alone read. The blurbs in the festival programme for the events featuring Richard Holloway and Nadeem Aslam respectively in 2013 are clear examples of this production of space:

Richard Holloway: 30 Years of Scottish Society. His gorgeous memoir was one of the finest books of last year, confirming the former Bishop of Edinburgh's status as one of Scotland's great public thinkers. A firm Book Festival favourite, Richard Holloway joins us today to celebrate the 30th anniversary of the world's leading literary event in a conversation with founding director Jenny Brown about three extraordinary decades of society, faith and storytelling in Scotland. (EIBF, 2013: 34)

Nadeem Aslam: A Secret Journey into Afghanistan. He's been described by Colm Tóibín as 'one of the most exciting and serious writers working in Britain now' and his new book will build his reputation still further. Nadeem Aslam, twice longlisted for the Man Booker Prize, presents *The Blind Man's Garden*, an unforgettable story set in Afghanistan and Pakistan after the 9/11 bombings. It's an evocative novel that sheds new light on a key moment in recent history. (EIBF, 2013: 15)

The chapter now examines some of these events and conversations to determine how the festival may be understood as a representation of Islamicate space.

THE FESTIVAL AS A REPRESENTATION OF ISLAMICATE SPACE

An analysis of the festivals listing compiled by the Alwaleed Centre (2012) reveals several broad themes discussed at the EIBF. These run the gamut from religion and politics to war and conflict as well as women and gender relations, all of which also feature in the other Edinburgh summer festivals as corroborated by my own compilation of Islamicate events at the festivals (Alibhai, 2013) and its associated research. More specifically within these categories, events at the Book Festival not only tend to revolve around human rights issues and captivity, fundamentalism, and the Middle East, but they are also explicitly titled as such, for example 'The Amnesty International Imprisoned Writers Series', which takes place daily, 'Maziar Bahari and François Bizot: Coming Face to Face with Your Captor' (EIBF, 2012: 30), 'Maajid Nawaz: One Man's Journey from Extremist to Democrat' (EIBF, 2012: 11) and 'Tom Holland: How Religion Shaped the Middle East' (EIBF, 2012: 25). Additionally, the act, process and genre of writing itself in the context of these specific themes are themselves an integral part of the festival's programming, as evidenced by events such as 'Raja Shehadeh: Palestine, Politics and Playwriting' (EIBF, 2012: 22). Similar examples can be found on the festival programme for 2013.

Given that this is a literary festival, it is unsurprising that, except for named series, events are fronted by the names of authors presenting them. The tasks, therefore, of (1) identifying 'Events relating to Islam and the World of Islam' (Alwaleed Centre, 2012), in other words, of Islamicate relevance, and (2) promoting this subset as such but without replicating existing marketing, and especially when this relevance is not immediately apparent, becomes a little trickier, if not more involved. In the case of the Alwaleed listing, it is easy enough to cite the festival programme's own title, 'Sadakat Kadri: Debunking the Myths About Shariᶜa Law' (EIBF, 2012: 45) without further explanation. But 'Youssef Ziedan and Andrés Neuman: Ancient Stories with Modern Twists' (EIBF, 2012: 44) requires the parenthetical gloss, 'discussion of their novels, *Azazeel* and *Traveller of the Century*, respectively set in ancient Egypt and nineteenth-century Prussia', on the Alwaleed listing, as does 'Jonathan Steele: One war that might never be won' (EIBF, 2012: 45) with '(Afghanistan)'. In the case of the festival's original title 'Elif Shafak: Cross-country story of a family' (EIBF, 2012: 32), the Alwaleed listing dispenses with it entirely, rendering it simply as 'Elif Shafak discusses her novel *Honour* (set in Kurdistan, Istanbul and London)'. These and other glosses, such as for Amnesty International's Imprisoned Writers

Series, '"The Arab Spring" (EIBF, 2012: 39) (readings from works about the uprisings in Egypt, Tunisia, Libya, Bahrain, Yemen and Syria)' point to the importance of geography in marking events as Islamicate. Indeed, the festival programme itself as a whole uses such spatial references, frequently citing cities, countries and regions in its event titles and accompanying blurbs.

As Lefebvre would note, these are fundamentally social spaces and, as such, they 'interpenetrate one another and/or superimpose themselves upon one another. They are not things, which have mutually limiting boundaries and which collide because of their contours or as a result of inertia' (Lefebvre, 1991: 86–7). Such spatial configurations and overlaps allow people, events, debates and narratives located in one part of the world to be physically and metaphorically transposed to another part of the world where they are further discussed, analysed and comprehended. In terms of Islamicate events at the festival, this transposition takes place chiefly through three lenses. The chapter discusses one of these lenses next.

ENCOUNTERS

Encounters take place between minds, peoples, cultures and civilisations. They may be mysterious – troubling, even. But fundamentally, experiences of first contact are explorations of curiosity and exercises in suspending judgement. Only afterwards do they develop into dialogue and understanding or degenerate into confrontation and conflict. Perhaps this is because encounters are fundamentally meetings of difference, with either creative (or, in Lefebvrian terms, productive) or destructive potential. They are memorable, out of the ordinary, questioning each other's paradigms, mental maps, world views and ways of being. In returning to them again and again, they are even dialectical. While repeated encounters may breed a degree of familiarity and, in turn, clichéd contempt, they may also breed understanding, but only insofar as a delicate balance is struck between stability and unpredictability, and especially where the encountering cultures and societies, kindred or not, perceive each other as equals. If this element of unknowing does not induce fear or is not perceived as threatening, the encounters remain fresh, creative and full of promise, generating dialogue, interaction, borrowing, adapting and adopting. In this regard, what is often termed a 'clash of civilizations' (Huntington, 1993) is perhaps more accurately a 'clash of ignorance' (Said, 2001).

In recent times, nowhere was this clash first made more manifest in the British context than in the aftermath of Ayatollah Khomeini issuing a death sentence against Salman Rushdie for his *The Satanic Verses* (1997). In the twenty-five or so years since Khomeini's edict, once referred to by V. S. Naipaul as an 'extreme form of literary criticism' (Jaggi, 2001), much ink has been spilled on the Rushdie affair. It marked the beginnings of a now *de rigueur* pattern of protest and counter-protest about the representation of Islam and Muslims that is almost unthinkingly accompanied by tropes about free speech on the one hand and licence on the other. But even as headlines fuel the inflammatory interventions by various state actors and public individuals, it is interesting to note that these debates are less about religion per se and more about society at large. Indeed, as Devji (2012) notes, in the case of Rushdie:

> the closest demonstrators came to a theological argument was to demand that their religion be included under Britain's blasphemy law. So in the UK at least, the controversy's only religious element had to do with the desire of Muslim immigrants to be integrated into British society. Otherwise Muslims demonstrating against Rushdie referred to their feelings of outrage at his depiction of Muhammad by using the secular language of libel, defamation and hate speech.

Rushdie's appearance at the Book Festival in 2013 to promote his memoir, *Joseph Anton* (2012), was eagerly anticipated, the event title and blurb on the programme reading as follows:

> Salman Rushdie: Defining a Literary Generation. In 1983, Salman Rushdie was shortlisted for the Booker Prize for his novel *Shame* and named among *Granta*'s inaugural Best of Young British Novelists. Only a few years later, he was forced into hiding by an Iranian *fatwa* after the publication of *The Satanic Verses*. Rushdie survived, became a passionate champion of free speech and emerged as the single most influential British writer of our times. We are thrilled to welcome him to reflect on a remarkable career with John Freeman, editor of *Granta*. (EIBF, 2013: 10)

But his ultimate reception was rather muted, the earlier drama surrounding him and his book largely dissipated and displaced by more recent controversies on representations of Muhammad, and blunter attacks on Islam and Muslims. This was evidenced not only by the number of return tickets for his event, comfortably accommodating about a dozen queuing waitlisters at the box office, despite it being sold out early on, but also in the surprisingly brief discussion set aside on *The Satanic Verses* at the event itself. In a sense, everyone had moved on: looking back on the publication of the novel, even Inayat Bunglawala, then a university student involved in the Rushdie protests who went on to become the Assistant Secretary General of the Muslim Council of Britain, acknowledged in the run-up to the publication of *Joseph Anton* that the protesters' demands

> were, in retrospect, totally over the top and very embarrassing. We may not have liked his book, but there could be no excuse for trying to deny others the right to buy it and read it for themselves. I would hope that if the same events were to be replayed today, UK Muslims would instead respond by publishing their own books offering their own narrative. (Bunglawala, 2012)

Rushdie is not a self-effacing man, but his deadpan humour was likeable, whether he interjected at the chair's introductory remarks recounting Khomeini's *fatwa* ('I remember V. S. Naipaul saying that Khomeini's was a very bad review', said Rushdie, pausing for the punchline: 'I think he meant it as a joke'), spoke about being exposed to novelist William Styron's testicles or narrated a surreal standoff, replete with a convoy of armoured Jaguars, between English and Scottish police forces as to whose jurisdiction prevailed in rural Ayrshire over his security. I turn now to a discussion of some of the characteristics of encounter-themed events at the festival.

Commonality and Difference

A fundamental feature of encounter narratives at the EIBF is that they highlight commonality over difference, whether in discussing the divine, the relationship between truth, doubt and faith, the role of religion in society or the supposed clash between East and West. As such, seemingly solid distinctions between 'us' and 'them', 'self' and 'the other' tend to evaporate into more nebulous affinities.

Although Rushdie described the absurdities of protection and living in confinement as sometimes being like 'a comedy routine', his remarks on *The Satanic Verses* were astute and reflective. They took the form of pithy observations on the nature of revelation, the historicity of people and events associated with Islam compared to the other Abrahamic faiths, and the spread of religious fundamentalism not being the preserve of a single tradition. Recalling how his father, fluent in Arabic and Persian, unlike him, told him the story of the first revelation, 'but from the point of view of a completely disbelieving person', Rushdie was not at all dismissive of the Prophet Muhammad:

> Put it like this. When Muhammad describes his own description of revelation he describes the angel, Gabriel, as being very very large. The angel

stood on the horizon and filled the sky [Rushdie gestures, holding his hands wide apart]. All right. Big angel [audience laughter]. So the question is, which my father asked me and I guess I asked myself afterwards, if you had been standing next to him, would you have seen the angel? And my view is, probably not. Right? And yet, he's not telling a lie. You know, he's not making it up. And so what is that? What is that event? You know, where he genuinely felt, what he genuinely sees, you know, and I would feel that if I was standing like you and I are next to each other I would not have seen the same thing. What does that mean? What is revelation? How does it work? And he gave me, my father gave ... me some of the stories which I went along and studied ... And when I was at university, I came across this incident, which is in the records, the sort of temptation of the Prophet, the incident of the satanic verses ... And I remember thinking, 'That's a good story', and you know, twenty years later I found out how good a story it was [audience laughter].

Good stories, if not excellent ones, are a fundamental requirement of literary festivals. Youssef Ziedan addressed similar issues at the EIBF just a year earlier than Rushdie, in 2012, for his novel *Azazeel* (2012). There is, first of all, the delicious parallel between the titles of arguably their most famous books, for not only was *Azazeel* awarded the International Prize for Arabic fiction, the 'Arabic Booker', in 2009, but also the word itself, as Ziedan noted, is 'the Hebrew and old Arabic name of the devil' and who 'here is a part of us, not an external figure'. Second, it is a novel steeped in history and philosophy: 'It's not for everyone,' said Ziedan, a scholar of Arabic and Islamic Studies, and Director of the Manuscript Centre and Museum associated with the Bibliotheca Alexandrina. Told in the form of an 'internal speech about Hiba' (or Hypa), a fifth-century Coptic monk fleeing his native Egypt for Syria in the wake of extreme violence propagated by dogma and corruption in early Christianity, *Azazeel*, too, revolves around the role and nature of religious texts. Third, it was popular and controversial in equal measure. According to Ziedan, it was in its ninth edition even before the prize and in its twenty-seventh by the time of his appearance at the festival, highly unusual for this genre. In the three years before, seven books for and against the novel had been published in response. But after 'the Italian translation and the Egyptian revolution,' Ziedan continued, 'they've reconsidered the novel, and the idea of God, [the] Devil, and ourselves'. Despite its explicit genre as a novel, Ziedan, like Rushdie, had to address issues of authenticity. Because it drew heavily from 'religious thinking and knowledge', Ziedan said that:

even specialists in Syria have asked if it's real. But it's not. The people are real, but I went through it and tried to make the history more real. History is *his* story. Histories tell us what they believe and we have many stories.

The form of the novel is particularly suited to encounter narratives, because it raises important questions without the expectation of definitive answers. In other words, it allows for the continuing exploration not only of fundamental questions about life and meaning without the hubris of resolution, but also of comparably more mundane concerns, about individual as well as societal development and change, where the elements of transposition and poetic licence allow one to say things in one context that they might find considerably difficult, for a variety of reasons, in another. This is true, for example, of Joanne Harris's novel *Peaches for Monsieur Le Curé* (2013), the genesis of which, as she revealed during her event 'Joanne Harris: Milk Chocolate and Minarets', was the sight of veiled women in her native Yorkshire. Interestingly, however, the programme blurb made no further reference to Islam (EIBF, 2013: 42).

It is ironic that such licence did not allow escape for Rushdie. However, that backlash resulted from a confluence of circumstances then impossible to predict and for which there was no precedent. But if the reaction was a measure of fundamentalism, Rushdie was quick to point out, as mentioned earlier, that Muslims certainly did not hold a monopoly on its expression. Ziedan, citing opposition from within both Jewish and Christian communities for his novels and for *Azazeel*'s portrayal of Cyril, the Patriarch of Alexandria, echoed similar sentiments at his festival event, arguing that 'Violence in the name of God is a problem in Judaism, Christianity and Islam.' This illustrates an important point: that where historical incidents inspire contemporary novel writing, fiction often triumphs over truth, and the authority exercised by the forces of history, tradition and historiography fades in the face of competing publics in many squares.

Of course, this does not obviate the need for discerning fact from fiction. If anything, it renders history, tradition and historiography as essential to human life, so closely is it tied to the creation of memory and meaning. Take, for example, Mustafa Cerić at 'Rethinking Islam: Is Radical Islam the World's Greatest Threat?', part of a popular debate series at the Book Festival in 2012. Introducing himself to an audience of around 120 men and women as the Grand Mufti of Bosnia-Herzegovina, a genocide survivor, Muslim and European, Cerić emphasised that Islam was not something out there in the Middle East, but a reality here, in

Europe, going back centuries. His linkage of the constituent elements of his identity to the promise of 'never again', in memory of and response to the history of war, destruction and genocide in Europe, demonstrates another kind of commonality. Note that this commonality, however, is spatial and not merely ideological, a point reinforced by his repeated reference to the history of genocide in Europe, as well as the use of the phrase 'we Europeans' throughout the debate. But the commonalities discussed above go hand in hand with the inescapable differences that I examine next.

Spatial and Temporal Diversity

The second characteristic emerging from these narratives is, conversely, the spatial and temporal diversity of these encounters. Even as the dichotomy between Islam and the West, if not a full-scale clash, is made explicit in the full title for 'Rethinking Islam' in 2012, and in others such as John Tolan's 'Islam and the West: More Complex Than You Might Think' in 2013, the festival does present the existence of multiple histories, traditions and historiographies of Islamicate cultures, each of which becomes a reservoir of changing memory and meaning.

In the case of 'Rethinking Islam', Cerić began a wide-ranging discussion by outlining the views of 'some historians' that there were twelve civilisations, seven of which were dead and five that were still living: Chinese, Japanese, Indian, Western and Islamic. He said he was interested in Western and Islamic civilisation, noting that, while Western civilisation was connected with geography and not religion, Islamic civilisation was connected to religion. This is an odd characterisation, particularly as he went on to speak of the West and Islam as 'Siamese twins' sharing a cosmology, cosmogony and eschatology. Cerić described their mode of engagement as being 'one of competition' and said that 'Recently, I think, they're competing in a bad way.' Invoking Baghdad of the eighth century and Cordoba of the tenth century, he said, 'We have to live together. There is no choice. We are Siamese twins, like it or not.' Reflecting on the title of the debate, he said that 'Rethinking Islam was appropriate for the present time' and that especially from the view of the West, 'we've had ten to twelve years of a really unhelpful, monolithic view'.

Having lived in Spain, Denmark and the UK, Cerić said he had 'seen what Islam in Europe is going through', but that we need to 'see Islam not as competing within the West'. He spoke of the 'challenge of people now living in Europe who see themselves as Europeans and Muslim', and that 'this conflict needs to be resolved or we are condemned to repeating the conflicts of the past'. Speaking of the Middle East, he said that what we are seeing there 'is an evolution of Islam'. Whereas the coup in Sudan in 1989 was 'a very brutal Islam ... looking like a dinosaur', the present situation in 'Egypt and Sudan is a kind of dialogue where Islam and democracy can be compatible', but that 'It's not going to happen tomorrow.'

Dilip Hiro, Cerić's co-panellist, was equally expansive. He set the scene by comparing Muhammad and Jesus, arguing that 'politics and religion were intertwined in Islam', because Muhammad represented both spheres, whereas Jesus 'was a carpenter'. He noted that while Islam was associated with the Arab world, 'the number of Muslims in Pakistan, India and Bangladesh equalled 300 million, which is the same number of all twenty-two members of the Arab League'. Starting from the abolishment of the (Ottoman) caliphate in 1924, Hiro surveyed the variety of forms of political Islam, covering the Muslim Brotherhood, the Mujahideen of Afghanistan in the 1980s ultimately spilling over into Pakistan and India, the Islamic Revolution in Iran, Sufi Islam in South Asia, the development of the Pakistani Taliban and the rise of the AKP in Turkey.

The panellists, who included the novelist Jamal Mahjoub, also covered the spread of Islam, European Islam, educational systems, the failure of secularisation in Muslim societies, Sunni-Shia tensions, the role of the state in intervening for religion in the public sphere, fundamentalism, the status of women, the application of sharia in various contexts and multiculturalism. They did not always agree with each other, each citing specific examples, but this served only to highlight the diversity of Muslim responses to the issues at hand. In light of Cerić's earlier remarks on an 'unhelpful, monolithic view' of Islam from the West, this was an important element of the event. As we shall see shortly, however, the demonstration of this diversity and its attendant complexity does not in itself facilitate greater understanding of the issues at stake among observers.

Cerić, however, dominated the floor, often interrupting even when the panel's chair, Ruth Wishart, directed questions to another panellist. On Islam as a whole, he said, 'Islam is more than religion, culture, geography, Shia or Sunni issue. It's a way of life. Because Islam is a civilisation.' On European Islam, he asserted, 'Unfortunately, we Europeans are not confident of developing our own theology because the Sun still rises in the East.' On the performance of religion in the public sphere, Cerić cited the presidents of the newly independent states of Central Asia after 1991 all very publicly going on the *hajj*, shops closing during

Ramadan and Pakistan under Zia ul-Haqq, who had army command-
ers lead the Friday prayer. On the appeal of Islamist parties, Cerić said,
'Go to a mosque in Cairo. You get food, employment, medical aid.
They were doing what the government should have been doing.' But
he also noted that in Egypt 'there's an internal battle', evidenced by
the exchange between the Speaker of Parliament 'arguing with a Salafi
calling on everyone to forcibly pray'. Pointedly, he stated, 'The question
is, who is going to hijack Islam and who is going to lead it?'

In response to an audience question about the transformation of
a cosmopolitan, liberal and civilised Kabul in the 1970s to how it is
now, Hiro spoke of villages, a feudal society, ideological fervour and
anti-imperialist attitudes. Cerić, in turn, argued that faith, religion and
morality were not the same, but he was jeered, unusually, for a festival
audience, when he spoke of God breathing life into man. When the
audience was silenced by one of its own, urging them to 'respectfully
listen', Cerić continued, 'You may be religious but not moral, or moral
and not religious. So there is always a relationship between religion and
the state. The possibility of both is different.' He further argued that
there should not be a confrontation between religion and the state, but
harmony, and that people lived in a forced secularisation when they
were not allowed to have a voice this way. This prompted another
audience member to comment that the debate had been 'enlightening,
and interesting to rethink' and as such that it 'might be worth looking
at similarities between the three great [monotheistic] faiths and not just
differences'. Cerić ended on a sobering note, highlighting yet another
spatial difference. He asserted that we should appreciate freedom here
because '70 per cent of all refugees in the world are Muslim. All the wars
today are in Muslim lands. Muslims nations haven't had freedom. The
Muslims need their own West.'

As suggested earlier, discussions on difference do not necessarily
enlighten. If anything, they make people uncomfortable and unsettled. As
one reviewer noted, this event 'was perhaps too ambitious. The panel ...
were all informed and explained their views well, but couldn't agree the
issues among themselves. Inevitably, the audience had a whole different
set of opinions. Little progress was made' (Stodel, 2012). But does this
assessment have more to do with a lack of cultural and religious literacy
specifically about Islamicate cultures? After all, Western religious diversity seems to be taken for granted – it is difficult to imagine, for example,
that anyone in the same context would suggest that Christians of various
stripes should completely agree on the same issues among themselves.

If the sheer diversity of themes and opinions on these themes at this event proved too messy to handle for some, the earlier-mentioned John Tolan's 'Islam and the West: More Complex Than You Might Think' (EIBF, 2013: 37) a year later in 2013 provided a much more concise presentation on rethinking the relationship between Islam and the West. Critically referencing the notion of a clash of civilisations, Ruth Wishart, again chairing, observed:

> The media as we know is fond of clichés, which often provide an easier route for them for analysis than joined-up thinking does [audience laughter], and a persistent cliché not least since 9/11 has been to characterise every incident involving cross-cultural acts of violence as a product of the ongoing clash of oriental and occidental civilisations.

Picking up on Wishart's initial remarks, Tolan provided a pithy observation of Huntington, who 'claimed that conflict was inevitable'. 'Huntington,' Tolan said, 'realises, of course, that this was a simplification, as the idea of the Cold War was also a simplification. In other words, if you liked the Cold War, you'll love the clash of civilisations!' Indeed, 'anyone who knows about the history of the Mediterranean world' knew that contact was rich and varied. Amidst laughter, Tolan said that Huntington bashing was 'easy sport, like shooting fish in a barrel. But we don't do that for 400 pages.'

Dedicating his talk to a co-author who had died of leukaemia a few months earlier, Tolan began by addressing the issue of the need for their book *Europe and the Islamic World: A History* (2013). First, he said, although it was ostensibly 'on a much covered subject', many other works tended to 'lack historical depth' and so this work had attempted to 'look at the importance of these relations over history'. Second, these other works 'were very much from a European perspective', but this one was a corrective in that it came from 'multiple perspectives, many languages, many cultures, which share the Mediterranean basin'. Here again, the attention drawn to spatial and temporal diversity, as it applies to encounters between Islamicate and non-Islamicate cultures and civilisations, is evident.

Tolan proceeded with the rest of his talk by presenting four vignettes of encounters between these peoples from his portion of the book: the Italian who dies in Toledo, the shipwrecked pilgrim, globalisation and the weeping sultan. These deftly woven tales covered the great translation movement though the example and efforts of Gerald of Crimona and described a thriving Muslim community in Sicily as seen through the eyes of Ibn Jubayah. They also demonstrated the remarkable exchange, facilitated by cross-cultural trade, between 'merchants, missionaries and mercenaries'. Finally, in the figure of a nephew of Saladin who had just won a major victory over the fifth crusade, they covered an example of empathy in suffering, and the possibility of a 'humane and philosophical conqueror' such that 'in the midst of war' was 'born the image of the wise and just sultan'.

In narrating the wealth and rich detail of these narratives dispersed deliberately over time and space, Tolan delivered on the promise of the event's title, providing examples of ambivalence and exchange and borrowing as well as conflict and collaboration in the historical relationship between Islam and the West. Again, however, audiences appeared to struggle in engaging with the complexity of this diversity. This time round, the gap between historical knowledge and how it related to understanding and addressing contemporary conflict was even starker. This was clear from the moment that Tolan concluded with the fourth of his vignettes. Indeed, the question-and-answer session that followed took a jarringly presentist turn from the outset, with Wishart immediately asking about the prospect of the Arab Spring turning. Subsequent questions continued this trend, with a discussion on the European Union, the war on terror and contemporary Shia–Sunni conflicts. Unsurprisingly, then, the audience took this lead and Tolan had to field questions about the difference in the 'Islamic diaspora' between France and the UK, and which had the 'better model' of multiculturalism, as well as larger issues about immigration, migrants and language, including the rise of Spanish as the second language of the USA. Tolan did try to steer back into more familiar historical territory, citing examples from conflict relations between the Ottomans and the Safavids in the context of civilisational clashes, the intellectual debt Europe owed to Ibn Sina (Avicenna) and precisely the dangers of presentism in discussing the 'sorry state' of affairs of contemporary intellectual life in the Arab world. But it was clearly a losing battle, and the event arguably 'jumped the shark' when an audience member asked Tolan what, in his view, were 'the things, the attractive things, that we could learn from the Arabic culture, the Islamic culture'.

It was a sincere question and Tolan's response was equally well meant. Invoking London and Paris, 'where there is a lot of exchange and conflict as well', Tolan stated that an 'increasingly globalised world' had

its negative sides as countries like China and India become more ... powerful all across the world. But what is it that we in Europe can appreciate from the Arab cultures now? I think that those of us who travel in the Arab world can come up with lots of examples ... [the] sense of hospitality, openness ... [of being] invited into people's homes. Even people in difficult economic situations will make an effort out of pure generosity to make people feel at home. It is something interesting for us to think about ... [in] other parts of the world as well ... [there is] more generosity and sharing where people have less.

But the question was vexingly, if perhaps inadvertently, utilitarian in its framing. After all, the entire talk preceding the question-and-answer session was didactic, premised precisely on addressing the amnesia or ignorance of historical interactions between Islam and the West. Tolan could not have presented more vivid and powerful examples of positive contact and exchange, 'for better or for worse', as he had said in bringing his talk and the last of the vignettes to a close. But these arguably self-evident lessons seemed only implicit to the audience. Thus caught off guard, Tolan's response to the question was hesitant, punctuated by pauses and almost bewildered, not only falling back on a cliché of generosity and hospitality, but also conflating 'Islam' with 'Arab' and thereby undermining the very diversity that he had been so careful to demonstrate. This was frustrating for several Muslims in the audience whom I spoke with immediately after the event. One confessed that she groaned inwardly when the question was asked and had seen the response coming. 'But it wasn't really his fault,' she said. 'He gave a historical point of view, but the questions just focused on what is happening now.' Sadly, the tyranny of immediacy looks set to prevail for some time still.

CONCLUSION

A number of other events also exemplified this notion of encounter. The two described above were sponsored by the Alwaleed Centre, whose sponsorship was certainly a result of its ongoing outreach agenda and in fulfilment of several of its stated objectives, not least:

> To improve radically knowledge and understanding of Islamic civilisation and of Muslims in Britain among policy-makers, the general public, and students of all ages in the UK through a comprehensive educational outreach programme, and by helping to integrate the study of Islamic civilisation into the school curriculum. (Alwaleed Centre, n.d.)

The centre's events at the EIBF are thus circumscribed by a discourse that is both academic and strategic. But, like a number of other, non-Alwaleed events discussed at length elsewhere, they did not entirely resonate with their intended public. For all the cool rationality evident in the titles of these events as well as other similarly themed ones, the actual discussions were invariably passionate and humanising in equal measure. Nonetheless, it would seem that there are limits to the extent that these events, at least in the short term, can fundamentally change the public and popular paradigm that conflates Islam, Islamdom and Islamicate. This problem is compounded when discussions on history are not perceived as bearing on contemporary circumstances, especially when they remain overwhelmingly framed by a discourse of conflict, violence and othering.

The EIBF is a remarkable site in its function as a public square. Its role, too, in both the production as well as the representation of an Islamicate space cannot be understated, particularly in the way that this contributes to wider public understandings of Islam and Muslims. Where encounters between Islamicate and Western cultures are narrated, commonality is an overriding theme. Spatial and temporal diversity, nonetheless, also feature, especially in relation to the politics and conflicts between modern nation states. But other seeds of Islamicate diversity, particularly of the histories and thought of many distinct communities of interpretation and, in turn, their notions of religious authority and leadership, ethics, governance and civil society, have yet to take root in Charlotte Square Gardens.

REFERENCES

Abou El Fadl, K. (2006). *The Search for Beauty in Islam: A Conference of the Books*. Lanham, MD: Rowman and Littlefield.

Alibhai, F. S. (2013). 'Religion, faith and spirituality at the Edinburgh summer festivals 2013: A compilation of Islamicate and other events', available at https://dx.doi.org/10.6084/m9.figshare.759605.v1

Alwaleed Centre (n.d.). 'The six key objectives of the centre', available at www. ed.ac.uk/literatures-languages-cultures/alwaleed/about/our-objectives

Alwaleed Centre (2012). 'Events relating to Islam and the world of Islam in Edinburgh's 2012 festivals', available at www.ed.ac.uk/files/imports/file-Manager/Festivals 2012.pdf

Aslam, N. (2013). *The Blind Man's Garden*. London: Faber and Faber.

Bahari, M. (2012). *Then They Came for Me: A Story of Injustice and Survival in Iran's Most Notorious Prison*. Richmond: Oneworld Publications.

Barley, N. (2011). 'Directing the Edinburgh International Book Festival'. *The Guardian*, 12 August, available at www.theguardian.com/books/2011/aug/12/edinburgh-international-book-festival-director

Barley, N. (2013). 'Celebrate 30 years of the world in words: What will the next 30 years bring?' *08.2013 Edinburgh International Book Festival: Celebrating 30 Years*, 2.

BBC (1989). 'Ayatollah sentences author to death'. *On This Day: 1950–2005*, available at http://news.bbc.co.uk/onthisday/hi/dates/stories/february/14/ newsid_2541000/2541149.stm

BBC (2013). 'Edinburgh International Book Festival celebrates 30 years'. *BBC Scotland*, 10 August, available at www.bbc.co.uk/news/uk-scotland-23578116

Bizot, F. (2012). *Facing the Torturer: Inside the Mind of a War Criminal* (C. Mandelle and A. Audouard, trans). London: Rider.

Bunglawala, I. (2012). 'Looking back at Salman Rushdie's *The Satanic Verses*'. *The Guardian*, 14 September, available at www.theguardian.com/books/2012/sep/14/looking-at-salman-rushdies-satanic-verses

Devji, F. (2012). 'Looking back at Salman Rushdie's *The Satanic Verses*'. *The Guardian*, 14 September, available at www.theguardian.com/books/2012/sep/14/looking-at-salman-rushdies-satanic-verses

EIBF (2012). *Edinburgh International Book Festival: 11–27 August 2012: The World, In Words*. Edinburgh: Edinburgh International Book Festival.

EIBF (2013). *08.2013 Edinburgh International Book Festival: Celebrating 30 Years*. Edinburgh: Edinburgh International Book Festival.

EIBF (2014). 'Edinburgh International Book Festival wraps up 17 days of dialogue, discussion and debate', available at www.edbookfest.co.uk/news/edinburgh-international-book-festival-wraps-up-17-days-of-dialogue-discussion-and-debate

Geller, P. (2011). *Stop the Islamization of America: A Practical Guide to the Resistance*. Washington, DC: WND Books.

Grim, B. J. and Karim, M. S. (2011). 'The future of the global Muslim population'. *Pew Research Center Forum on Religion and Public Life*, available at www.pewforum.org/2011/01/27/the-future-of-the-global-muslim-population

Harris, J. (2013). *Peaches for Monsieur Le Curé*. London: Black Swan.

Hirschkop, K. (1990). 'Heteroglossia and civil society: Bakhtin's public square and the politics of modernity'. *Studies in the Literary Imagination*, 23(1), 65–75.

Hodgson, Marshall G. S. (1977). *The Venture of Islam: Conscience and History in a World Civilization* (3 vols), Vol. 1: *The Classical Age of Islam*. Chicago, IL: University of Chicago Press.

Holland, T. (2012). *In the Shadow of the Sword: The Birth of Islam and the Rise of the Global Arab Empire*. New York: Doubleday.

Huntington, S. (1993). 'The clash of civilizations?' *Foreign Affairs*, available at www.foreignaffairs.com/articles/48950/samuel-p-huntington/the-clash-of-civilizations

Jaggi, M. (2001). 'A singular writer'. *The Guardian*, 8 September, available at www.theguardian.com/education/2001/sep/08/artsandhumanities.highereducation

Jones, C. (2014). 'Is Islamic State medieval?' *Research the Headlines*, 18

September, available at https://researchtheheadlines.org/2014/09/18/is-islamic-state-medieval/

Kadri, S. (2011). *Heaven on Earth: A Journey Through Shariʿa Law*. London: Random House.

Lefebvre, H. (1991). *The Production of Space*, trans. D. Nicholson-Smith. Oxford: Blackwell.

Light, A. and Smith, J. M. (eds) (1998). *The Production of Public Space*. Lanham, MD: Rowman and Littlefield.

Manji, I. (2003). *The Trouble With Islam Today: A Muslim's Call for Reform in her Faith*. London: St Martin's Press.

Nawaz, M. and Bromley, T. (2012). *Radical: My Journey from Islamist Extremism to a Democratic Awakening*. London: W. H. Allen.

Neuman, A. (2012). *The Traveller of the Century*. London: Pushkin.

Petley, J. and Richardson, R. (2011). *Pointing the Finger: Islam and Muslims in the British Media*. Oxford: Oneworld Publications.

Poole, E. (2002), *Reporting Islam: Media Representations of British Muslims*. London: I. B. Tauris.

Rushdie, S. (1995). *Shame*. London: Vintage.

Rushdie, S. (1997). *The Satanic Verses: A Novel*. London: Owl Books.

Rushdie, S. (2012). *Joseph Anton*. London: Vintage.

Said, E. (1978). *Orientalism*. London: Penguin.

Said, E. W. (2001). 'The clash of ignorance: Labels like "Islam" and "the West" serve only to confuse us about a disorderly reality'. *The Nation*, available at www.thenation.com/article/clash-ignorance?page=full

Shafak, E. (2012). *Honour*. London: Viking.

Shehadeh, R. (2012). *Occupation Diaries*. London: Profile Books.

Steele, J. (2012). *The Ghosts of Afghanistan: The Haunted Battleground*. London: Portobello.

Stodel, B. (2012). 'Edinburgh Festivals 2012'. BobView.com, 19 August, available at http://bobview.com/tag/mustafa-ceric/

Tolan, J., Veinstein, G. and Laurens, H. (2013). *Europe and the Islamic World: A History*. Princeton, NJ: Princeton University Press.

Ziedan, Y. (2012). *Azazeel*. London: Atlantic Books.

13

INTEGRATION
Halal Scots: Muslims' Social Integration in Scotland

Reza Bagheri

INTRODUCTION

Since the 1970s, we have seen increasing interest in the integration of Muslims as the most visible ethno-religious minority group in Britain. The term 'integration' as used in this chapter is concerned with the social aspect of a process in which Muslims, as well as other minority ethnic people, required and/or would like to participate in society. More elaboration of different theoretical and academic interpretations of this term is discussed later in this chapter. The social aspects of integration mainly revolve around the maintenance of Muslims' distinctive identity and practice (Modood, 2005, 2007; Parekh, 2008; Vertovec and Wessendorf, 2010). This chapter looks at Scottish Muslims' integration strategies (based on gender, generational and level of religiosity) and introduces the idea of 'halal integration' which entails fitting into society while maintaining their religious identity. This refers to the life of many Scottish Muslims, whom I refer to as 'halal Scots' – those who integrated into many aspects of Scottish society while maintaining their religious identity and practice. Some examples of such integration are adopting alternative ways of socialising such as meeting at cafés, running family and social events in non-alcoholic environments, and taking part in voluntary and charitable work.

Previous research reported that Muslims in northern parts of England, for instance, had developed separate rather than integrated lives (Cantle, 2001: 9), though this report was highly contested and more recent surveys have reported that there was more residential mixing in the 2000s (Simpson, 2012). Recently, for instance, David Cameron (British Government, 2011), then the British prime minister, announced at the Munich Security Conference that 'state multiculturalism' had encouraged 'different cultures to live separate lives, apart from each other and apart from the mainstream'. Muslims' distinctive identity and practice has sometimes even been perceived as a national identity threat (Goodhart, 2004; Chakraborti and Garland, 2009: 45) or has been seen as creating potential enemies within (see Ahmed, 2003). It is, however, important to note that Muslims in the Scottish context established a more mixed and integrated way of living with the majority from the outset (Hussain and Miller, 2006: 19), which was associated partly with the smaller population of Muslims in Scotland (Penrose and Howard, 2008: 95). For example, a British Council Scotland Survey showed that both Muslim and non-Muslim participants believed that 'integration in Scotland is easier than in England' (2010: 8) and also found that around 60% of Scots believed that 'Muslims in Scotland are integrated into everyday Scottish life' (ibid.: 5) and only 27% felt that they were not.

The importance of integration lies in the fact that some minority groups, including Muslims, often sought to maintain their own ways of life and also to teach such ways of life to their children, while the host country sought to maintain a sense of common national identity and cultural continuity. The problem was seen as a matter of finding a way for a society to incorporate its minorities so that it could both satisfy the minorities' aspirations to maintain cherished ways of life and at the same time maintain itself as a (historical) community of common belonging. Therefore, incorporation of these new members into society is a question of growing importance. Different scholars' responses to this question have mainly revolved around the concepts of assimilation and integration. Assimilation refers to a process in which the newcomers become similar to their host society (Brubaker, 2001), whereas the term integration, mainly proposed by multiculturalists, refers to a state of 'recognition and respect' (Kymlicka, 1995; Hall, 2000; Parekh, 2006; Modood, 2007). The term 'integration' is contested, and there is no single definition or theory of immigrant integration (Castles et al., 2002; Phillimore and Goodson, 2008). One common theoretical approach to integration was through distinguishing integration from assimilation (Kymlicka, 2001; Parekh, 2006; Modood, 2007; Pfeffer, 2014) or through parallelising them (Brubaker, 2001). Pfeffer (2014: 354) proposes three main distinctions; first, based on integration, a host society would invoke 'laws to incorporate its immigrants in a way that is respectful of, and is willing to celebrate their diverse practices', whereas, based on assimilation, a host society would seek 'to attenuate differences between minorities and the host society'. Second, 'assimilation is often a unidirectional process insofar as it places most of the expectations on immigrants ... Conversely, integration ought to be viewed as a dialogical process meaning that it should be achieved through the cooperation and deliberation of both actors' (Pfeffer, 2014: 354). Finally, 'integration can be defined on the basis of participation in, as opposed to degree of similarity with, the host society ... However, just because integration requires convergence on liberal democratic values does not mean that cultural groups need to give up traditional practices' (Pfeffer, 2014: 354). Immigrants' integration is also debated and theorised from more practical and functional perspectives, which highlights the interaction between the social and functional dimensions and the influence of the state (Berry 1997; Hale, 2000; Korac, 2003; Ager and Strang, 2008; Hickman et al., 2008; Fekete, 2008). Further to social and structural issues, relational and cultural barriers were also important in minorities' integration. This revolves around issues such as 'relationships with the host community, the importance of retaining one's own cultural connections, shared values and the need to ensure safety and security' (Phillimore and Goodson, 2008: 309). From this perspective, the importance of relational and cultural issues, such as religious boundaries and cultural barriers, is better highlighted.

Religion and religious identity, for many Muslims, are central to their sense of who they are and how their behaviour in all spheres of life should be (Jacobson, 1997; Modood, 2005). Joppke (2012) also argues that the religious identity of practising Muslims creates boundaries for Muslims' cultural and social integration. The significance of Islam in practising Muslims' lives is related to the crucial emphasis of teachings of Islam upon right and correct action (Jacobson, 1997; Esposito, 2011). Islamic law, which constitutes 'the ideal social blueprint for the believer who asks, *what should I do?*', has remained important to Muslims' identity and practice (Esposito, 2011: 158). These pervasive religious boundaries can affect Muslims' social integration, because they affect their wider social relation with non-Muslims – the majority – and their daily lives (Jacobson, 1997; Joppke, 2012). Jacobson (1997) highlights the differences in socialising patterns between Muslims and non-Muslims, and suggests that the dominance of drinking alcohol in the social lives of most young Britons can result in the isolation of Muslims. Muslims' identity politics, however, has also been seen as an important trigger for increased civic integration (Choudhury, 2007; Meer, 2010). As Hussain and Miller (2006) argue, Muslims' Scottish identity was adopted as a tool of integration rather than separation. Therefore, Muslims' religious identity and practices can function as a cultural boundary and barrier (Joppke, 2012), a trigger for increased civic integration (Choudhury,

2007; Meer, 2010) or a tool of integration (Hussain and Miller, 2006). It is, however, important to note that Muslims' affiliation with religious identity can vary on the basis of their commitment to their religion, and this can also be different from the level of their religious practice (Ameli et al., 2004; Maliepaard and Phalet, 2012). Thus, this chapter discusses the importance of religious identity for integration among practising and less-practising Muslims.

In this research, with regard to the importance of religiosity, participants are divided into three main categories of practising, less-practising and non-practising. Practising Muslims are those participants who make a full commitment to the religion and observe Islamic law, especially the 'five pillars of Islam' (Meer, 2010: 59; Esposito, 2011: 18). In contrast, non-practising Muslims are those people who identify themselves as Muslim in terms of culture, ethnicity or birth (Ameli et al., 2004: 21), but who do not practise any religious observances such as the five pillars of Islam or the Islamic dietary law. The less-practising Muslims are those who do not fit into the first two categories. More specifically, it refers to those people who identify themselves as Muslim, but do not practise all Islamic rules – for example, they do not read daily prayer or fast during Ramadan, but they do still practise some other rules, such as avoiding alcohol consumption and consuming only halal meat.

Integration, or acculturation, can differ 'among generations, as indicated by the differences that can be observed between immigrants and their children and grandchildren' (Phinney, 2003). The differing values that are associated with the private and public spheres may require second-generation Muslims to develop different identity strategies and to switch cultural 'codes' (Ballard, 1994: 33). By highlighting the long-term and intergenerational nature of integration, Modood (2007) and Pfeffer (2014) argue that, in some areas, the integration of second generations still remains problematic. By taking generational dynamics into consideration, I will discuss the importance of generational difference in Muslims' integration. Previous research also pointed to a gendered process of exclusion in observing that both structural factors (such as discrimination and racism) and cultural pressures (Qureshi and Moores, 1999; Masud, 2005; Cassidy et al., 2006; El-Nakla et al., 2007; Lewis, 2007) affect Muslim women's social integration. Lewis (2007), for example, suggests that young Muslims – particularly young women – are often overprotected by their anxious families. Qureshi and Moores (1999) also suggest that young British Asians live between two sets of cultural values: on the one hand, the social world of family, community and religion, and, on the other, the Western world as experienced through education and media. They suggest that 'the Islamic tradition make[s] any translation between those value systems especially difficult for second-generation girls' (Qureshi and Moores, 1999: 318). This chapter reflects on these gendered processes and highlights the importance of gender dynamics in Muslims' social integration in Scotland by addressing the experiences of both men and women.

This chapter draws on research that involved forty-three semi-structured interviews with Muslims, differentiated by generation and gender, in 2011 (July to December). These in-depth interviews started with a topic guide, but relied on open-ended and broad questions with prompts and probes. The length of interviews varied (from 30 to 120 minutes), according to the respondent's available time and how much discussion each question provoked, but around three-quarters of the interviews (thirty out of forty-three) lasted around forty minutes. The location for the interview was also chosen according to the respondent's preference, and included places such as the respondent's or my home, Islamic centres and mosques, and university meeting rooms and cafés. As the category 'Muslim' is ethnically, socially and denominationally a diverse category, I tried to gain access to different participants from different ethnic, social and denominational backgrounds in order to reflect this diversity. For example, in terms of ethnic background, twenty-eight respondents were of Pakistani origin, five were Iraqi, five Kenyan, two Malawian, one Egyptian and one was of Lebanese background. There was also a White Scottish convert woman whose father was an Iranian, but as she was brought up by her White Scottish mother as a non-Muslim, she considered herself to be a White Scot. In terms of social differences, these respondents came from different social positions: sixteen were employed, fifteen were self-employed, seven were students and five were housewives and social volunteers. They had also reached different levels of education; fourteen had been educated to Standard Grade level, twenty-two had a higher-education degree and the rest (first-generation participants) had been educated to primary level in their country of origin. In terms of denomination, they were also from different backgrounds; the majority (thirty-one) were Sunni Muslims and the remaining twelve Shia Muslims. As there is not an official sample of Muslims, the most convenient way to access Muslims was through university Islamic societies, mosques, Islamic centres, Muslim organisations and social groups. The process of data analysis in this study is influenced by the grounded theory method because of its well-described, well-organised and systematic process of qualitative data analysis (Glaser and Strauss, 1967). It should be noted that the respondents' names mentioned in this chapter are all pseudonyms.

Integration of ethnic minority people has been studied from different perspectives and aspects, but much of what has been discussed about integration 'starts from the *majority* vantage point, [and] little attention is paid to the views of minorities' (Fekete, 2008). There is also a dearth of research about Muslims' integration, especially social integration, in Scotland. Most studies have paid less attention to social integration by focusing more on economic or educational integration (Hussain and Miller, 2006; British Council Scotland Survey, 2010; Kidd and Jamieson, 2011). The data from my research demonstrates the problematic nature of social integration for Muslims in the Scottish context, and this is the focus of this chapter. Most existing studies of Muslims in Scotland have focused on major urban areas such as Edinburgh and Glasgow (Hopkins, 2004; Hussain and Miller, 2006; Virdee et al., 2006; Kyriakides et al., 2009). This chapter, therefore, will extend such research by covering the experiences of Muslims across Scotland's major cities and small towns.

FITTING IN: ALTERNATIVE WAYS OF SOCIALISING

The first aspect of Muslims' social integration was making friends and socialising with majority group members (White Scottish non-Muslim people). Some participants stated that they had both White Scottish non-Muslim and Muslim friends. Educational settings such as school and university were the most common places in which participants established or developed friendships and social relationships with majority group members. For example, Akram was one of ten participants who mentioned the importance of school in the development of her first social relationships with the majority. She was a less-practising second-generation Muslim woman and was born and brought up in Dundee. Akram, an accountant, stated that she had a good relationship with English and Scottish people and that this started at school:

> I have English and Scottish friends as well as Muslim friends and most of my clients are White Scottish people. Actually, this was started from school. Throughout my education, there was a lot of integration with the Scottish people and I did not have any problem with them and they did not have problem with me either. (Akram, 43, female, Dundee)

This can imply the importance of school in developing some Muslim children's social friendships with the majority. In another example,

Batool, a young second-generation Muslim woman from Glasgow, noted that during her school years, even though there were some Asian girls in her class, she intentionally tried to form close relationships with Scottish girls. These two examples highlight that these participants' first contact with the White Scottish people, the majority, started from their experiences of attending school. This shows the importance of schools and spaces of education in the development of Muslims' social integration with the majority.

Another important issue about school is that when there is a greater chance of gaining familiarity with Muslims this may have an effect on White Scottish pupils' welcoming attitudes and thus facilitate Muslims' friendship with the majority. If children at school are in close contact with Muslim pupils, they can become more familiar with them, and thus reduce prejudice and develop social friendships. Familiarity with Muslims could decrease Islamophobia and prejudiced attitudes. This supports previous research findings that more contact and knowledge about Muslims plays an important part in decreasing Islamophobia (Hussain and Miller, 2006; Ormston et al., 2011). Decreasing Islamophobia and being in daily contact with Muslim pupils can make the process of setting up a social friendship much easier for both Muslim pupils and the majority children.

The data suggests that when these social relationships develop at a later stage of life, more cultural and social barriers come into play. For example, if these relationships were to develop outside of school, for example in people's homes, they would face certain limits (such as daytime interaction and the no-alcohol environment). Wahed, who was a second-generation Muslim man studying at Glasgow University, for instance, stated that even though he had some White Scottish friends, most of the time he tended to interact with his Pakistani Muslim friends. Wahed highlighted that the issue of drinking and going out is so dominant in Scottish culture and normal conversations are often centred on that topic. Even though he self-identified as Scottish, as he did not drink alcohol he could not relate to such issues; thus, he preferred to interact with Muslims with whom he had more in common from a cultural and religious point of view. When alcohol becomes central and with events often taking place in pubs and bars, Muslims may limit their social relationships to a certain extent. As a result, some Muslims tried to meet people socially in places such as cafés and coffee shops.

Akram, the less-practising second-generation Muslim woman, who was born and brought up in Dundee and was a skilled self-employed accountant with a college degree, expressed that she would meet her

Scottish friends in places such as coffee shops where alcohol was not available:

> I have got some Scottish friends as well ... they are all girls and we meet out for a coffee; sometimes I go to my friends' houses, but they are Muslims too. But for meeting up with White Scottish girls in the towns, we usually go to places such as cafés. (Akram, 43, female, Dundee)

This quote highlights how even skilled second-generation Muslims can limit their social integration because of religious observations. It further implies that, first, Akram's social friendship with White Scottish people was limited to girls; second, her social meetings with Scottish girls were limited to places outside the home; and third, meeting outside the home was further limited to no-alcohol environments such as cafés. Akram's comment thus illustrates how avoiding alcohol consumption and mixed-sex meetings can affect Muslim women's social integration. Akram was a less-practising Muslim; however, she stated that she preferred to meet people socially in places where alcohol is not served.

The next example is Azadeh, a second-generation practising Muslim woman with a college degree. She was a housewife, yet very active in many Muslim and non-Muslim groups. She stated that she does not drink alcohol and prefers not to be present at places where it is served. She explained, however, that she managed her social integration by leaving events just as the alcohol was about to be served. Azadeh highlighted that, although her religion limited her to some extent, such as leaving parties at drinking time, it did not make her isolated or cause her to miss out on socialising.

Leaving events as alcohol was about to be served was also evident in the example of Sanaz, another second-generation Muslim woman with a university degree. She said that she had attended a Christmas party at her school but did not go for drinks afterwards. This suggests that approaches to avoiding being present in places where alcohol is served can differ, even among practising and less-practising Muslims. Some do not attend the event at all, while others attend but leave before alcohol is served. Taking different strategies to avoid being around alcohol can be context-dependent. For example, none of the practising Muslims and some of the less-practising Muslims would attend pubs and bars; however some did attend academic or work-related parties where alcohol would be consumed at some point during the event. Some of the respondents, such as Batool, Fatima and Fazel, avoid such events from the beginning, while others, such as Akram, Sanaz and Sadiq, simply leave the event when people start drinking. This might suggest better integration for those with more open interpretations of avoiding being present in places where alcohol is served than those with a more restricted interpretation.

In other contexts, such as community or family events when Muslims are the main organisers or are on the decision-making committee, the participants made sure that the events were held in places where alcohol was not served at all, thus removing a barrier for the greater social integration of Muslims. Running voluntary and charitable groups could enable Muslims to observe their religious consideration for social integration. For example, in events run by these groups there was no alcohol consumption or mixed-sex meetings.

I now consider the collective effort of some female Muslims to arrange such halal social meetings. Arezo, another second-generation Muslim woman, was involved in arranging many events for Muslim women at Edinburgh Central Mosque. She stated that they arranged their events with non-Muslims at the mosque or another place where alcohol was not involved. Arezo highlighted that, because of the drinking culture, Muslims cannot attend the majority's social events and therefore sought to organise their own. Another example of such efforts to reserve a special space, a non-alcoholic place, is Sadiq's organisation of a university conference in a restaurant where halal food was served and alcoholic drinks were not available. Sadiq, a practising Muslim who was studying at Glasgow University, highlighted his own experience of organising a university conference in a restaurant that did not serve alcohol. These examples suggest the importance of space in the development of practising and some less-practising Muslims' social integration, and that the effort for halal integration was not only limited to Muslim individuals but also involved some Muslims or Muslim groups in some public institutions, who suggested or negotiated alternative spaces for their greater social integration.

Muslims' alternative ways of integrating was not limited to spatial changes; my analysis of the data suggests that timing is also important. Six participants (Jafar, Fazel, Sadiq, Hareb, Azim and Zahra) reported their concerns about evening socialising. For example, Azim, another second-generation practising Muslim, stated that he does not take part in the Scottish nightlife culture. He said that the main reason for avoiding Scottish nightlife was the dominance of alcohol consumption and the possibility of being pushed by friends to take part in such culture. This suggests that, for some Muslims, social integration with the majority can be limited to daytime events and, as discussed earlier, mostly to non-alcoholic environments. Socialising in the evening might be more difficult for Muslim women as there is more family control over young Muslim women than over their male counterparts. For example, Hareb, a first-generation practising Muslim from Stirling, allowed his son to stay overnight at his Scottish friends' home, but he did not let his daughters socialise in the same way. This suggests that boys here have a fuller and more active social life, as concerns about alcohol and mixed-sex interaction do not arise for them. However, such participation was not allowed for girls and their socialising was limited to daytime meetings. The increased parental control over Muslim women was also highlighted in the example of Akram:

> The social integration is more difficult for female Muslims. It has a lot to do with the peer pressure and the parents as well and how they see things. A lot of first-generation Muslims like my parents were not happy with their children's integration with the Scottish people. Such objection was more about female because they tended to (self) control female Muslims a lot more than men. For example, they wanted to know what female Muslims were up to rather than what male Muslims were up to.

The examples of Hareb's daughters and Akram suggest that some Muslim women might be under parental or peer pressure to manage their social integration in certain ways, such as interacting only with girls and during the day. The parental control of young Muslim women may be associated with controlling female Muslims' sexuality (Brah, 1996). Muslim women's lack of participation in nightlife culture can also be associated with the observation of patriarchal family values, in which women are considered as 'culture-bearers' (Esposito, 2011: 98). The latter was demonstrated in the example of Zahra, a second-generation practising Muslim woman. She stated that some Muslim women would not participate in nightlife culture for a range of reasons, such as 'morals, commitment and love for the family'. Her example shows that even those Muslim women who work, which is already a departure from the practice of patriarchal ideology, can still observe other values such as devotion to the family. It is, however, important to note that if it was only the women who were expected to be so devoted, such practice can be seen as patriarchal. Another important point is that those women who participate in the dominant socialising culture can also manage their time in such a way as to be devoted to their families as well. The example of Zahra, however, implies that staying with one's family and taking care of children can limit some Muslim women's socialising at night. Zahra also stated that, rather than taking part in this culture of evening socialising, she prefers instead to participate in voluntary work and family events. It can be deduced that, as the former is usually done during the daytime and with little or no involvement of alcohol and the latter involve children and family members, there would be no barrier to Zahra and Muslim women like her participating in voluntary work and family events.

Social friendship with the majority can for some other Muslims be even more limited than daytime meetings in cafés. For example, Wahed and Azim preferred to socialise with their Muslim friends rather than with their White Scottish friends. This was also highlighted by Jafar, a second-generation practising Muslim man from Glasgow. He stated that, while his White Scottish friends are going drinking or clubbing, he attends community programmes. Jafar said that activities such as drinking and clubbing restricted his social relationships with his White Scottish friends to doing charity and academic work and that having more in common with other Muslims in his community leads him to communicate with his Muslim friends in the evening when his Scottish friends are out drinking. Such time management in socialising with Muslim and non-Muslim friends was also evident in the examples of Wahed and Akram, who stated that the dominance of drinking in Scottish social culture limited their social friendships with White Scottish people to a certain extent. All these examples suggest that some Muslims' friendships with White Scottish people are often limited by religious or cultural considerations connected with being Muslim. This implies that such restrictions would apply less to less-practising Muslims, but the example of Akram, who was a less-practising Muslim woman, suggests that even some less-practising Muslims may commit to such restrictions. In other words, even the category of 'less-practising Muslims', which adds to the dichotomy of 'practising' and 'non-practising', does not represent a homogeneous group. For example, Hamid, a first-generation less-practising Muslim man, stated that he has some White Scottish friends with whom he has developed a mutual close social relationship:

> I have got some White friends, I play cricket with White folks. They are very good friends. They come to my house and we go to their house and we have got a very good interaction between each other. (Hamid, 28, male, Edinburgh)

Hamid is unusual among my participants, since almost none of the others reported close personal relationships with their White Scottish friends. This was mainly related to the dominance of alcohol consumption in such relationships. There was only one other example of a respondent mentioning strong social interaction with White Scottish friends, that of

Hareb's son, and in this case, of course, alcohol was not served when he was at his Scottish friends' house. Conversely, in the example of Hamid, alcohol was served when he was at his Scottish friends' house, but he did not see it as a barrier. Hamid used to go to pubs and bars and was a less-practising Muslim who did not mind being present in places where alcohol was served, even though he avoided drinking alcohol. The example of Hamid suggests the importance of flexibility around being present in places where alcohol is served in improving some less-practising Muslims' social integration. It may also imply that those who have no commitment to the religion at all, such as non-practising Muslims, will not have such cultural barriers in developing their social friendships with White Scottish people. Other barriers, such as racism and Islamophobia, can affect social integration. Given the importance of commitment to the religion, further research on Scottish non-Muslims' attitudes towards social integration would be useful.

SOCIAL AND SHARED ACTIVITIES

Another form of social integration preferred by Scottish Muslims was organising and/or participating in shared social activities such as voluntary work, and inter-faith and charity events. For example, thirteen participants (out of forty-three) were active in such activities; some of them (Arezo, Sadiq, Zahra and Jafar) explicitly stated that they preferred to develop or maintain their social relationships with majority Scots through voluntary work. The importance of this form of social integration stems from Muslims' active role in organising and running such activities, which also hints at their civil integration. The popularity of these activities, especially among second-generation Muslims, can be grounded in the absence of alcohol and the accommodation of Muslims' religious needs. Running voluntary and charitable groups could enable Muslims to observe their religious duties, and in events run by these groups there was no alcohol consumption or mixed-sex meetings. For example, Jafar, one of the thirteen participants active in social and charitable work, highlighted his involvement in these activities as a good example of halal integration. This example highlights how respondents were keen to integrate, and sought innovative and acceptable means of doing so. Jafar was a second-generation practising Muslim man and a full-time student at Glasgow University, and the data suggests that all thirteen participants who were active in this type of social and charitable work had been educated at least to Standard Grade level, suggesting the importance of education in Muslims' social integration. Although halal integration remained important for these individuals, mixing and interacting with the Scottish majority group members was key to these activities. Many participants asserted that their activities were in cooperation with Scottish majority group members, as well as Muslims, and were thus beneficial for both. For example, Arezo, a self-employed second-generation Muslim woman, said that she worked on a voluntary basis with Scottish children, including non-Muslims:

> I used to volunteer a lot. I started to volunteer with Muslim groups and then I just thought, why I am volunteering only with Muslim groups; it is not just the Muslim groups need help, everybody needs help, then I started volunteering with a group that teaches English to people with learning disabilities and they are all Scottish people. (Arezo, 50, female, Edinburgh)

Educated Muslims' voluntary work and civil participation was not limited to social and charitable work. There were three particular participants (Zahra, Saleh and Samad) who reported high levels of political participation. Saleh, a first-generation practising Muslim man, was politically active in many groups, such as the Muslim Council of Scotland. He is a retired professor and has lived for twenty-eight years in East Kilbride. Saleh stated that he was working with the Scottish Parliament to improve racial equality in Scotland.

Out of the thirteen participants who were active in social and shared activities, eleven were second-generation Muslims. This suggests the importance of generational dynamics in Muslims' social and political participation. However, the examples of Saleh and Samad, as two first-generation Muslims, challenge the exclusion of the first generation from social and political integration. These two examples suggest that even first-generation Muslims may be active in such civil and political participation. It is, however, important to note that both Saleh and Samad had higher-education degrees from Scottish universities. The fact that all thirteen participants in this section had been educated at least to some extent in Britain suggests the importance of this in Muslims' social and political participation. Having been educated in Scotland and thus being more familiar with Scottish cultural, social and political systems can make educated Muslims more confident and capable of taking part in social and political activities. This was highlighted further in the examples of Zahra and Nader, who asserted that second-generation Muslims naturally integrate into society. The lesser participation of first-generation participants in such activities can also be explained by this argument, suggesting that most of the first-generation participants had not been educated at all in Scotland and struggled with language, which diminished their participation in civil and political issues. It is important to note that other issues such as the poor economic status of most first-generation participants could also limit their participation in social and shared activities or civil and political integration. For example, my data suggests that many of the first-generation participants were unskilled workers and the main provider for their extended family; they had to work very hard, and in some cases had two jobs, to make an acceptable life for themselves and their families. Therefore, they lacked the time to take part in voluntary or social activities. In contrast, second-generation Muslims were not interested in long working hours and had their parents' financial support for their higher education. Therefore, this suggests the importance of second-generation Muslims' increased skills, education and language fluency, as well as simply having more time, in their further integration in social and political activities.

SPORTING ACTIVITIES

Participating in sporting activities is another mechanism whereby Muslims integrate socially in Scotland. Consistent with earlier forms of social integration, interacting with White Scottish people was highlighted in sporting activities too. For example, Nader, a second-generation Muslim man, stated that he was in a football team in which he was the only 'Asian' and the only Muslim. Nader stated that for him, as a second-generation Scottish Muslim, integration was a matter of course. This supports my earlier argument that social integration for second-generation Muslims, thanks to their same educational, cultural and linguistic attribution, is normal. However, the dominance of alcohol consumption in the face of its prohibition in Islam was the main barrier for second-generation Muslims' greater social integration. Muslims' participation in sporting activities points to the absence of such barriers in sport. This was highlighted in the example of Fazel, a second-generation practising Muslim man. He stated that, even though he could not take part in the drinking culture, he could play football with White Scottish people and that because there was little or no alcohol involvement in football matches, he could enjoy such activities. In another example, Azim, also a second-generation practising Muslim man, stated that instead of taking part in drinking and clubbing, he plays football with White Scottish people. Nader's, Fazel's and Azim's experiences highlight the important role of football in their social integration as opposed to drinking or clubbing. It is, however, important to note that many football teams have a culture of going out for a drink afterwards, which would limit the extent to which Muslims can take part. Other sports also played a role in Muslims' social integration. Zahir, a second-generation practising Muslim man from Glasgow, stated that he used to take part in many sporting activities, including hockey and rugby, with White Scottish people.

All the above examples suggest the importance of the absence of alcohol in the development of second-generation Muslims' social integration in sporting activities. However, there were two first-generation participants (Hamid and Samad) who highlighted issues other than alcohol in their social integration. As mentioned earlier, Hamid, a less-practising Muslim man, stated that he has some White Scottish friends with whom he has developed a mutual close social relationship through playing cricket. This shows that engagement in sporting activities can extend beyond the pitch. Unlike other participants who highlighted the absence of alcohol consumption in sporting activities, Hamid explained that through sport he has developed close friendships and visits the homes of White Scottish people. Later in the interview, he also mentioned that if this group of friends drink at home or go to places where alcohol is served, he can still spend time with them but will simply avoid drinking alcohol himself. It is important to note that this approach was very rare among practising participants; none of the others reported such close personal relationships with their White Scottish friends, which was mainly related to the dominance of alcohol consumption in such relationships. Hamid was a less-practising Muslim and would go to pubs and bars, so did not object to being present in places where alcohol was served, which may have helped him develop such close relationships with some of his White Scottish friends.

The example of Hamid implies that those who have less or no commitment to their religion, such as less-practising and non-practising Muslims, will not have such religious barriers in developing their social friendships with White Scottish people. However, other cultural barriers, such as language barriers, a preference for socialising only within their own ethnic group and racism still can affect their social integration. This was highlighted by Samad, a first-generation practising Muslim man from Dunfermline. Samad explained how he and his Muslim friends in a Scottish cricket club split from a White majority Scottish team and made a Muslim majority team. Samad explained that issues such as the language barrier and cultural differences, such as feeling more comfortable with other Muslims, led them to form a Muslim team within a Scottish club. This demonstrates the limitations to some Muslims' social integration due to their socialisation only with people from the same ethnic and religious background (cf. Wimmer and Lewis, 2010; Platt, 2012). Unlike those who highlighted the barrier of alcohol, Samad suggests that the main reason for their split was the perception of racism, cultural and language issues. Given the strong association between sporting teams and alcohol, this may also have played a role.

Considering the second-generation Muslims' socioeconomic status, being advantaged by having a Scottish education, knowing the English language and having greater links with Scottish culture, it may be that their perspectives on social integration would be different from those of first-generation Muslims, who mostly lacked such attributes. Considering the importance of sociological variables in their participation in sporting activities, the data suggests that the majority of those who participated in sporting activities were second-generation Muslims (sixteen out of eighteen). This may imply the importance of a generational dynamic in Muslims' participation in sporting activities. However, the examples of two first-generation Muslims, Hamid and Samad, challenge this.

Participants' involvement in sporting activities was not limited to male interviewees. There were seven Muslim women (Sanaz, Shakila, Kathryn, Zainab, Akram, Arezo and Rafiqah) who reported taking part in sporting activities. Muslim women's participation in sporting activities, however, involved different barriers from those reported by Muslim men. Muslim women's participation was interlinked with their religious concerns, more specifically the prohibition of mixed-sex meetings. The data suggests that all seven Muslim women took part only in women-only sessions. However, it was evident that all practising women participants in this research tended to respect some gender segregation in sporting activities. For example, Sanaz, a second-generation Muslim woman from Edinburgh, stated that she preferred women-only sessions because of hijab issues and feeling more comfortable. In another example, Shakila, a second-generation practising Muslim woman from Glasgow, stated that the MWAE (Muslim Women Association of Edinburgh) organised several women-only sessions for teenage girls for religious reasons and because they 'feel more comfortable'. These two examples imply the importance of the hijab and Muslims' preference for attending women-only session sporting activities.

Participation in women-only sessions was not limited to practising Muslim women. There were three less-practising Muslim women (Kathryn, Zainab and Akram) who also only attended women-only sessions. For example, Kathryn, a second-generation less-practising Muslim woman, stated that she did not feel 'comfortable' attending mixed-sex sessions because it was prohibited in Islam. Even though Kathryn was a less-practising Muslim, in parallel to the examples of Sanaz and Shakila, she highlighted that religious concerns and feeling more comfortable were the main reasons for attending women-only sessions. Other less-practising Muslim women also attended women-only sessions. This implies that observing the prohibition of mixed-sex meetings can be common among less-practising and practising Muslim women alike. Such communality was also evident regarding the issue of alcohol, as none of the above less-practising Muslim women drank alcohol. This implies that even though some less-practising Muslim women may not observe hijab, daily prayer or Ramadan fasting, they may nonetheless observe the prohibition of alcohol and mixed-sex meetings in sporting activities.

Muslim groups had to contact their local authority to arrange any women-only sporting activities. This was highlighted by Arezo, a second-generation Muslim involved in arranging many sporting activities for Muslim women. She said that booking any women-only sessions requires greater engagement of Muslim women with public institutions:

> It is a long process of applying for funding, looking for suitable female tutors (there are many more male tutors in the sports and exercise field than female), finding suitable venues, advertising to get a suitable number of girls attending, getting disclosures for all the tutors and helpers and also the insurance. The local authorities help whenever they can, but usually there is a lack of venues which are suitable. (Arezo, 50, female, Edinburgh)

The examples of Shakila and Arezo, who were active in arranging women-only sporting activities for Muslim women, suggests the civic integration of some Muslim women in Scotland too. These examples also suggest that there was a high demand for women-only sessions among Muslim women, and that some Muslim women organisations' civic engagement to accommodate this demand was fulfilled by the local authorities. It is, however, important to note that these sessions were inclusive of all women, regardless of their ethnic and religious background, and so White Scottish women could also take part in these sessions. This was highlighted by Rafiqah, a second-generation practising Muslim woman; she stated that women-only sessions were very welcoming and well attended by Muslim and some non-Muslim women, and they became a permanent feature of Muslim women's social life in Scotland.

These examples suggest that the organisation of such sessions in response to Muslim women's demand was a form of civic integration that Muslim women engaged in and has led to greater engagement in civic participation. This finding supports previous research suggesting that Muslims' identity politics can be an important trigger for more civic integration (Choudhury, 2007; Meer, 2010). For Muslim men and women alike, sport can offer a safe arena in which to interact, because it does not involve alcohol. Muslim women's engagement, however, can be more constrained, but the search for gender-segregated sessions had led to increased civic participation.

CONCLUSION

This research suggests that even though Muslims in Scotland deal with different social and cultural barriers, they try to fit into the different aspects of Scottish society. The most common strategy was halal integration, which meant fitting into society while maintaining their religious identity. Even though the adoption of this strategy implies the importance of Muslims' religious identity, the strategy of fitting in and integration varied depending on Muslims' gender, generational dynamics and religious practice. Considering the importance of generational dynamics, the integration of second-generation Muslims in social life is often stronger than that of first-generation Muslims. The second-generation Muslims' greater integration comes as a result of their Scottish education, knowing the English language and being more confident in socialising and communicating with White Scottish people. Such greater integration was evident in their interest in social and civil participation. My findings therefore challenge simplistic representations of Muslims as living parallel lives, characterised by segregation and separation.

Another important issue which can affect Muslims' integration is religious practice and moral observation (such as lack of alcohol consumption and avoiding being present where alcohol is served). Muslims who do not mind being around alcohol tend to develop closer social relationships with White Scottish people. In contrast, practising Muslims' social integration can be limited to daytime and non-alcoholic environments. The social integration of non-practising Muslims is sometimes different, and perhaps more developed, from that of practising or less-practising Muslims. However, gender is important here. Some less-practising Muslim women did not drink alcohol and avoid attending places where it was served, and nor did they take part in mixed-sex sporting activities. Such commitment to abstinence among some less-practising participants might be due to family and/or community pressure (Runnymede Trust, 1997; Lewis, 2007; Murji, 2011), rather than religious practice.

Due to the importance of alcohol consumption in hindering Muslims' integration, as one of my participants pointed out, at public events where Muslims' participation is expected, it is important to consider using a location where alcohol is not served and making halal food available. Alternatively, if no such venue is possible, then some tables with halal food and non-alcoholic drinks should be reserved for Muslims. Such simple steps would send out a strong symbolic message that majority Scots are keen to interact and engage with Muslims, and that integration is not a one-way street. This may assist in reinforcing the sense of belonging to Scotland that many of my respondents already possess.

REFERENCES

Ager, A. and Strang, A. (2008). 'Understanding integration: A conceptual framework'. *Journal of Refugee Studies*, 21(2), 166–91.

Ahmed, A. (2003). *Islam under Siege: Living Dangerously in a Post-honor World*. Cambridge: Polity Press.

Ameli, S. R., Elahi, M. and Merali, A. (2004). *Social Discrimination: Across the Muslim Divide*. London: Islamic Human Rights Commission.

Ballard, R. (1994). 'Introduction: The emergence of *Desh Pardesh*'. In R. Ballard (ed.), Desh Pardesh: *The South Asian Presence in Britain*, pp. 1–34. London: Hurst.

Berry, J. W. (1997). 'Immigration, acculturation and adaptation'. *Applied Sociology*, 46(1), 5–34.

British Council Scotland Survey (2010). *Muslim Integration in Scotland*. Ipsos MORI Scotland, available at www.britishcouncil.org/scotland-society-muslims-integration-in-scotland-report.pdf

British Government (2011). *Number 10*, available at www.number10.gov.uk/news/speeches-and-transcripts/2011/02/pms-speech-at-munich-security-conference-60293

Brubaker, R. (2001). 'The return of assimilation? Changing perspectives on immigration and its sequels in France, Germany and the United States'. *Ethnic and Racial Studies*, 24(4), 531–48.

Cantle, T. (2001). *Community Cohesion: A Report of the Independent Review Team*. London: Home Office, available at http://resources.cohesioninstitute.org.uk/Publications/Documents/Document/DownloadDocumentsFile.aspx?recordId=96andfile=PDFversion

Cassidy, C., O'Connor, R. and Dorrer, N. (2006). *Young People's Experience of Transition to Adulthood*. York: Joseph Rowntree Foundation.

Castles, S., Korac, M., Vasta, M. and Vertovec, S. (2002). *Integration: Mapping the Field*. London: Home Office, available at www.homeoffice.gov.uk/rds/pdfs/rdsolr2803.doc

Chakraborti, N. and Garland, J. (2009). *Hate Crime: Impact, Causes and Responses*. London: Sage.

Choudhury, T. (2007). *The Role of Muslim Identity Politics in Radicalisation*. London: Communities and Local Government, available at http://kms1.isn. ethz.ch/serviceengine/Files/ISN/116369/ipriadoc_doc/52b115be-7829-4914-84c8-4db3bd599a96/en/1431_identity.pdf

El-Nakla, N., Macbeth, G. and Thomas, F. (2007). *Muslim Women's Voices: Report Presenting the Findings of a Scotland-wide Listing Exercise Conducted with Muslims*. Glasgow: Muslim Women's Resource Centre.

Esposito, J. (2011). *What Everyone Needs to Know about Islam*, 2nd edn. Oxford: Oxford University Press.

Fekete, L. (2008). *Integration, Islamophobia and Civil Rights in Europe*. London: Institute of Race Relations, available at www.irr.org.uk/pdf/ Integrationreport.pdf

Goodhart, D. (2004). 'Too diverse?' *Prospect*, 65(February), 30–7.

Hale, S. (2000). 'The perception and resettlement of Vietnamese refugees in Britain'. In V. Robinson (ed.), *The International Refugee Crisis*, pp. 280–90. Basingstoke: Macmillan.

Hall, S. (2000). 'Conclusion: The multicultural question'. In B. Hesse (ed.), *Un/settled Multiculturalism: Diasporas, Entanglements, Transruptions*, pp. 209–41. London: Zed Books.

Hashmi, N. (2002). *A Muslim School in Bristol: An Overview of the Current Debate and Muslim Schoolchildren's Views*. Bristol: CECS, University of Bristol.

Hickman, M., Crowley, H. and Mai, N. (2008). *Immigration and Social Cohesion in the UK*. York: Joseph Rowntree Foundation, available at www. jrf.org.uk/sites/files/jrf/2230-deprivation-cohesion-immigration.pdf

Hopkins, P. (2004). 'Young Muslim men in Scotland: Inclusions and exclusions'. *Children's Geographies*, 2(2), 257–72.

Hussain, A. and Miller, W. L. (2006). *Multicultural Nationalism: Islamophobia, Anglophobia, and Devolution*. Oxford: Oxford University Press.

Jacobson, J. (1997). 'Religion and ethnicity: Dual and alternative sources of identity among young British Pakistanis'. *Ethnic and Racial Studies*, 20(2), 238–56.

Joppke, C. (2012). *The Role of the State in Cultural Integration: Trends, Challenges and Ways Ahead*. Washington, DC: Migration Policy Institute.

Kidd, S. and Jamieson L. (2011). *Experience of Muslims Living in Scotland*, Edinburgh: Scottish Government Social Research, available at www.scot land.gov.uk/Resource/Doc/344206/0114485.pdf

Korac, M. (2003). 'Integration and how we facilitate it: A comparative study of the settlement experiences of refugees in Italy and the Netherlands'. *Sociology*, 37(1), 51–68.

Kymlicka, W. (1995). *Multicultural Citizenship: A Liberal Theory of Minority Rights*. Oxford: Oxford University Press.

Kymlicka, W. (2001). *Politics in the Vernacular: Nationalism, Multiculturalism and Citizenship*. Oxford: Oxford University Press.

Kyriakides, C., Virdee, S. and Modood, T. (2009). 'Racism, Muslims and the national imagination'. *Journal of Ethnic and Migration Studies*, 35(2), 289–308.

Lewis, P. (2007). *Young, British and Muslim*. London: Continuum.

Maliepaard, M. and Phalet, K. (2012). 'Social integration and religious identity expression among Dutch Muslims: The role of minority and majority group contact'. *American Sociological Quarterly*, 75(2), 131–48.

Masud, M. (2005). *'Muslim Women talk': Experiences of Muslim Women in Scotland Since the London Bombings*. Muslim Women's Resource Centre, available at www.mwrc.org.uk/wp-content/uploads/2016/06/ScottishMWT-Report.pdf

Meer, N. (2010). *Citizenship, Identity and the Politics of Multiculturalism: The Rise of Muslim Consciousness*. Basingstoke: Palgrave Macmillan.

Modood, T. (2005). *Multicultural Politics: Racism, Ethnicity and Muslim in Britain*. Edinburgh: Edinburgh University Press.

Modood, T. (2007). *Multiculturalism: A Civic Idea*. Cambridge: Polity.

Murji, S. (2011). 'Identity formation and Muslim women in the UK: The roles of religion, family and education'. In K. Gallagher (ed.), *Multiculturalism: Critical and Interdisciplinary Perspectives: At the Interface*, available at www.inter-disciplinary.net/at-the-interface

Ormston, R., Curtice, J., McConville, S. and Reid, S. (2011). *Scottish Social Attitudes Survey 2010: Attitudes to Discrimination and Positive Action*. Edinburgh: Scottish Government Social Research, available at www.scotland.gov.uk/Publications/2011/08/11112523/17

Parekh, B. (2006). *Rethinking Multiculturalism: Cultural Diversity and Political Theory*. Basingstoke: Palgrave.

Parekh, B. (2008). *A New Politics of Identity*. Basingstoke: Palgrave.

Penrose, J. and Howard, D. (2008). 'One Scotland, many cultures: The mutual constitution of anti-racism and place'. In C. Dwyer and C. Bressey (eds), *New Geographies of Race and Racism*, pp. 95–112. Burlington: Ashgate.

Pfeffer, D. (2014). 'The integration of groups'. *Ethnicities*, 14(3), 351–70.

Phillimore, J. and Goodson, L. (2008). 'Making a place in the global city: The relevance of indicators of integration'. *Journal of Refugee Studies*, 21(3), 305–25.

Phinney, J. (2003). 'Ethnic identity and acculturation'. In K. Chun, P. Organista and P. Marin (eds), *Acculturation: Advances in Theory, Measurement and Applied Research*, pp. 63–81. Washington, DC: American Psychology Association.

Platt, L. (2012). 'Exploring social spaces of Muslims'. In A. Waqar and Z. Sardar (eds), *Muslims in Britain: Making Social and Political Space*, pp. 53–83. Milton Park: Routledge.

Qureshi, K. and Moores, S. (1999). 'Identity remix: Tradition and translation in the lives of young Pakistani Scots'. *European Journal of Cultural Studies*, 2(3), 311–30.

Runnymede Trust (1997). *Islamophobia: A Challenge for Us All*. London: Runnymede Trust.

Simpson, L. (2012). *'More Segregation or More Mixing?' Dynamics of Diversity: Evidence from the 2011 Census*. Centre on Dynamics of Ethnicity (CoDE), University of Manchester, available at www.ethnicity.ac.uk/census/869_CCSR_Bulletin_More_segregation_or_more_mixing_v7NW.pdf

Vertovec, S. and Wessendorf, S. (eds) (2010). *The Multiculturalism Backlash: European Discourses, Policies and Practices*. London: Routledge.

Virdee, S., Kyriakides, C. and Modood, T. (2006). 'Codes of cultural belonging: Racialised national identities in a multi-ethnic Scottish neighbourhood'. *Sociological Research Online*, 11(4), available at www.socresonline.org.uk/11/4/virdee.html

Wimmer, A. and Lewis, K. (2010). 'Beyond and below racial homophily: ERG models of friendship network documented on Facebook'. *American Journal of Sociology*, 116 (2), 583–642.

Index

Page numbers in italic indicate an illustration; 't' indicates a table

EU representative:
Easy Access System Europe
Mustamäe tee 50, 10621 Tallinn, Estonia
Gpsr.requests@easproject.com